Embedding Artificial Intelligence into ERP Software

Siar Sarferaz

Embedding Artificial Intelligence into ERP Software

A Conceptual View on Business AI
with Examples from SAP S/4HANA

 Springer

Siar Sarferaz
SAP SE
Walldorf, Germany

ISBN 978-3-031-54248-0   ISBN 978-3-031-54249-7   (eBook)
https://doi.org/10.1007/978-3-031-54249-7

This Springer imprint is published by the registered company Springer Nature Switzerland AG
The registered company address is: Gewerbestrasse 11, 6330 Cham, Switzerland

Paper in this product is recyclable.

Preface

Enterprise resource planning (ERP) systems digitalize all business processes of companies to increase the level of automation and optimization. ERP solutions integrate data and business processes from sales, marketing, finance, supply chain, manufacturing, services, procurement, and human resources to operate as a central system of record for many organizations. Enterprises are driven by data and insights. It's not just about having the right data but having the insights from that data associated with core business processes. This is where artificial intelligence (AI) can help, as it reveals knowledge from structured and unstructured data to facilitate intelligent ERP solutions. Artificial intelligence is typically defined as the ability of a machine to perform cognitive abilities we associate with human minds, such as perceiving, reasoning, learning, and problem-solving. It requires a system to correctly interpret external data, learn from such data, and use those learnings to achieve specific goals through flexible adaptation. Artificial intelligence, instead of explicitly programming rules, learns from data to make sense of raw data and uncover hidden insights and relationships. Artificial intelligence is increasingly becoming a significant part of ERP systems. The relevance of artificial intelligence for ERP stems from the potential of artificial intelligence to drastically enhance the efficiency, accuracy, and functionality of ERP systems. Here are some examples why artificial intelligence is relevant and transformative for ERP systems:

- Improved decision-making: Artificial intelligence can analyze vast amounts of data quickly and accurately, providing insights that can improve decision-making processes. AI-enabled ERP systems can predict trends, identify potential issues, and suggest appropriate actions, thus helping businesses make more informed and timely decisions. Algorithms can help businesses understand their operations, customers, and markets better by analyzing and interpreting large amounts of data.
- Automation of routine tasks: Artificial intelligence can automate repetitive tasks, reducing the need for manual input and allowing employees to focus on more complex tasks. This automation can lead to significant improvements in productivity and efficiency. For example, algorithms can automate tasks like data entry, invoice processing, or inventory management in ERP systems.
- Supply chain optimization: Artificial intelligence can help optimize supply chains by predicting demand, optimizing delivery routes, and identifying

potential supply chain disruptions before they occur. Algorithms can analyze historical data and identify patterns to make accurate forecasts. This can be particularly useful in areas such as sales forecasting, demand planning, and inventory management.

- Risk management and fraud detection: Artificial intelligence can analyze transaction patterns to detect anomalies that might indicate fraudulent activities. It can also predict potential risks and provide alerts, thus enhancing the security and reliability of ERP systems. This can save businesses a lot of money and protect their reputation. Algorithms can easily scale to handle larger amounts of data as a business grows. This can make it easier for businesses to grow and expand without having to make significant investments.

- Improving customer service: Artificial intelligence can enhance customer service by providing personalized experiences, quicker response times, and more accurate information. For example, AI-powered chatbots can handle customer inquiries 24/7, providing immediate responses and escalating complex issues to human agents. Artificial intelligence can analyze customer behavior and predict what they are likely to want or need in the future. This can help businesses tailor their services to individual customers, improving customer satisfaction and loyalty.

- Predictive maintenance: Artificial intelligence can analyze large volumes of data to predict potential equipment failures before they occur. This allows businesses to shift from a reactive maintenance approach to a proactive one, significantly reducing downtime and associated costs. This can prevent unexpected equipment downtime, save money on repairs, and improve overall operational efficiency. Algorithms can provide insights into the impact of maintenance activities on other areas of the business, aiding in strategic decision-making. For instance, it can help determine whether it's more cost-effective to repair or replace a piece of equipment.

From our perspective, the rich data foundation and the strong focus on business processes of ERP systems optimally facilitates embedding artificial intelligence. However, incorporating artificial intelligence into ERP solutions is a challenging task due to the complexity of these systems. For instance, SAP's ERP product contains over 250 million lines of code and 143,000 tables. It supports 25 industry verticals, localizations for 64 countries, and over 100,000 business processes. We must solve two substantial challenges regarding embedding artificial intelligence into the ERP software: (1) How can we systematically integrate artificial intelligence into ERP business processes for ease of consumption? (2) How can we make artificial intelligence enterprise-ready covering ERP qualities like compliance, lifecycle management, extensibility, or scalability? Considering those challenges and providing for them an adequate solution is the objective of this book. In the first part, we describe the history and future trends of the ERP software. In addition, we also propose reference processes and reference architecture for ERP systems that build the foundation for the suggested solution concept. Furthermore, we suggest a method for operationalizing intelligence for ERP business processes. In the second part, we propose concepts of embedding artificial intelligence into ERP software. In this context, we depict the suggested solution architecture and resolve specific topics like data integration, model validation, explainability, data protection and privacy, model degradation, and performance. In the last part, we suggest an implementation framework that practically enables the introduced concepts. The framework harmonizes the development and operations of artificial intelligent ERP applications. This part concludes with case studies considering artificial intelligence scenarios of SAP's ERP as a well-known product. Those use cases in ERP areas of logistics, finance, and sales apply the defined solution approach and framework outlined in this elaboration. This proves the added value and the real-world feasibility of those new inventions we suggested. Finally, ethical aspects of artificial intelligence are briefly discussed in the epilogue. Business AI refers to the application of artificial intelligence technologies within the business environment to improve efficiency, enhance decision-making, and generate insights that would otherwise be difficult or impossible to obtain with traditional techniques. These applications can span a wide range of business functions, including sales and marketing, customer service, human resources, finance, and operations. As enterprises run ERP systems to operate their business processes, our solution for embedding artificial intelligence into the ERP software operationalizes business AI. The review of Prof. Dr. Axel Winkelmann and Prof. Dr. Guenther Gust are sincerely appreciated and gratefully acknowledged.

Walldorf, Germany   Siar Sarferaz

Disclaimer

This publication contains references to the products of SAP SE or an SAP affiliate company. SAP products and services mentioned herein as well as their respective logos are trademarks or registered trademarks of SAP SE or an SAP affiliate company. For SAP product screenshots included in this publication copyrights are reserved by SAP. All other product and service names mentioned are the trademarks of their respective companies. Data contained in this document serves informational purposes only. National product specifications may vary. SAP is neither the author nor the publisher of this publication and is not responsible for its content. SAP Group shall not be liable for errors or omissions with respect to the materials. The only warranties for SAP Group products and services are those that are set forth in the express warranty statements accompanying such products and services, if any. Nothing herein should be construed as constituting an additional warranty.

Contents

Methodology

1

In this chapter, we depict the goals and the content of the elaboration. The written composition is structured into the main parts ERP fundamentals, concepts for embedding artificial intelligence, implementation framework, and case studies. We also briefly explain the problem space, our solution proposal, the approach for deducing the results, and the added value of our findings. For deriving the business requirements and resolving them, we analyzed 60 artificial intelligence ERP use cases and 20 ERP products, which are also itemized in this chapter.

1.1 Scientific Approach

There are various science theories that provide the ground for information system research. Design science research, for example, focuses on the development and evaluation of artifacts, such as constructions, models, or methods, to solve real-world problems and improve existing solutions (Gregor & Hevner, 2013; Venable et al., 2016; Winter, 2008). The main goal of design science research is to create knowledge through the design and analysis of innovative artifacts, which can be used to address relevant and significant problems in various domains, such as information systems, engineering, and business (Goldkuhl, 2002; Hevner & Chatterjee, 2010). My honored science philosophy professor Peter Janich provides an even more comprehensive framework for science theory by arguing that science is not only reflections of an objective reality but is constructed by human beings through language, practices, and communication (Janich, 1997, 2005, 2006). Scientific knowledge, according to Janich, is developed through a process of social negotiation and consensus among scientists and is evaluated based on their coherence, simplicity, and effectiveness in solving particular problems. In his view, science is a social activity that involves finding general and objective explanations of observable relationships by drawing on empirical data and a common methodological approach. The common ground of those science theories we can condense to three questions

© The Author(s), under exclusive license to Springer Nature
Switzerland AG 2024
S. Sarferaz, *Embedding Artificial Intelligence into ERP Software*,
https://doi.org/10.1007/978-3-031-54249-7_1

(Wilson, 2002) concerning the research contribution: Is it true? Is it new? Is it interesting? Those questions we answer in context of embedding artificial intelligence into ERP software. We begin with the last question as the relevance of the problem being addressed is the most crucial aspect of research contribution.

1.1.1   Is It Interesting?

ERP software is essential for companies as it builds the backbone for enterprises by integrating crucial functions and processes into a single, unified system. Thus, ERP software adds value to organizations:

- ERP streamlines and automates business processes, improves data flow and communication, and provides real-time access to accurate and consistent information across different departments.
- By automating routine tasks and standardizing business processes, ERP reduces manual work and human errors, leading to increased productivity and efficiency.
- ERP provides real-time access to accurate and consistent data, which helps employees make informed decisions based on relevant and up-to-date information.
- By breaking down information silos and providing a single source of truth for all departments, ERP improves communication and collaboration across the organization.
- Through better resource management, process optimization, and reduced operational redundancies, ERP helps organizations save costs and improve their business.
- ERP can be easily scaled and adapted to accommodate organizational growth and changing business requirements.

In addition to optimize companies, ERP systems also impact the daily life of ordinary persons. Billions of worldwide transactions are processed by ERP systems day to day, for example, people buying their beverages in the supermarket, paying per bank transfer, visiting hospital for admission, claiming an insurance case, making a request to public authority, or booking flights. Conversely, ERP software is relevant to be considered in the elaboration. From the historical reflection of ERP software (*Chapter 2*), we know that today's ERP solutions are using rule-based execution to automate processes, facilitate compliance, and guarantee data consistency. No doubt, rule-based automation has significantly increased efficiency over time but has already reached its limits, especially as rule-based systems cannot learn and evolve without human being adding and adapting rules. Artificial intelligence helps to close this gap and increases the level of automation and optimization of business processes based on self-learning algorithms. Processes can be improved faster and with less human involvement and knowledge due to artificial intelligence. Intelligent ERP systems make the best use of both artificial intelligence and rules-based techniques, freeing up humans to concentrate on high-value tasks. Increased productivity from incorporating artificial intelligence into business processes fosters creativity and opens the door to new business models. Let's illustrate with some examples how artificial intelligence can improve ERP functionality (Sarferaz, 2022):

- High-tech equipment failure is a crucial business issue for manufacturers. The health of these machines can be predicted by combining sensor data with business data from ERP systems and applying artificial intelligence models. Thus, proactive business processes can be developed for maintenance scheduling, logistics planning for spare parts, and allocation of the repair crew.
- Success depends on being able to predict local market trends early on and providing the precise products that the market demands. Artificial intelligence algorithms can examine purchasing patterns and suggest products to be included or removed from a business's offering. They can assist in determining which variants, segmented by particular markets, are not currently selling well and which ones will go on to become the top sellers in the future.
- Final quality assurance and shipment readiness checks for products include confirming that a product has been manufactured precisely in accordance with its specifications and configuration. This human-centric process can be supported by image recognition algorithms making use of visual product quality checks. As a consequence, the accuracy and automation level of quality processes in production can be increased, which results in fewer returns, better customer satisfaction, and improved profitability.
- The foundation for ERP business processes is high-quality master data, which is essential. To ensure data consistency, artificial intelligence models can automatically identify and apply validation rules. Furthermore, the interaction with end users is simplified, and costs are reduced by the artificial intelligence–based autocompletion of attribute values while maintaining master data.
- Reconciliation between different companies takes a lot of time during the financial close. To enhance and accelerate local and group closes, artificial intelligence algorithms aid in automating and controlling end-to-end, intragroup invoicing, payment, and settlement scenarios. Artificial intelligence models aid in spotting and fixing discrepancies in reconciliations, producing accurate data for month-end corporate group reporting, and improved intercompany management transparency.

Thus, artificial intelligence enables disruptive innovation in many ERP domains and has a major impact on the ERP software market. There is a consensus among market analysts that ERP products evolves toward intelligent ERP solutions with the aim of autonomous processing (*Chapter 2*). IDC market research (IDC, 2022a) predicts that by 2026, all business technologies will have features that are driven by artificial intelligence, and 60% of organizations will actively use these features to improve outcomes without relying on technical artificial intelligence talent. Globally, companies are projected to spend $118 billion on artificial intelligence solutions in 2022. This spending is anticipated to rise by $301 billion between 2021 and 2026 at a compound annual growth rate (CAGR) of 26.5%. The global IT spending CAGR over the same 5-year period was 6.3%, which is more than four times higher than this.

According to McKinsey, the market for artificial intelligence applications will be worth $127 billion worldwide by 2025 (Sarferaz, 2022). According to PricewaterhouseCoopers, artificial intelligence could increase gross domestic product growth by up to 26% and contribute nearly $16 trillion to the global economy by 2030 (Sarferaz, 2022). By 2023, artificial intelligence will automate 60% of manual tasks, predicts Gartner. Almost all sectors and industries will reap benefits (Sarferaz, 2022).

We conclude that ERP software is relevant as it impacts the business of companies and the daily life of people. The current rule-based level of automation of ERP business processes can be increased with artificial intelligence techniques, for example, improved forecasting, optimized operations, more personalized customer services, and enhanced user experiences. ERP analysts outline the increasing market volume and importance of artificial intelligence in the domain of business applications. Thus, identifying and solving the challenges of embedding intelligence into ERP software as objective of the elaboration is relevant and valuable.

1.1.2   Is It New?

There are various publications concerning artificial intelligence in the business domain (Akerkar, 2019; Canhoto & Clear, 2020; Chen et al., 2021; Cubric, 2020; Guenole & Feinzig, 2018; Kerzel, 2020; Soni et al., 2020). However, typically, they are focusing on specific artificial intelligence scenarios and their individual implementations, explaining the data science approach for business problems, or offering general views on social, economic, and ethical implications of artificial intelligence. What is missing is a comprehensive consideration of how artificial intelligence can be embedded into digitized business processes. This gap we would like to close by providing an end-to-end perspective from identification of the business requirements to resolving them conceptually and proving their feasibility with case studies.

After analyzing the problem space based on numerous user cases, we pinpointed two key obstacles that need to be addressed when it comes to embedding artificial intelligence into ERP software as illustrated in Fig. 1.1. We will explain our

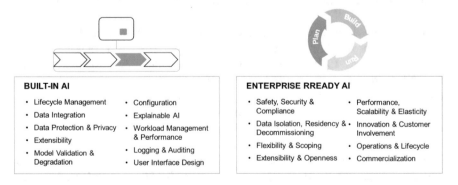

Fig. 1.1 AI challenges in the context of ERP

methodology of detecting and resolving those challenges in the next section. From our perspective already the identification of those requirements is a new finding as no prior art is known reflecting these holistically. As shown in Fig. 1.1, to embed artificial intelligence into business processes, corresponding enterprise requirements must be met. Incorporating artificial intelligence functionality into ERP software must result, for example, into compliant, secure, and performant business processes. Those qualities we refer to as Enterprise Ready AI (*Chapter 6*).

Typically, consumers of business processes are not educated in data science and are also not technical minded. Conversely, it is crucial that artificial intelligence capabilities are deeply integrated into business processes and user interfaces of ERP software for ease of consumption, which we referred to as Built-in AI in Fig. 1.1. Thus, artificial intelligence features must be provided to the right person, at the right place, and at the right time. To meet this requirement, corresponding concepts must be provided. Those concepts must facilitate the Built-in AI demand while ensuring the Enterprise Ready AI requirement. For resolving these artificial intelligence aspects, we depict the business requirements and propose novel concepts for life cycle management (*Chapter 8*), data integration (*Chapter 9*), data protection and privacy (*Chapter 10*), configuration (*Chapter 11*), extensibility (*Chapter 12*), model degradation (*Chapter 13*), explainable AI (*Chapter 14*), workload management and performance (*Chapter 15*), legal auditing (*Chapter 16*), model validation (*Chapter 17*), and user interface design (*Chapter 18*). We have filed patents for various of these concepts. Patents protect new and non-obvious inventions. Conversely, they prove the novelty of our solution proposals, particularly as the patent authority conducts intensive investigations on the aspect of novelty. For illustration, we list the abstracts for some of our patents exemplary, which are published on https://patents.justia.com/inventor/siar-sarferaz:

- Automatic enforcement of data use policy for machine learning applications (patent number 11494512): "Techniques and solutions are described for restricting data that is provided to a machine learning application. Restrictions can be based on use status information, such as use status information associated with a retention manager and indicating whether data is blocked from use. Data identifiers used by a cloud-based system can be correlated with archiving objects of a local system so that the cloud-based system can receive use status information to avoid using blocked data. Restrictions can include restricting data based on whether a data subject has provided consent that allows the data to be used by the machine learning application. A data view can be defined that filters query results to those where consent exits. The data view can join, such as an inner join, a table providing consent information with a data having data subject data."
- Detection of machine learning model degradation (patent number 11625602): "A method may include training, based on a first training dataset, a machine learning model. A degradation of the machine learning model may be detected based on one or more accuracy key performance indicators including a prediction power metric and a prediction confidence metric. The degradation of the machine learning model may also be detected based on a drift and skew in an input dataset and/

or an output dataset of the machine learning model. Furthermore, the degradation of the machine learning model may be detected based on an explicit feedback and/or an implicit feedback on a performance of the machine learning model. In response to detecting the degradation of the machine learning model, the machine learning model may be retrained based on a second training dataset that includes at least one training sample not included in the first training dataset. Related systems and articles of manufacture are also provided."

- Embedded machine learning (patent number 11507884): "Systems and methods are provided for receiving a request for data associated with a particular functionality of an application, identifying a first attribute for which data is to be generated to fulfill the request, and determining that the first attribute corresponds to data to be generated by a first machine learning model. The systems and methods further providing for executing a view or procedure to generate data for input to the first machine learning model, inputting the generated data into the first machine learning model, and receiving output from the first machine learning model. The output is provided in response to the request for data associated with the particular functionality of the application."

- Facilitating machine learning configuration (patent number 11580455): "Techniques and solutions are described for facilitating the use of machine learning techniques. In some cases, filters can be defined for multiple segments of a training data set. Model segments corresponding to respective segments can be trained using an appropriate subset of the training data set. When a request for a machine learning result is made, filter criteria for the request can be determined and an appropriate model segment can be selected and used for processing the request. One or more hyperparameter values can be defined for a machine learning scenario. When a machine learning scenario is selected for execution, the one or more hyperparameter values for the machine learning scenario can be used to configure a machine learning algorithm used by the machine learning scenario."

- Machine leaning facilitated data entry (patent number 20210342738): "Techniques and solutions are described for facilitating data entry using machine learning techniques. A machine learning model can be trained using values for one or more data members of at least on type of data object, such as a logical data object. One or more input recommendation functions can be defined for the data object, where an input recommendation method is configured to use the machine learning model to obtain one or more recommended values for a data member of the data object. A user interface control of a graphical user interface can be programmed to access a recommendation function to provide a recommended value for the user interface control, where the value can be optionally set for a data member of an instance of the data object. Explanatory information can be provided that describes criteria used in determining the recommended value."

- Facilitating machine learning using remote data (patent number 20210264312): "Techniques and solutions are described for facilitating the use of machine learning techniques. In some cases, a system suitable for providing a machine learning analysis can be different from a remote computer system on which training data for a machine learning model is located. A machine learning task can be defined that includes an identifier for at least one data source on the remote computer system. Data for the at least one data source is received from the remote computer system. At least a portion of the data is processed using a machine learning algorithm to provide a trained model, which can be stored for later use. Data on the remote computing system can be unstructured or structured. Particularly in the case of structured data, a remote computer system can make updated data available to the machine learning task."

- Machine learning life cycle management (patent number 20210241170): "Systems, methods, and computer program products for managing a lifecycle of a machine learning (ML) application from a consumer point of view are described herein. Execution of an intelligent scenario for training of the ML application is initiated. An integrator component generates a training pipeline. The training pipeline includes training logic associated with a defined workflow for the training. An application having an input dataset trains the ML application using the training pipeline. The integrator component determines training metrics associated with the trained ML application. The training metrics are indicators of a level of accuracy of the trained ML application. A centralized component provides the training metrics for characterization of the trained model."

- Automated, progressive explanations of machine learning results (patent number 20210192376): "Techniques and solutions are described for analyzing results of a machine learning model. Disclosed technologies provide for progressively providing explanation of machine learning results at increasing levels of granularity. A global or local explanation can be provided for given set of one or more machine learning results. A global explanation can provide information regarding the general performance of the machine learning model. One type of local explanation can include results calculated for considered, but unselected options. Another type of local explanation can include analysis of features used in generating a particular machine learning result. By automatically calculating and providing analysis of machine learning results, users may better understand how results were calculated and the potential accuracy of the results, and may have greater confidence in using machine learning techniques."

- Machine learning performance and workload management (patent number 20210004712): "Systems and methods are described herein for reducing resource consumption of a database system and a machine learning (ML) system. Data is received from an ML application of a database system. The data includes a first inference call for a predicted response to the received data. The first inference call is a request to a ML model to generate one or more predictions for which a response is unknown. An ML model using the received data generates an output comprising the predicted response to the data. The output for future inference calls is cached in an inference cache so as to bypass the ML model. The generated output to the ML application is provided by the ML model. A second inference call is received which includes the data of the first inference call. The cached output is retrieved from the inference cache. The retrieving bypasses the ML model."

We conclude that the considered problem and the proposed solution are new contributions to scientific knowledge. The novelty is well proved by corresponding patents.

1.1.3   Is It True?

Traceability of how results have been produced is an important aspect of scientific knowledge contribution. For verifiability, we describe in Fig. 1.2 the deduction of our results.

For understanding the problem space, we first analyzed around 60 artificial intelligence use cases in the ERP domain. The key questions we considered in this context were the following: Should the underlying problem be resolved with artificial intelligence, or could rule-based techniques be a better alternative? What technical functionality is required to implement the artificial intelligence use case? Table 1.1 lists those use cases and provides brief description of them. To have a broad coverage, the use cases are originated from the ERP core business processes *idea to market*, *source to pay*, *plan to fulfill*, *lead to cash*, *recruit to retire*, *acquire to decommission*, *governance*, and *finance*. Around 30 of the use cases will be described in detail in Part 3 where the case studies are explained. From use case analysis, we drove the business requirements as illustrated in Fig. 1.1. Furthermore, we identified artificial intelligence application patterns. We additionally validated those business requirements and application patterns (*Chapter 6*) with customers and domain experts. The artificial intelligence application patterns categorize the use cases along similarity of business functionality and realization approach. The rationale behind is that we don't want to provide for each use case an individual technical implementation but to resolve at least one or better more artificial intelligence application patterns with the same solution architecture. This approach results typically into a more lean and powerful solution concept. For embedding artificial intelligence into ERP, we must consider the underlying software architecture. This is comparable with constructing a new room in a house where the existing architecture cannot be ignored too. In the context of ERP software, the challenge is that there is

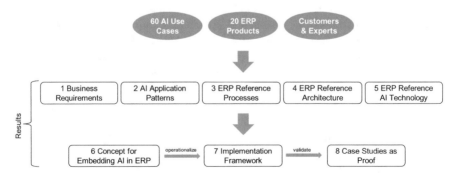

Fig. 1.2 Approach for deducing of results

Table 1.1 Analyzed AI use cases, [a]Scenario is explained as case study in Part 3 of the book

ID	Scenario name	Scenario description	ERP reference process
1[a]	Receivables Line Item Matching	Accounts receivable involves tracking money owed by clients for goods and services, and artificial intelligence technology can be used to automatically digitize payment advice, match and clear payments with open receivables, streamlining the payment process	Finance
2[a]	Matching with Payment Advice Information Extraction	A payment advice is a crucial source of information for accounting departments, and artificial intelligence algorithms can be used to automatically extract and process relevant data from unstructured documents to optimize the clearing process	Finance
3[a]	Matching with Lockbox Information	The increasing use of electronic payments has led to challenges in identifying payers and receivables due to decoupled remittance information and varied data quality; to address this, artificial intelligence can be leveraged to enrich lockbox entries, which can then be confirmed by accountants and cleared using lockbox functionality, with auto clearing as a possible option	Finance
4[a]	Payables Line Item Matching	Outgoing payments, which are debit items in a customer's bank statement, and vendor-initiated payments, which are triggered by vendors and deducted directly from the customer's bank, can be effectively managed and cleared by an artificial intelligence service that learns from account behavior, works immediately, and adapts continuously without the need for ongoing maintenance, overcoming the limitations posed by minimal information on bank statements	Finance
5[a]	Clear Goods Receipts and Invoice Accounts	Good receipts and invoice account reconciliation is an exception-handling process addressing discrepancies between goods and invoice receipts, involving substantial manual effort in report creation, data gathering, and root cause investigation, which causes delays in period-end closing but can be made more efficient with artificial intelligence–driven recommendations, ultimately leading to better P&L results, reduced write-offs, and improved cost and inventory valuation for companies	Finance
6[a]	Accruals Management	The accruals prediction functionality can utilize artificial intelligence to estimate and predict accruals for cash flow planning, addressing challenges like asynchronous projects and outdated reported values, by leveraging historical purchase order data and grouping similar orders, ultimately improving the efficiency of closing annual books, reducing errors and finance costs, and automating accrual calculations for more accurate totals, benefiting customers and portfolio management resources	

(continued)

Table 1.1 (continued)

ID	Scenario name	Scenario description	ERP reference process
7[a]	Predictive Accounting	The predictive accounting based on artificial intelligence revolutionizes traditional accounting by automating closing activities and providing real-time, forward-looking data based on incoming sales orders, enabling organizations to make informed decisions and strategize for future business operations	Finance
8	Monitoring of Goods and Invoice Receipts	The G/L accountant must verify if supplier invoices match received goods and manually analyses and process uncleared finance documents, as reconciling and explaining significant differences in goods receipt/invoice receipt reconciliation is crucial for period close tasks, which can be improved with artificial intelligence analyzing uncleared postings, clearing postings within predefined thresholds, and recommending next steps for finance postings on purchase order items	Finance
9	Intelligent Accrual	Accrual estimation involves an accountant adjusting linear values based on their knowledge, business owner feedback, and reported values; however, artificial intelligence can enhance this process by analyzing current and historical purchase orders, past payments, and grouping similar purchase orders to provide recommendations for more reliable accruals during manual review, ultimately allowing for high-confidence accrual predictions	Finance
10	Bank Reconciliation	The month-end reconciliation procedure requires a general ledger accountant to match closing balances and line items from bank statements with corresponding journal entries, which can be time-consuming and labor-intensive, especially for companies with numerous bank accounts or high transaction volumes, but by implementing an automated reconciliation process based on artificial intelligence, this manual effort can be significantly reduced	Finance
11	Intelligent Intercompany Reconciliation	Intercompany accounting, a major challenge for many companies due to its time-consuming, error-prone, and labor-intensive nature, can lead to significant issues in financial statements and closing processes; however, intercompany matching and reconciliation based on artificial intelligence can offer real-time transaction-level matching, user-defined matching and reconciliation rules, and a fully automated process from company to corporate close	Finance
12	Risk of Late Filing	The risk of late filing can be reduced with artificial intelligence by determining risk score for taxpaying organizations potentially missing tax return deadlines, feature catalogs for identifying high-risk factors, automatic risk score generation with top influencing factors, and personalization of collections or follow-on processes	Finance

13	Process Outsourced Billing Documents	This about application of artificial intelligence in the utilities billing process to understand agents' past behavior and to either automatically release or suggest a release of all noncritical exceptions, for efficient reduction in the amount of manual work	Finance
14	Risk of Late Payment	The risk of late payment can be reduced with artificial intelligence by determining risk score for taxpaying organizations potentially missing due dates, feature catalog, automatic risk score generation with top influencing factors, personalization of collections or follow-on processes. This reduces the risk for a taxpaying organization not paying an outstanding bill, invoice, or assessment by the due date	Finance
15	Predicted Days to Payment	Artificial intelligence is used to forecast the early or late payment of open invoices for each customer in public sector and finance processes, enabling personalized collection strategies through predefined variables and event catalogs	
16[a]	Contract Consumption	Procurement leaders must renegotiate soon-to-expire contracts for better conditions, overcoming challenges in tracking expiration dates, with artificial intelligence sourcing and procurement functionality offering early supplier renegotiation, improved pricing, predicted contract expirations, enhanced purchasing compliance, and streamlined management of spend across categories	Source to Pay
17[a]	Resolution for Invoice Payment Block	The invoicing process is highly digitized and automated, but manual intervention is required for payment blocks due to issues like unplanned additional costs, quantity/price deviations, or other blocking reasons, making the process time-consuming and expensive, while the integration of artificial intelligence can help analyze, track, and solve these issues, improving processing time and preventing lost cash discounts for buyers	Source to Pay
18[a]	Supplier Delivery Prediction	During the purchasing process, materials are often supplied by multiple suppliers, and delays can impact production and assembly lines, but by using artificial intelligence algorithms, purchasers can predict supplier delivery delays, improving communication with the product life cycle management (PLM) department and maintaining material requirements planning (MRP)	Source to Pay
19[a]	Proposal of New Catalog Item	A purchasing manager faces challenges in managing the acquisition of goods, updating the internal catalog, and analyzing vast amounts of user-generated free-text items, but the proposing catalog items with artificial intelligence could automate investigative actions and purchase order creation, optimize catalog coverage, reduce error-prone purchases, and ultimately help achieve the goal of minimizing free-text items	Source to Pay

(continued)

Table 1.1 (continued)

ID	Scenario name	Scenario description	ERP reference process
20[a]	Proposal of Material Group	Operational purchasers must rectify misassigned material groups for free-text items to minimize incorrect category purchases, facing challenges like resource-intensive manual tasks; automating this process with artificial intelligence can yield benefits like reduced costs, improved efficiency, and better decision-making, by assisting in assignment of material groups to lower misallocations during purchase requisition creation	Source to Pay
21[a]	Materials without Purchase Contract	Purchasers must identify materials without contracts and create and prioritize requests based on similar materials with existing contracts; artificial intelligence can reduce off-contract spend by prioritizing the materials without purchase contracts, suggesting options, and overcoming challenges in executing corporate procurement tasks to reduce off-contract spending, streamline the request creation process, and enable early supplier renegotiations for better purchasing prices	Source to Pay
22[a]	Image-Based Buying	By utilizing artificial intelligence for procurement, the purchasing experience can be enhanced by automatically generating purchasing demand through image recognition and cross-catalog searches, resulting in improved user efficiency, reduced delays, and significant cost savings by minimizing the discrepancies between user and purchaser descriptions and validating demand ahead of time	Source to Pay
23[a]	Intelligent Approval Workflow	Artificial intelligence can streamline the purchase approval process by automatically approving requests with over 90% historical approval likelihood, leveraging historical data to identify patterns and increase efficiency while reducing costs and providing a confidence level for the approval of each purchase requisition	Source to Pay
24	Central Invoice Management	Artificial intelligence algorithm identifies invoice documents and related content, automatically digitalizing unstructured invoices and matching extracted information with master data while extracting header data for all invoices, taxes on purchase invoices, and line item details	Source to Pay
25[a]	Stock in Transit	Customers track and manage stock transport orders between storage locations or plants, addressing challenges like lack of visibility into delayed deliveries and estimating stock transfer durations, ultimately improving planning, scheduling accuracy, and reducing safety stock inventory, by incorporating artificial intelligence to predict the arrival date of shipments, thus ensuring on-time delivery and minimizing negative impacts on downstream finished products	Plan to Fulfill

26[a]	Demand-Driven Replenishment	With applied artificial intelligence, the inventory manager ensures timely material delivery and monitors replenishment planning, execution, and buffer levels, with the goal of optimizing data-driven buffer levels to balance customer service and bound capital through demand-driven replenishment, lead time prediction, and dynamic buffer level adjustment, reducing safety stock, carrying costs, days in inventory, and obsolescence while improving overall supply chain efficiency	Plan to Fulfill
27[a]	Defect Code Proposal with Text Recognition	The quality technician and engineer handle defect processing through reporting and analyzing; artificial intelligence can assist them by proposing defect code groups and codes based on textual descriptions and images, providing recommendations and suggestions	Plan to Fulfill
28[a]	Early Detection of Slow and Nonmoving Stocks	The production and inventory planner can utilize artificial intelligence to optimize stock quantities across various locations, such as plants, warehouses, and dealers, by analyzing historical data, detecting slow and non-moving inventory in advance, and proactively suggesting material movements based on incoming purchase requisitions, sales orders, and spares demand to prevent stagnation	Plan to Fulfill
29[a]	Automate Root Cause Analysis	In a traditional quality engineering process, issues are detected, analyzed, and documented through various means, while the artificial intelligence–driven solution efficiently analyses historical data and defect characteristics, suggesting potential root causes for defects and enabling quality engineers to quickly implement fixes, reduce downtime, and improve inspection management by presenting the most relevant information for easy filtering and prioritization	Plan to Fulfill
30[a]	Optimize Inspection Plans	In the traditional process, production operators and quality inspectors review quality characteristics and inspection results and then adjust inspection plans based on customer requirements, but artificial intelligence solution utilizes historical data to streamline the process, reducing manual effort for quality engineers and considering various inspection purposes while maintaining a similar structure to routing plans, with the plan header containing crucial information and inspection operations organized similarly to routing operations, allowing for multiple inspection characteristics per operation	Plan to Fulfill
31[a]	Defect Recording	Artificial intelligence–driven image recognition streamlines defect code proposals, allowing quality technicians to focus on finding more defects while exploring overlaps with text recognition use cases and how defects are categorized with relevant data being taken from the manufacturing order for production defects	Plan to Fulfill

(continued)

Table 1.1 (continued)

ID	Scenario name	Scenario description	ERP reference process
32	Visual Inspection	Inspection, crucial for maintaining product quality across the value chain, is currently a manual, costly, and error-prone process; however, artificial intelligence can leverage advancements in computer vision technology to expedite defect identification and seamlessly integrate computer vision into inspection processes	Plan to Fulfill
33		Artificial intelligence facilitates prescriptive scheduling and simulation, which dynamically adjusts to weighted KPIs, utilizing rule and event-based simulation for shop floor scheduling, optimization, and execution, with the aim of enhancing efficiency, enabling what-if analysis, and offering alternative solutions for addressing bottleneck situations	Plan to Fulfill
34[a]	Predict Conversion of Sales Quotations	Sales representatives must track and improve sales quotation conversion rates to boost sales volumes while facing challenges such as manual effort and difficulty identifying underperforming quotations; artificial intelligence can help by automating data collection and analysis, providing accurate predictions of conversion rates and potential sales volumes, and enabling representatives to focus on high-potential quotations and improve overall sales efficiency, contributing to a company's top-line growth	Lead to Cash
35[a]	Predict Sales Forecasts	Sales planning, a complex process involving data collection, analysis, and human experience, faces challenges such as high manual effort, time-consuming tasks, and data accuracy; however, artificial intelligence–driven sales performance prediction can offer benefits like higher revenue growth, reduced effort, and better support for inexperienced staff by automating data analysis, simplifying insights, and enabling informed, fact-based decisions through early detection of deviations and a focus on key performance indicators	Lead to Cash
36[a]	Predict Delivery Delay	Delivery performance, a key KPI in supply chains, faces challenges like delays, lack of transparency, and customer escalations, but leveraging artificial intelligence services can help sales representatives predict, analyze, and address delays by learning from past data, increasing customer satisfaction, retention, and overall efficiency, while current methods like available-to-promise (ATP) planning fall short in considering future deviations	Lead to Cash
37	Personalized Product Re-commendation	Personalization, crucial for enhancing customers' online experiences, can be achieved through artificial intelligence algorithms that analyze customer click behavior on Web shops to generate tailored product recommendations based on their preferences	Lead to Cash

38	Optimized Marketing and Sales	Artificial intelligence can help enhance marketing and customer service strategies, sales planning, budgeting, and forecasting while building an organizational network, increasing pipeline yield through deal-focused recommendations, and boosting forecast accuracy with automated pipeline health assessments	Lead to Cash
39	Marketing Execution	Utilizing artificial intelligence to improve marketing execution, segmentation, pricing, promotions, and lead generation while boosting email channel revenue through personalized product recommendations and optimizing email engagement with send time and delivery optimization	Lead to Cash
40	Opportunity Optimization	Artificial intelligence helps to enhance sales processes such as quotation, configuration, and pricing by providing discount recommendations to boost closing rates, personalized cross-sell suggestions to grow deal sizes, opportunity scoring to identify top prospects, personalized product recommendations for Web channel revenue, scoring to predict customer purchasing intent, and visually similar cart recommendations to increase sales of new in-stock items	Lead to Cash
41[a]	Project Cost Forecasting	For a project manager, maintaining budgets and avoiding overruns is crucial for project success, and leveraging artificial intelligence services can help address common challenges like inadequate data and imperfect forecasting techniques by utilizing historical data to establish objective reference data, create an ideal work breakdown structure (WBS), improve cost forecast accuracy, and provide continuous monitoring and decision support for project management, ultimately increasing customer satisfaction and mitigating budget overrun risks	Idea to Market
42[a]	Digital Content Processing	Many organizations still rely on inefficient paper- and document-based processes, but artificial intelligence algorithms can help in digitizing unstructured sources and implementing automated classification; they can significantly improve efficiency, reduce errors, and enhance business value through cost savings, increased automation, and agile customer-specific scenarios while addressing customer pain points by fixing underperforming solutions, removing obstacles, mitigating risks, and lowering upfront investment costs	Idea to Market

(continued)

Table 1.1 (continued)

ID	Scenario name	Scenario description	ERP reference process
43	Project Portfolio Forecasting	Project financial controller requires various cost forecast alternatives for simulating future project cost evolution by employing simple approaches like using plan plus actual for future periods, manual forecast data, or cost performance index (CPI) from earned value management, as well as artificial intelligence that leverages historical data from similar projects and surrounding conditions, allows the project financial controller to understand and adjust parameters, considers additional information such as weather and raw-material costs, and continuously learns from parameter adjustments to optimize the process	Idea to Market
44	Project Early-Warning	Artificial intelligence can help automatically derive current project status and predict future status, enabling early identification of deviations, risks, and trends while aggregating overall status from incomplete or outdated data, minimizing dependency on project managers' experience, and proactively supporting decision-making and issue resolution, ultimately transforming project management from a reactive to an action-oriented process	Idea to Market
45	Context specific Recipe Development	Artificial intelligence can analyze and identify cluster patterns between ingredients in recipes, enabling it to support employees by making proposals during the development process, optimizing search results in the context of a recipe, and assisting recipe developers throughout the formulation process	Idea to Market
46	Guided Configuration	During the ordering process, artificial intelligence could guide users in configuring products by offering suggestions based on historical data to achieve desired individual configurations, reduce errors, and increase conversion rates, ultimately leading to simplified, smart product configurations and less manual rework by experts in sales orders	Idea to Market
47	Configurable Bill of Material	Inconsistent sales orders for configurable products can lead to difficulties in identifying matching components at the subcomponent level, but artificial intelligence can address this issue by automatically matching input properties with available components, reducing the need for manual reconfiguration by experts in sales orders	Idea to Market

48	Automatic Time Confirmation	Artificial intelligence automatically generates time confirmation proposals by analyzing data from various workflow tools, enabling project team members to confirm or modify them within a week, ultimately reducing effort and ensuring more accurate time tracking that reflects the real situation while also learning from historical patterns to enhance predictions.	Idea to Market
49	Requirement Driven Development	The early design phases involve rapid innovation cycles, generating numerous ideas, and selecting the most promising concepts for further development, utilizing artificial intelligence to draw upon company knowledge of successful and failed solutions, past developments, and product feedback, leading to accelerated development cycles, consideration of a wider range of alternatives, and early rejection of unsuccessful concepts, thus preventing wasted investments	Idea to Market
50	Workforce Assistant	As a hiring manager experiencing a resource bottleneck, artificial intelligence can autonomously guide on hiring temporary or permanent staff, upskilling existing employees, or outsourcing to contractors by consolidating information on the contracting market, training offers, and available budgets, ultimately alleviating time-consuming processes, expediting decision-making, and reducing training and support requirements for growth managers	Recruit to Retire
51	Personalized Recommend-ation	Artificial intelligence helps analyze individual data such as user attributes, preferences, learning history, and peer recommendations, to provide targeted, personalized course suggestions from the user's learning library, considering similarity with completed courses and other users' learning histories, as well as user-specified topics of interest while avoiding recommending courses that are already in the user's learning plan, bookmarked, or completed	Recruit to Retire
52	Career Explorer	Artificial intelligence can recommend personalized career opportunities to employees based on similar career paths within the organization, allowing them to explore roles, analyze skill gaps, and update preferences while also serving as a data source for marketplace to help employees discover relevant opportunities, including unconventional roles and career moves from outside their job hierarchy	Recruit to Retire
53	Image based Expense Management	Artificial intelligence can streamline expense reporting by allowing employees to capture receipt images, automatically generating, categorizing, and itemizing expense entries, thus reducing paper clutter, increasing spending visibility, improving budget management, saving time on report filing, and accelerating the reimbursement process	Recruit to Retire

(continued)

Table 1.1 (continued)

ID	Scenario name	Scenario description	ERP reference process
54	Predictive Maintenance	Artificial intelligence supports to enhance operational asset management by increasing service profitability, reducing maintenance costs, and boosting asset availability through the identification of asset health using learning algorithms enabling engineers and domain experts to compute health indicators using customer-specific models that reflect physical conditions and reveal hidden patterns and dependencies within sensor data to detect anomalies, predict failures, and oversee an entire fleet	Acquire to Decommission
55		Artificial intelligence can help in failure curve analytics to enable assessment of equipment failure likelihood and age by utilizing failure curves for groups of equipment with similar operating conditions, providing insights such as current age, probability of failure, confidence intervals, predicted failure date, and remaining useful life, allowing early detection of potential risks and proactive prevention planning	Acquire to Decommission
56	Emission Forecast	Environmental managers in emission-heavy industries must collect, monitor, and report emissions data, ensuring compliance with operational permits, and can utilize artificial intelligence to forecast future emissions, identify potential deviations or non-compliance, and proactively prevent unwanted events while also planning for regulatory changes and operational adjustments that may impact their emission inventory and permit requirements	Acquire to Decommission
57	Implausible Meter Reading Results	Using artificial intelligence in the utilities metering process helps analyze agents' historical actions and autonomously release or recommend the release of noncritical exceptions, ultimately streamlining the process and significantly decreasing manual labor requirements	Acquire to Decommission
58[a]	Business Integrity Screening	Artificial intelligence services in governance, risk, and compliance help organizations manage change, navigate risks, and adhere to regulations by analyzing risks, managing regulations, and monitoring compliance, which improves risk management, fraud prevention, and audit management and assists fraud investigators and screening specialists in prioritizing impactful cases using predictive detection methods, ultimately enhancing efficiency, profitability, and decision-making while reducing the risk of disruptions to critical business processes	Governance

59	Tax Compliance	Constantly changing corporate regulatory requirements necessitate centralization of business processes, including continuous transaction-level tax compliance, for growth and visibility; artificial intelligence can address compliance and risk challenges based on historical accounting documents, enabling integration of detection methods into business integrity screening strategies, automated correction measures, and learning from new decisions	Governance
60	Business Rule Mining	With artificial intelligence, enterprises can employ rule mining to uncover patterns in existing master data, analyze it using mining runs, collaboratively determine the business relevance of proposed rules, create and link data quality rules from accepted ones, and utilize information from rule mining in implementing data quality rules	Governance
61	Job Description and Interview Question with generative AI	Leveraging generative artificial intelligence in recruitment can streamline the creation of consistent, compelling job descriptions and personalized interview questions, improving efficiency, quality of hires, and employer branding while reducing bias and time and cost expenditures	Recruit to Retire
62	Delivery Note Processing with generative AI	Generative artificial intelligence in transportation management extracts information from documents to accelerate delivery note processing, reducing time per truck from 10 to 3 minutes, decreasing manual checks, expediting the unloading process, and improving accuracy up to 70%, resulting in an overall savings of 11%	Plan to Fulfill

[a]Scenario is explained as case study in part 3 of the elaboration

no standardized architecture definition available. This is due to the varying functional scope of the ERP products, different implementation strategies, and the fact that the product architecture is often a closely guarded secret of the ERP vendors. To overcome this gap, we proposed an ERP reference architecture (*Chapter 4*). However, to suggest such an ERP reference architecture, we had first to define ERP reference processes (*Chapter 3*), which specify the functionality of ERP systems. The reference processes describe the WHAT, while the reference architecture depicts the HOW. In defining the ERP reference processes, we investigated around 20 ERP products, which are listed in Table 1.2. We selected those ERP products according to IDC analysis (IDC, 2020) of the ERP vendors with the highest market share. We took into consideration key aspects such as the capabilities offered by the products and, if available, the technical realization approach provided by the vendor. In addition, we explored and abstracted the artificial intelligence technologies ERP products incorporating for implementation of corresponding use cases (*Chapter 5*). With the results 1 to 5 of Fig. 1.2, we had the necessary foundation to define the solution concept for embedding artificial intelligence into ERP software (*Chapters. 7–19*). We operationalized those concepts we operationalized with an implementation framework (*Chapter 20*) to simplify their consumption by developers. Thus, the framework applies the concepts as far as possible automatically while developers can focus on the implementation of the business logic. This reduces the total cost of development but also increases the quality of coding. While the framework concepts are generally valid, we introduce a concrete implementation as feasibility proof based on the ERP platform of SAP, especially as we utilize this technology also for the implementation of the case studies. The case studies prove the real-world feasibility of the proposed solution. Artificial intelligence use cases from the ERP domain sales and research (*Chapter 21*), sourcing and procurement (*Chapter 22*), inventory and supply chain (*Chapter 23*), and finance (*Chapter 24*) were realized successfully based on the suggested solution concept and implementation framework. Development of artificial intelligence applications in the context of ERP shall consider ethical aspects, which are discussed finally (*Chapter 25*).

To recap, we explained how our results were deducted and validated so that the scientist community can retrace and verify them.

Table 1.2 Analyzed ERP products selected from the IDC list (IDC, 2020)

ID	ERP product	Vendor	Considered information
1	SAP S/4HANA, SAP SuccessFactors, SAP Customer Experience	SAP	https://www.sap.com/products/
2	Oracle Fusion Applications Suite, NetSuite Applications	Oracle	https://docs.oracle.com/en/
3	Infor LN, Infor M3	Infor	https://www.infor.com/solutions/erp
4	Sage X3, Sage 100	Sage	https://www.sage.com/en-us/products/
5	Microsoft Dynamics 365	Microsoft	https://docs.microsoft.com/en-us/dynamics365/
6	Workday Finance, Spend Management & HCM	Workday	https://www.workday.com/en-us/products/
7	Customer 360, Sales Cloud, Service Cloud, Commerce Cloud, Marketing Cloud	Salesforce	https://www.salesforce.com/products/
8	Kinetic	Epicor Software	https://www.epicor.com/en-us/industry-productivity-solutions/
9	TurboTax, QuickBooks, Mailchimp, Mint	Intuit	https://www.intuit.com/products/
10	SYSPRO ERP	Syspro	https://eu.syspro.com/product/erp-software/
11	IFS Cloud	IFS Global	https://www.ifs.com/ifs-cloud/ifs-cloud-overview
12	Visma.net ERP	Visma	https://www.visma.com/enterprises
13	3DEXCITE, 3DVIA, BIOVIA, CATIA, DELMIA	Dassault Systems	https://www.3ds.com/products-services/
14	Acumatica Cloud ERP	Acumatica	https://www.acumatica.com/cloud-erp-software/
15	Mago ERP, Mago Cloud	Zucchetti	https://www.zucchetti.com/
16	Aptean ERP	Aptean	https://www.aptean.com/en-US/solutions/erp
17	Ramco ERP	Ramco	https://www.ramco.com/products/erp-software/
18	Teamcenter PLM	Siemens	https://plm.sw.siemens.com/en-US/teamcenter/
19	Mainpac	Constellation	https://mainpac.com/
20	Clover	Fiserv	https://docs.clover.com/docs/home

Part I
ERP Fundamentals

We begin this part with a historical view of ERP systems. The first software solutions for enterprises had been best of breed products, which were developed for very specific use cases. The resulting gap of integration among those numerous solutions was closed with monolithic ERP systems later. In turn, the high implementation and operations efforts of monolithic systems have been compensated nowadays with cloud-based ERP solutions where hardware is shared among multiple deployments. However, intelligent ERP is the future direction. These products apply artificial intelligence technology to automatize business processes toward an autonomous solution. Although there is a long journey to go, the first use cases in this domain are very promising. Market analysts also foresee high potential and expect billions of dollar growth in this area. Consequently, researching in the new field of embedding artificial intelligence into ERP software is essential to resolve the underlying challenges and leverage the huge opportunities as we do with this elaboration. We also briefly discuss the application of artificial intelligence in context of ERP systems in terms of increasing automation of business processes. In this context, we also provide an answer to the question, "What makes an ERP system intelligent?" For embedding artificial intelligence into ERP software, we must know the architecture of ERP systems to incorporate systematically artificial intelligence. However, the functionality and architecture of ERP solutions depend on the vendors and differ accordingly. Therefore, we first propose a reference process specification, which constitutes the functionality of ERP solutions. All enterprises cover the domains develop products and services, generate demand, fulfill demand, plan and manage, and have to digitalize the underlying business processes. We suggest business processes for those domains and derive from them a reference architecture for ERP software. The suggested reference processes we use to specify which part of a business process shall be enriched with artificial intelligence capability (the WHAT), while the proposed reference architecture we utilize to determine where and how to incorporate artificial intelligence technology (the HOW). Especially the concepts we later define are founded on those reference models and are therefore commonly valid. As a side benefit, the reference processes and refence architecture can be additionally reused for assessing ERP products. This part is based on our investigations in Sarferaz (2022, 2023). As exemplary listed, there are numerous publications regarding ERP software. However, their main focus is not on future trends, reference processes, and reference architecture but on aspects like:

- ERP selection criteria (Kumar 2003; Verville 2003; Fischer 2004; HAN 2004; Wie 2005; Keil 2006; Lall 2006; Ayag 2007; Yang 2007; Bueno 2008; Aberdeen 2006, 2007; Ratkevicius 2012; Bhatt 2021; Chang 2020; Yurtyapan 2021; Alaskari 2019; Chen 2019; Czekster 2019; Aydogmus 2021; Beskese 2019; Thanh 2022; Polivka 2021)
- ERP success factors (Grabski 2003; Ewusi 1997; Glass 1998; Laughlin 1999; Swan 1999; Parr 2000; Soh 2000; Sumner 2000; Motwani 2002; Stapleton 2004; Wei 2004; Anexinet 2006; Kimberling 2006; Ibrahim 2008; Lindley 2008; Parijat 2009; Menon 2019; Kiran 2019; Barth 2019; Al-Okaily 2021; Mahraz 2020; Gavali 2019; Tongsuksai 2019)
- ERP value proposition (Chen 2006; Gibson 1999; Gobeli 2002; Gunasekaran 2006; Krumbholz 2000; Rebstock 2000; Robinson 1999; Somers 2000; Davenport 1998; Dong 2000; Jacobs 2003; Akkermans 2003; Tarantilis 2008; Prahalad 2008; Rosemann 2000; Ross 2002; Stewart 2000; Willis 2002; Ruivo 2020; Hadidi 2020)
- ERP implementation (Avital 1999; Brancroft 1998; Becerra-Fernandez 2000; Gobeli 2002; Gattiker 2005; Jacobs 2003; Soh 2000; Vincent 2003; Boersma 2005; Bonner 2000; Brown 1999; Ranganathan 2006; Umble 2003; Al-Mashari 2003; Nohria 2003; Cotteleer 2006; Adam 2000; Gattiker 2000; Purnendu 2003; Olhager 2003; Pawlowski 1999; Rohit 2021; Alsharari 2020)

Intelligent ERP

2

In this chapter, we take the reader through a journey of the history of ERP systems and show the strengths and weaknesses of ERP solutions and how the providers deal with the constant change in requirements. In this context, ERP vendors and their market share are briefly introduced. The first material resource planning (MRP) systems were provided as best of breed solutions for more than 50 years ago. Monolithic ERP systems followed, overcoming the integration challenges of MRP products. Today, cloud-based ERP solutions are in focus, which aim to reduce hardware and operations cost with cloud computing techniques. However, the future is intelligent ERP systems that make use of artificial intelligence to mimic cognitive capabilities of human being for increasing the automatization of business processes. This is a completely new research area for which we suggest answers in the elaboration.

2.1   ERP Evolution

ERP stands for enterprise resource planning system, but what does it entail? ERP refers to a multi-modular software designed to manage and regulate a variety of activities that support enterprises. Functions such as data collection, storage, product planning, parts procurement, inventory management, purchasing, customer service, and order monitoring can all be facilitated through ERP. Additionally, ERP encompasses financial and human resource management application modules. In essence, ERP software strives to digitize all enterprise processes to enhance overall optimization. Implementing an ERP system requires significant business process reengineering and employee retraining. The rapid advancement of information technology and the continuous digitization of both private and business sectors have increased the demand for advanced ERP systems. Factors contributing to this demand include the need for prompt delivery of goods and services, as well as a fast, simple, and secure method for conducting transactions across multiple instances.

© The Author(s), under exclusive license to Springer Nature
Switzerland AG 2024
S. Sarferaz, *Embedding Artificial Intelligence into ERP Software*,
https://doi.org/10.1007/978-3-031-54249-7_2

Let us delve into the evolution of ERP systems and the changes in requirements and functionalities.

The origins of ERP systems can be traced back to the 1960s or 1970s, depending on the source. It all began with MRP systems, which stands for material requirements planning systems. Initially, these systems were primarily designed for the manufacturing industry and were used to calculate the materials and components needed to produce a product (Essex et al., 2020). Joseph Orlicky, an IBM engineer, invented the MRP system in 1964. However, MRP systems had some limitations, such as their narrow focus and lack of feedback mechanisms for production plans when material plans were infeasible due to capacity shortages. Over time, MRP systems evolved, and it became evident that a more comprehensive, holistic approach was necessary to integrate other processes and the entire organization. This evolution included establishing connections between manufacturing execution and production planning activities, known as the master production schedule (MPS), among other developments. Various approaches were also developed for capacity planning and financial planning. These improvements led to the creation of more advanced MRP systems, called MRP II systems. In the early 1970s, several companies emerged that focused on standard software for businesses. These start-ups initially concentrated on finance, using a single database and real-time processing. At that time, these systems were available as mainframe software on large computers. Gradually, back-office processes like human resources and accounting were combined, and by the 1980s, all business functions within a company were integrated. This progress was made possible by the rapid and continuous advancements in computer technology, both in hardware and software. MRP II, which stands for manufacturing resource planning, was introduced by management expert Oliver Wight in 1983 (Wight, 1984). Wight defined MRP II as a comprehensive market and resource-oriented planning system for sales, production, and inventory levels, starting at the executive level. The development and integration of various company departments led to the idea of a unified database and a single system, as separate systems often resulted in inconsistencies and increased time expenditure. MRP II systems, with the help of advancing computer technology, offered the ability to perform simulations based on data sets in addition to providing a company-wide information base. These simulations aided companies in making various operational decisions without altering the actual data sets in the database. As a result, MRP II systems had three key features: interfunctional coordination, closed-loop planning, and what-if analysis capability. Despite these advancements, MRP II systems had a significant drawback: they were primarily focused on production, which excluded non-manufacturing companies and other sectors of the economy. This shortcoming led to the development of the next stage in the evolution: ERP systems, which aimed to fill the market gap. ERP systems emerged in the 1990s, as depicted in Fig. 2.1 (Saueressig et al., 2021a, 2021b). Gartner research analysts, as cited by Essex et al. (2020), identified the necessity for a consistent nomenclature and led the effort to establish it. They drew inspiration from business software providers such as SAP, PeopleSoft, Baan, and more. Although the terms MRP and MRP II are no longer widely used, they are seen as the precursors to modern ERP systems. Many of their concepts and ideas continue to be employed in today's ERP systems. In most cases, MRP solutions are incorporated into ERP systems as a standard feature.

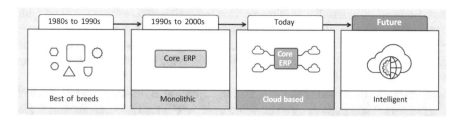

Fig. 2.1 Evolution of ERP software

So, what exactly is an ERP system? ERP systems are versatile solutions that support major business processes across various industries and company types. Not only do they handle production workflows, but they also manage other general business processes. A key feature of ERP systems is their applicability to all sectors, since every organization, regardless of its industry, must issue invoices and engage with other businesses in some manner. As ERP systems evolved, they faced the challenges of localization, global markets, and international networks. This led to the development of multilingual and multicurrency systems, including conversion capabilities, to keep up with the ever-changing global market landscape and competition. ERP systems had to address numerous hurdles, such as creating distributed systems, custom data views, and processing capabilities for different roles and employees. By 2000, typical functionalities of an ERP system included engineering, technical change control and documentation, procurement or purchasing, materials management, manufacturing, human resources, cost accounting, finance, marketing, and sales. The advent of the ERP concept prompted system vendors to reevaluate their approach, shifting from mainframe computers to server-client architectures, which facilitated multi-user operations. User interfaces were gradually improved, and early ERP systems allowed real-time software usage at individual workstations. Additional features introduced during this period included distributed relational databases with query and reporting capabilities, electronic data interchange for communication with suppliers and customers, decision support systems for managers, graphical user interfaces, and standard application programming interfaces. However, technological progress did not stop in 2000. Over the next decade, a new trend emerged: data needed to be accessible and retrievable at any time and from any location. Cloud computing became a buzzword in this context, enabling real-time communication between companies. Some businesses transitioned from traditional desktop applications to browser-based user interfaces. From the 2010s until now, numerous technological advancements have continued to present new challenges for ERP system providers. These include artificial intelligence and machine learning, blockchain, predictive analytics, and other emerging technologies that require the cloud's advanced computing power, big data, and Internet connectivity. As a result, the long-term future of ERP systems involves the development of autonomous solutions referred as intelligent ERP. Progress in artificial intelligence have significantly impacted process automation, dynamic analytics, and user experiences based on voice, vision, and messaging. Artificial intelligence enables users to eliminate mundane routine tasks by automating business processes, ranging from HR to payment processing, purchase order approvals, and sales execution. Proactive analysis of new data types and detection of unfamiliar patterns provide unprecedented insights for identifying opportunities and threats. Artificial intelligence capabilities facilitate human interaction by leaving only non-automated tasks for users to handle. Advanced bot techniques, such as ChatGPT, can even generate code, allowing intelligent ERP systems to adapt to changes autonomously.

In 2021, the ERP market was valued at $92.1 billion as illustrated in Fig. 2.2. The largest market competitors by share value were SAP with 13.0%, Intuit with 8.7%, Oracle with 6.1%, Workday with 4.9%, and Microsoft with 2.6%. Combined, these companies accounted for nearly a third of the entire global ERP market. The increased market share of tech giants like Microsoft, Oracle, and SAP can be attributed to their unique historical backgrounds and diverse strategies. For instance, Microsoft achieved success in the ERP market by offering dynamic products and fully integrated tools, along with strategic acquisitions such as Great Plains (Davidson, 2020). On the other hand, SAP has been a frontrunner in business applications since introducing its first ERP system in 1972 (Davidson, 2020), catering to clients in over 180 countries with a wide range of ERP solutions tailored to various use cases and business sizes. The software's scalability also contributes to its advantage. Oracle, primarily recognized for selling databases, platform software, cloud systems, and enterprise software products, emerged as a top ERP company following several acquisitions in the early 2000s. Their acquisition of NetSuite in 2016 further solidified their position in the ERP cloud systems realm. Meanwhile, Sage, much like SAP, has a long-standing history in ERP software dating back to 1981, primarily focusing on small businesses. Their ERP solutions are known for their modularity and customization options.

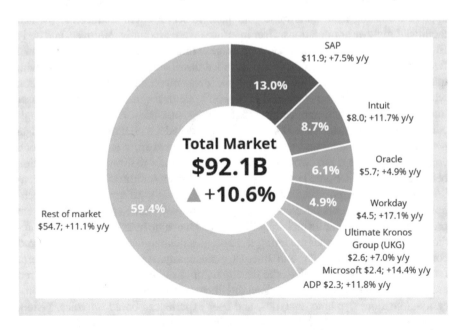

Fig. 2.2 Worldwide ERP market share in 2021 (IDC, 2021). Note: 2021 Share (%), Revenue ($B), and Growth (%)

Infor has become a leading player in the small and medium business sector after aggressively modernizing their product line since 2010 and utilizing acquisitions to provide ERP software for various industries. To stay ahead in the market, competitors apply different strategies, which can be grouped into revenue growth, technology, and industry. Despite these diverse approaches, a common thread among them is the desire to leverage emerging technologies like artificial intelligence and cloud services, enabling clients to gain deeper data insights and enhance business processes. Generally, the emphasis is on customer-centric, cloud-based, and intelligent solutions.

Exploring the traits and functionalities of ERP systems and their recent implementations, architectural advancements have allowed these solutions to excel in the market, offering high performance, reliability, and adaptability. As customer needs evolved, ERP providers faced new challenges, leading to the emergence of seven essential features for modern ERP systems (Saueressig et al., 2021b): high performance and scalability, user experience, extensible architecture, streamlined and standardized implementations, intelligent ERP processes, cloud and on-premise deployment options, and security encompassing data protection, compliance, and data isolation.

2.2   ERP Future

As explained in Sarferaz (2022), an intelligent ERP system is a software solution that incorporates artificial intelligence, machine learning, and advanced automation technologies to perform tasks, make decisions, and manage processes with minimal or no human intervention. This type of ERP system aims to improve efficiency, reduce errors, and adapt to changing business conditions with self-managing business processes and self-diagnosing capabilities. Traditional ERP systems require substantial manual input and management, while intelligent ERP systems can learn from historical data, analyze patterns, and predict future trends. Some exemplary key features of an intelligent ERP might include:

- Advanced analytics and forecasting: The system can analyze large volumes of data to identify trends and make accurate predictions, helping businesses make more informed decisions.
- Intelligent automation: Intelligent ERP systems can automate routine tasks such as data entry, invoicing, and order processing, freeing up employees to focus on more strategic work.
- Continuous improvement: The system can learn from its own performance and user feedback to continuously improve its capabilities and provide better insights and recommendations over time.
- Enhanced security: With built-in artificial intelligence and machine learning, an intelligent ERP can identify potential security threats, vulnerabilities, and compliance issues more effectively than a traditional system.

• Personalization: The system can adapt to individual users' preferences and needs, providing a more tailored experience and improving productivity.

An intelligent ERP can be an excellent solution for businesses looking to optimize their operations and stay competitive in the rapidly evolving digital landscape. However, implementing such a system may require significant investment in terms of technology, infrastructure, and training. To accomplish this, modern ERP systems need to become smarter. Intelligence is typically a quality attributed to humans and other living beings, characterized by the ability to learn, comprehend, and reason logically. In the context of ERP systems, artificial intelligence is utilized to imbue business processes with intelligence, increasing the automation and optimization levels. Data science techniques are applied for this purpose. Data science's objectives can be distilled into two main points: solving a specific problem and deriving insights from a dataset, with the latter serving as a means to achieve the former. As the volume of data generated and stored grows exponentially, leveraging data to resolve problem statements becomes increasingly appealing, offering more opportunities for data science to provide solutions. The data science process can be broken down into the following stages phases Varga (2019) and Shah (2019):

• Project initiation and problem statement definition.
• Data acquisition or gathering the necessary data to solve the problem outlined in step 1.
• Data preparation and quality assessment to ensure the collected data is fitting for its intended purpose. While data science cannot glean insights from poor-quality data, it can certainly do so when applied correctly to a dataset of adequate quality.
• Data modelling, which involves each step and technique to apply to the data in order to achieve the specified goal and executing these steps.
• Reporting and communicating insights. This step, along with the subsequent utilization of these insights, relies heavily on the results and insights obtained in step 4 and the target audience.

Management decisions require the highest-quality information available, and data science is crucial in delivering this information to leaders. In addition to this strategic aspect, data science also helps keep a business operational. Connecting data science principles with data collected in ERP systems adds value. This not only enhances the functionality of operational processes but also allows companies to unlock the full potential of their data. By transforming data into valuable knowledge and insights, businesses can gain a deeper understanding of their customers and the functioning of their processes. This information can be used to tailor products to customer needs, optimize processes, and identify the factors that drive a business's success. By leveraging the data produced in ERP systems through everyday operations, companies can accelerate the transition to intelligent ERP by gaining valuable insights. Since ERP systems typically hold vast amounts of transactional business process data, it is logical to assume that useful insights can be extracted from this information. By applying artificial intelligence techniques to this data, companies can address specific problem statements, such as predicting material requirements for upcoming quarters or identifying the factors that influence customer purchasing decisions. Using the same dataset, businesses can analyze financial data and forecast significant financial events, allowing them to take action proactively. As the shift toward connected assets under the keyword of Industry 4.0 and the Internet of things (IoT) continues, an increasing volume of real-time sensor data becomes available, further expanding the applications of data science. The advent of new services related to asset maintenance and automation, such as automated anomaly detection and predictive maintenance, has transformed the industry. However, delivering effective solutions in this domain is a challenging task. It demands not only a profound knowledge of data science techniques but also a comprehensive understanding of the assets and machinery involved. By applying natural language processing and computer vision systems, businesses can automatically extract essential information from documents like invoices, streamlining the invoicing process. Similar approaches can be used to categorize documents, such as customer tickets, and automatically assign them to the appropriate call center employee. Chatbots, when connected to analytical tools, can help employees obtain information from various data sources. Reports with drill-down capabilities can be used to convey complex information to management in a simplified manner, improving data transparency and ease of insight. While artificial intelligence and ERP systems have been around for some time, the synergies between them are a recent development. Data scientists are now exploring innovative ways to derive meaningful insights from data to benefit their organizations. The growing research on applying artificial intelligence algorithms to solve everyday problems has paved the way for novel solutions to age-old challenges. Effectively leveraging data science offers numerous advantages for businesses, including increased return on investment, enhanced operational efficiency, and reduced human errors. It also enables companies to respond faster to changes in products, services, pricing, or availability, ensuring they remain competitive. Failing to capitalize on the benefits of artificial intelligence and the resulting enhancements to business processes may lead to a decline in customer satisfaction. Current ERP systems largely do not utilize artificial intelligence, making the path to fully intelligent ERP a lengthy one. Achieving a completely intelligent ERP may be impossible due to technical, legal, and functional constraints. However, intermediate steps toward an intelligent ERP, such as integrating intelligence into specific processes, are valuable. One example is the already-mentioned prediction of high-tech equipment failure, which is crucial for manufacturers. By combining sensor data with business information in ERP systems and using artificial intelligence models, the health of machines can be anticipated, transforming maintenance scheduling and logistics planning for spare parts and repair crew management into proactive processes. Another example is the importance of verifying that a product is manufactured precisely according to specifications and configuration before shipping, which is an important step in final quality assurance. Image-recognition algorithms can be used to conduct visual product quality inspections, increasing the accuracy and automation of production quality processes. This leads to fewer returns, higher customer satisfaction, and better profitability. A third example outlines the importance of high-quality master data as the foundation for ERP processes. Artificial intelligence can be applied to automate the identification and implementation of validation rules, ensuring data consistency. Autocompleting attribute values using artificial intelligence while maintaining master data streamlines interactions with end users and reduces manual tasks, saving costs. These intelligent processes can be classified into application patterns such as recommendation, prediction, or ranking scenarios. ERP systems should offer a standardized framework for each pattern, enabling development teams to apply artificial intelligence application patterns as reusable building blocks and expedite implementation. In conclusion, while fully intelligent ERP may remain a visionary concept that may never be entirely achievable, a symbiotic relationship between humans and machines will continue to evolve. In this relationship, machines will support users and augment human capabilities.

Let's also consider analyst reports emphasizing the growing importance of artificial intelligence in business applications and conversely, outlining the relevance of solving the challenge of embedding artificial intelligence into ERP software. According to IDC's Worldwide Semiannual Artificial Intelligence Systems Spending Guide (IDC, 2022a), which tracks artificial intelligence (AI) software, hardware, and services across industries and use cases, enterprises worldwide are expected to invest \$118 billion on artificial intelligence solutions in 2022. This spending is expected to grow to \$301 billion at a compound annual growth rate (CAGR) of 26.5% for the 2021–2026 period. This is more than four times greater than the 5-year CAGR of 6.3% for worldwide IT spending over the same period. In addition, worldwide intelligent process automation (IPA) software will reach \$49 billion in 2026, growing at a CAGR of 19.4% for the 2021–2026 period. According to IDC by 2026, AI-driven features will be embedded across business technology categories, and 60% of organizations will actively use such features to drive better outcomes without relying on technical AI talent. The market for artificial intelligence life cycle platforms is growing rapidly worldwide with IDC data predicting a 36.2% CAGR in product revenue through to 2026, but adoption of AI-powered technology within organizations will be dominated in the coming years by "silent" embedded AI features within other technologies. AI-powered features are finding their way into every layer of technology that organizations use from optimization and automation within modern networks and infrastructure management tooling to assisted software development tools leveraging smart code completion and automated testing to advanced threat detection in modern enterprise security platforms to the provision of advanced predictions, recommendations, and even asset creation for business users of CRM, ERP, and financial software applications. Vendors are racing to embed these features to help organizations automate aspects of their technology installation, configuration, administration, development, and customization. These systems leverage organizations' own data, often combined with anonymized data from larger customer populations, to provide intelligent recommendations and predictions to business users, helping them be more effective. IDC FutureScape (IDC, 2022b) highlights that intelligent ERP and associated applications are undergoing a plethora of changes from the days of legacy on-premises systems to SaaS and cloud-enabled applications chalked full of artificial intelligence and automated workflows. These modern, modular, and intelligent systems can manage vast amounts of data in real time, changing up the performance capabilities of an organization nearly overnight. IDC predicts that by mid-2025, 50% of end users will leverage AI-infused applications, moving from systems of record to systems of intelligent planning, providing a lens toward better outcomes. Furthermore, by 2028, 30% of employers will use intelligent processes to augment the shortfall in labor and by doing so will increase the organization's agility, resilience, and performance. According to a recent IDC report (IDC, 2022c), the global AI software market is projected to expand from $340.4 billion in 2021 to $791.5 billion in 2026, with a compound annual growth rate (CAGR) of 18.4%, as illustrated in Fig. 2.3.

AI-centric software refers to applications where AI technologies are vital to their functionality, without which they would cease to function. These programs require AI (e.g., supervised, unsupervised, reinforcement) and user/data interaction (e.g., natural language processing, image/video analytics, and vision) or knowledge representation capabilities. In contrast, AI-non-centric software denotes applications where AI is integrated into the software but is not essential to its core functionality. These applications can still operate without AI and may include machine learning, user/data interaction, or knowledge representation capabilities. AI is now prevalent throughout the technology stack. IDC's AI software market encompasses AI platforms, AI applications, AI systems infrastructure software (SIS), and AI application development and deployment (AD&D) software (excluding AI platforms). A May 2022 survey by IDC involving over 2000 IT and line-of-business (LOB) decision-makers confirms that AI adoption is on the rise globally. Organizations are expected to increase their AI spending by 4% in 2022 compared to 2021. AI has a significant impact on businesses and organizations across various industries. Early adopters have reported a 35% improvement in innovation and a 33% enhancement in sustainability by investing in AI over the past 3 years. AI investments have also led to a 32% increase in both customer and employee retention. Organizations are boosting

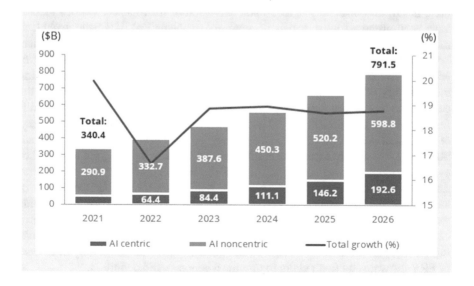

Fig. 2.3 Worldwide artificial intelligence software forecast 2022–2026 (IDC, 2022c)

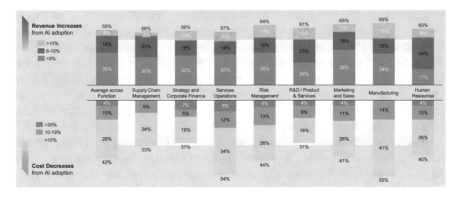

Fig. 2.4 Revenue and cost improvements from AI adoption (McKinsey, 2023)

their AI expenditures this year, with accelerated innovation as the primary business objective for AI adoption. Approximately 50% of large enterprises consider this their top driver. The COVID-19 pandemic has also sped up AI-powered automation plans across all regions. Figure 2.4 very well outlines the impact of artificial intelligence adoption to different ERP domains.

2.3 Applying Intelligence on ERP

ERP software has progressed from a best-of-breed strategy in the 1980s to monolithic systems in the 1990s. Presently, the emphasis is on cloud-based ERP, with the goal being the development of intelligent ERP software. However, what exactly constitutes an intelligent ERP system? Despite extensive research and discussion, there is still no universally agreed-upon definition of intelligence. Various models have been proposed by scientists to represent mathematical, linguistic, technical, musical, and emotional intelligence, but none have gained widespread acceptance. So, how can we create intelligent ERP software without a clear understanding of what that entails? To address this issue, we propose applying the operationalization methodology, which has its roots in philosophy. This method is used to resolve the conundrum and render the concept of intelligence quantifiable by establishing different levels of automation, akin to how psychologists use IQ values. In the context of ERP, intelligence is not merely an end goal; rather, it is about enhancing automation to achieve a more autonomous ERP system, thereby reducing the total cost of ownership (TCO) through expedited process runtimes or optimized resource utilization. Consequently, the following principle holds true: the greater the degree of automation in a business process or system, the higher its intelligence level. In this section, we present a methodology for measuring the intelligence of business processes facilitated by ERP software, and we discuss both the business and technological aspects. We underline that we consider the term intelligence only in context of ERP software and don't claim to provide a general valid definition.

2.3.1 Methodology

ERP systems function as the core mechanism for managing an organization's various business operations. Crucial question for determining the level of automation revolve around comprehending the common structure of all these business processes.

As depicted in Fig. 2.5, there are four aspects to be taken into account for automation in a business process, according to Parasuraman et al. (2000). This widely accepted standard has been adapted specifically for ERP software. Each dimension is assessed on a scale of 1 (low) to 5 (high) based on its degree of automation. By evaluating the automation level of each dimension for a specific business process or system, the overall automation level can be identified. This allows for the determination of the current and desired intelligence levels and the creation of an implementation plan to enhance the intelligence of the business process.

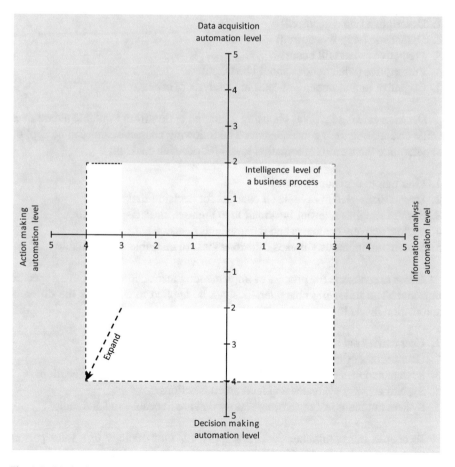

Fig. 2.5 Methodology for operationalizing intelligence

Data acquisition involves entering data into ERP systems using devices like keyboards, scanners, disks, or voice input. The following characteristics can be applied to determine the various automation levels for data acquisition:

1. Manual entry by the user
2. Manual entry combined with data integration
3. Data integration with occasional manual entry
4. Conversational AI and data integration
5. AI-based data extraction and integration (e.g., a PDF document is converted into structured data and input by a robotic bot)

Information analysis entails examining and interpreting data to derive meaningful insights. The following characteristics can be applied to determine the different automation levels for information analysis:

1. Descriptive (what occurred)
2. Diagnostic (why it occurred)
3. Predictive (what will occur)
4. Prescriptive (what actions should be taken)
5. Cognitive (autonomous self-learning analysis of events)

Decision-making involves choosing a rational option from available alternatives while considering their consequences. The following characteristics can be applied to determine the various automation levels for decision-making:

1. User makes decisions manually.
2. User utilizes system events and changes for decision-making.
3. System supplies relevant information to the user for decision-making.
4. System actively evaluates and recommends decisions.
5. System autonomously makes decisions that are traceable and auditable.

Action execution is the process of implementing instructions to achieve a specific objective. The following characteristics can be applied to determine the different automation levels for action execution:

1. User carries out actions manually.
2. User utilizes system events and changes to perform actions.
3. System supplies relevant information to the user for performing execution.
4. System actively evaluates and recommends actions.
5. System autonomously performs actions that are traceable and auditable.

To deepen our comprehension, let's apply this methodology to a sales performance use case: A sales plan is a strategy outlining revenue objectives and the steps required to achieve those targets.

Typically, creating such a sales plan involves manually analyzing historical data to forecast revenue as a key metric. This process could be enhanced by using artificial intelligence to predict future sales development. As a result, by offering improved insights for taking necessary actions, the manual labor involved in sales planning can be reduced, and the actual sales volume can be increased. Figure 2.6 illustrates the implementation of this method to determine the present and desired levels of intelligence for the described sales performance situation. It is evident that by forecasting sales revenue using artificial intelligence, the automation levels for decision-making and action-taking dimensions are increased. Nonetheless, the automation levels for data acquisition and information analysis dimensions remain unaltered, as no extra intelligence is incorporated into them.

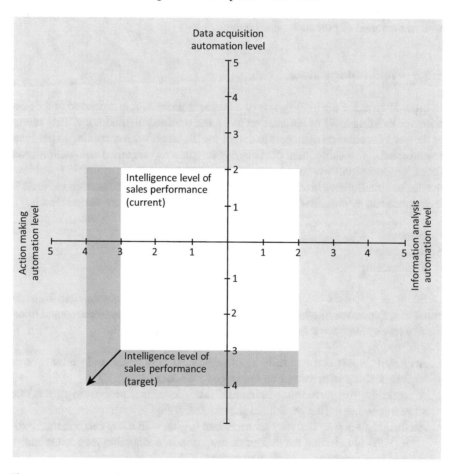

Fig. 2.6 Example of applying methodology

2.3.2   Business View

Companies of all sizes strive to enhance their revenue and profit margins by using modern ERP systems. By incorporating intelligence into business processes, these systems assist in realizing these objectives through the generation of novel insights from data or by facilitating data-driven automation. Nevertheless, the specific value of incorporating intelligence is contingent upon the context or application in which it is utilized. For instance, even an incremental enhancement via rule-based methodologies can be perceived as more intelligent compared to the existing state, thereby contributing additional value to the business. The suggested framework lays the groundwork for an impartial dialogue among diverse stakeholders (e.g., customer, ERP vendor) regarding the present and prospective state of a business process, as well as the range of potential value creation.

2.3.3   Technology View

In order to enhance the intelligence of a business process, it is crucial to first determine the existing level of automation using the outlined methodology. This serves as the basis for solution managers to determine the target level according to business requirements. The subsequent challenge is to attain the specified automation level for each dimension. A range of concepts and technologies are available to achieve the desired intelligence level for the respective dimensions. As illustrated in Fig. 2.7, techniques can be classified into different categories for realizing various levels:

- Manual
- Rule-based
- Self-learning

Business processes can be operated manually without any automation. To overcome this, numerous rule-based methods can be used to boost automation and intelligence levels. Here are a few examples of rule-based techniques:

- An ABAP report that conducts input or process validations and presents error messages along with resolution guidance to the user
- A workflow for performing individual tasks/decisions, progressing from one stage to another until a predefined process is finished
- An insight-to-action analytics scenario that begins with a key performance indicator (KPI) tile alerting the user of drifting trends, conducting root-cause analysis, and implementing corrective measures
- A situation-handling application that notifies the user of an issue, supplies the necessary data for resolution, and suggests predefined actions

To reach level 5, rule-based methods are usually not adequate and must be supplemented with self-learning techniques. These approaches analyze raw data to

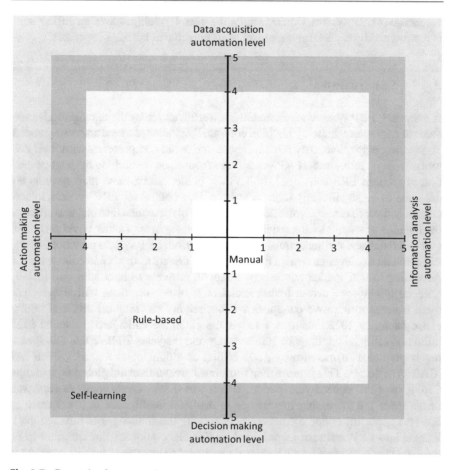

Fig. 2.7 Categories for automation technologies

uncover hidden insights and relationships by learning from the data, rather than relying on explicitly programmed rules. Some instances include:

- Deep learning for image recognition
- Conversational AI for natural language processing (NLP)
- Bots or intelligent applications that leverage artificial intelligence models to autonomously make decisions and execute actions

In the context of ERP software, rule-based technologies are well established, so this elaboration concentrates on self-learning methods based on artificial intelligence to increase the intelligence level of business processes. The proposed approach offers a framework for determining a strategic direction for ERP systems in terms of enhancing their intelligence. To imbue ERP systems with more intelligence, additional business processes must advance to levels 4 and 5, aiming for an autonomous ERP system. Consequently, the overall intelligence of an ERP system is represented by the intelligence level of its constituent business processes.

2.4 Conclusion

In summary, ERP systems are incredibly powerful, driven by the relentless advancement of computer technology, which continually challenges vendors to stay ahead. To remain competitive, they must innovate and avoid complacency with their current offerings. Today, most ERP vendors are focused on developing the next generation of modern ERP solutions. Unlike their predecessors, these new systems are designed to be significantly more adaptable. It is crucial for ERP vendors to stay current and continuously evolve, as technologies like machine learning and artificial intelligence advance rapidly. Additionally, the emergence of other novel technologies could demand further action and innovation from ERP system providers. Cloud and artificial intelligence remain key technology drivers as they enable those trends. According to IDC market analysis by 2026, all business technologies will include artificial intelligence driven features, and 60% of organizations will actively use these features to improve outcomes without relying on technical artificial intelligence talent. In 2022, businesses across the globe are anticipated to spend $118 billion on artificial intelligence solutions. During the years 2021–2026, this spending is predicted to increase by $301 billion at a compound annual growth rate (CAGR) of 26.5%. This is more than four times greater than the global IT spending CAGR over the same 5-year period, which was 6.3%. These numbers very well demonstrate the increasing importance of artificial intelligence in the domain of business applications and the necessity of solving the challenges of infusing intelligence into ERP software as provided by this elaboration. A key question to be resolved is, what makes an ERP system intelligent? The answer for this question is not simple, as there is no commonly accepted definition of the term intelligence. From our perspective, rule-based business applications that are coded or implemented as workflows are already intelligent as they perform complex tasks. However, the corresponding rules are determined by human being and coded accordingly as software. In case of artificial intelligence, the algorithms learn from data and determine the underlying rules without human being. Thus, from our point of view, there are different levels of intelligence and conversely disparate level of automation for ERP business processes. Thus, in this chapter, we proposed a methodology of applying artificial intelligence systematically on ERP software. Our idea is to operationalize the term intelligence and repatriate it with the level of automation of business processes. All business processes in an ERP system have the dimensions data acquisition, information analysis, and decision- and action-making. For each dimension, the level of automation can be improved by applying artificial intelligence techniques. With the increasing level of intelligence of the underlying business processes, also the ERP system becomes more intelligent toward an autonomous ERP.

ERP Reference Processes

3

Although ERP solutions have been around for years, there is no common definition of its functional scope. As a result, market analysts and ERP suppliers offer their own, highly subjective, interpretation of ERP functionality. However, to embed systematically artificial intelligence into ERP software, we must have a clear understanding of the ERP functionality. In this chapter, we propose a reference process that acts as a functional specification for ERP systems. The reference processes outline the functional richness of ERP software and conversely the complexity of embedding artificial intelligence into it but also emphasizes the high potential of applying artificial intelligence for improving those business processes. Furthermore, the reference processes build the foundation of the ERP reference architecture of the next chapter. The refence processes can as well be used to compare the functionality of different ERP products.

3.1   Introduction

Let's begin with the problem statement. Despite the existence of ERP solutions for many years, there is no universally agreed-upon definition of their functional scope. In the realm of database systems, the SQL standard outlines the primary functionality of a database system. However, no such standards exist for ERP systems. As a result, market analysts and ERP vendors offer their own interpretations of the functional scope, which are often highly subjective. To address this issue, we propose a reference business process definition for enterprises, which serves as a functional specification for ERP systems. This business process description can be used to verify the functional coverage of ERP solutions or to compare the functionality of various ERP products. In this chapter, we provide a brief overview of these business processes to highlight the functional richness of ERP software and, conversely, the enormous potential of artificial intelligence to increase the automation level of ERP systems. The description of the key business processes underscores the complexity

© The Author(s), under exclusive license to Springer Nature
Switzerland AG 2024
S. Sarferaz, *Embedding Artificial Intelligence into ERP Software*,
https://doi.org/10.1007/978-3-031-54249-7_3

of ERP software and, consequently, the significant challenge of integrating artificial intelligence into them. The explained business processes (the What) lay the ground-work for the reference ERP architecture (the How) that we will introduce in the next chapter. The reference ERP architecture forms the foundation for the technical solution concerning the incorporation of artificial intelligence into ERP software.

The value chain encompasses the entirety of an enterprise's processes. It can be used as an initial analysis approach for identifying and creating strategic competitive advantages. As illustrated in Fig. 3.1, the value chain considers all interconnected activities involved in delivering products or services as components within a complex chain. Each component of the value chain incurs costs and contributes to the final product's value. Consequently, it is essential to analyze each component of the chain. A company's activities are divided into two categories: primary activities and support activities. Primary activities provide an immediate value-added contribution to the creation of a product or service, while support activities enhance the efficiency and effectiveness of primary activities. Primary activities consist of inbound logistics, manufacturing, outbound logistics, marketing, sales, and service, while support activities encompass procurement, technological development, human resources management, and enterprise infrastructure.

The value chain can be segmented into four distinct enterprise domains: the customer domain, the supply domain, the corporate domain, and the products and services domain. Departments associated with the products and services domain focus on the development of products and services, while those linked to the customer domain concentrate on generating demand. Departments within the corporate domain are tasked with planning and managing the enterprise, and those connected to the supply domain are responsible for meeting customer demand. The foundational business processes for these four domains involve developing products and services, generating demand, fulfilling demand, and planning and managing the enterprise, as illustrated in Fig. 3.2. The *Idea to Market* process supports the

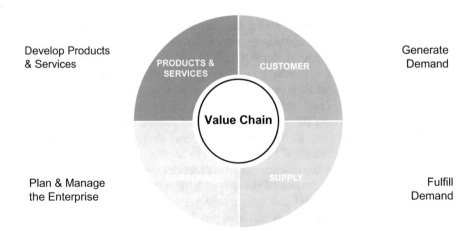

Fig. 3.1 Enterprise domains

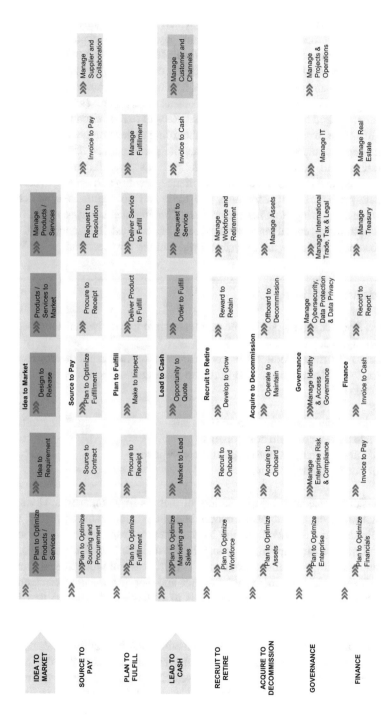

Fig. 3.2 Reference business processes

ideation, requirement analysis, and design of products and services. This output is then utilized in the *Source to Pay* process, which involves contracting suppliers, procuring necessary materials and services, and paying the corresponding invoices. The *Plan to Fulfill* process encompasses the receipt and inspection of goods, as well as the manufacturing of products or provisioning of services. Marketing activities that generate leads and convert opportunities into quotes and orders are facilitated by the *Lead to Cash* process. In addition to these core processes, supplementary processes are required to support an enterprise. *Recruit to Retire* manages the entire employee life cycle, from recruitment and onboarding to development, rewards, and retirement. *Acquire to Decommission* handles the planning, acquisition, onboarding, operation, and offboarding of assets such as manufacturing machines. Companies must also manage risks and compliance, identity and access, cybersecurity and data privacy, IT infrastructure, and trade and tax regulations, which are ensured by the supporting *Governance* process. The *Finance* process covers invoice to pay and cash management, as well as treasury and real estate management.

Those business processes are described briefly in the next sections.

3.2   Idea to Market

The process from idea to market can be segmented into five individual subprocesses as shown in Fig. 3.3.

The Plan to Optimize Products/Services encompasses in general the Product and Service Portfolio Management. The portfolio management is responsible for the following tasks:

1. Assemble and delineate portfolio components
2. Define and assess portfolio components
3. Compare and make decisions on portfolio components
4. Monitor portfolio components

These tasks are executed using a variety of metrics for comparison. The actual implementation of each component occurs later in project management. In summary, the Product and Service Portfolio Management is responsible for overseeing product and service strategies, managing the product and service portfolio, and planning and tracking portfolio investments. The Process from Idea to Requirement comprises Ideation Management and Product and Service Design Management. The primary focus of ideation management is to systematically capture new ideas for products/services or their variations, as well as to systematically document new ideas for enhancing or modifying existing products/services. Ideation management involves not only recording ideas but also evaluating their feasibility. Several evaluation criteria, such as cost and competitive analysis, are necessary for this assessment. It is crucial to conduct exploratory research before defining new concepts. Subsequently, new ideas and requirements are analyzed. Upon completing ideation management, the Product and Services Design Management phase begins, which

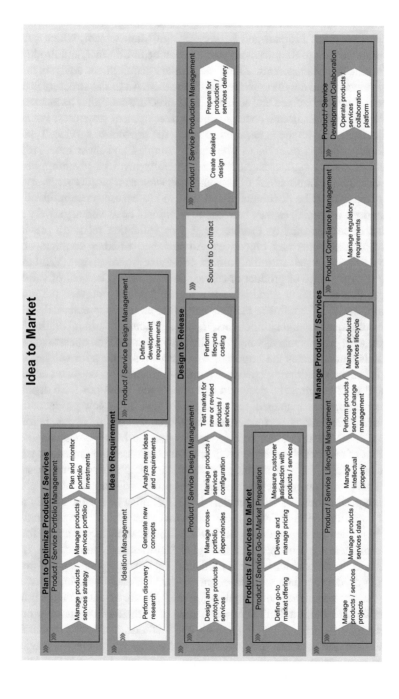

Fig. 3.3 Process of idea to market

includes defining requirements. It is essential to consider the Business Process Segment, a group of business activities and capabilities that generate a specific value or outcome for a stakeholder. The Design to Release process consists of three distinct sub-processes: Product and Service Design Management, which partially occurs during the Idea to Requirement process, Source to Contract, and Product and Service Production Management. Once the primary requirement analysis is completed, the concept and detailing phase can commence. An initial structure is developed and continuously refined and adjusted. This structure can either be independent or a combination of functional, conceptual, and development structures. For subsequent validation, a prototype is required to verify the product or service. Typically, the developed products or services are highly complex and must meet stringent quality and efficiency standards. Assurance generally involves planning, controlling, and executing examinations of the outcome, such as a prototype. Every malfunction or error must be documented and resolved to ensure success. Identifying all malfunctions is crucial, as they can lead to additional costs and negatively affect the product or service quality. Product or service validation relies on previously established requirements and objectives. All insights, whether conflicts or successes, must be integrated into the product or service improvement. Validation is necessary at every stage of product or service development. The goal of validation is to ensure that all quality standards are achievable and to optimize the process. Regular monitoring of employee budgets and other expenses is essential. Product validation comprises several components, including document administration, quality management, process management, product management, and operational maintenance. This demonstrates the importance of advance planning for validation and the need for regular validation checks throughout the entire process. In summary, services and products must be designed and prototyped, cross-portfolio dependencies and configurations managed, test markets for revised or new products identified, and life cycle costing performed and monitored. All of this occurs before the Source to Contract and Product and Service Production Management stages. The management of product and service production encompasses the intricate design of a product or service, as well as the groundwork for actual production or service delivery. This process involves the integration of product development and production. During production, the bill of materials (BOM) must be systematically monitored and controlled. The BOM is a comprehensive list of all materials and their required quantities for a given process. BOM administration serves as the foundation for implementing concepts such as digital factories and Industry 4.0. Digital factories act as intermediaries between product development, planning, and production, linking production data with development data for manufacturing. Modelling tools and various simulation and visualization methods are essential in this process. The objective is to adopt a digital approach and create three-dimensional products. While Industry 4.0 does not supply the tools and methods, it supports digital factories in real time and oversees their operation and optimization. Once a product or service has been designed and provided, market entry can be planned. This involves defining the go-to-market offering, developing and managing pricing, and measuring customer satisfaction with the products or services. This entire process falls under the Products and Services to Market category, which outlines the market entry process and its preparation. The final process in the Idea to Market framework is the Management of Products and Services, which comprises Product or Service Life Cycle Management, Product Compliance Management, and Product and Service Development Collaboration. Product and Service Life Cycle Management entails managing product and service projects, data, intellectual property, performance, change management, and life cycle. Product Compliance Management deals with regulatory requirements, which must always be monitored. Alongside this is the Product and Service Development Collaboration, which involves operating the product or service collaboration platform. Establishing an appropriate project structure, led by a project manager or project financial controller, is crucial for all project-related planning, execution, and monitoring activities. The project creation process ranges from structuring simple projects with single accounting objects to complex projects with a hierarchy of work packages, depending on the requirements. Early-stage cost planning for a project often demands considerable effort. However, since expertise is frequently based on personal bias or strategic considerations, it can be inaccurate or even entirely overlooked.

3.3   Source to Pay

The process from source to pay can be segmented into six individual subprocesses as shown in Fig. 3.4.

The initial subprocess in the Plan to Optimize Sourcing and Procurement involves an organization identifying and sourcing its requirements before purchasing goods or services. Sourcing entails matching the organization's needs with a supplier capable of providing the necessary goods or services. The sourcing process includes steps such as identifying and understanding requirements, narrowing down potential suppliers, requesting information and bids, awarding the purchase to the best proposal, and transitioning to the procurement process through purchase orders or contracts. The first subprocess focuses on analyzing a company's general purchasing strategies. This involves investigating the organization's spending profile, planning expenditures, and clarifying purchasing needs to gain an overview of required purchases. The Source to Contract subprocess occurs through an RFx (Request for x), which is a procedure for organizing an invitation to tender. RFx typically comprises three components: Request for Information (RFI), Request for Quote (RFQ), and Request for Proposal (RFP). The RFx process begins with the RFI, followed by the RFQ and RFP, during which potential suppliers are compared. The RFx phase concludes when a source is chosen. After selecting a source, the final step involves defining purchasing quotas for various products and services with the chosen source. In the context of Procurement Contract Management, business terms are negotiated, and contracts are established. The subsequent process, Plan to Optimize Fulfillment, accompanies crucial steps to achieve optimal order fulfillment. Sourcing activities can range from daily requirements like finding office suppliers to more strategic tasks such as projecting and forecasting demand in a key spend category and

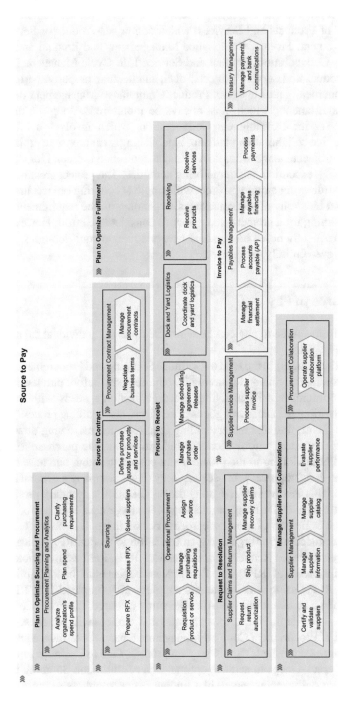

Fig. 3.4 Process of source to pay

negotiating the best prices with an optimal supplier mix. Sourcing is not solely about price; a supplier may offer the best price but fail to deliver or face external challenges, leading to supply chain disruptions or reduced end-product quality. Procurement typically begins where sourcing ends, creating purchase requisitions and issuing purchase orders for goods or services to the supplier identified during the sourcing process. Overall, the Procure to Receipt process describes the journey from procurement to goods receipt. The initial phase in the process is Operational Procurement, which aims to identify the necessary products or services for production. Based on this information, appropriate sources are allocated to each required product and service. After selecting a source, the subsequent step involves generating relevant orders and releasing the scheduling agreement. Dock and Yard Logistics manage the coordination of loading bays and traffic within the plant premises. The final subprocess in goods movement is Receiving the ordered items. The reception of products and services varies; services are consumed, while products are stored in a warehouse. Depending on the company's production strategy and capacities, incoming goods may also be processed immediately. In numerous industries, there is an increasing shift from traditional business models focused on producing and selling goods to bundling various offerings, such as goods, warranties, ongoing maintenance, and licenses, into a comprehensive service package. A common example is offering a driving experience through leasing options instead of selling a car, along with a service plan, guaranteed work, and standard repairs. Consequently, services are increasingly permeating the core of the business world. Employees play a crucial role in operational procurement. When an employee identifies a need, they enter it into the system to place an order. Operational procurement typically involves three main types: stock, consumables, and external services. Stock procurement is often used for direct procurement activities and involves purchasing stock items and storing them in inventory for management and distribution. Consumable items, which are usually indirect items consumed and replenished regularly but not managed as inventory in the system, include items like pens, paper, and coffee for the office kitchen. These items may be ordered by the office manager or directly by an employee who notices a shortage. This kind of indirect purchasing is generally low value and high volume, and due to its high volume, it significantly impacts an organization's overall expenditure. Consumable spending is an ideal area for managing procurement through self-service processes in a system, enabling buyers to concentrate on strategic spending within the organization and allowing the requesting employee to choose precisely what they need without bypassing the organization's standard approval and spending procedures. External services procurement encompasses the purchase of services such as building maintenance, consulting, or other tasks suitable for contingent labor. External services are supplied by individuals or groups who are not part of the organization but are engaged solely for a specific project or task. These services can be part of both direct and indirect procurement activities. Procurement of products or services can sometimes fail, leading to the Request to Resolution process, which handles complaints and returns. When goods or services do not meet expectations, claims arise. After recording and resolving claims with the supplier, the return process begins, usually requiring the supplier to coordinate return transportation. Analyzing claims helps identify gaps and improve processes and products continuously. The Invoice to Pay process concludes with payment, involving the receipt and processing of invoices in subsequent stages. Although payments typically occur at the end of a procurement process and the start of a sourcing process, some procurement scenarios challenge the idea of a one-size-fits-all sequence. The end-to-end process Finance manages the Invoice to Pay process, which is crucial for procuring goods as it deals with invoice payments. A supplier invoice is a document from a supplier for delivered materials or performed services. Supplier Invoice Management involves processing supplier invoices, obtaining the invoice, and initiating payment. Financial settlements are incorporated based on accounts payable, and financing payables initiate payments. Financial settlements are the primary element within the process, and accounts payable are processed starting from these settlements. Treasury Management focuses on communicating with banks to process payments and assist with treasury processes such as cash and liquidity management, debt and investment management, and foreign exchange risk management. Manage Suppliers and Collaboration is divided into two subprocesses. The goal of Supplier Management is to organize and analyze existing suppliers. The first step is to certify and validate existing suppliers based on internal criteria, allowing for better classification. Next, supplier information is managed, covering master data and various RFx documents. An up-to-date and comprehensive list of all relevant information is crucial for selecting the right supplier. Suppliers are categorized in a catalog, which can be used for source selection. A final step, conducted in conjunction with suppliers, is performance evaluation. This step enables the company to decide which source to choose for a new order based on previous deliveries. Access to supplier networks is vital, and supplier collaboration platforms are used for this purpose.

3.4   Plan to Fulfill

The process from plan to fulfill can be segmented into five individual subprocesses and starts with Plan to Optimize Fulfillment as shown in Fig. 3.5.

Prior to initiating a service or producing a product, it is essential to establish a supply chain network. This network encompasses various policies that need to be implemented, as well as a strategy for managing materials. Supply chain planning enables businesses to predict and handle customer demands, inventory, and operational risks and opportunities. It is important to develop and manage a manufacturing strategy to maintain an organized and structured manufacturing phase in a product's life cycle. Manufacturing Strategy Management allows users to document a manufacturing strategy for a specific business unit and plan accordingly. Once a strategy is in place, it is necessary to determine the required resources and their quantities. Consequently, creating and managing a service resource plan is a vital component of Service Fulfillment Strategy and Planning. Demand Planning involves a range of processes and functionalities related to demand management, statistical forecasting, promotion, and life cycle planning. It is a critical aspect of an

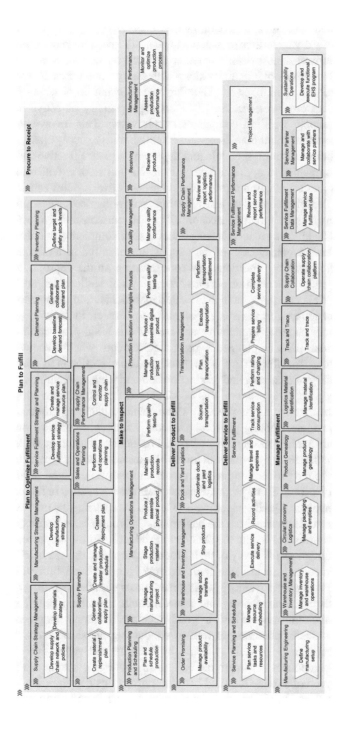

Fig. 3.5 Process of plan to fulfill

organization's Sales and Operations Planning Process, which includes developing a baseline demand forecast and generating a collaborative demand plan. Inventory Planning enables organizations to plan the ideal stock levels for products at specific locations. Companies must decide whether to stock or destock at a location and calculate the economic order quantity along with safety stock for each product location. This approach minimizes stockholding and ordering costs while ensuring a high level of customer service. Supply Planning's primary objective is to align demand with supply within a company's supply chain. This involves creating a material and replenishment plan, generating a collaborative supply chain, and managing the master production schedule and deployment plan. Effective supply planning allows companies to optimize inventory levels and resource utilization while ensuring customer satisfaction through timely order delivery. Sales and Operations Planning is a flexible forecasting and planning activity that sets sales, production, and other supply chain targets based on historical, current, and projected future data. Supply Chain Performance Management assists companies in enhancing the effectiveness and responsiveness of their supply chain in the face of complex and rapidly changing market conditions. By concentrating on the appropriate process metrics, companies can monitor performance, pinpoint bottlenecks, and discover opportunities. This approach facilitates both departmental and organizational performance management. In the context of Make to Inspect, material requirements planning ensures material availability and carries out basic production planning. Adequate supplies must be planned to meet requirements, whether they stem from sales orders, stock transfer orders, or production. The objective is to guarantee the timely availability of customer and production demand while preventing disruptions due to missing parts. The primary goal of Manufacturing Operations Management is to oversee the manufacturing process, which entails organizing production materials, creating and assembling physical products, maintaining production records, and conducting quality testing. In contrast, Production Execution of Intangible Products concentrates on non-material assets like services, with the main objectives being to manage the production project, create and assemble digital products, and perform quality testing. Since production materials are not needed in this case, there is no staging involved. Quality planning is essential for ensuring the quality of products, processes, and services from the beginning. Customers have high expectations regarding order promises within the Deliver to Product to Fulfill subprocess, as they desire quick and reliable delivery of their products. Knowing the exact delivery date is crucial for customers, making the management of product availability the primary goal of Order Promising. Inventory Management deals with the recording and tracking of materials based on quantity and value, including planning, entry, and documentation of stock movements such as goods receipts, goods issues, physical stock transfers, and transfer postings, as well as conducting physical inventory. While Inventory Management focuses on stocks by quantity and value, the Warehouse Management component considers the unique structure of a warehouse and oversees the allocation of storage bins and transfer transactions like shipping within the warehouse. Dock and Yard Logistics aim to speed up gate-in and gate-out processes, enabling faster execution of activities and increased yard throughput. This ensures optimized resource usage and supports planning, execution, and billing with integrated yard logistics management. Transportation Management, on the other hand, aims to reduce costs and enhance service by streamlining transportation management processes. It covers the entire transportation management life cycle for both domestic and international freight, ultimately improving customer satisfaction. Service Planning and Scheduling, a part of Deliver Service to Fulfill, is necessary for executing optimized Just-in-Time productions. Companies must plan service tasks and required resources, as well as develop resource scheduling to maintain a functional supply chain with minimal downtime. Service Fulfillment encompasses various tasks that need to be executed, such as managing service delivery, recording activities, handling travel and expenses, tracking service consumption, performing rating and charging, preparing service billing, and completing service delivery. Service Fulfillment Performance Management emphasizes reviewing and reporting performance. Before initiating the manufacturing phase of a product's life cycle, it is crucial to determine how this step should occur within the context of Manage Fulfillment. Manufacturing Engineering assists in establishing and developing a product's manufacturing process and defining the manufacturing setup for seamless production. Warehouse Management empowers users to oversee their warehouse activities, adapting to fluctuating demand while minimizing expenses. Circular business approaches emphasize reusing resources and reducing waste to nearly zero, making sustainability and circularity highly profitable strategies. The increasing prevalence of these practices is driven by urbanization and consumer preferences for sustainable products, services, and brands. Consequently, managing packaging and empty containers is a crucial aspect of Circular Economy Logistics. It is essential to manage a product's genealogy, including forward and backward traceability from the primary material to its subcomponents. Real-time insights into material and product availability are crucial for reducing supply chain risks and optimizing costs, making Track and Trace an important aspect. Traceability is a fundamental capability for efficiently orchestrating goods to market and mitigating risks. Supply Chain Collaboration aims to ensure that all stakeholders work effectively together in a network, resulting in various organizational benefits. During the service fulfillment process, data is collected, archived, recorded, and analyzed. This generates a significant amount of data that must be managed and organized for analysis. Service Fulfillment Data Management assists users in managing and organizing this recorded data. Service Partner Management concentrates on optimizing partner relationships, which may include resellers, brokers, service providers, distributors, or other collaborating entities. These partnerships can facilitate idea sharing and the delivery of superior content. Sustainability Operations designs and implements an effective Environment, Health, and Safety (EHS) program. By continuously analyzing operational data and providing relevant information, this process engages the workforce, identifies potential hazards, and takes action before safety is compromised. EHS performance is enhanced by integrating risk management into daily operations through unified business processes, shared data, and workflows.

3.5   Lead to Cash

The process from lead to cash can be segmented into seven individual subprocesses and starts with Plan to Optimize Marketing and Sales as shown in Fig. 3.6. In the Marketing Strategy and Planning subprocess, the initial step involves formulating an appropriate marketing strategy and setting corresponding marketing budgets. It is also advisable to create and oversee a well-suited customer loyalty program. The Customer Service and Planning aspect aids in devising a customer care and service strategy to foster a distinctive customer experience. Sales Planning and Performance Management facilitates the generation of a sales forecast, followed by the establishment of a comprehensive sales budget, sales objectives, and metrics. Furthermore, sales commissions can be determined and administered. Within the Market to Lead subprocess, Marketing Execution encompasses the primary stages of executing the marketing process. This includes identifying market segments and planning and defining sales prices.

Simultaneously, promotional efforts are devised and supervised, with specific customer demographics identified to target the appropriate audience. This allows marketing initiatives to be implemented effectively. The resulting data enables the analysis of and response to customer insights, identifying potential buyers interested in particular products or services. Within the Opportunity to Quote subprocess of Sales Execution, various channels like the Internet or local stores are utilized for sales purposes. Moreover, shopping carts and checkouts are managed through self-service, along with the handling of leads, opportunities, and points of sale. It is also essential to review sales proposals, received bids, and quotes, adapting and managing the configuration of products and services, and determining and calculating sales prices. Following successful customer acquisition, negotiating and processing a customer contract is necessary within the Order to Fulfill context. Such contracts are defined in the Customer Order and Contract Management subprocess and stored in the relevant system. This allows for the management of customer contracts and orders, as well as the orchestration of the fulfillment process. Ultimately, entitlements can be managed, and once a customer order is completed, production processes commence. However, orders with special requests may result in alterations to the overall design. Order to Fulfill also involves processes like project management, which includes planning the optimization of order fulfillment and delivering the product or service for fulfillment. An internal sales representative's main duties involve order capture and fulfillment. The primary objective of Request to Service is to manage customer service and support. In the past, the emphasis on brand building and loyalty was placed on creating and producing exceptional products. While providing excellent service has its advantages, businesses primarily focused on the products they sold, with service often considered secondary. This is alluded to by the term *after-sales service*, which refers to fixing broken items. Good service was mainly employed to enhance a product's reputation and price, while the service itself was viewed as a cost center. The shortcomings of this previous approach are now evident. As companies seek comprehensive experiences rather than just products, the service function is becoming an essential

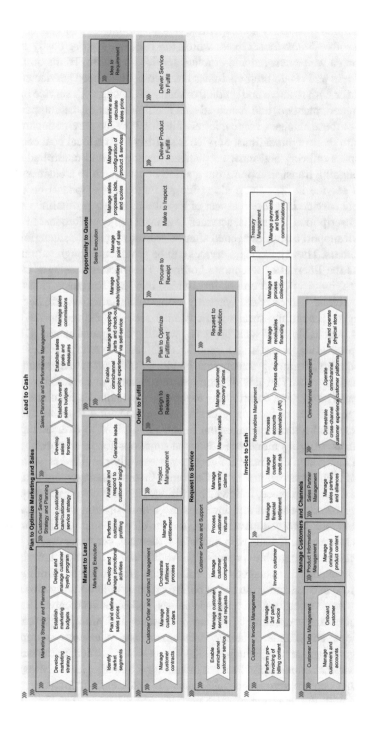

Fig. 3.6 Process of lead to cash

component of the overall offering and value proposition, as well as a source of profit. Additionally, in today's competitive landscape, businesses cannot depend solely on reactive *break-fix* services, which are invariably more costly and less profitable than a well-managed and efficient service operation. To maximize their service business and retain their customer base, companies need service contracts that account for both reactive and predictive scenarios, along with service offerings that are designed, planned, and managed as a profitable part of the company portfolio. To drive these changes, companies are altering how the service department is integrated into their organizations. Service is shifting from a local cost center to a central business offering and must be planned, managed, and controlled accordingly. The ongoing transformation from a strictly cost-driven to a business-driven approach to service is happening alongside an increasing emphasis on solution selling, where service is just one aspect of a deal that boosts profitability through products, subscriptions, contracts, services, and even projects. Request to Service focuses on all support activities needed after delivering tangible or intangible products to customers. These customer services can be provided through various channels, such as the Internet or telephone hotlines. This process manages customer service issues, inquiries, and complaints, which can lead to returns that are also overseen by Request to Service. Warranty claim management is another crucial aspect, along with handling recalls and customer recovery claims during the service process. A reliable after-sales process, including complaint handling, repairs, and returns processing, is essential for most businesses. The returns process should be of high quality, featuring transparent handling, efficient management, and a prompt refund process. The sale of returned, refurbished, or recycled products is becoming more prominent, contributing to the development of a circular economy. Return and refund clerks face daily challenges in managing these intricate processes. Accelerated returns management in sales is utilized to oversee buyer and supplier returns, offering numerous advanced functions for returns management. Following a completed customer delivery, a successfully provided service, or the fulfillment of a customer contract, the Customer Invoice Management subprocess of Invoice to Cash takes place, followed by billing. This step covers the preparation of pre-billing invoice content and includes the administration of third parties if subcontractors are involved. Eventually, the invoice is sent to the customer. Receivables Management deals with financial settlement, customer credit risk control, and accounts receivable processing. Additionally, disputes are resolved, receivables financing is managed, and collections are processed. Billing clerks play a vital role in overseeing the entire billing process, collaborating closely with internal sales representatives, shipping specialists, and accounts receivable accountants to ensure timely creation of billing documents and prompt customer payments without complaints. Manage Customers and Channels encompasses Customer Data Management, which handles all customer and account information, as well as customer onboarding. Product Information Management focuses on providing product content across multiple channels. Sales Partner Management primarily deals with the handling of sales partners and alliances. The Omnichannel Management subprocess orchestrates cross-channel customer experiences, supports the operation of omnichannel customer platforms, and plans and operates physical stores.

3.6 Recruit to Retire

The process from recruit to retire can be segmented into eight individual subprocesses as shown in Fig. 3.7. The Plan to Optimize Workforce subprocess commences with the organization and examination of financial and human resource needs. To accomplish this, objectives are established, and the requisite resources are projected. The Strategy and Planning of Human Resources (HR) encompasses the formulation of the HR strategy, which guides the workforce toward realizing the outlined goals. Moreover, comprehensive policies for the entire workforce are delineated and brought to completion.

Prior to finalizing the workforce budget, the projected human and financial resources must be authorized by the management. Organizational Management is responsible for creating the organizational structure and determining employee resourcing requirements, which includes identifying the necessary resources and skill sets to achieve the specified objectives. The goal of the Recruit to Onboard process is to acquire new talent based on prior planning and optimization efforts. This begins with the development of a corporate branding strategy for the organization. Once the required positions are approved, corresponding job requisitions are generated, providing a foundation for potential candidates to apply for open positions. Submitted applications are then matched to available positions, and the most suitable candidates are recruited. Purchasing requisitions and orders are used to acquire essential equipment for new employees, such as hardware or software. Upon hiring, new employees undergo onboarding, where they are introduced to their tasks, policies, strategies, and other necessary information to become productive. The Develop to Grow process focuses on employees' growth aspirations and development needs, aiming to strike the ideal balance between individual development goals and organizational and departmental objectives. Managers and employees should engage in ongoing dialogue to support each employee's short-, medium-, and long-term development, enabling them to apply their strengths and abilities to the company's advantage. Total target cash often comprises a base salary paid monthly, and variable pay or bonuses. Bonuses may be awarded annually or more frequently, such as quarterly, and are given for exceptional achievements by a department or individual employee. High-performing employees are rewarded, for example, by recognizing the employee with the highest sales revenue. The Reward to Retain subprocess aims to retain employees by offering rewards and incentives. In addition to direct financial compensation, companies may provide a comprehensive benefits package to motivate employees to perform at their best and maintain a healthy work-life balance. Benefit offerings are designed to enhance health and productivity while safeguarding employees against risks to future income. These offerings may vary by country and encompass local statutory benefits and requirements, such as sports facilities or health checks. These benefits must be consistently

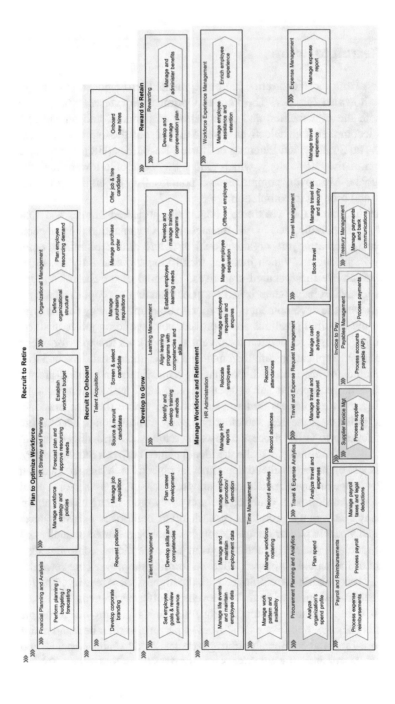

Fig. 3.7 Process of recruit to retire

managed and administered. Within the context of HR Administration, employment and employee data are maintained, including administrative information like names, addresses, and ages, as well as contractual data such as full-time employment, salaries, or fixed-term contracts. Depending on career development plans and goal achievement, employees may be promoted to higher levels or, in less favorable cases, demoted. Promotion guidelines must be transparently communicated to employees and managers. To enhance processes and better serve employees' needs, HR departments regularly conduct reporting and analytics. In an increasingly globalized world, teams may be relocated and restructured, potentially necessitating the physical relocation of employees to other regions. The process of relocation encompasses various aspects such as modifying employment contracts, covering moving costs, and altering pension contributions. In their daily work, employees often have numerous inquiries related to payroll, contracts, or overtime hours. These inquiries must be systematically managed by the HR administration, for instance, by employing a ticketing solution to process requests efficiently and effectively. Offboarding employees is another crucial aspect, with reasons for termination ranging from changing employers to retirement or fixed-term contracts. Additionally, the employee assistance and retention subprocess focuses on enhancing the employee experience. The Time Management subprocess ensures that employees record their work and absence times, which is vital for financial and workforce planning, as well as payroll and labor law compliance. Supporting different work patterns and availability, such as part-time jobs and variable workforce rostering, is essential. Typically, working hours are recorded at the activity level, and absence time due to vacations or illness must also be documented. Accurate analysis of an organization's spending profile and planning is a prerequisite for the Travel and Expense subprocess. Employees often need to travel for various reasons, necessitating the establishment of a travel and expense process that begins with analyzing travel needs and ends with managing expenses. A travel booking solution that reflects the company's travel policies is required. Some expenses, like hotel accommodations, are paid by the company in advance, while others, such as taxi fares, are usually paid by the employee and reimbursed later through the reimbursement process. Unpredictable and ad hoc expenses are typically covered by the employee and later requested for reimbursement. Invoices must be submitted and refunded based on the reimbursement process of Payroll and Invoice Pay. The submission and processing of expense invoices are generally automated, as the relevant solutions can convert unstructured documents into relational system records. Apart from expenses, the monthly salary must be paid to the employee through the payroll process, which takes into account taxes and legal deductions. Examples include church rates, payroll tax, health insurance, and pension insurance, which must be withheld and transferred directly to the respective parties. The Invoice to Pay process deals with supplier invoices and manages payables, while Treasury Management handles actual payments with the bank. This involves managing communication with the bank and transferring salaries to employees' bank accounts.

3.7   Acquire to Decommission

The process from acquire to decommission can be segmented into five individual subprocesses as shown in Fig. 3.8.

In order to enhance maintenance procedures and asset performance, businesses must consistently evaluate and refine their maintenance programs to ensure safe, reliable, and efficient asset operation. This is the primary objective of the Plan to Optimize subprocess. Utilizing best-practice methodologies such as reliability-centered maintenance, reliability engineers assess asset risks to identify optimal maintenance and service strategies that minimize costs and decrease the likelihood of failure for critical assets. Next-generation asset performance management transforms these established methods into data-driven processes. The Plan to Optimize Assets subprocess is initiated before the actual asset life cycle commences. This subprocess involves planning the acquisition of the asset and the overall acquisition strategy, which can be divided into two components: asset strategy and planning and asset maintenance strategy and analysis. The asset strategy and planning process outlines the approaches for acquiring new assets. First, a company-wide asset strategy must be established, considering requirements from other processes like Governance. Second, the property strategy must be defined, determining whether an asset should be owned or leased, with financial considerations playing a crucial role. Lastly, an asset investment plan must be created. For the maintenance strategy, the asset maintenance policy needs to be defined, followed by an analysis of the assets and maintenance performance. Reliability engineers define asset maintenance strategies by conducting an asset risk and criticality assessment, which generates scores for specific impact categories and allows for prioritization of the most important assets. Based on a thorough understanding of the asset's potential failure patterns, engineers can choose from various maintenance strategies, such as reactive maintenance (also known as run to failure); time-, usage-, or condition-based maintenance; or predictive or prescriptive maintenance. The suggested maintenance strategy encompasses more than just dedicated repair work to keep the asset operational; it may also include inspection requirements, design changes, and other measures to reduce the probability of potential failures. A reliability engineer may revise a maintenance strategy for improved business outcomes, and a maintenance planner can review and understand the recommended strategy and actions, implementing them in a collaborative process. The next stage in an asset's life cycle is its acquisition and onboarding. The Acquire to Onboard subprocess consists of asset acquisition, asset construction, and asset commissioning. First, the asset must be either acquired or leased, a decision that must be made in consultation with financial processes, as it affects the company's cash flow and overall liquidity. This decision may also be made by functional and non-functional departments focusing on specific qualities. In some cases, assets must be constructed and built by the company itself, which can be cost-effective if the necessary skills and materials are available in-house. Typically, acquired or leased assets must be assembled, requiring the management of a capital project for the asset. Additionally, asset construction must be designed and planned, with the construction project managed to assemble the asset. Before

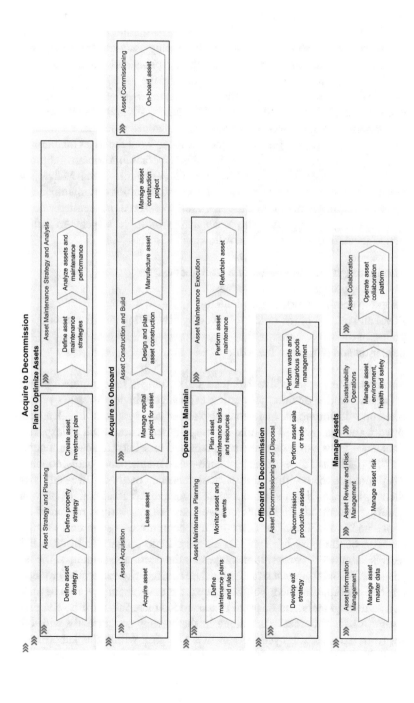

Fig. 3.8 Process of acquire to decommission

assets can be effectively utilized, they need to be integrated within the context of commissioning. One of the most crucial and likely the longest-lasting subprocess commences immediately after the asset has been integrated. The Operate to Maintain subprocess encompasses two primary subjects: asset maintenance planning and asset management execution. In the process of planning asset maintenance, several steps must be undertaken. Initially, the maintenance plans and guidelines must be established, which is highly reliant on the nature of the asset, as different assets require varying maintenance intervals. Subsequently, the asset and its related events must be monitored. Periodically, the asset maintenance tasks and assigned resources need to be organized. When executing planned or unplanned asset maintenance, two steps are necessary. First, qualified personnel must carry out the asset maintenance. Following that, the asset must be refurbished. The Operate to Maintain subprocess continues for as long as the asset is in use or until it is decommissioned. Maintenance management facilitates the ability to request, plan, and implement maintenance to better serve the requirements of a next-generation workforce. In maintenance execution, end-to-end processes typically span across multiple stages. An industry best-practice scenario encompasses the following phases:

- Initiation through the submission of a work request
- Review and approval of the work request
- Transition to detailed work-scope planning
- Approval and release of the order, followed by scheduling and dispatching
- Execution of the work
- Confirmation and closure of the work

In conventional terms, proactive maintenance is arranged for equipment before it deviates from tolerance or fails, preventing expensive scheduled repairs or emergency fixes and downtime. A maintenance planner can strategize in advance the scope of work and time needed for time- or usage-based actions such as inspections and maintenance tasks using maintenance plans and task lists. Instead of a generic approach with traditional time- or performance-based maintenance plans, condition-based and predictive or prescriptive maintenance methods are employed. Consequently, businesses can shift to a more personalized asset maintenance program, featuring optimized timeframes and work scopes, resulting in enhanced asset performance and availability. The Offboard to Decommission subprocess signifies the conclusion of the asset life cycle. If an asset is no longer useful or is being replaced, this subprocess occurs. It encompasses the decommissioning of the asset and its disposal. Initially, an exit strategy must be devised. Subsequently, productive assets must be decommissioned. Following that, the asset should be sold or traded. Lastly, waste management and disposal of hazardous materials must be addressed. The Manage Assets subprocess is unique in that it runs concurrently with other processes from the asset life cycle perspective. One task within this subprocess is asset information management, which involves managing the asset master data that must be consistently maintained and regularly updated. Another ongoing task is the inherent review and management of asset risks. This process includes identifying, evaluating, and mitigating threats related to assets. If necessary, mitigation procedures are carried out based on the risk management plan. By systematically addressing potential risks before they arise, a company can save money and safeguard its assets. Another crucial task is sustainability operations, which focuses on managing the environment, health, and safety surrounding the asset. This ensures daily operations are safe, and the workforce is encouraged to identify and address hazards before they impact safety. By maintaining operational continuity, asset integrity is preserved, and production is optimized by minimizing unplanned downtime and outages through proactive identification and mitigation of safety issues. The final task is asset collaboration, which deals with operating the asset collaboration platform. These market trends create a higher demand for collaborative business services and network concepts. Securely and standardly sharing asset data is essential for supporting peers in the maintenance and service industry.

3.8 Governance

The process of governance can be segmented into seven individual subprocesses and starts with Plan to Optimize Enterprise as shown in Fig. 3.9. The initiation of this subprocess involves handling the business models, as they are perpetually evolving. A prime illustration of this is Amazon's business model: at its inception, the company solely dealt in books. Presently, Amazon offers an extensive range of products and services, effectively altering its business model from exclusively selling books to marketing a diverse array of items. Consequently, it is crucial to continuously refine and adapt the business model. To guarantee this, a suitable operating model strategy is formulated. Furthermore, it is essential to devise a plan for managing business information, given that a company's data is both sensitive and legally significant and should not be accessed without proper authorization. The governance procedure entails comprehensive coordination of all end-to-end processes to enable seamless integration in planning. Particular focus must be given to unexpected occurrences, which need to be counterbalanced and alleviated to prevent adverse effects on the organization. Especially, it is essential to establish a corporate branding approach that, for instance, influences the company's reputation and public relations.

All of a company's business processes are interconnected, and as such, they must be considered holistically to achieve a high degree of optimization. To accomplish this, business processes are designed and modelled on a global scale to establish a consistent foundation for implementation. In addition to optimizing the enterprise, the governance process is responsible for Managing Enterprise Risk and Compliance. This enables an organization to effectively address risk, control, and assurance tasks. To minimize risks and ensure compliance, audits and assurances must be conducted. Business integrity must be maintained, and measures to prevent fraud must be put in place. Regulatory compliance must also be managed by defining appropriate action plans and execution processes. The subprocess of Managing Identity and Access Governance is responsible for the technical access to critical infrastructure and systems. This subprocess determines which employees can access specific information within the company through authentication. The entire life cycle management

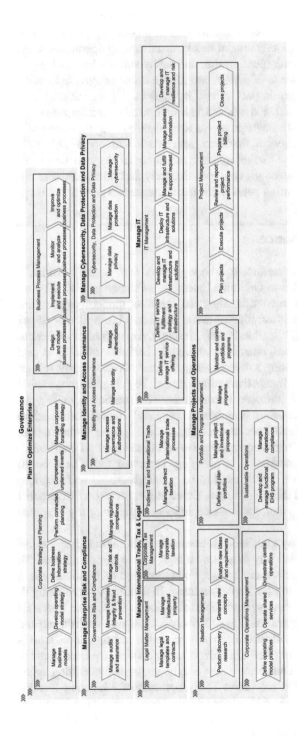

Fig. 3.9 Process of governance

of identities, from provisioning to decommissioning, must be covered. Relevant policies, authentication mechanisms, and corresponding implementation strategies must be defined for this purpose. This also applies to authorizations concerning data, processes, and systems. In addition to information, identity and access governance must also cover other assets, such as buildings. The subprocess of Managing Cybersecurity, Data Protection, and Data Privacy addresses these critical aspects of the governance process, as the name suggests. There is an increasing number of data privacy and security requirements, such as the General Data Protection Regulation (GDPR) and the California Consumer Privacy Act, which must be considered for legal compliance within enterprises. Moreover, business data is highly sensitive and valuable, making it a prime target for cybersecurity threats. Successful security attacks can lead to significant financial losses and damage a company's public credibility. As a result, data privacy measures must be implemented to ensure legal compliance, data protection procedures must be applied to protect business data from unauthorized access, and cybersecurity mechanisms must be deployed to defend the company from security vulnerabilities. The subprocess of Managing International Trade, Tax, and Legal matters ensures that the company adheres to international regulations. In the context of legal matter management, relevant templates and contracts are defined and made available for reuse. This also applies to indirect taxation, which is typically collected by a producer or retailer and paid to the government. International trade involves the exchange of goods and services between countries, allowing consumers and nations access to products and services not available domestically. The subprocess of Managing IT begins with defining and managing various IT service offerings based on the company's needs. The demand for IT services depends on the industry in which the company operates. To meet these IT requirements, a service fulfillment strategy and infrastructure concept must be defined. These form the basis for developing and managing the IT infrastructure and software solutions. When using IT solutions, issues or bugs may arise. Users must be able to report these problems and receive assistance in resolving them. To achieve this, IT support must be established to manage and fulfill user requests. The subprocess of Managing Projects and Operations comprises five distinct processes, the first of which is ideation management. A company typically employs many individuals, each with their own thoughts and ideas. These ideas can be valuable to the company, and ideation management facilitates the submission of ideas by employees. This boosts employee motivation by valuing their ideas as significant. It's also essential to recognize those employees whose suggestions are put into practice. Portfolio and program management are vital for businesses since they deal with a variety of products and services. As a result, the portfolio must be outlined and planned in line with the company's product or service strategy. The process of defining a portfolio is already intricate, involving numerous stakeholders and objectives, which may require the establishment of a program for successful implementation. Programs are made up of several concurrently running projects that require coordination and synchronization. Companies have numerous tasks that necessitate the creation of programs for execution. As a result, a standardized methodology must be devised to harmonize the programs, making them more comparable and efficient. Continuous monitoring and control are necessary for portfolio and program management to achieve predefined objectives and enhance underlying processes. Daily tasks in enterprises are frequently organized around projects, such as market opportunity analysis, portfolio definition, or product design. Therefore, project management must be optimized within companies in terms of methodologies and tools for planning, executing, and closing projects. In the context of corporate operations management, operating model practices are established. Companies can choose whether to outsource operations to shared services or manage them internally. Generally, a hybrid strategy is applied, combining both options. The final subprocess of the Manage Projects and Operations process involves managing sustainable operations. For businesses, sustainability is not only about environmental protection but also about enhancing their image and brand. Being a sustainable company also aids in regulatory compliance and avoiding financial penalties.

3.9   Finance

The process of finance can be segmented into five individual subprocesses as shown in Fig. 3.10. The initial subprocess in Finance involves the Plan to Optimize Financials. This subprocess can be broken down into three stages: planning, execution, and analysis. During the planning stage, it is crucial to determine which key performance indicators (KPIs) need to be monitored during the execution stage and establish the duration for budgeting and forecasting activities. To provide a roadmap for the execution stage, budgets for all departments are devised, and expenditure and revenue projections are made. In the execution stage, each department is allocated a budget and must maintain accurate financial records through effective accounting management. Both income and expenses must be documented. Management accounting focuses on identifying, measuring, analyzing, interpreting, and conveying financial data to managers to help them monitor the organization's goals. This information equips managers with the necessary insights to make well-informed business decisions.

Cost accounting, a subfield of management accounting, focuses on capturing the total production costs by considering both variable and fixed expenses. This enables managers to identify and reduce unnecessary expenditures while maximizing profits. In the analysis phase, plans are compared to the information recorded during the operational phase, allowing for the identification of deviations and the implementation of corrective measures. The objective of the Invoice to Pay process is to ensure that bills are paid and to monitor the company's outstanding debts. Supplier invoice management handles invoices from suppliers after a service has been provided or a product delivered. Payables management is in charge of tracking financial assets, starting with managing financial settlements and continuing with processing accounts payables to maintain a comprehensive financial overview. This process also includes payables financing, which is responsible for clearing supplier invoices and making payments to the appropriate creditors. Accounts payable, an account within the general ledger, represents an organization's obligation to pay off debts to its creditors or suppliers. The total outstanding amounts owed to suppliers are shown

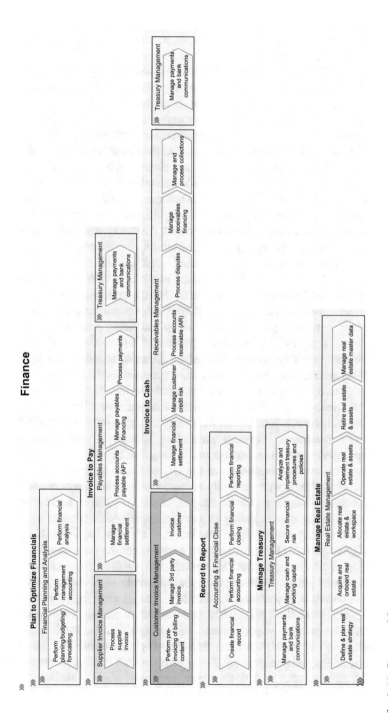

Fig. 3.10 Process of finance

as the accounts payable balance on the company's balance sheet, with increases or decreases from the previous period reflected on the cash flow statement. Payable financing is a type of credit where companies borrow money from a supplier to purchase products and goods. Invoice to Cash, similar to Invoice to Pay, involves customers owing debt to the company. Customer invoice management handles pre-invoicing of billing content, as well as managing third-party invoices and incorporating them into the invoice sent to the customer if necessary. Receivables management ensures orderly receipt of payments, beginning with financial settlements management and continuing with customer credit risk management. Accounts receivable and disputes are processed, and receivable financing and collection processing are carried out. Accounts receivable represents the balance of money owed by customers for goods or services received. Recorded on the balance sheet as a current asset, accounts receivable reflects the amount of money owed by customers for credit purchases. Comparable to accounts payable, accounts receivable focuses on money to be received rather than money owed. Accounts receivable can be analyzed using the turnover ratio or days sales outstanding to estimate when the money will actually be received. Receivables financing is relevant when customers receive funding based on issued invoices for purchased goods or services but payment has not yet been received. Treasury management deals with bank interactions and finalizes the payment process. The Record to Report subprocess consists of creating a financial record, performing financial accounting, executing financial closing, and generating financial reports. The process of generating information for management to assess the company's status is facilitated by financial accounting, a branch of accounting that documents, consolidates, and communicates the numerous transactions arising from business activities over a specific period. These transactions are condensed into financial statements, including the balance sheet, income statement, and cash flow statement, which reflect the organization's operational performance during a given timeframe. Financial accounting adheres to various established accounting principles, which are subject to the company's regulatory and reporting requirements. For instance, businesses in the United States must conduct financial accounting in compliance with generally accepted accounting principles (GAAP), ensuring consistent information for investors, creditors, regulators, and tax authorities. Financial closing is a recurring process in management accounting, where accounting teams verify and adjust account balances at the end of a specified period (e.g., annually or quarterly) to create financial reports for the company. The objective is to inform management, investors, lenders, and regulatory agencies about the company's financial position. Closing the books involves consolidating transactions from multiple accounts, reconciling the data to ensure its accuracy, and identifying discrepancies and anomalies. It is crucial that the total of all debits equals the total of all credits. The general ledger accountant, closing specialist, business analyst, and consolidation expert are the four primary roles responsible for maintaining accounting accuracy and transparency. Every company has bank accounts that handle incoming and outgoing cash flows due to payments, which must be monitored and managed. In small businesses, accounting or management may handle this task, but as a company grows, larger and more complex payment transactions typically require one or more full-time positions, such as a treasurer or treasury department.

The primary objective of treasury management is to maintain the company's solvency by controlling its liquidity. Treasury Management tasks also include risk management in corporate finance, asset management, and capital procurement. Treasury management is often considered a subfield of financial management in many organizations. While financial management focuses on managing financial resources to meet revenue targets, treasury management emphasizes ensuring liquidity at all times. Financial management outlines the financial plan containing strategies for achieving the company's financial objectives, while treasury management ensures the implementation of strategies defined for short- to medium-term goals. One responsibility of treasury management is liquidity or cash management, which involves capturing and controlling cash flows of liquid funds for the company's internal and external financing, with the goal of maintaining solvency. Corporate financial risk management is also a key focus of treasury management. To ensure a company's success, it is crucial to manage payment flows in a way that prevents any deficits that could lead to late payments. Efficient management of these cash flows necessitates the implementation of treasury management. The task of liquidity management involves ensuring that a company's working capital is utilized in the most efficient and effective manner, ultimately helping the organization achieve its long-term financial goals, such as increasing revenue and reducing costs. Real Estate Management plays a crucial role in overseeing a company's property assets. This process starts with the development and planning of a real estate strategy and extends to the acquisition and integration of properties. Focusing on profit-driven and value-based procurement, management, and marketing of real estate, Real Estate Management is particularly important for organizations that do not have real estate as their core business. These properties are often referred to as corporate real estate. After allocating the real estate and workspace, operational processes such as rent payments, regular inspections, and maintenance are carried out. When the real estate is no longer required, it is retired. The management of real estate master data is a vital task and is also taken into consideration.

3.10 Conclusion

Even though ERP systems have been in existence for quite some time, there is no widely accepted understanding of their functional range. To address this issue, we proposed a reference business process definition for organizations, which acts as a functional blueprint for ERP systems. In this chapter, we touched upon these business processes to illustrate the potential of artificial intelligence in enhancing the automation capabilities of ERP functions. All organizations revolve around four key domains: customer, supply, corporate, and products/services. The fundamental business processes within these domains include idea to market, source to pay, plan to fulfill, lead to cash, recruit to retire, acquire to decommission, governance, and finance. We provided a concise overview of these reference business processes, which are the foundation for defining an ERP reference architecture, in the next chapter.

ERP Reference Architecture

4

For embedding artificial intelligence into ERP software, knowing the underlying architecture is necessary. However, the solution architecture of ERP varies according to the various vendors. In order to address this issue, we abstract from the various ERP products and propose a reference architecture. Thus, we can systematically incorporate our suggested artificial intelligence concepts into the ERP reference architecture and guarantee their validity independent of the underlying ERP vendor. But how to obtain the reference architecture? To resolve this challenge, we reuse the reference processes from the previous chapter to derive the common reference architecture and define the software modules research and development, sales, supply chain, procurement, manufacturing, service, asset management, finance, and human capital management. As a side result, the reference architecture can also be used to evaluate the architecture of different ERP products.

4.1 Introduction

Let's begin with the problem statement. To embed artificial intelligence into ERP software, we must know the underlying architecture. However, the solution architecture depends on the different ERP vendors and vary accordingly. To resolve this challenge, we abstract from the various ERP products and suggest a reference architecture for ERP software. Thus, we can integrate the later introduced artificial intelligence concepts systematically into the ERP reference solution architecture and ensure in addition their validity independent of the ERP vendor. The reference solution architecture implements the reference business processes of enterprises, which we explained in the previous chapter based on corresponding modules. Therefore, embedding artificial intelligence on business process level is also considered. As a side benefit, the proposed reference architecture can be also used to compare the functional and non-functional capabilities of different ERP products.

© The Author(s), under exclusive license to Springer Nature
Switzerland AG 2024
S. Sarferaz, *Embedding Artificial Intelligence into ERP Software*,
https://doi.org/10.1007/978-3-031-54249-7_4

As illustrated in Fig. 4.1, the reference architecture is built upon various software layers. The database system serves to store master, transactional, and configuration data. Master data pertains to an object's attributes and remains constant over long periods. This type of data includes information needed on a recurring basis; products is an example for master data. In contrast, transaction data is dynamic and encompasses the data for all executed business processes. Generally, transactional data is restricted to a specific timeframe and undergoes frequent changes. Instances of this data include information generated from daily transactions, such as changes in purchase orders or invoices.

Finally, configuration data refers to the technical details that govern and tailor business processes, which are maintained during the implementation phase of ERP systems. Examples of configuration data include settings for organizational structures or fiscal year definitions for finance. The data model of ERP systems has been grown over time, encompassing tens of thousands of tables with intricate networks of relationships and cryptical field names, making it difficult to consume and comprehend. To address this issue, a semantic layer is provided atop the database tables to conceal the complexity and enable human-readable and efficient access to business data. This semantic layer is typically known as a virtual data model since it does not necessitate additional materialization of data and tables. The software

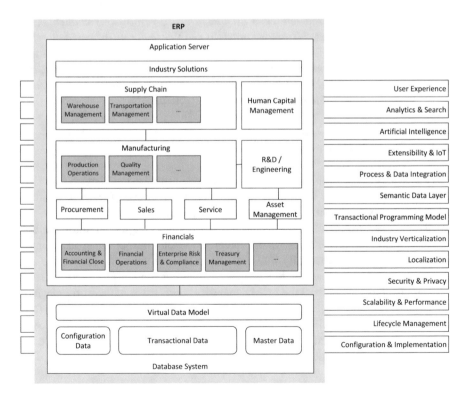

Fig. 4.1 Reference ERP architecture

modules on the application server offer reusable functionality to implement the reference business processes discussed in the last chapter. There is no one-to-one correspondence between application modules and core/supporting processes; usually, features from multiple software modules are needed to execute a single core/supporting process. R&D/Engineering is responsible for a significant portion of the core process Idea to Market, while Procurement, Supply Chain, and Manufacturing handle the core processes Source to Pay and Plan to Fulfill. The core process Lead to Cash is primarily managed by Sales and Services, while Recruit to Retire is overseen by Human Capital Management software modules. Asset Management primarily handles Acquire to Decommission reference process, and the supporting process Finance is mainly managed by the Finance component. Governance applies various technical features of the ERP platform, such as identity and access management, information lifecycle management, or risk management. Industry Solutions are built on top of the core modules, enhancing core functionality with industry-specific features for various verticals like retail, banking, insurance, automotive, or the public sector. ERP software must ensure numerous product qualities, such as facilitating compliance, delivering high performance, and supporting extensibility. These nonfunctional requirements must be addressed uniformly across all ERP application modules using the concepts and frameworks shown on the right side of Fig. 4.1. To embed artificial intelligence into the abovementioned ERP application modules, it is essential to understand their structure. Therefore, in the following sections, we will suggest reference solution architectures for each of them. The core application modules in Fig. 4.1 can be distributed across multiple application servers and combined with various deployment types (e.g., on-premises, public cloud, private managed).

4.2 Research and Development/Engineering

The Idea to Market reference process is primarily executed by the R&D/Engineering application module, as illustrated in Fig. 4.2.

Core Portfolio and Project Management is split into two components: Project Financials Control and Project Logistics Control. Project Financials Control is responsible for planning and monitoring expenses and budgets, enabling cost tracking that is closely integrated with essential business operations. This cost and budget tracking helps prevent additional expenses and safeguard the project. Project Logistics Control allows for the creation of project structures composed of work breakdown structures and network structures, planning and scheduling project activities, managing procurement processes in conjunction with core business processes, and offering insights into all logistics-related execution aspects of a project. Product Engineering is divided into two the components: Product Development Foundation and Variant Configuration. The Product Development Foundation supplies a product platform that serves as the foundation for the entire development process. It promotes product design, initiates master data and product structures, and integrates change and configuration management. The Product Development

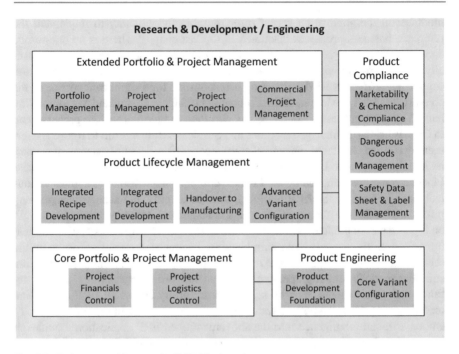

Fig. 4.2 Reference architecture for R&D/Engineering

Foundation also encompasses the bill of materials (BOM), which is a list of all necessary materials and their corresponding quantities for a given process. Variant Configuration enables customers to design their own product models, with users defining the product's rules and designs themselves. Simultaneously, an appropriate work plan and bill of materials for production are generated. The component shall also provide additional features, such as price calculation. Product Compliance encompasses three distinct sub-components: Marketability and Chemical Compliance, Dangerous Goods Management, and Safety Data Sheet Management and Hazard Label Data. The first sub-component, Marketability and Chemical Compliance, aids in managing material and ingredient information while adhering to legal and customer requirements. It gathers compliance data from suppliers and customers, making this information publicly accessible. Moreover, the component automatically monitors regulated substance volumes and evaluates products and materials against various compliance requirements, such as mandatory registrations and allowed quantities. Dangerous Goods Management centralizes dangerous goods information for all products, regions, and transportation modes. It automates the classification of dangerous goods and utilizes built-in regulatory content. The component shall ensure that all shipments comply with dangerous goods regulations by conducting integrated checks, providing appropriate packaging, determining accurate transportation methods and routes, and automating the generation and distribution of dangerous goods documents. The purpose of Safety Data Sheet Management and Hazard Label Data is to centrally manage substance and regulatory information, streamline component and product classification, and automate the creation of safety data sheets and labels. It applies regulatory content to minimize effort and maintain ongoing compliance while automating label printing and safety data sheet distribution as part of logistics processes. Product Life Cycle Management comprises Integrated Recipe Development, Integrated Product Development, Handover to Manufacturing, and Advanced Variant Configuration. Integrated Recipe Development is a component for describing product manufacturing or process execution. Recipes contain information about products, process components, required resources, and the steps to be executed. Recipe types are also included in the development process. Integrated Product Development is designed for discrete manufacturing and accelerates design by incorporating product life cycle management into a unified, real-time environment. The component manages complex product structures, including hardware and software compatibility, and enables the creation of individualized products by defining and reusing variant product structures across the supply chain. It encompasses embedded systems development, visual instance planning, visual asset planning, 3D visual enterprise manufacturing planning, access control management, and engineering change and record management. Advanced Variant Configuration streamlines information exchange within the company and up to customer delivery. It shall use a comprehensive simulation environment for variant configuration models and offers user-friendly classification capabilities. The integrated advanced variant configurator should support multi-level variant configuration models.

Extended Portfolio and Project Management enhances efficiency and automation, providing insights into product and project performance in terms of cost, time, scope, resources, and quality. It combines Portfolio Management, Project Management, Project Connection, and Commercial Project Management. For instance, Project Connection shall automate and streamline the bidirectional exchange of project information with external scheduling tools, orchestrating the exchange through business rules that define the sequence of creating and modifying project elements. Commercial Project Management covers end-to-end processes, including selling, planning, executing, monitoring, and controlling projects.

4.3   Procurement

The Source to Pay reference process is primarily executed through the Procurement application module, as illustrated in Fig. 4.3. Operational Procurement is composed of multiple elements and commences with the handling of purchase requisitions. A purchase requisition refers to a request for a specific quantity of materials or services with a predetermined delivery time. This marks the beginning of the purchasing process. However, a demand from a material requirement planning (MRP) task can also lead to a purchase requisition. Typically, purchase requisitions follow a release strategy or initiate an approval process based on the workflow engine. A purchase order is a request made to an external supplier to deliver a certain amount of material at a specified time or to carry out specific services within a defined time

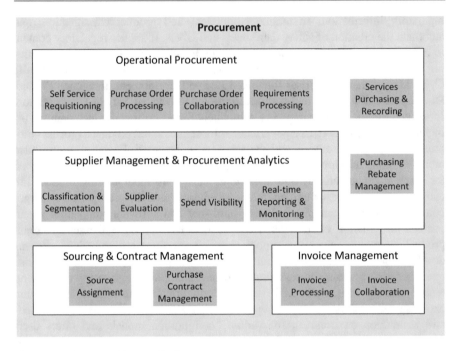

Fig. 4.3 Reference architecture for Procurement

frame. Self Service Requisitioning shall offer a user-friendly interface and cross-catalog search, allowing employees to adopt procurement processes and policies more easily. It also should support an enhanced workflow for completing purchase requisitions, including a workflow inbox. Purchase Order Processing and Collaboration facilitate both indirect and direct procurement. The component includes analytical capabilities for monitoring the status of purchase orders. Requirement Processing enables control over automation and manual intervention, when necessary, while also supporting human decision-making through analytical visualizations embedded within transactional applications. Service Purchasing and Recording streamline the procurement of goods and services. The process simplifies limit (value-only) purchase order items to maintain control over unplanned services and record relevant details. Lastly, Purchasing Rebate Management oversees the entire purchasing rebate lifecycle, from planning and tracking to settling and analyzing rebate agreements.

The process of procuring goods and services involves not only identifying the ideal supplier but also encompasses strategic activities such as projecting and forecasting demand in key spending categories for a business. This includes negotiating the best prices with an optimal mix of suppliers, which is the goal of Sourcing and Contract Management. However, even if suppliers offer the most competitive prices, they may not be chosen due to quality issues or delays in delivery. As a result, Source Assignment is a crucial aspect of the procurement process. Purchase Contract Management shall offer analytical applications to monitor the status of contracts and agreements. An outline purchase agreement between a supplier and a company procuring specialized materials or services is known as a purchase contract. Invoice Management is split into two components: Invoice Processing and Invoice Collaboration. Supplier invoices are generated after receiving an invoice from the supplier and can be created with or without reference to a purchase order. To verify the accuracy of the supplier invoice, invoice verification checks are conducted. The supplier invoice can be simulated before posting the document to display account movements. Invoice Processing and Collaboration facilitate the uploading of supplier invoice attachments and enable fully automated implementation without user intervention. The component shall assist in managing supplier invoices and payment blocks, as well as uploading scanned invoice copies for manual invoice processing with optional integration with OCR. Supplier Management and Procurement Analytics aim to continuously assess, classify, and allocate suppliers to segments of varying importance through the classification and segmentation of suppliers. This allows purchasers to concentrate on suppliers that are strategically significant and critical to the business, thereby enabling the development and management of their business relationships. Purchasing categories allow buyers to manage suppliers based on specific goods and services, such as hardware and software or installation and inspection. Classification Segmentation and Supplier Evaluation should support evaluation by defining supplier criteria like weighting and scoring. The component enables real-time analysis of the parts per million score to discuss potential quality improvement activities with the supplier. Spend Visibility and Real-time Reporting & Monitoring shall provide a real-time, multidimensional spend report that can be manipulated like a pivot table and includes drill-down functionality.

4.4   Supply Chain

The primary execution of the Plan to Fulfill reference process is carried out by the Supply Chain and Manufacturing application modules, with this section concentrating on the Supply Chain aspect. Figure 4.4 illustrates the reference architecture for Supply Chain. Inventory management shall ensure transparency and control over inventory levels and stock quantities, facilitating smooth material flow throughout all inbound and outbound logistics operations. Efficient warehousing enables the effective storage and handling of goods and materials, enhancing asset utilization, boosting throughput, and promoting precise, timely order fulfillment with optimal warehouse transparency. The Goods Movement module shall use simplified postings for transfers and scrapping of goods, benefiting from real-time, high-volume processing using sensor data. Inventory Analytics & Control refines inventory and material flows based on real-time analytics. Returnable Packaging Logistics oversees the shipping and receiving of reusable packaging materials to and from business partners, increasing visibility in material distribution and minimizing overall material volume by consolidating logistics information into a unified version of the truth. Physical Inventory allows for real-time reporting on warehouse stocks and inventory, documenting the physical quantities of warehouse stocks, owned stocks,

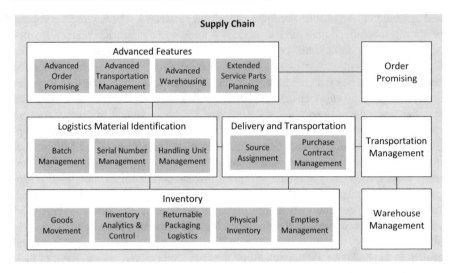

Fig. 4.4 Reference architecture for Supply Chain

and other stock types. Empties Management monitors empty containers to and from business partners, gathering detailed data, and accurately recording high-volume transactions for empty returns and associated deposits.

Warehouse Management enables real-time visibility into the handling and processing of materials, allowing for streamlined warehouse operations. This process begins with organizing the warehouse by defining its physical structure, storage types, and creating storage bins. The entire warehouse can be represented in the system, down to the level of individual storage bins. Logistics Material Identification includes Batch Management, which enhances product quality, ensures comprehensive traceability, and minimizes customer and legal risks. This component allows for the creation of batch master records, assignment of specific batch numbers, classification of batches, assignment of characteristics, automatic compliance with legal requirements through batch genealogy, and batch tracking. Serial Number Management distinguishes individual items of a material or equipment, enabling the creation of serial number profiles, serial number master records containing crucial data on serialized materials, and identification of single items for tracking in inventory management, physical inventory, and equipment. Handling Unit Management represents packing-based logistics structures and monitors the movements of entire handling units instead of individual materials. Delivery and Transportation includes Delivery Management, which shall automate the execution and confirmation of transportation demands from various sources (sales orders, purchase orders, stock transport orders), reducing redundancies and human error through electronic collaboration. The goods receipt step for inbound deliveries is the final activity organizations undertake before receiving goods. Transportation Management supports the entire transportation chain, managing transportation demands through planning, tendering, and settlement of freight processes. It also allows for booking carriers in compliance with hazardous goods requirements. Transportation Management is applicable for domestic and international transportation in the shipper industry, as well as inbound and outbound freight management. It enables the creation and use of central master data, such as business partners and products for transportation-related processes, and the establishment of transportation networks. Freight agreements, which are contracts between business partners outlining their commitment to conduct business in a specific manner, can also be utilized. Internal sales representatives and order fulfillment specialists require mechanisms to configure, execute, and monitor availability checks and optimize supply distribution, which are the goals of Order Promising. This is especially crucial when the availability of materials needed to fulfill requirements is limited. As a result, the available-to-promise (ATP) check has to be supported, allowing users to determine the date and quantity a sales order requirement can be confirmed based on a specific checking rule and the current stock situation for the specified material. Advanced Order Promising shall ensure quick and accurate order commitments by automatically considering relevant stock in real-time while safeguarding business priorities and profitability objectives. Advanced Transportation enhances transportation efficiency by managing all inbound and outbound freight comprehensively. Advanced Warehousing optimizes orders using features such as cross-docking, workforce management, slotting, inventory optimization, transit warehousing support, and connectivity to warehouse automation equipment. Extended Service Parts Planning accurately plans service parts inventory across distribution networks based on parts volumes, velocity, and segments, strategically calculating trade-offs between costs and service.

4.5 Manufacturing

As previously noted, the primary implementation of the reference process, Plan to Fulfill, is carried out by the Supply Chain and Manufacturing application modules, with the emphasis in this section being on Manufacturing. The reference architecture for the Supply Chain is illustrated in Fig. 4.5. Production Engineering is split into two components. The product engineering phase involves the design and development of products. New products or product lines are created to leverage existing process technology and enhance quality and reliability. Existing products may be modified in response to changing market or customer needs. The outcome of this product phase includes corresponding drawings and a list of all necessary parts for product production, known as the bill of material (BoM). Production BoM Management organizes products to manage components and assemblies and establishes separate BoMs for various areas (e.g., Engineering, Production, Sales, and Services). The component identifies the appropriate BoM version for the specific date, production version, and purpose. Routing Management Recipe Development plans operations during manufacturing activities. Operations form the foundation for scheduling dates, capacity requirements for work centers, and material consumption. Recipes outline the product formulation process and the development of

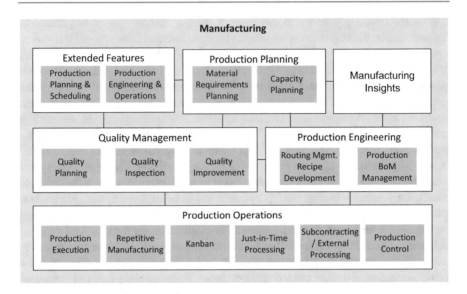

Fig. 4.5 Reference architecture for Manufacturing

manufacturing products. Work centers/resources represent machines, production lines, employees, or groups of employees. Along with BoM and routing/master recipes, work centers/resources are among the most critical master data in the production planning and control system. They are utilized for scheduling, costing, capacity planning, and simplifying operation maintenance. The goal of Production Planning is to plan products and components to initiate internal and external procurement. Managers must take into account two factors: Material Requirements and Capacity. Companies must plan raw materials based on BoM explosion of finished product requirements. Additionally, proposals for internal and external procurement based on quantities and date requirements must be generated. To plan capacity, the production planner must balance production requirements with the available capacity of respective work centers and shift calendars, which is the focus of Capacity Planning. Material requirements planning (MRP) ensures demand coverage by supply elements without considering available capacity. The capacity planning's role is to assist MRR planners in adjusting the production plan to account for capacity constraints while maintaining demands in terms of time and quantity.

Production Execution is a component of Production Operations that encompasses the execution, control, monitoring, and verification of the manufacturing process using real-time data from the shop floor, contract manufacturers, and suppliers. Repetitive Manufacturing processes can be streamlined through mass processing and the simplification of financial controls in periodic actions. In this type of manufacturing, material flow can be planned and monitored with a higher level of precision. Planned orders are employed to model, plan, and initiate material flow, while product cost collectors gather the associated costs. Kanban inventory management allows for automatic replenishment by implementing self-regulating control circuits, such as empty bins that trigger procurement processes. Kanban is a methodology for managing production and material flow based on the physical stock of materials in production. The core concept is to maintain a consistent supply of materials needed regularly in small quantities within the production environment. Production Control shall offer centralized cockpits to minimize bottlenecks and reduce risks. As a result, production operators must oversee the entire shop floor production process, including handling materials, Bills of Materials (BoMs), recipes, routings, components, work centers, and resources, up to the completion of finished products. This management and regulation of the manufacturing process are typically carried out by a production supervisor responsible for assigning production tasks to individual machines and implementing measures to address machine breakdowns or component shortages. Subcontracting can be utilized to outsource production through subcontracting procurement, requiring companies to supply components to the contractor based on the BoM structure. External Processing shall allow organizations to outsource production operations to third-party providers or other production units within the company. This can be managed through external operations in routings and production orders. Just-in-Time Processing eliminates inventory buffers by delivering components and subassemblies directly to the customer's production line. With just-in-sequence, assembly is delivered in the order specified by the requested requirements. Quality Management should offer tools to inspect production processes and goods receipts, managing inspection lots and implementing usage decisions to enhance manufacturing output. Quality Management encompasses quality planning, inspection, and improvement. Quality Planning is crucial for planning the quality of products, processes, and services. Manufacturing Insights assists in analyzing manufacturing data for process enhancements, decision support, and reporting and documentation purposes. The component provides exception-based management alerts, with real-time notifications based on production bottlenecks such as time or component delays or resource constraints, which can be used to minimize shortfalls and scrap with high efficiency. Extended Production Planning and Scheduling shall improve core production planning and scheduling functionality by leveraging the visual planning board. The component automates consumption-based replenishment through demand-driven MRP and employs simulation capabilities with predictive MRP. Extended Production Engineering and Operations designs and operates production processes, bridging the gap between product engineering and manufacturing operations by transforming product design into production process design, which serves as the basis for production order management and shop floor execution.

4.6 Sales

The primary implementation of the Lead to Cash reference process is carried out by the application modules Sales and Service, with the emphasis of this section being on Sales. The reference architecture pertaining to Sales is illustrated in Fig. 4.6.

Fig. 4.6 Reference architecture for Sales

The Order and Contract Management component is composed of six essential sub-components that ensure uniform master data, including pricing, throughout the organization. Sales Master Data Management shall enable the use of simplified data models and a centralized business partner, allowing for the creation, modification, or display of sales master data in a unified user experience. Customer materials definition comes into play when customer product identifiers differ from those used by the company. Price Management oversees price master data definition and carries out price calculations, setting up the pricing process in business documents and determining how net values are computed. Sales Contract and Quotation Management should support various contract types, such as sales contracts, condition contracts for settlement management, scheduling agreements, or trading contracts. This component allows for the creation, modification, or display of customer quotations, which are triggered by a request for quotation (RFQ) from customers. In response to the RFQ, a quotation is provided, which the customer may accept or reject. Sales Order Management and Processing should offer a comprehensive view of sales order execution and help prevent overall delivery delays through embedded predictive analysis. This component enables the execution of business transactions based on sales documents, such as inquiries, quotations, and sales orders, defined within the system. Sales and Solution Billing encompasses both manual and automated billing and invoicing scenarios, allowing external billing data to be combined with sales documents into a single invoice. Billing documents can be created, posted to financial accounting, and output through various channels. Sales Rebates, Incentive, and Commissions Management facilitates the handling of volume-based sales rebates using condition contract settlement. Claims, Returns, and Refund Management helps reduce customer service and support costs by streamlining return processes and customer return analysis, improving tracking, expediting request processing, and lowering operational expenses. This component enhances the capture and handling of all complaints and returns, triggering logistical follow-up actions such as product inspection, issue resolution, and claims and refunds management. Sales Monitoring and Analytics allows for the monitoring and analysis of core sales business processes, from quotations and contracts to sales orders and their fulfillment to invoicing. Sales plans can be created, modified, released, and displayed, enabling the analysis of sales target achievement and providing insights into current sales performance. Sales Force Support covers the entire presales life cycle, from appointments to lead and opportunity creation. Sales Lead Management aims to gather potential sales information at the beginning of the sales pipeline, automating the initial presales process and linking initial interest to sales. Opportunity Management, on the other hand, records identified sales possibilities and tracks progress throughout the sales cycle, controlling sales opportunities that describe sales prospects, requested products or services, budgets, potential sales volumes, and estimated sales probabilities. Activity Management assists in planning, tracking, and organizing sales activities throughout the entire customer relationship life cycle, recording all company employee activities, including appointments and task creation. Account and Contact Management provides the sales force with a comprehensive view of each customer, including key contact and account data, managing and granting easy access to accounts and contacts. Sales Performance Management helps motivate sales forces and drive revenue through attractive incentive and compensation policies. By implementing compelling variable compensation programs, the component for incentive and commission management can improve the company's sales performance. Organizations can manage programs for employees and partners, creating and maintaining accurate and strategically aligned incentive and compensation plans to retain and motivate top performers and achieve corporate objectives.

4.7 Service

As previously noted, the Lead to Cash reference process is primarily executed through the Sales and Service application modules. This section concentrates on Services, as illustrated in Fig. 4.7, while the reference architecture for Sales is depicted in Fig. 4.6. Service Master Data and Agreement Management is responsible for managing customer asset records, service history, and commercial agreements, and it plans preventive maintenance services using the available relevant information. Technical Assets, Structure, and History provides accurate information about customer locations and installed equipment to call centers, field service, depot repair, and sales personnel. This also enables planning and performing maintenance services with comprehensive records of equipment or systems through equipment master data, maintenance plans, measuring points, task lists, and bills of materials.

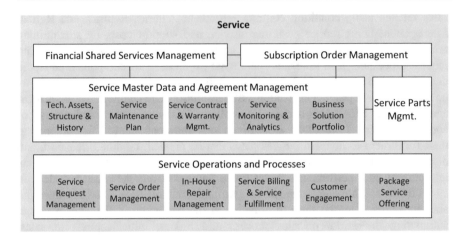

Fig. 4.7   Reference architecture for Service

Service Maintenance Plan facilitates the scheduling of service commitments and significant maintenance events, such as shutdowns and turnarounds, allowing for preventive and predictive service activities based on time, counter, condition, or risk. Service Contract Management and Warranty Management addresses service agreements, pricing arrangements, and customer entitlements in a unified repository, enabling automatic periodic billing. Contracts are long-term service agreements between companies and their customers that outline the services' content and scope, which are guaranteed within specific tolerance limits for certain parameters, like within a predetermined time frame. Warranties define the services' scope and parts usage that organizations perform in case of damage or issues. This process ensures the processing of service deliveries with automatic warranty agreement checks. Service Monitoring and Analytics and Business Solution Portfolio enable the monitoring of service businesses' operations and outcomes by comprehensively capturing and measuring service performance and profitability using operational reporting and dashboards.

Service Request Management, a component of Service Operations and Processes, allows users to generate, monitor, and handle service requests while maintaining full visibility of current and historical service agreements and activities. By utilizing solution quotations, users can create quotes for various product types, such as tangible products, services, and service contract items. Service Order Management equips frontline field service teams with the latest information on service history and equipment configuration, enabling them to expertly carry out maintenance service tasks. This component streamlines the management of the service life cycle, from generating and processing service order quotations to creating and processing service orders and confirmations. In-House Repair Management aids businesses that provide in-house repair and maintenance services for products. By integrating the repair process across multiple lines of business, planning and executing in-house repairs become more efficient and transparent. These services are conducted in-house at repair centers and encompass core repair and maintenance activities such as prechecking, quotation processing, planning, repairing, and billing for repair objects. Service Billing and Service Fulfillment ensures the efficient delivery of services, ranging from simple to highly complex, through planning, scheduling, parts provisioning, service work, and billing. This approach results in reduced costs and comprehensive logistical and financial insights. Customer Engagement promotes effective issue resolution through multichannel customer engagement and intelligent interactions. Packaged Service Offerings automatically bundle items and initiate corresponding follow-on processes up to the billing stage. Service Parts Management streamlines spare part stock processing based on usage and availability, enhancing efficiency in parts fulfillment, planning, procurement, and warehousing. This is achieved through integration with core materials management and finance functions, as well as support for language and localization requirements. The component addresses all aspects of service parts management, including planning, execution, fulfillment, collaboration, and analytics, and comprises service parts planning and execution scenarios. Subscription Order Management and Financial Shared Services Management enable customers to offer their business solutions as a mix of products and service subscriptions. These may include recurring fees, usage-based charges, and one-time fees based on a consumption pricing model. The component manages all parties involved in business transactions and all data related to subscription products, handling products, and product bundles consisting of various product and subscription combinations. Financial Shared Services Management involves using service management capabilities natively integrated into end-to-end processes to generate synergies and enhance efficiencies within a single working environment. The component supports efficient and scalable operations by simplifying and automating the execution of key financial processes across departments, ultimately improving quality and compliance by delivering standardized, consistent, and repeatable services across diverse business systems.

4.8   Human Capital Management

The primary implementation of the Recruit to Retire reference process is carried out by the Human Capital Management application module, as illustrated in Fig. 4.8. The purpose of human capital management is to assist organizations in achieving their strategic objectives by attracting, developing, and effectively managing employees. Personnel Administration, a component of Personnel Management, handles administrative tasks related to employee master data, such as personal information, addresses, banking details, and employment contract details. The data in Personnel Administration is usually valid for a specific time frame, like an employee's bank information being valid from March 1, 2021, to October 30, 2021. Organizational Management is used to develop an organizational plan that outlines a company's functional structure, encompassing elements like organizational units, positions, tasks, jobs, and more. This component is utilized to assess headcount, determine reporting hierarchies, and allocate agents to workflow tasks, among other

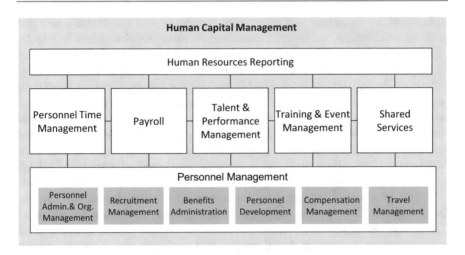

Fig. 4.8 Reference architecture for Human Capital Management

things. Recruitment Management enables job seekers and candidates to explore job opportunities, join a talent pool, and submit their applications online, thereby supporting the entire recruitment process from applicant data creation to filling open positions. Benefits Administration offers services for inquiries related to various benefit plans, such as health, insurance, savings, credit, miscellaneous, stock purchase, flexible spending accounts, and flexible spending account claims. These benefits play a crucial role in the overall compensation packages that employers provide to attract and retain top talent.

Personnel Development encompasses activities aimed at fostering employee growth, such as identifying potential and qualifications, planning careers and succession, and devising development plans. This component allows for the planning and execution of targeted personnel and training measures to enhance employees' professional growth while ensuring that staff qualification requirements are met and planned. Compensation Management enables businesses to implement innovative reward strategies, including performance- and competency-based pay, variable pay plans, and long-term incentive reward programs. It also facilitates the analysis and comparison of compensation packages using internal and external salary data to maintain market competitiveness. Travel planning offers access to booking services (e.g., flights, hotels, rental cars, rail), enforces travel policies for queries and bookings, establishes custom hotel catalogs, takes into account agreements with travel service providers, and stores travelers' personal preferences. Travel expense reporting shall support the creation of general data for travel expense reports, the settlement of travel expenses, and the payment of expenses through financial accounting and payroll. Personnel Time Management assists with all processes related to planning, recording, and evaluating internal and external work and absence data. Time and labor data can be recorded centrally by a time clerk or individually by each employee. Payroll supports all processes related to employee remuneration. Based on an employee's time records and work contract, the payroll application calculates gross and net pay, which includes individual payments and deductions calculated during a payroll period. Talent and Performance Management helps develop and nurture talent within organizations. It assists in hiring personnel, furthering education and development of talents, identifying and shaping future management personalities, and aligning employees with company goals and compensation. Training and Event Management offers a wide range of robust functions for planning and managing various business events, from training sessions to conventions, efficiently and effectively. It includes analytics and evaluation capabilities. Event Management features a comprehensive range of functions, such as business event preparation, establishing hierarchical structured business event catalogs, calculating business event costs and suggesting prices, booking individual and group attendees, handling billing, evaluating attendees and events, and reporting on all event-related data. Training Management consists of course offerings, which involve course planning and catalog creation, and training administration, which includes booking activities. Shared Services standardizes and automates shared services processes and self-services for employees and managers. Uniform processes and services can be implemented across the organization to reduce operational lead times and ensure a consistently high level of service. The self-services component allows for the creation and management of employee self-services and manager self-services. To improve processes and services, comprehensive and real-time analytics for human resources are needed, which is the focus of Human Resources Reporting. As Human Capital Management contains all relevant employee data, the necessary analytical operations can be performed to support decision-making. Numerous standard reports can be provided, enabling companies to report on data along hierarchical structures and access standard analytics with ease.

4.9   Asset Management

The Acquire to Decommission reference process is primarily executed by the Asset Management application module, as illustrated in Fig. 4.9. Maintenance Management uses a comprehensive strategy that encompasses planning, execution, enhancement, and collaboration. The foundation for various Asset Management solution processes is formed by maintenance master data. Key features include organizing technical objects hierarchically and horizontally, generating master records for functional locations and equipment, and creating maintenance bills of materials. Maintenance Demand Processing enables users to generate and handle a wide range of work requests, from traditional corrective methods to condition-based, predictive, or prescriptive maintenance approaches. Maintenance work can be requested and described using mobile devices or desktop computers to report technical issues. Maintenance Planning allows for the scheduling of maintenance tasks and the identification of the most suitable technician to utilize the appropriate tools, resources, and perform maintenance activities. Additionally, a comprehensive view of asset status, maintenance expenses, and breakdown causes is provided. Maintenance

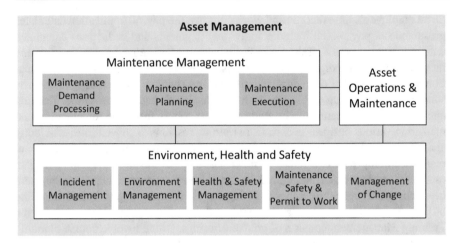

Fig. 4.9 Reference architecture for Asset Management

costs can be minimized by effectively utilizing labor, materials, equipment, and schedules. Another feature is the classification of maintenance plans to facilitate improved search, analysis, and monitoring of maintenance expenses. Operations can be categorized into pre-work, main work, and post-work. Maintenance Execution enables the processing of planned or emergency maintenance and provides access to relevant information on any device. Employees shall be able to remotely access, transfer, complete, and manage assigned work orders while gaining real-time insights into asset performance for informed, timely decision-making. They shall also be able to review ongoing maintenance activities and reschedule multiple times per day if necessary. Asset Operations and Maintenance expands core planning functionality with advanced scheduling capabilities and resource planning. Maintenance Scheduling helps users minimize excessive downtime and reduce costs by implementing the right systems and processes. It considers availability windows for maintenance, work center capacity, and maintenance plans. The component incorporates resource scheduling, allowing for insights into maintenance workload and control over available capacities for current and upcoming maintenance activities. Multi-resource management streamlines and automates processes for defining and meeting project resource demands. It also shall offer functionality for tracking, assigning, and scheduling resources, collecting assignment approvals, and generating relevant reports such as demand overview and resource utilization reports.

Environment Health and Safety (EHS) plays a crucial role in overseeing business operations related to environmental protection and the health and safety of individuals. This component allows to plan and execute activities necessary for adhering to emission-related environmental regulations. Moreover, it provides the ability to document and analyze incidents, safety observations, and near misses. Through Incident Management, EHS enables the recording of incidents, near misses, and observations, fostering transparency and standardization with the help of templates, task tracking, and automated analytical reporting. This can lead to reduced injury, illness, and incident rates, as well as decreased EHS penalties, fines, and unplanned downtimes. Environment Management shall apply predictive learning algorithms and statistical methods to project emissions data based on historical information. This allows for the management of greenhouse gas emissions and other air or water emissions in order to meet legal requirements while promoting proactive data transparency and monitoring. Health and Safety Management assists in managing general and equipment-related safety instructions centrally, preventing incidents and minimizing EHS risks through a standardized, cost-effective approach to operational risk management. This component aids in reducing workplace exposures and their associated health impacts, overseeing industrial hygiene and monitoring by planning and executing workplace sample campaigns and related measurements. Maintenance Safety and Permit to Work ensures the proper control of maintenance work by providing clear safety instructions and permits, connecting EHS information to technical equipment and plant maintenance tasks. This component offers flexible permit levels that are natively integrated with the work-order process in enterprise asset management, automating the permit process and enforcing fully auditable procedures that encourage consistent behavior. Lastly, Management of Change streamlines change requests, further enhancing the effectiveness of EHS systems in managing environmental and safety concerns.

4.10 Finance

The primary implementation of the Finance reference process occurs through the Finance application module, as illustrated in Fig. 4.10. Financial Operations monitors incoming and outgoing payments in real time, offering a comprehensive view

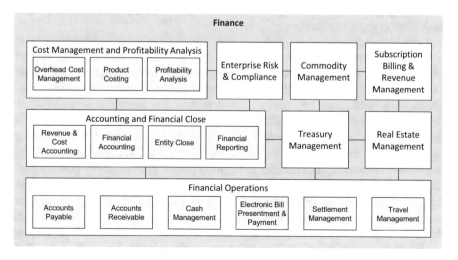

Fig. 4.10 Reference architecture for Finance

of an organization's financial status by tracking all financial activities within the company. Accounts Payable displays the company's debts to its creditors as liabilities on the balance sheet, providing an overview of outstanding amounts and their respective due dates. Efficient management of customer accounts receivable is handled by Accounts Receivable, which deals with funds owed to the company for goods delivered or services provided. Cash Management allows the company to centrally manage cash and liquidity by monitoring real-time cash flow, ensuring adequate liquidity is maintained. In the modern digital landscape, Electronic Bill Presentation and Payment is essential, offering electronic billing and online payment options. This function also assists companies in generating electronic invoices for their customers in accordance with company format guidelines. Settlement Management deals with intricate, high-volume financial payment processes offered to business partners. Travel Management oversees all aspects of business travel and related expenses, tracking costs and reimbursing employees as needed. Accounting and Financial Close ensures the company's financial records are well organized and accurate. The general ledger created within this component serves as the foundation for the company's finances. Revenue and Cost Accounting maintains detailed records of incoming and outgoing cash flows, allowing the company to enhance accuracy by staying current with cost accounting changes. Automating revenue and cost recognition processes can reduce audit expenses, shorten the time required to close annual books, and decrease overall finance costs. Financial Accounting facilitates real-time reporting by streamlining financial processes and providing granular information. This function enables financial reporting and real-time, self-service analytics derived from highly detailed operational data, supporting asset management and year-end book closing. Entity Close finalizes the books at year-end and generates financial statements in the desired format, adhering to international financial reporting standards. Financial Reporting delivers information that reveals an organization's financial position to management, investors, and government entities, aiding managers in making informed decisions and supporting the company in audits and compliance matters.

Cost Management and Profitability monitors the expenses and profitability of products and services, allowing companies to modify their product lineup or optimize costs. By comparing costs to revenue, a profitability analysis is generated. Overhead Cost Management shall offer transparency and insights into the overhead allocation process, with cost centers, profit centers, and margin analysis available for both actuals and plans. Product Costing allows for the creation of group-level financial statements, calculating the costs incurred in producing individual products or services without the need for extract, transform, and load processes, enabling continuous accounting. Profitability Analysis provides an overview of product profitability, including risks and costs, with centralized data storage facilitating real-time analysis and aiding in product portfolio creation. Treasury Management handles cash management and bank communication, supporting cash, liquidity, and risk management, as well as integrated financial reporting. It streamlines working capital, risk management, and compliance activities related to cash, payments, liquidity, and risk. Real Estate Management covers all aspects of the real estate life cycle, such as investment and construction, sales and marketing, lease and space management, and maintenance and repair. It handles tasks ranging from portfolio analysis and investment tracking to lead qualification, lease posting, rent escalation, and maintenance and repair service orders. Real estate object management offers both architectural and usage views of master data. Enterprise Risk and Compliance helps manage risks, controls, and regulatory requirements in business operations. To minimize risk and ensure compliance, all incoming and outgoing payments are checked, with automatic alerts sent to responsible parties for faster response and reaction times. Commodity Management identifies and qualifies financial risks related to commodity price fluctuations in sales and procurement. It tracks suppliers, resources, and price developments, enabling companies to make informed procurement decisions or hedge risks with commodity derivatives. The module also monitors exchange rates for services provided in different countries and currencies, supporting material management contracts from commodity pricing to risk analytics and facilitating mark-to-market queries, stock logistics documents, and financial derivatives. Subscription Billing and Revenue Management allows organizations to adopt flexible payment models, including subscriptions and usage-based billing. Key features include subscription business models with recurring and one-time charges, rating and billing of millions of usage transactions from multiple platforms, complex volume-based discounts and surcharges, and revenue sharing and partner settlement. Subscription order management enables customers to offer their business solutions as a mix of products and services.

4.11   Conclusion

In this chapter, we suggested a reference architecture for ERP software. The reference consists of various application modules for implementing the reference business processes explained in the previous chapter. The reference architecture builds the technical foundation for embedding artificial intelligence into ERP solutions. The Idea to Market reference business process was realized with the application module Research and Development/Engineering. The reference business process Source to Pay was covered by the application module Procurement. The application modules Supply Chain and Manufacturing implemented the reference business process Plan to Fulfill. Lead to Cash was mapped to the application modules Sales and Service. Human Capital Management handled the Recruit to Retire reference business process. The application module Asset Management covered the Acquire to Decommission reference business process, while the Finance module managed the Finance business process. The reference business process Governance was implemented with various components of the underlying ERP technology platform and therefore was not discussed further.

ERP Reference Artificial Intelligence Technology

5

In this chapter, we explain the artificial intelligence technologies that are used in ERP systems to implement corresponding business applications. We identified two types of technology provisioning in the context of ERP systems. There are artificial intelligence technologies that are embedded into the database system and application server of ERP systems. For scalability reasons, artificial intelligence infrastructure (e.g., GPU computing) is also provided side by side to the ERP platform. We will introduce both types of ERP technology so that a general understanding is provisioned. However, from our perspective, it is not valuable to consider this topic abstractly. Therefore, we will depict as a concrete example SAP S/4HANA as the well-known ERP product and reflect the contained artificial intelligence technologies. This is also helpful in understanding the case studies and implementation framework introduced in the last part of the elaboration. The goal is to describe what those technologies are intended to be used for and not to explain all features and functions in detail.

5.1 Introduction

By investigating on different ERP products (see objective and methodology chapter) and the used artificial intelligence technologies, we concluded the ERP reference artificial intelligence technology as shown in Fig. 5.1. There are two variants of artificial intelligence technologies provided in context of ERP software. Basic libraries and runtimes are available on the ERP platform for implementing simple scenarios. In addition, AI technology platforms like AWS AI, Azure AI, Google AI, IBM Watson, Alibaba AI, or SAP AI are supported side by side to the ERP platform for complex scenarios. These AI technology platforms typically share a similar structure, offering infrastructure for training, inference, data storage, GPU hardware, operations, and monitoring. They also support data science environments and generic services like image recognition and text translation. All those components

© The Author(s), under exclusive license to Springer Nature Switzerland AG 2024
S. Sarferaz, *Embedding Artificial Intelligence into ERP Software*,
https://doi.org/10.1007/978-3-031-54249-7_5

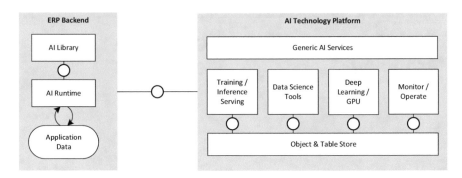

Fig. 5.1 ERP reference artificial intelligence technology

are self-explanatory and will be discussed in Chap. 7 so that instead of describing them abstractly, we will depict the artificial intelligence technologies concretely for SAP S/4HANA as an exemplary ERP solution. This will be particularly helpful in understanding subsequent chapters where case studies based on SAP S/4HANA are explained, serving as proof points for the proposed approaches. Our aim is to give an overview of some of SAP's most significant artificial intelligence technologies. While this document does not cover all the features and functionalities of these technologies, it does offer guidance on their usage and recommendations on which technology to use in specific situations, as some have overlapping capabilities. SAP provides a range of artificial intelligence technologies to its partners, clients, and internal stakeholders for their own projects. We will discuss SAP HANA, SAP Data Intelligence, SAP AI Core, and SAP Analytics Cloud and conclude with SAP AI Business Services and SAP AI Launchpad. Based on the ERP reference artificial intelligence technology shown in Fig. 5.1, we can classify SAP HANA as embedded technology of the ERP platform, while all the other listed technologies are provided side by side on the AI technology platform of SAP.

SAP HANA's key feature is its multipurpose database, which allows users to store, process, train, and serve all their data and artificial intelligence processes in memory and in real time. As all customer-initiated actions and operations are executed immediately within SAP HANA's in-memory database, there is no need to transfer data to another system for processing. The specialized machine learning (ML) libraries [Automated Predictive Library (APL) and Predictive Analytics Library (PAL)] built into SAP HANA applications support a wide range of artificial intelligence use cases. For data scientists' convenience, all training methods offer a native scripting interface (SQLScript), which can be used directly or wrapped in Python and R libraries.

When it comes to complex orchestration situations, data categorization, and data quality procedures, SAP Data Intelligence excels in these areas. It can seamlessly integrate unstructured, streaming, or cloud application data in various formats scattered across the organization and write it to the desired endpoint. With connections to R, Python, APL, and PAL libraries, SAP Data Intelligence provides a unified graphical design interface for both data ingestion and transformation. SAP Data Intelligence is suggested for situations where artificial intelligence use cases involve multiple diverse data sources that need to be merged and managed in SAP HANA, with an R Server, or directly in a Python environment. It also supports data orchestration to external artificial intelligence environments. When advanced hardware resources like GPUs or intricate orchestration of workflow steps are required, SAP AI Core is the recommended solution for managing and controlling training and serving workflows in a scalable AI runtime. It is designed for AI engineers with strong coding skills and a need for flexibility. SAP AI Core aims to operate scalable, cost-effective, and customizable artificial intelligence models while maintaining privacy and compliance. It ensures the high level of scalability for every artificial intelligence scenario through auto-scaling, scale-to-zero, multi-model serving, and a broad array of resource types, including GPU support. Focusing on life cycle management, SAP AI Core collects various metrics, primarily by integrating with the AI API for life cycle handling, which reduces the time to value for artificial intelligence applications designed for SAP systems. For analytical and business users, SAP Analytics Cloud offers built-in predictive capabilities with a simple user interface. Its prediction engine is constructed using the APL library from SAP HANA. Live datasets can be created on top of SAP HANA on-premises systems, and data can be collected from multiple source systems. Forecasts made using SAP Analytics Cloud's predictive capabilities are typically consumed through SAP Analytics Cloud stories. SAP AI Business Services provide strategic machine learning capabilities that enhance customer experiences by automating and optimizing business operations. These services and applications are available as reusable, generic offerings that can be immediately utilized. Most of these services use SAP AI Core as the underlying artificial intelligence environment. SAP AI Launchpad serves as a centralized tool for managing the life cycle of artificial intelligence models, deployments, and other operations-related information across all deployment scenarios and landscapes. It also allows users to manage supporting AI runtimes like SAP AI Core, SAP HANA, and SAP Data Intelligence. SAP AI Launchpad becomes the standardized user interface for managing and operating any artificial intelligence use cases provided by SAP or custom-developed, due to the centrally regulated AI API for life cycle management. Based on the AI API abstraction, third-party artificial intelligence offerings can also be utilized for implementing artificial intelligence applications.

In the next sections, the mentioned artificial intelligence technologies are explained using the five phases of data science process described in the last chapter.

5.2   Data Preparation

5.2.1   SAP HANA

To create artificial intelligence models based on relational data, SAP HANA offers a comprehensive suite of tools. There are four primary tools for data preparation:

1. Crafting standard SQL scripts and SAP HANA data modeling
2. Utilizing the internal functions of the Predictive Analysis Library (PAL)

3. Using the default features of the Automated Predictive Library (APL)
4. Leveraging the SAP HANA Machine Learning Python and R client

SAP HANA's multi-model database enables artificial intelligence scenarios to take advantage of its diverse features. Both Calculation View and Smart Data Integration Flowgraphs play a vital role in SAP HANA data modeling, offering the flexibility of pure SQL and SQL Script data manipulation. Calculation Views enable common analytical model operations on relational tables, such as joins, unions, selections, and complex calculations using SQL Script Table Functions. These views serve as transparent data structures, facilitating real-time access to live data from complex virtual data models without storing any data. In contrast, data integration Flowgraphs support SQL operation-based data flow modeling, including custom logic implementation through SQL script procedures. Although both Calculation Views and Flowgraphs are useful for general data preparation, they were not specifically designed for tasks like normalization, imputation, dimensionality reduction, or imbalance handling. SAP HANA's AI libraries excel at addressing these specialized tasks. The Predictive Analysis Library (PAL) caters to data science experts, providing optimal performance and dedicated algorithm parameterization, while the Automated Predictive Library (APL) targets business analysts and developers with limited data science experience. APL's focus on automation allows it to handle common data issues like skewness, missing values, or value level differences without user intervention. Conversely, PAL offers an extensive toolkit for tackling various data pre-processing challenges, with its reference guide detailing the available tools. The methods discussed so far require direct interaction with the SAP HANA database and the necessary expertise to utilize them. Recognizing the widespread use of R and Python in data science, SAP HANA provides native machine learning client libraries for these languages. The R and Python client packages allow data scientists to work in their preferred environment, similar to using any popular open-source library, while delegating all operations to a remote SAP HANA instance without data movement or the need for powerful data science workstations. This has two implications for data preparation. Firstly, all SAP HANA AI library functions are accessible via the Python and R clients. Secondly, the libraries offer common data manipulation capabilities akin to the DataFrame features of the respective languages. Although it may seem like working with a native DataFrame in R or Python, all operations are translated into SQL statements executed on the database, without necessarily transferring data to the client. Depending on the intended operationalization scenario, the relevant generated SQL statements can be captured and integrated into database SQL Script or data model artifacts.

In summary, using SAP HANA for artificial intelligence projects provides access to a powerful, enterprise-grade in-memory database with a wide array of tools and options for data preparation and manipulation. The specialized machine learning libraries offer additional features for artificial intelligence-specific planning tasks. For structured, tabular projects that require live data access and involve large data sets, consider incorporating embedded machine learning in SAP HANA.

5.2.2   SAP Data Intelligence

SAP Data Intelligence, the company's cloud data management solution, addresses data cataloging, data quality, and various intricate orchestration scenarios. Artificial intelligence teams often face several challenges during the data preparation stage, such as:

- Identifying available information for use
- Assessing the reliability of the data
- Organizing and formatting data for model creation
- Adjusting data for feature creation or extraction during training

If all data is structured (tabular) and already exists within an SAP solution like SAP HANA or SAP Data Warehouse Cloud, the built-in features of SAP HANA (mentioned earlier) may suffice. However, teams often need information scattered across the organization in different locations. These situations may involve a mix of unstructured data (e.g., images, documents), streaming data (e.g., IoT data, weblogs), cloud application data, and traditional relational data, which could be stored in SAP HANA. SAP Data Intelligence proves useful in these cases, as it can integrate various data types and allow end users to model pipelines that channel this data to the desired endpoint for training data. While processing, SAP Data Intelligence can transform and clean up the data. Each pipeline is reusable, scalable, and features a graphical modeling interface with numerous operators for low-code pipelining. Additional capabilities that aid data preparation include defining data quality rules applicable to data sets, generating a historical profile of quality in each data set over time, and indexing all connected data sources for end users to search across data using a free-form search.

In summary, SAP Data Intelligence is recommended for moving, cleaning, and transforming data when the application data for a use case is not centrally located in SAP HANA or is unstructured in nature.

5.2.3   SAP AI Core

Argo Workflows, an open-source container-native workflow engine designed for orchestrating parallel tasks directly on Kubernetes, provides a comprehensive set of features through SAP AI Core. Argo can be likened to a machine that manages and nourishes a Kubernetes cluster. With SAP AI Core, it becomes effortless to define, schedule, and coordinate intricate workflows and applications on Kubernetes. SAP AI Core boasts numerous capabilities, including:

- Handling complex tasks with a combination of parallel and sequential steps and dependencies
- Managing Kubernetes cluster deployments for sophisticated, distributed applications

- Establishing policies for time-based workflow execution

In SAP AI Core, each task is executed in a pod, simplifying the process of performing multiple tasks simultaneously. The generic workflow engine offers a high degree of flexibility for implementing most data preparation and integration pipelines. Various Argo Software Development Kits (SDKs) are available, enabling the programmatic definition of SAP AI Core compliant workflows, such as those in Python. SAP AI Core is specifically tailored for the AI Engineer persona, who possesses extensive coding skills and requires the highest level of flexibility. This persona also necessitates enterprise-grade security and governance for SAP AI Core. We have full control over the hyperscaler on which SAP AI Core will be installed, and we can connect to any hyperscaler object storage (AWS, Alibaba Cloud, Azure, GCP) as well as SAP HANA Data Lake files. It is ensured that raw and processed data does not leave specific geographic regions or even particular hyperscalers, especially when adhering to stringent security standards. Utilizing SAP HANA and SAP Data Intelligence in an enterprise setting and transferring application data to an object store accessible by SAP AI Core is a logical choice, as these solutions offer a wide array of data preparation and management options with a user interface. However, SAP AI Core is the optimal choice if the artificial intelligence solution must be deployed in a scalable, programmatic, and flexible manner, operating autonomously without relying on centrally managed or governed data.

In summary, use SAP HANA or SAP Data Intelligence for central data management solutions. These tools can load data into a persistent store for SAP AI Core to access. If the objective is a stand-alone artificial intelligence solution with intricate tasks, dependencies, and GPU support, the data preparation features of SAP AI Core present an advantageous alternative.

5.2.4   SAP Analytics Cloud

In SAP Analytics Cloud, predictive scenarios are supported by two types of data models: datasets and planning-enabled models. Datasets can contain information from various sources and can be obtained from different source systems. In this case, the source data is replicated in SAP Analytics Cloud. SAP HANA on-premises systems can facilitate the creation of live datasets, which are equivalent to SQL views and SAP HANA table data. Here, the source data is not replicated in SAP Analytics Cloud but remains entirely in SAP HANA. Classification, regression, and time series forecasting models can utilize datasets as their data sources, whether they are replicated or real-time data. The end-to-end data flow when using datasets involves gathering data from source systems, building predictive scenarios with datasets, and providing predictions as datasets for use in stories. SAP Analytics Cloud features two categories of models: planning models for planning purposes and analytic models primarily used for reporting purposes. Both account-based and measure-based structures can be employed to create models. Time series forecasting models can be derived from planning-enabled models, which can receive data from various sources. The end-to-end data flow when using planning models includes integrating source system data, delivering predictive forecasts, building predictive scenarios, consuming predictive forecasts in stories, and exporting predictive forecasts to source systems if needed. In the context of different data models (datasets and planning models) and stories, SAP Analytics Cloud provides lightweight data preparation and blending. These capabilities can support simple time series forecasting models but may not be advanced enough to handle the data preparation requirements for classification and regression models. In such cases, SAP Analytics Cloud may need to be used alongside another platform, like SAP Data Intelligence, to manage complex tasks related to feature generation and selecting appropriate observations for input and target variables. SAP Analytics Cloud's focus on citizen data scientists and business users ensures that algorithm hyperparameterization and data prerequisites are automatically managed in predictive scenarios, making it inaccessible to end users. This approach allows end users to focus on gathering data and conducting data experiments to enhance predictive models.

In summary, SAP Analytics Cloud's data preparation capabilities are specifically designed to generate datasets and planning-enabled models for use in predictive scenarios. The measure-based planning model serves as the reference data model for SAP Analytics Cloud.

5.3 Modeling

5.3.1 SAP HANA

The APL and PAL libraries within SAP HANA are designed to work with training inputs in a relational format, as they are database-embedded AI engines. These libraries can handle various data structures, such as Calculation Views, SQL Views, Table Functions, persisted tables, federated remote data sources from other SAP HANA databases, or even third-party data sources. SQLScript serves as the native scripting interface for preprocessing, and to facilitate usage by data scientists, all methods have been wrapped in Python and R libraries. Consequently, these methods can be called from any Python or R environment and executed remotely in the SAP HANA dataset instance without requiring data transfer. Both PAL and APL support a wide range of common artificial intelligence scenarios, offering assistance for link prediction, recommender systems, cluster analysis, regression, time series forecasting, and association analysis. Additionally, PAL provides specific algorithms for outlier detection use cases. As the more advanced library, PAL includes a unified interface for classification and regression scenarios, enabling easy implementation of various algorithms using the same procedure interface without needing modifications at the application integration level. The algorithms also support automated hyperparameter search and model evaluation during training, as well as a dedicated comparison feature to automatically compare different algorithms for an expanding range of algorithms. Recently, PAL in SAP HANA Cloud introduced algorithm pipelining and an AutoML engine for classification, regression, and time series forecasting scenarios, aiding data scientists in developing the best possible machine learning models. APL, on the other hand, focuses on automating workflows. When artificial intelligence models need to be segmented by specific sub-groups in the data (e.g., regions, locations, or times), PAL leverages SAP HANA's parallelization capabilities to enable automatic parallel training of the required models, delivering optimal performance while creating thousands of models simultaneously. SAP Integrated Business Planning is an example of an SAP application that utilizes this feature. Moreover, the Python machine learning client supports the creation of function pipelines, allowing for the stacking of multiple artificial intelligence method calls into complex scenarios. SAP HANA provides workload management capabilities to regulate system resources allocated to artificial intelligence training workloads, while algorithm libraries offer multi-threading options to accelerate training processes. SAP HANA Cloud also presents new scalability and elasticity options to efficiently scale system resources for artificial intelligence workloads in both pure cloud and hybrid on-premises/cloud scenarios.

In summary, any artificial intelligence initiative based on structured, tabular data can take advantage of the comprehensive toolkit offered by SAP HANA's embedded machine learning. The two specialized libraries, APL and PAL, provide a simple yet effective entry point into the artificial intelligence domain for various target audiences. Python or R interfaces are the preferred means of interacting with these libraries to facilitate adoption and integration.

5.3.2 SAP Data Intelligence

The SAP HANA APL and PAL engines, as mentioned earlier, are supported by SAP Data Intelligence as part of its modeling engine, which also offers the ability to script in R and Python. To provide Python users with a user-friendly Integrated Development Environment (IDE) for model development and training, the solution incorporates a JupyterLab notebook. The ML Scenario Manager offers a single location within the solution to monitor all artifacts related to a specific use case, including pipelines, data sets, notebooks, and training runs. Furthermore, the pipeline modeling user interface contains native operators for SAP HANA ML, R, and Python. SAP HANA ML users can access a low-code interface that enables them to utilize any of the APL and PAL engines' functions without needing to write SQL scripts. It is also possible to integrate open-source R, Python, ABAP, Node.js, and C# programming languages with SAP HANA ML in a single pipeline. This allows for more comprehensive training, which can now include creating end-to-end pipelines necessary for taking data from its original source, training a model (or using an existing model as part of a pipeline), and connecting the results to the locations where the scored data needs to be sent. It is essential to note that model training occurs on the standard SAP Data Intelligence node, which does not utilize GPUs. For situations requiring GPU support, such as deep learning scenarios that need to be completed quickly, SAP AI Core is recommended. If the GPU train/serve environment has the necessary API endpoints, SAP Data Intelligence can still be utilized to pipeline the data to an external training or serving environment, like SAP AI Core, and to direct the scored data to its final destination.

In summary, if SAP HANA ML will be used alongside other data from outside SAP HANA that may also involve the use of R/Python or if a graphical interface is desired for SAP HANA ML, then SAP Data Intelligence is recommended. It functions as a single, easy-to-use graphical design interface for data ingestion and transformation that integrates with R, Python, APL, and PAL libraries.

5.3.3 SAP AI Core

In the preceding section, it was noted that Argo Workflows serve as the workflow execution engine for SAP AI Core. Utilizing SAP AI Core for training offers several benefits, including:

- Running any workload that can be executed in containers
- Using Kubernetes for efficient orchestration of parallel tasks
- Flexible resource allocation plans, encompassing GPU resources

SAP AI Core conducts model training and pre-/post-processing workflows in batch mode. GitOps mechanisms can be employed to deliver training workflows, facilitating declarative content distribution. To develop an Argo Workflow template, any code editor (e.g., Visual Studio Code) or Argo SDKs can be used. Frameworks like Netflix's Metaflow or Kubeflow expedite artificial intelligence scenario delivery from experimentation to production, providing enhanced support for specific artificial intelligence processes. The aim is to broaden the content package approach for more prevalent use cases, allowing a focus on transitioning experiments into production. SAP AI Core supplies content packages for common use cases, such as computer vision, and offers comprehensive GPU support for training single or multiple models. Typically, the experimentation phase occurs in the data scientist's local environment, like JupyterLab, since SAP AI Core's training capabilities emphasize artificial intelligence scenario productization. After determining the necessary hyperparameters, a model can be trained on SAP AI Core using a training workflow. Alternatively, a pre-trained model can be brought in and advanced to the next stage. A distinguishing feature is multi-tenancy, which enables serving a global artificial intelligence model while granting each tenant access to unique trainable artificial intelligence models by segregating stakeholders into tenants. This allows stakeholders to train with their own data, catering to their specific requirements. Partners can separate clients for security and regulatory compliance, while customers can divide board components to ensure governance. SAP AI Core's integration with hyperscaler object stores, such as AWS S3, allows for incorporating customer-managed data sets in the relevant support landscapes. Another option is storing data in SAP HANA Data Lake files. SAP AI Core's life cycle management capabilities enable the collection and storage of self-defined metrics, parameters, and training job statistics, which can be exposed via AI API to SAP AI Launchpad for monitoring. Several SAP AI Business Services utilize SAP AI Core as the AI runtime to deliver frequently needed capabilities.

In summary, SAP AI Core is the optimal solution for managing and operating training workflows in a scalable AI runtime when sophisticated hardware resources like GPUs or complex workflow step orchestration are necessary.

5.3.4   SAP Analytics Cloud

Leveraging automated machine learning methods and an intuitive user interface, SAP Analytics Cloud enables end users to create time series forecasting models, classification models, and regression models. The predictive engine employed by SAP Analytics Cloud offers features similar to those found in SAP HANA's Automated Predictive Library (APL). In SAP Analytics Cloud, users cannot explicitly select and parameterize the underlying algorithms, ensuring that the capabilities are accessible and comprehensible to end users. Classification and regression models can be applied to new observations, generating new datasets with predictions that can be integrated into SAP Analytics Cloud stories. Time series forecasting models have various applications and can be based on a single time series or up to a thousand combinations using entities (dimension combinations). These models can be constructed on top of datasets from SAP Analytics Cloud or models with planning capabilities. Predictive forecasts can be written back directly into planning model versions or datasets (predictive planning).

In summary, SAP Analytics Cloud's predictive scenarios offer ready-to-use forecasting capabilities through automated machine learning and user-friendly workflows designed for analytical end users. The strategic investment focus is on automated time series forecasting workflows to address planning forecasting needs.

5.4   Evaluation

Due to the fact that SAP HANA's integrated artificial intelligence is based on industry norms, the applied algorithms deliver all the conventional metrics needed to assess the performance of the artificial intelligence model, as one would expect from any library. These metrics are typically generated by default during training, cross-validation, or score function runs and are included in the standard output. They can be directly displayed or saved for later use or comparison. As mentioned earlier, most algorithms have built-in features for automatically evaluating models and searching for parameters, along with a unique function for comparing different regression algorithm models. The APL library also includes two exclusive metrics for model performance, Predictive Power and Prediction Confidence, which are intended to provide business users with a more intuitive understanding of model performance. Of course, all generated metrics can be natively accessed through the machine learning clients for Python and R. Model performance evaluation can be done using SAP Data Intelligence based on the metrics specified in the R or Python model during scripting/development. A wide range of metrics can be set up and collected since SAP AI Core places a significant emphasis on artificial intelligence lifecycle management. The AI Engineer has full autonomy to choose the most suitable metrics for each use case, including error rate, confusion matrix, and others. Metrics tracking is part of the AI API, allowing us to store and retrieve metrics using GET/PATCH/DELETE requests. These metrics and parameters can then be evaluated using either a third-party user interface or SAP AI Launchpad. SAP AI Core focuses on the productization of artificial intelligence use cases, so the standard evaluation phase of an experiment is not the main concern. Metrics are collected with the goal of operating and productizing artificial intelligence processes and evaluating them later. SAP Analytics Cloud provides simple evaluation metrics in predictive scenarios to assess the effectiveness of predictive models (e.g., Predictive Power, Prediction Confidence, RMSE, Expected MAPE), specifically designed for business users. Additionally, stories make it easy to evaluate models on the fly. SAP Analytics Cloud's analytical and visualization capabilities simplify the comparison of predictions and results.

In summary, while SAP HANA provides a standard toolkit for model evaluation and some automated features for assistance, building complex models still necessitates proper data science expertise. SAP AI Core, with its strong focus on life cycle management, can collect various metrics, especially when integrated with the AI API. APIs enable programmatic interaction to retrieve metrics tracked by SAP AI Core. For those who prefer a user interface for tracking metrics, SAP AI Launchpad is available. SAP Analytics Cloud offers both business user-centric model evaluation and ad hoc model evaluation using stories.

5.5 Deployment

5.5.1 SAP HANA

The implementation of SAP HANA artificial intelligence scenarios primarily focuses on objects capable of holding SQL code, as SQL and SQLScript function as native interfaces to the embedded artificial intelligence in SAP HANA. This can be as straightforward as SQLScript files prepared for manual execution. Ideally, the script should be stored in central objects that can be automated for productive use, such as SAP HANA stored procedures that run automatically or on-demand. Database Table Functions may also include calls to artificial intelligence libraries and can be incorporated into Calculation Views to create virtual data models like real-time predictions each time a Calculation View is queried. SAP Business Technology Platform Fiori and Cloud Application Programming (CAP) applications support embedding their respective SQLScript objects within SAP HANA native artifacts. Consequently, any process or workflow based on these applications can leverage all deployment techniques of these tools and incorporate artificial intelligence capabilities. Numerous options are available when using machine learning clients for Python and R, with scripts created in this way being converted into the appropriate SQL statement and executed each time a Python or R script runs, allowing integration into any Python or R code deployment. The Python client's support for this feature enables easy integration of training and prediction design-time artifacts into application projects. Integration with SAP applications that utilize the artificial intelligence model, such as SAP S/4HANA, is a critical aspect of deployment. This is crucial for two main reasons: firstly, data-driven insights are most valuable when closely integrated with relevant business processes and applications and, secondly, artificial intelligence initiatives should maximize the use of existing tools and knowledge. Making intelligent solutions accessible through existing tools is an essential first step in their democratization. ABAP Managed Database Procedures (AMDPs) serve as the primary component for this, as they are ABAP classes that encapsulate SQLScript code in ABAP standard objects and syntax, making it available to all ABAP-based applications and creating a connection between ABAP-based applications and SAP HANA. All other options, aside from raw SQL files, support multi-landscape scenarios. Standard development objects can be used for transporting and deploying both SAP HANA and SAP applications in this context. It is essential to deploy the corresponding artificial intelligence models along with the SQL-based runtime objects, which are always common tables for embedded artificial intelligence in SAP HANA. These model tables can be extracted, transferred, and stored using any data management tool and can also be queried from remote systems using SAP HANA's remote access capabilities. The APL library provides a unique deployment option by supporting the export of trained models as JavaScript code snippets, enabling support for more clustered landscapes and architectures that can be deployed wherever a JavaScript engine is present. SAP HANA embedded artificial intelligence can utilize all standard operational tools, such as monitoring, auditing, integration with Git repositories, or the internal SAP HANA repository. To accommodate requirements where applications share the same database resources, these resources can be allocated and limited. For optimal performance, SAP HANA can be configured to store specific artificial intelligence models in the main memory, ensuring constant availability. A dedicated model storage and management system introduced by the Python API supports model versioning and specific usage of model versions.

In summary, SAP HANA provides deployment flexibility, accommodating various use cases and architectures. It is recommended to leverage existing IT operations knowledge in the relevant environment, such as Python or ABAP application skills, over SAP HANA native development methods. SAP HANA does not place a strong emphasis on operationalizing models, necessitating more custom implementations. Using other applications with more predefined tools is advised.

5.5.2   SAP Data Intelligence

Creating a custom operator simplifies and promotes reusability in model deployment by encapsulating R or Python code into a versatile building block that can be integrated into any pipeline. Users with appropriate permissions can duplicate and modify any operators or pipelines, as they are all designed for reusability. In SAP Data Intelligence, each operator operates within its own Docker container, allowing for resource scaling as needed. Moreover, pipelines can automatically scale based on resource load. To manage the complete data delivery process to the model for scoring and the distribution of scored results, models are deployed as pipelines, with SAP Data Intelligence capable of connecting to multiple data sources and targets. Monitoring and pipeline metrics are provided, and any pipeline can be scheduled for continuous operation. Integration with Jenkins and Git for CI/CD is also supported. However, Data Intelligence lacks dedicated operational life cycle management tools focusing on model divergence and retraining.

In summary, SAP Data Intelligence is recommended for scenarios where operationalizing artificial intelligence use cases requires consolidating and orchestrating various data sources with SAP HANA, an R Server, or directly in a Python environment, or orchestrating data to external artificial intelligence.

5.5.3 SAP AI Core

SAP AI Core excels in key areas such as cloud-native architecture and Continuous Integration/Continuous Delivery (CI/CD) deployments for artificial intelligence-related use cases. It is generally advised to keep source code in a centrally managed Git repository for efficiently operating use cases. This repository enables automatic syncing, access to the latest code, and automation of the entire deployment process. SAP AI Core offers configuration and content management options based on GitOps principles, allowing for system configurations and artificial intelligence use case workflows to be solely based on the Git repository's information. This provides benefits such as content management, tracking configuration changes, reviewing and approving changes, and having an auditable change log through Git history. By integrating with a Docker registry, we can demonstrate successfully operating artificial intelligence use cases using only the docker images we trust. The multi-tenancy option prevents data, models, and deployments from interfering with each other and offers enhanced enterprise-level security. Features like auto-scaling, scale-to-zero, multi-model serving, and GPU support ensure use case scalability and better cost control. SAP AI Core is reliable for deployments with applications, enabling artificial intelligence capabilities integration into any business processes based on these applications. SAP AI Core offers a secure environment that operates effectively and at scale, with a centrally defined AI API that is easy for developers to work with. Developers can rely on AI Engineers to provide the latest updates via the controlled AI API without needing to know any specifics, streamlining and accelerating the entire delivery process with less maintenance required. Use cases can be managed and operated through SAP AI Launchpad, allowing for workflow and artifact adaptation, version tracking, and other monitoring aspects. There are multiple ways to run use cases, such as programmatically training runs, deploying models, or retrieving logs. However, if a user interface is preferred, it is recommended to perform operational and administrative tasks in SAP AI Launchpad. One essential aspect of operations is keeping models running while updating the artificial intelligence use case to ensure accurate results over time with minimal downtime. This is achieved by maintaining the deployment URL while updating a running deployment with a new configuration, ensuring that business applications can access use cases without constantly exchanging URLs. The calling business application remains operational at all times, and the last known running configuration is recorded for quick restoration in case of deployment failure due to incorrect configuration. SAP AI Core provides advanced options for configuring and managing development and productive environment parameters in the central Git repository. This allows for selecting appropriate behavior for different environments, such as development and test spaces, which may have smaller, more specific parameters across all data centers and hyper scalers. As a result, configuration life cycle management requires less time and effort from operations personnel.

In summary, SAP AI Core offers a scalable, enterprise-stable, and security-enabled runtime environment for productizing and deploying artificial intelligence use cases. AI Engineers can focus more on delivering use cases and less on running a Kubernetes cluster that meets all necessary industry security standards. SAP AI Core emphasizes the operation phase of the artificial intelligence life cycle, highlighting possibilities such as running new training runs, deploying models, or updating deployed models while maintaining the inference URL. It is recommended to use SAP AI Core for managing various artificial intelligence use cases and monitoring them using a user interface like SAP AI Launchpad.

5.5.4   SAP Analytics Cloud

In SAP Analytics Cloud, predictive models and scenarios are developed and stored. These predictions are usually accessed by end users through stories after being created in datasets or planning model versions. Additionally, SAP Analytics Cloud's table export features allow for the distribution of predictive forecasts and predictions as flat files. The data exporting capabilities of SAP Analytics Cloud enable the writing back of predictive forecasts, created using time series forecasting models in planning models, to their source systems. All predictive models are designed and implemented within SAP Analytics Cloud, which also handles the complete model life cycle management. For models based on datasets for classification, regression, and time series forecasting, predictions must be manually updated after the predictive models are retrained with the latest data. However, scheduling the retraining of time series forecasting models built on planning models is supported, and the delivery of predictive forecasts can be automated. In summary, predictions generated by SAP Analytics Cloud's predictive features are primarily consumed through SAP Analytics Cloud stories, and predictive forecasts can be returned to source systems using data exporting functions. While the updating of time series forecasting models can be automated in SAP Analytics Cloud, models for regression and classification require manual updates.

5.6 Conclusion

In this chapter, we discussed the artificial intelligence technologies commonly found in ERP systems, using SAP S/4HANA as a specific example. We examined the artificial intelligence solutions SAP HANA, SAP Data Intelligence, SAP AI Core, and SAP Analytics Cloud across the five stages of the data science process: Data Preparation, Modeling, Evaluation, and Deployment. We conclude now with details regarding SAP AI Business Services and SAP AI Launchpad, which were briefly mentioned above.

By utilizing algorithms for recommendation, matching, classification, and document processing, a broad spectrum of artificial intelligence scenarios can be addressed. SAP AI Business Services provide reusable artificial intelligence capabilities that enhance customer experiences by automating and optimizing business processes. These services ensure that artificial intelligence can be easily consumed across the entire organization by offering reusable and generic services and applications aimed at the artificial intelligence scenarios mentioned earlier. By delivering generic machine learning and artificial intelligence capabilities that can be readily applied to various business processes using simple REST-APIs or the AI API, customers can utilize machine learning services without needing data science expertise. The modular and API-based architecture allows for easy integration across different processes and solutions. Reliable APIs, such as the AI API, are available for training and inference, and SAP provides deployment, monitoring, ongoing operations, and support. Some services also allow for the creation of custom models using proprietary data, in addition to pre-trained models optimized for specific use cases (e.g., extracting structured data from invoices). The SAP Business Technology Platform features the multi-tenant SaaS application SAP AI Launchpad, which enables the management and execution of artificial intelligence scenarios across various AI runtime instances. This application serves as the single point of access to all artificial intelligence content throughout the SAP landscape. SAP AI Launchpad not only offers transparency but also the ability to reuse content across different landscapes and AI runtimes. It organizes, explores, and discovers artificial intelligence content by storing all relevant information in a centralized location. In terms of operations, SAP AI Launchpad allows users to view and examine metadata generated by supported AI runtimes. The standardized AI API facilitates integration between SAP AI Launchpad and supported AI runtimes. The application provides a comprehensive view of all metrics and artifacts available through the integrated AI runtimes, focusing on supporting the life cycle management and operations of artificial intelligence processes. This feature enables the analysis and evaluation of critical production KPIs. Customers can also directly deploy models using SAP AI Launchpad by productizing existing training models of supported AI runtimes or triggering jobs. Re-deployments of the current production landscape are another crucial aspect. A system administrator can manage administrative tasks for their SAP AI Core runtime, such as the necessary authentications in their artificial intelligence workflows.

Part II

Concepts for Embedding Artificial Intelligence

In this part, we deal with the solution concept for embedding artificial intelligence into ERP software. We begin with a discussion of the technical and business challenges involved with implementing artificial intelligence in context of ERP systems. Those challenges constitute the problem statement and, conversely, the business requirements to be resolved. We outline that those challenges cannot be taken as granted but required lasting investigations as artificial intelligence in context of ERP is a new research field. When implementing artificial intelligence for ERP software, enterprise-readiness must be ensured. This includes qualities like compliance, life-cycle management, data and process integration, extensibility, and performance. For those aspects, we specify the business requirements and propose corresponding solution concepts. For the success of artificial intelligence in terms of consumption by business users, from our perspective, it is important that the artificial intelligence capabilities are deeply integrated into business processes and user interfaces of ERP software. Thus, artificial intelligence functionality can be provided to the right person, at the right place, and at the right time. The solution architecture that we propose encounters this aspect. We provide an overview of this solution architecture before we take a closer look at the technical dimensions for so-called embedded and side-by-side approach. There is no one solution fits all as the requirements of the artificial intelligence use cases vary. Therefore, we suggest a scalable architecture that resolves simple scenarios with embedded artificial intelligence method and complex use cases with side-by-side approach. The already explained ERP reference processes, ERP reference architecture, and the identified ERP application patterns in the next chapter build the foundation for the proposed solution architecture for embedding artificial intelligence into ERP software. This part is based on our investigations in Sarferaz (2021) and our patents (https://patents.justia.com/inventor/siar-sarferaz). There are a moderate number of publications regarding applied artificial intelligence. However, they do not provide any approaches for systematically embedding artificial intelligence into ERP software. As exemplary listed, typically, the publications focus on data science for specific use cases, suggest enterprise AI strategies for management, or outline the value of artificial intelligence for businesses: Kleppmann (2017), Huyen (2022), Lakshmanan (2020), Hilpisch (2020),

Katsov (2022), Jarvinen (2020), Krishnan (2020), Natarajan (2021), Gordon (2021), Reid (2023), Haq (2020), Earley (2020), Dhamija (2020), Charlier (2017), Bersin (2018), Growth (2017), Casati (2019), Davenport (2018), Moll (2019), Woollacott (2019), Bourrasset (2018), Insights (2018), Mahmood (2019), Juma (2020), Kerzel (2020), Zadeh (2020), Hechler (2020), Carmona (2019), Al-Ghourabi (2023), Chaubard (2023), Nelson (2020), Maione (2021), Zdravkovic (2021), Schuler (2021), Kaddoumi (2022), Yathiraju (2022), Goundar (2021), Parthasarathy (2023), Biolcheva (2022), Aktürk (2021), Anguelov (2021), and Manoilov (2023).

Business Requirements and Application Patterns

In this chapter, we determine the challenges of applying artificial intelligence in the context of ERP systems. Identifying and solving those challenges is the added value resulting from this elaboration. Artificial intelligence must be deeply integrated into business processes and user interfaces of the underlying ERP systems in order to gain benefit for users. Typical ERP users are business experts with nearly no knowledge about data science or statistical techniques. ERP software must be enterprise-ready, for example, legally compliant, extensible, or configurable. However, this requirement has not yet been resolved for artificial intelligence and is worked out in this composition. In the course of our investigations regarding implementation projects, we determined various artificial intelligence patterns in the context of ERP software. Identifying the relevant ERP application patterns for artificial intelligence is also a new finding and vital for driving the appropriate solution architecture.

6.1 AI Business Requirements of ERP

Enhanced computational capabilities, advanced algorithms, and the accessibility of vast data sets are driving the adoption of machine learning to incorporate intelligence into back-office operations and deliver intelligent ERP systems. ERP systems underlying in-memory databases accelerate processing, combine analytical and transactional data, and foster innovation through the integration of artificial intelligence features. As a result, artificial intelligence can be seamlessly incorporated into ERP systems, allowing organizations to streamline business operations, enhance employee satisfaction, and improve customer service. Conversational AI offers a natural language interface for ERP solutions, transforming user interactions with the system by enabling hands-free applications based on speech. However, embedding artificial intelligence capabilities into ERP solutions is a complex endeavor due to the intricate nature of these systems. For example, SAP S/4HANA consists of 143,000 tables and over 250 million lines of code, supporting thousands

S. Sarferaz, *Embedding Artificial Intelligence into ERP Software*, https://doi.org/10.1007/978-3-031-54249-7_6

of business processes across 25 industry sectors and 64 localizations. When we began our research, we believed that identifying the optimal artificial intelligence algorithm was the primary challenge. Over time, we realized that in the context of ERP software, this is not the only issue. Two main problem areas must be resolved:

1. How can we systematically incorporate artificial intelligence into business processes for easy consumption?
2. How can we ensure artificial intelligence is enterprise-ready?

To be successfully utilized by customers, ERP systems must guarantee numerous product qualities. Facilitating those product qualities is referred as enterprise-ready. These product qualities must also be ensured for artificial intelligence functionality. Figure 6.1 outlines the key product qualities that impact the solution architecture for embedding artificial intelligence into ERP systems. While conventional artificial intelligence applications primarily focus on identifying the best algorithm and model, in the context of business applications, additionally, also those product qualities must be enabled. Our experience with numerous artificial intelligence ERP applications revealed that approximately 20% of the effort was dedicated to data science, while 80% of the work involved implementing the ERP product qualities. *Identifying* this significant difference, *deriving* the resulting requirements, *resolving* them conceptually, and proposing technical implementation are the added value *provisioned with this elaboration.*

6.1.1 Safety

Legal compliance, such as adherence to governance legislation, security standards, breach prevention, data security, and privacy, is essential for ERP software. Clients

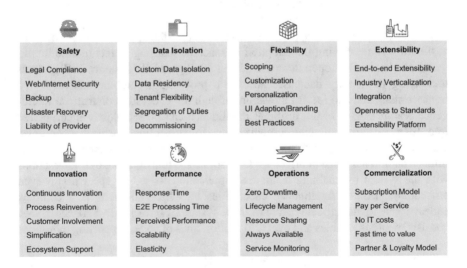

Fig. 6.1 ERP qualities to be ensured for artificial intelligence

should have access to audited reports, certifications, and attestations. Global standards from organizations like ISO or the Cloud Security Alliance apply to nearly all ERP customers. Additionally, there are region or nation-specific regulations and standards, as well as industry-specific rules. The cost benefits for cloud service providers stem from their ability to scale multiple clients across shared resources. However, compliance can be challenging, as regulations often necessitate encryption, auditing, and data separation, which increase hardware requirements and restrict resource sharing. Cloud compliance demands a collaborative partnership between the customer, who owns the data and bears the legal responsibilities for data handling, and the cloud vendor, who processes the data and must also comply with regulations. An example for implication of legal compliance on artificial intelligence implementation is that training and inference processes must consider the General Data Protection Regulation (GDPR) and must exclude application data without available consent. Another example is that reasoning behind inference results must be explained to end users and recorded for legal auditing.

Web servers inherently create a connection between the network and the outside world. The level of Web security depends on server maintenance, Web application updates, and Web site coding. Therefore, cutting-edge Web security standards must be implemented for ERP applications, such as protection against XSS, CSRF, SQL injection, URL manipulation, fake requests and forms, cookie visibility and theft, session hijacking, remote system execution, file-upload abuse, denial of service, phishing, and malware. Regular security patching is also necessary. In the context of artificial intelligence, uploaded files containing training data must be scanned for vulnerabilities before processing.

Every component must guarantee the ability to perform online *backups* for all business application data, meaning that backups can be done without shutting down the component. To reduce the likelihood of data loss, it is essential for customers to regularly back up their business data. In the context of artificial intelligence, for example, trained models stored in the ERP database should be backed up frequently. *Disaster recovery* refers to the capacity to retrieve data following a loss. Recovery from backups should be feasible across distributed landscapes and data centers, which entails special handling of replicated data on the application side, such as maintaining data consistency. The backup and restore process should not result in unavailability during data recovery. If a component within a scenario crashes, it should be possible to restore the entire scenario to a consistent state. This necessitates that the scenario backup concept includes information about data dependencies between components and the steps required to achieve a consistent state for the entire scenario. For instance, during recovery procedures, trained models must be reloaded in real time into the serving runtime. Both the consumer and provider should identify and transparently manage security and data protection risks for all services, ensuring a secure service life cycle that safeguards customers and avoids liability risks. They should also agree on and implement a joint organizational interface, including service level agreements (SLAs), to discuss and resolve potential or actual information security incidents.

Provider liability remains a critical aspect in the continued integration of artificial intelligence into all business areas. When a company considers moving its data and processing to the cloud for artificial intelligence purposes, two factors are crucial: the associated risks and the benefits to be gained. It is necessary to strike the right balance between assigning rights and liabilities among the parties and diversifying risks through insurance. Furthermore, new strategies for protecting intellectual property rights in the digital realm are being developed, along with the corresponding obligations of providers.

6.1.2 Data Isolation

Data ownership refers to customer data that is solely possessed by the customer. This data must be distinct from other customers' data, a concept known as *data isolation*. Techniques should be implemented to ensure data and network isolation for each tenant's service. To lower the total cost of ownership (TCO), particularly in cloud computing, network resources and shared data should be minimized in terms of system deployments and databases. However, this consolidation of data and resources introduces new risks, such as sharing infrastructure with potentially untrustworthy tenants. To address these risks, cloud infrastructure providers or Software-as-a-Service (SaaS) solutions must offer robust data isolation guarantees. Regardless of the chosen solution, customers should retain exclusive ownership of their data. These requirements also apply to artificial intelligence, where the training data of different customers must be clearly separated.

Data residency pertains to the physical or geographical location of an organization's data or information. It is closely related to data sovereignty, which involves the legal or regulatory requirements imposed on data stored within a specific country or region. For instance, the Energy Technology Development and Demonstration Program (EUDP) mandates that cloud systems and services for European customers be managed by a team based in the EU. Additionally, full transparency regarding data center and storage locations must be provided upon request. Cloud computing, which allows businesses to offer artificial intelligence services over the Internet, can raise concerns about data residency. Cloud users often lack knowledge of their data's physical location, as providers store data across multiple global data centers. Consequently, artificial intelligence service users must be aware of their cloud provider's data center locations and the various data residency policies that apply to each site.

Tenant flexibility refers to reorganizations that result in the consolidation or division of IT systems, leading to the relocation, splitting, or merging of artificial intelligence service application data. Support for moving a tenant from one data center to another is also necessary. Subsidiaries or sub-companies are often the first to adopt cloud computing in a two-tier model. As a company expands, changes such as reorganizations, acquisitions, or mergers become inevitable. Moving legal business entities to different geographical areas requires flexibility in transferring data and artificial intelligence services, including deployed models for inference, between data centers.

Segregation of duties is an internal control that ensures at least two individuals are responsible for separate parts of a task to prevent errors and fraud. Sensitive data must be managed according to user roles and responsibilities, necessitating distinct authorizations. Applications with excessive privileges may be exploited by attackers to gain unauthorized access to data and system resources. Adhering to minimal privilege rules not only provides defense in depth but also aids in data classification and access definition. No single individual should have the authority to execute two conflicting duties. This requirement becomes even more critical when certain administrative tasks are delegated to third parties, either through outsourcing or employing third-party resources. In the context of artificial intelligence applications, tasks such as adjusting model hyperparameters and consuming inference results must be performed by separate users with different privileges.

Decommissioning refers to the automated formal process of removing or retiring something from active service. A data return concept and a self-service scenario should be available. After a contract ends or a tenant moves, there must be an option to return and destroy the data, which is typically a legal requirement. Customers may request the export of their data in an appropriate format, such as .csv or another standard format. Application data for model training and batch inference are subject to this obligation and must be addressed for artificial intelligence applications.

6.1.3   Flexibility

Scoping involves the careful selection of necessary scenarios, business processes, and functionalities by customers within a controlled environment. ERP systems are very rich in functionality, which presents new challenges in terms of discovery and implementation. To tackle these challenges, sophisticated techniques are employed to help customers choose the right services. In a consumption-based business model, it is crucial to enable only the services that have been requested.

Customization encompasses configuration options, branding tools, and theme designers. Many organizations require support for similar processes, but despite these commonalities, there is a need to accommodate local variations and adapt to customer requirements. Solutions must be provided that allow for the individual configuration of intelligent applications while maintaining shared features. For instance, a financial business application that leverages artificial intelligence for automated reconciliations should support the training of multiple models based on different regional configurations.

Personalization pertains to the ability to manage local settings and user preferences. As users are exposed to a wide array of applications, their expectations may increase. Personalization is just as important in business applications as it is in Web or mobile applications. The degree of explainability for artificial intelligence-based supplier rankings, for example, could be personalized by the user, with their preferred settings used as the default value the next time they access the intelligent business application.

UI adoption and branding involve adapting user interfaces or other assets provided by the ERP vendor as a standard offering. Branding connects applications with specific colors or layouts to facilitate user interaction. UI adoption and branding capabilities must also be available for intelligent business applications, with additional requirements such as specific coloring for prediction accuracy thresholds.

Best practice features should be accessible and meet customer needs from beginning to end. Pre-delivered content, business processes, and standard code lists should be provided, along with industry and country-specific best practices and legal compliance supported out-of-the-box. Intelligent business applications should adhere to standards and legal requirements by default. Best practices are valuable because customers want to minimize effort on standard Lines of Business (LoB) processes and concentrate on core competencies and differentiating tasks. Generic artificial intelligence services, like invoice extraction from PDF documents, exemplify best practice content. Configuration data must be kept separate from application and system data, but coding and content should utilize similar processes and infrastructures. Transitioning from initial activation support to a comprehensive product life cycle, including introduction, maintenance, extension, upgrade, and potential retirement, necessitates a reevaluation of fundamental configuration delivery principles. Ensuring a seamless and smooth business configuration experience for development, partner development, cloud operations, and customers is essential. Rapid and straightforward customer system setup is only achievable through high-quality content and extensive automation.

6.1.4 Extensibility

End-to-end extensibility emphasizes the capacity to expand standard services and processes across all layers, from table extensions to UI field extensions, as well as the extensibility of related APIs. This enables vertical extensions of processes or services. Partners who extend core services may require an additional extension layer for their clients. Each extension should be autonomous and protected from upgrades and updates. For instance, in a provided artificial intelligence scenario, customers anticipate enhancing the data source for training and the corresponding data transformations.

Industry verticalization involves augmenting core functionality with industry-specific solutions, addressing the unique needs of various sectors, from healthcare to retail. The demand for more customized solutions tailored to specific industries has grown, replacing one-size-fits-all software with more modular, verticalized approaches. Companies are now investing in multiple industry businesses, necessitating support for industry verticalization in artificial intelligence. A layered extensibility concept is needed, allowing an artificial intelligence application to be enhanced first by industry solutions, then by partners, and finally by customers, all without mutual interference.

The quality of *integration* encompasses anchor points, integration platforms, out-of-the-box integration, and communication structures. Historically, data and process integration has been the sole responsibility of IT experts who connect various systems. The tools employed in crafting integration solutions are typically intricate and necessitate a background in programming. Moreover, these tools have a steep learning curve and can be expensive to maintain. However, contemporary business users, also known as citizen integrators, demand out-of-the-box integration or seek to achieve similar tasks effortlessly using integration tools. Additionally, public APIs must exhibit robustness in terms of non-incompatible modifications. Since applications that utilize APIs are susceptible to alterations, APIs inherently involve a contract. This contract offers a degree of confidence that the API will evolve compatibly over time, ensuring that the application relying on it will not malfunction. Such requirements apply to APIs related to artificial intelligence, such as inference APIs or data replication APIs.

Openness to standards involves offering public APIs, API management, open cloud development environments and extension platforms, and support for standard programming languages like Java and JavaScript. Customers and partners desire an extension infrastructure that enables integration, portability, interoperability, and innovation, as well as the ability to combine artificial intelligence services from various providers. To facilitate integration with other solutions, intelligent applications should expose public APIs through standard Web interfaces, such as REST, and provide comprehensive documentation. A separate platform is necessary to extend artificial intelligence services and business processes while maintaining core stability, enabling solution flexibility and innovation.

An *extensibility platform* is essential for implementing large new modules, while in-app extensibility can be used to enhance the core. In-app extensibility involves implementing extensions within the core application using predefined extension points, with both the kernel and the extension running on the same server and using the same database instance. For artificial intelligence scenarios, an extensibility platform is crucial due to the scalability of training and inference loads from the core ERP to the extension platform.

6.1.5   Innovation

Continuous innovation involves the regular introduction of new artificial intelligence features, condensed release cycles, rapid adoption of advancements, and reduced lead times. As technology advances daily, traditional IT processes struggle to keep up with the pace. The success of Software-as-a-Service (SaaS) models demonstrates users' appetite for swift innovation. Modern computing is driven by business needs that can be met through frequent software adjustments, sometimes even within a day. However, today's business environment demands more than just speed; innovation—the ability to create new artificial intelligence offerings, assess their potential market adoption, and deploy successful ones—is equally crucial. Cloud computing is better suited than traditional on-premise approaches, as cloud services are instantly available and make it easy to test new offerings. ERP providers can quickly gather user feedback on artificial intelligence applications instead of waiting months for market testing.

Process reinvention emphasizes enhancing business processes by applying new technologies or reimagining the entire process flow. Artificial intelligence has enormous potential to redesign business processes, as cognitive tasks can be transferred from humans to machines, increasing automation and optimization. Artificial intelligence models have been developed by data scientists for years, but they often remained in specialized tools and were only used by experts, adding little value. To bridge this gap, artificial intelligence capabilities must be systematically integrated into business processes, ensuring intelligence is delivered to the right person, in the right place, and at the right time.

Customer involvement prioritizes early engagement, customer and stakeholder interaction, online feedback, embedded participation in the ideation process, design thinking, agile development, and innovation platforms. The goal is to create meaningful and usable artificial intelligence applications that meet end users' needs. Cloud computing offers greater opportunities to influence software development decisions and adopt innovations early. Hosting artificial intelligence applications, monitoring activities, and sharing resources enable immediate feedback. Cloud services are used by many, so any system inconsistency or misbehavior impacts all users.

The IT sector is compelled to embrace *simplicity* as a core principle. IT departments aim to transition from managing technology's daily requirements to fostering the innovation it enables. Companies seek to streamline their existing network and data center infrastructure while anticipating the adaptability and effectiveness of artificial intelligence applications. For ERP providers, simplification is essential for maintaining an efficient cloud environment. This includes minimizing data model complexity, adhering to the principle of one, utilizing standard tools, promoting harmonization, offering an intuitive user experience, and maintaining a low data footprint. These attributes must also be present in artificial intelligence applications to support a consistent programming model. Historically, organizations have developed extensive custom code to supplement, modify, or even replace ERP software, resulting in a fragmented IT landscape and an ERP system that is challenging to upgrade. These extensive modifications to standard software have trapped companies, hindering their progress toward digital transformation. In the digital age, standardization is crucial, and while businesses strive to minimize customization, they still require significant flexibility. This involves reducing complexity through standardization and simplifying business processes based on artificial intelligence. Customers anticipate that artificial intelligence applications will provide harmonization in user experience, business processes, data integration, and domain model alignment across all services, without needing to understand the technical underpinnings. Consequently, approaches like the principle of one are expected, avoiding multiple frameworks for addressing the same issue. As a result, the implementation, usage, and management of artificial intelligence applications must be standardized.

Ecosystem support entails systematic collaboration with partners to offer artificial intelligence products that an ERP provider alone could not provide. While the ERP core must be highly standardized and stable, there is a need to fill gaps and accelerate innovation by collaborating with partners. Today, there are product and technology players in a highly collaborative and intricately orchestrated community. This results in a win-win situation for all parties and a one-stop shop for customers, backed by a single service-level agreement (SLA) and a single point of support. The trend of partner ecosystems in the artificial intelligence field has made the long-standing concept of complete vertical integration from one organization obsolete. It is now necessary to allow partners to extend and operate artificial intelligence services and solutions. To achieve this, life cycle management dependencies, partner programming models, organizational setups, partner access, and authorization concepts must be established. For instance, hyperscalers like Google, Microsoft, or Amazon offer powerful artificial intelligence services on their platforms, which are reused by ERP providers in context of partner programs for building new intelligent applications.

6.1.6   Performance

In the realm of artificial intelligence transactions, which are often characterized by backend calls, it is crucial to maintain satisfactory *response times* even when the system is under significant load. To pinpoint performance bottlenecks, a suitable performance testing mechanism should be implemented, and response times in production should be documented. This is beneficial because it is impossible to predict and test every scenario in a simulated environment. Rapid response times are particularly vital for interactive user experiences, such as when artificial intelligence generated results are displayed on a user interface.

Moreover, artificial intelligence services necessitate optimized *end-to-end processing times*, which encompass the duration from login to the completion of a task or job, including network latency. The primary performance indicators are response time and throughput. Expedient response times are especially important for user interactions with intelligent business applications. For instance, procurement portals may lose business if users perceive them as sluggish. Network latency is often the most significant factor contributing to poor response times when using Wide Area Networks (WAN), as it substantially increases end-to-end response times.

Perceived performance refers to the apparent speed at which a software feature executes its task, taking into account the system's reaction time and the quality of the outcome. Humans are generally impatient, so it is essential to consider both the active and passive modes of a person using an artificial intelligence service or application. In active mode, users are unaware of any waiting time, while in passive mode, their brain activity decreases, and they become bored. When actual performance cannot be improved due to physical limitations, techniques must be utilized to enhance the end user's experience and boost perceived performance, which is essentially how quickly a user believes the artificial intelligence application operates.

Artificial intelligence applications must be able to *scale* horizontally by adding more service instances (scale out) or vertically by augmenting virtual CPUs or memory to existing instances (scale up). Traditional businesses were limited by physical constraints, such as hard drive space and memory, which hindered scalability. Classic IT systems were optimized for specific situations and customer needs. However, cloud computing replaces these constraints with an infrastructure that can scale up or down (usually up) and adapt in accordance with a business's requirements. A scalable system is one where the workload it can handle grows proportionally to the resources provided; in other words, its capacity scales with available resources. Additional aspects of this quality include auto-scaling, economy of scale, and capacity on-demand without significant service degradation. For example, artificial intelligence model training often necessitates scalability, such as using CPUs for regression algorithms and GPUs for deep learning.

Elasticity pertains to the ability to deliver consistent service levels regardless of the current load. To achieve this, the system must dynamically adapt to workload changes, taking into account high frequency, peaks, low activity, and inactivity. The artificial intelligence platform itself must support an on-demand and elastic approach, expanding with actual demand, thereby increasing overall utilization and reducing costs. Elasticity is also crucial in artificial intelligence environments where resources are billed per usage. Typically, an elastic system requires scalability; otherwise, additional resources have minimal impact. Elasticity involves dynamically adjusting resources to handle loads, expanding resources as the load increases and contracting as demand decreases and resources become superfluous. Consequently, if the load increases, more resources must be added to minimize unused capacity, and if demand decreases, resources must be constrained to reduce wasted capacity. To mitigate the effects of unexpected peaks, scaling should closely match actual demand while keeping wasted capacity to a minimum. For example, training neural networks to process natural language in the context of ERP service management can be resource-intensive. However, since this training job is performed only once a month for a day, the system resources must be elastically increased and decreased accordingly.

6.1.7   Operations

Zero downtime refers to a quality where end users experience no noticeable service interruptions. In particular, updates or patches are applied seamlessly without requiring the application to enter maintenance mode, allowing users to access the application at any time. Unplanned outages can lead to user frustration, and for business-critical applications, they may result in financial losses or lost sales. For instance, artificial intelligence applications must continue working after updates and patches, ensuring that model training jobs do not disrupt inference processing.

In the traditional on-premises environment, customers have control over the *life cycle management*, allowing them to apply updates according to their own schedule.

Cloud computing, on the other hand, enables more rapid innovation cycles by frequently releasing patches or new features, sometimes even multiple times per day. This is possible because the provider manages the software and can update it at any time. To achieve this, a high level of automation is necessary for the update process, particularly in ensuring that the new code meets the required quality standards before deployment. This level of frequency can only be maintained through extensive automation. For artificial intelligence applications, life cycle management processes must be seamless and cost-effective. Continuous delivery of artificial intelligence services must be executed without manual intervention. A life cycle automation system is essential to guarantee a high level of automation across the board, such as a build pipeline that supports upgrades, patches, and migrations, regardless of the underlying products involved.

Resource sharing leads to significant economic efficiencies, allowing development teams to write code once, implement features in a single codebase without duplication, and serve multiple customers. By sharing a single codebase, artificial intelligence applications and data can be updated and patched more quickly. ERP providers can choose from various levels of resource sharing, from sharing hardware using virtual machines to sharing processes through intelligent programming. A computing architecture that enables providers to share resources in a public or private cloud is necessary. Training artificial intelligence models based on neural networks typically requires GPUs and large amounts of RAM, which are expensive and must be shared among tenants for economic reasons, especially since training jobs are performed intermittently.

Artificial intelligence services must be *always available* and accessible on any device. If one service fails, the remaining services should continue running, and if one availability zone fails, traffic should be redirected to another. Customer service centers should be available at all times with immediate responses. High availability of computing infrastructure is crucial for business continuity, including response times to user requests. Customers expect 24/7 access to business data and artificial intelligence applications, regardless of their device or location. The increasing use of mobile devices for business applications highlights this requirement. Artificial intelligence applications should be designed to handle latency, poor response times, and service unavailability of downstream systems gracefully. They should be error-tolerant and resilient to temporary issues such as latency, peaks, outages, and asynchronous interface call interruptions. Unavailability of artificial intelligence applications can lead to dissatisfied users and potential financial losses or lost sales for business-critical applications. Implementing artificial intelligence applications in a distributed manner can introduce multiple risks, such as network communication problems, lost messages, long-running requests, or outages of dependent systems. Resilience is essential for mitigating these critical situations and achieving a reliable system composed of unreliable components.

Service monitoring involves observability to gain an overview of active artificial intelligence services and to respond quickly to failures or inconsistencies. Debugging multi-tenant solutions in production is challenging, and the application's real state is constantly changing. Therefore, applications must generate comprehensive log information to facilitate post-failure analysis and meet product standards, such as audit logs. Traceability between artificial intelligence services and end users, for example, using correlation IDs, is crucial for monitoring at the business process level. Artificial intelligence applications should also be easily monitorable at run-time to detect non-application failures, such as slow networks or unresponsive downstream systems. Each artificial intelligence service should be monitored to assess its performance and enable corrective actions in case of failure, including monitoring model degradation in terms of reduced predictive power. Service-level agreements (SLAs) are typically used as contracts between two parties to define requirements, service quality, responsibilities, and obligations. SLAs may encompass a range of service performance metrics, each paired with corresponding service-level objectives (SLOs). As such, it is crucial to measure the values of these associated metrics, as defined in the SLA, during the usage stage to determine if the specified service level objectives have been met. Additionally, service and resource utilization must be tracked and monitored as needed to facilitate dynamic scaling capabilities. ERP providers must ascertain whether the innovations they deliver have a tangible impact on the customer side and if their investment efforts are warranted. Analyzing and evaluating this usage data allows product and portfolio decision-makers to more effectively establish their market presence and continually enhance product features. By concentrating on the most relevant use cases and products, development capacity can be directed toward areas that offer greater value and benefits for customers. It is essential to augment product scorecards with high-level usage metrics. Feature flags are employed to test and verify functionality with select customers before rolling out features more broadly.

6.1.8   Commercialization

Under a *subscription model*, users pay a fee on a per-user basis, either monthly or annually, granting them access to the software for the duration of the subscription. Rather than owning the software, customers lease it. The subscription fee covers software licenses, support services, and access to new software versions as they become available. This pricing model is relevant for all service models, including Infrastructure-as-a-Service (IaaS), Platform-as-a-Service (PaaS), and Software-as-a-Service (SaaS). Traditional pricing models, such as perpetual licenses and application bundles, are not suitable for cloud-based software products. Instead, customers consume artificial intelligence services without owning the software. A transparent and systematic pricing framework is necessary for customers or organizations to purchase or subscribe to an ERP vendor's artificial intelligence services for a specific period at a set price. Subscriptions typically involve a monthly or annual commitment.

The *pay-per-service* model starts with a zero balance, provisions cloud resources on demand, and charges customers based on actual consumption (pay-as-you-go). To facilitate digital transformation and provide more flexibility and quick access to new artificial intelligence functionality, ERP providers offer a usage-based commercial model (pay-per-use) for artificial intelligence services.

The *no IT costs* model involves paying only for services rather than hardware, software, power, and support to keep these items secure, stable, and functioning properly. There are no additional costs for setting up, maintaining, or upgrading standard stacks (SaaS), underlying platforms (PaaS), or infrastructure (IaaS). Upgrades are included in the monthly fees, eliminating the need for administrative work and IT expertise. Cloud computing removes the need for on-premises servers, allowing customers to avoid large upfront investments in hardware and software required to run their networks. In artificial intelligence-enabled ERP environments, these costs, along with network maintenance expenses, are included in a flat monthly fee. When servers, network backbones, and artificial intelligence services need upgrading, the ERP provider is responsible for doing so at no extra cost to the customer.

In many organizations, lines of business (LoB) lead discussions about *fast time to value* from artificial intelligence services in the cloud. Traditional IT departments can be quickly outpaced by buy-and-go cloud artificial intelligence services, as maintenance, patching, and upgrading are all managed by the ERP provider. Companies want to quickly establish their artificial intelligence computing arrangements with out-of-the-box services. This necessitates rapid availability, timely provisioning of productive systems, quick go-live, pre-delivered content, best practice processes, guided configuration, seamless data integration, user-friendly interfaces, minimal training effort, legacy system conversion/migration, and online tutorials.

Partner models necessitate new original equipment manufacturer (OEM) or value-added reseller (VAR) license agreements for artificial intelligence services, including partner usage rights, compliance obligations, and service level agreements (SLAs). Typically, OEMs assemble components from other vendors to create a new product sold under their own brand. VARs purchase products from manufacturers, add value in some way (e.g., by adding a new service), and resell the product under their own brand. A VAR agreement outlines the legal contract for this process. ERP providers gain firsthand information about customer purchases, active application usage, user types, and usage duration. Access to customer data helps maximize up-sells and cross-sells through loyalty programs. These programs enable ERP providers to discover desired artificial intelligence capabilities and encourage customer retention (renewal). In addition to customer retention programs, internal user engagement programs should also be offered.

6.2   AI Patterns of ERP

Let's start with the problem statement: In order to establish a solution architecture, it is essential to comprehend the technical capabilities needed for executing various artificial intelligence scenarios. Importantly, we aim to avoid separate architectural approaches for each artificial intelligence use case, as this would significantly increase development and operational efforts within the context of ERP systems. To overcome this issue, we first examined a multitude of artificial intelligence use cases and grouped them based on their similarities. As a result, we identified several artificial intelligence application patterns, which are detailed in this section. Our strategic objective is to offer a consistent concept and framework for each pattern's implementation. Consequently, these artificial intelligence application patterns can serve as reusable components for development teams, expediting the execution of artificial intelligence use cases while also standardizing and streamlining operational aspects. The later proposed solution architecture will facilitate all those application patterns. *Abstracting* from numerous analyzed use cases *to artificial intelligence application patterns* of ERP systems is an *added value of this elaboration.*

6.2.1   Matching

Matching involves establishing relationships and identifying similarities and discrepancies within a dataset. For instance, as a master data expert, our goal might be to minimize duplicate entries during consolidation. Manual matching can be quite labor-intensive, but intelligent systems applying artificial intelligence techniques can greatly expedite the process. These systems can offer one or more strategies, along with their quality, for linking similar items. Users only need to accept or reject the recommendations or modify them as needed. Matching is necessary when at least two artifacts share a certain level of similarity. The matching process adheres to a set of rules that can be dynamically adapted, or learnt, by the system. These learned rules may evolve over time due to user input or other factors. Matching can be applied to various content types, such as:

- Text (e.g., search and replace) or images (e.g., identifying all dogs in a collection of photos)
- Audio (e.g., natural language processing, where an audio stream corresponds to a query)
- Video (e.g., determining which company logos appear and their frequency during a soccer match)
- Complex business objects (e.g., matching invoices to goods receipts or identifying a customer's duplicate)

The content being matched greatly influences the output type and its presentation. One aspect of matching is the quality of a match, which means that objects can either fully or partially match. A full match occurs when all specified parameters are satisfied, while a partial match only meets some of the required parameters. The more parameters that match, the higher the match quality. The following matching types have been recognized so far:

- **Relationship matching**
  Establishes logical connections between objects of different types, such as associating multiple invoices with a single payment

- **Compatibility matching**
  Pairs objects of different types with shared properties to create a cohesive system, like assembling a high-/medium-/low-end computer (A computer is composed of various components like a motherboard, CPU, memory, and display, which must be compatible, and the CPU, for example, only fits into motherboards with a specific socket.)
- **Similarity matching**
  Combines similar objects of the same type into one, like merging multiple similar business partners because they are the same type of object.

To develop matching patterns, frequently used algorithms include multiclass classification algorithms like XGBoost/multilayer perceptron, clustering algorithms like K-means, and nonparametric methods like the k-nearest neighbors' algorithm.

6.2.2   Recommendation

Recommendation suggests datasets or actions based on the current situation. For instance, when working as a material requirements planner, we may need to find potential solutions for addressing a material shortage problem. Intelligent systems can aid users by recommending relevant content or by proposing an action or input that the user might prefer. In this context, we refer to a recommendation pattern and its influence on the user interface. We can distinguish between three kinds of recommendations:

1. **Content recommendation**
   The system narrows down content that might be of interest to the user, based on their behavior or the content's attributes. Common content recommender systems include Amazon and Netflix.
2. **Input assistance**
   The system helps the user by inputting data or filtering it. Typical examples include search phrase suggestions, suitable form templates, or a collection of suggested default values for specific fields, based on the user's input and interaction history.
3. **Solution proposal**
   The system assists users in tackling complex problems by recommending particular actions or proposed solutions. In some cases, this may be combined with a simulation of the potential outcome. Solution proposals usually involve various decision-support systems. Example use cases encompass payment and invoice matching, as well as material shortage situations.

To implement recommendation patterns, we must possess historical data about actions taken and inputs given during business processes. For the solution proposal recommendation type, logging business processes is essential; for content recommendation, the required historical data might be obtained from application data. For the input assistance recommendation type, additional texts or descriptions may be necessary. Commonly used algorithms for recommendation patterns include social analysis, multiclass classification algorithms like XGBoost or multilayer perceptron, text analysis or mining, and recurrent neural networks (RNNs).

6.2.3 Ranking

Ranking serves to differentiate between more relevant and less relevant datasets of the same kind, depending on the current context. For instance, when purchasing, we want to identify the top suppliers for a specific product within the context of a particular purchasing request. By presenting the best choices first, ranking simplifies intricate decisions for business users. Items within a group are ranked by comparing criteria pertinent to the user's business context, such as quantity, priority, or score. In a ranked table or list, the results are always sorted to display the highest-ranked items at the top. We distinguish between two types of ranking:

1. **Ranking by inherent value**
   This type of ranking relies on a value already present in the existing dataset, like the price. Users typically know and understand this value, so no further explanation is needed.
2. **Ranking by score**
   This ranking method is based on a computed grade, mark, or score. Users may need to comprehend the calculation behind the score, particularly if artificial intelligence techniques are employed.

While we can rank a list of items according to their rating, it is important to note that ranking and rating are distinct concepts. A rating positions a single item on a pre-established scale, such as rating a service provider on a scale of 1 (very bad) to 5 (very good). Ranking, on the other hand, always involves comparing a common value across a group of items. In the user interface, rankings are typically displayed for a list or group. To develop relevance and ranking patterns, popular algorithms include classification algorithms like XGBoost, clustering algorithms like K-means or the Gaussian mixture model, and nonparametric methods like the k-nearest neighbors' algorithm.

6.2.4 Prediction

Predictive models utilize historical data to anticipate future trends and outcomes by identifying patterns and considering all relevant information. For instance, as a master data manager, we may want to determine the number of change requests a team will need to handle in the upcoming quarter to optimize workload distribution. Intelligent systems employing predictive models substantially lower the expenses associated with forecasting business results, environmental influences, competitive insights, and market conditions.There are two primary categories of predictive models: parametric and nonparametric. A third class, semiparametric models, can be formed by merging features from both categories. Generally, parametric models involve specific assumptions regarding one or more population parameters that define the underlying distribution. In contrast, nonparametric models usually have fewer assumptions about structure and distribution but often include strong assumptions about independencies. Various algorithms for predictive models encompass ordinary least squares, generalized linear models (GLM), logistic regression, random forests, decision trees, neural networks, and multivariate adaptive regression splines (MARS). Each algorithm serves a specific purpose, addresses a particular question, or is suited for a certain type of dataset.

6.2.5   Categorization

Categorization involves allocating datasets to pre-established groups or classes. For instance, as a customer service representative, we might want to sort incoming requests by priority (high, medium, or low) based on their content to enhance customer support. Additionally, categorization can identify new groupings (clusters) within datasets, such as organizing customers into segments for tailored product offerings, targeted advertising, or fraud detection. Categorization is a complicated task where intelligent systems can boost automation levels by applying artificial intelligence techniques for classification and clustering. These methods are utilized to categorize objects into one or more classes and clusters according to their characteristics. Classification and clustering share similarities, but there is a subtle distinction. In classification, predefined labels are assigned to each input instance based on its attributes, while clustering lacks these labels. Since classification utilizes labels, it necessitates training and testing datasets for model validation, which is not required for clustering. Typically, classification is more intricate than clustering due to its multiple levels, while clustering only involves grouping. To create categorization patterns, frequently used algorithms encompass classification techniques like XGBoost, neural networks such as CNN/RNN/GAN, dimensionality reduction algorithms like principal component analysis, and clustering algorithms like K-means and the Gaussian mixture model.

6.2.6   Conversational AI

Conversational AI facilitates interaction with systems through natural language dialogue, promoting a hands-free approach. For instance, imagine generating a purchase order by conversing with a digital assistant. This ability to engage in discussions with a virtual aide to carry out business operations is a crucial aspect of the user experience in intelligent applications. Conversational AI can comprehend common natural language patterns, allowing it to search for business entities using different parameters, locate specific entities by name or ID, obtain an attribute's value for a particular entity, and establish basic new entities, including line items. This technology provides a more human-like user experience for applications, enabling tasks to be completed within the context of business data. As a result, natural language interactions with applications are supported, and the creation of business objects with information derived from conversational contexts is guaranteed. Conversational AI also allows for the sharing of notes, screenshots, and business objects with other users during a conversation. This technology enables the synthesis of business transactions from multiple SAP applications at a single interaction point. Additionally, custom skills for utilizing a digital assistant can be developed and implemented across various applications and channels.

6.3   Conclusion

In this chapter, we discussed the complexities of embedding artificial intelligence into ERP systems. Identifying the ideal algorithm and model is often the primary objective in artificial intelligence projects. However, when dealing with ERP systems, it is crucial to ensure various product qualities for artificial intelligence applications. We outlined the ERP product qualities, such as safety, data isolation, flexibility, extensibility, innovation, performance, operations, and commercialization, and illustrated their impact on artificial intelligence applications. Typically, 20% of the development effort in artificial intelligence-based ERP projects is allocated to data science, while the remaining 80% focuses on implementing the aforementioned qualities. The value derived from this elaboration includes identifying the significant differences between traditional and ERP-based artificial intelligence applications, determining the associated requirements, resolving them conceptually, and proposing technical implementations. In the context of ERP, it is essential to establish a consistent solution architecture and programming model for artificial intelligence applications. Thus, the development and operations of all artificial intelligence applications are harmonized, resulting in reduced Total Cost of Development (TCD) and Total Cost of Ownership (TCO). To accomplish this objective and prevent heterogeneous solutions for each use case, we derived application patterns for artificial intelligence by abstracting from numerous existing scenarios. These application patterns for artificial intelligence serve as the basis for the solution architecture, which will be discussed in the following chapter. Identifying those application patterns for ERP systems and deduce corresponding requirements is also an added value of this written composition.

Solution Architecture

7

In this chapter, we define the solution architecture for embedding artificial intelligence into ERP software. The previously discussed ERP product qualities, ERP reference processes, ERP reference architecture, and ERP application patterns for artificial intelligence build the foundation for the solution architecture that we propose in this chapter. There are simple use cases like trending and predictions, which can be served with classic algorithms as regression and clustering. Usually, those algorithms also not require a lot of data, memory, or computing power. Therefore, we propose to implement this type of use cases within the ERP platform and call them embedded artificial intelligence. However, there are more complex user cases like image recognition or processing of natural language that need neuronal networks and deep learning. These algorithms demand high volume of data and system resources. To avoid that the critical business processes in ERP systems are negatively affected from excessive hardware consumption, we suggest scaling out this category of use cases to corresponding AI technology platform and called side-by-side artificial intelligence. While we focus in this chapter on the overall architecture, we will discuss additional aspects (e.g., data protection, extensibility) in the next chapters.

7.1 Guiding Principles

We define the solution architecture for artificial intelligence based on key guiding principles of modern ERP solutions, which we'll describe in this section, as depicted in Fig. 7.1. Let's walk through these principles:

In conventional ERP systems, the fundamental data model for business entities, such as customers, products, and sales orders, is often repeatedly modeled for various objectives due to the need to accommodate minor domain-specific metadata. As a result, technology solutions for integration, user interfaces, analytics, and transactions each require their own distinct business object models, leading to an increased

© The Author(s), under exclusive license to Springer Nature
Switzerland AG 2024
S. Sarferaz, *Embedding Artificial Intelligence into ERP Software*,
https://doi.org/10.1007/978-3-031-54249-7_7

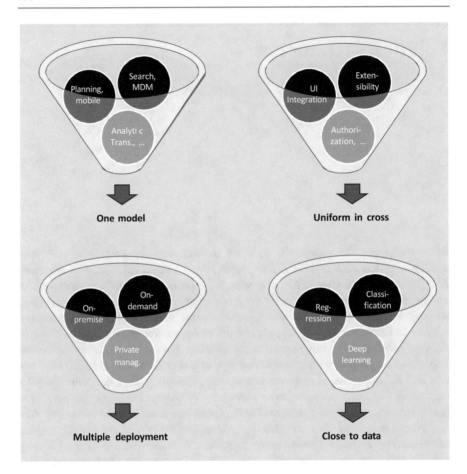

Fig. 7.1 Guiding principles for solution architecture

total cost of development (TCD) since the same information must be repeatedly provided. Furthermore, the presence of incompatible metamodels means that cross-functional issues like UI integration, extensibility, and authorization must be addressed multiple times, resulting in a high total cost of ownership (TCO) and hindering the adoption of solutions by customers. In contrast, modern ERP systems are built upon a single core data model that is repurposed for various contexts through domain-specific enhancements. For the suggested artificial intelligence architecture, we presume the existence of a modern ERP system with a unified core data model, which we will expand to accommodate the domain of artificial intelligence.

The data model of modern ERPs is built upon views that are established on top of database tables containing business data. Generally, ERP data models consist of thousands of cryptical database tables with intricate relationships. To make this data model accessible for business applications, views are created on top of these tables.

These views transform the underlying structures and relationships into a core data model that is easier for humans to understand. For instance, sales orders are stored in multiple related tables, which are then encapsulated by a single view representing the sales order business object. As is common in the database domain, these views are defined using SQL statements that combine (e.g., JOIN, UNION) different tables and rename columns as needed. In the context of modern ERPs, this view technology is enhanced to include business semantics in the form of annotations. This allows domain-specific semantics to be added to the entire view or individual fields within the view. For example, the sales order field *revenue* could be enriched with a *currency* annotation, enabling ERP engines to automatically apply currency conversions. Similarly, the *estimated revenue* field could be enhanced with a *prediction* annotation, allowing the underlying artificial intelligence engine to forecast the value. This approach avoids redundant data modeling, reducing development costs and increasing comprehensibility. Additionally, cross-topics for artificial intelligence, such as extensibility and security, are addressed uniformly since they are all based on the same core data model.

Modern ERP products cater to market demands for hybrid deployment models by offering consistent data models and compatible business processes. Typically, multiple deployment options are supported, including on-premise, public cloud, and private managed cloud. Private managed cloud refers to a cloud environment hosted entirely for one an organization, containing all relevant cloud components which are managed by the ERP vendor. From the customer's perspective, private cloud is a deployment model where the cloud infrastructure is exclusively used by a single organization with multiple consumers (i.e., single tenant) and accessed via a virtual private network (VPN). It is owned, managed, and operated by the customer. In contrast, public cloud is a deployment model where the cloud infrastructure is shared among multiple customers and accessed via the Internet. The ERP vendor typically owns and manages the infrastructure and business software for public cloud. On-premise ERP software is installed and runs on computers at the customer's location, rather than at a remote facility like a server farm or cloud on the Internet. The proposed artificial intelligence solution architecture is invariant across different deployment options and works in on-premise, privately managed, and public cloud environments.

In the context of artificial intelligence, a crucial principle is to bring algorithms to the ERP data rather than the other way around. Algorithms are typically composed of a few lines of code, are self-contained, and can be deployed flexibly. In contrast, application data is voluminous and contains numerous dependencies. As a result, replicating or extracting application data is often a complex and TCO-intensive task (e.g., handling deltas, meeting performance requirements, interpreting data semantically) and should be avoided. This consideration is taken into account in the suggested artificial intelligence solution architecture, which minimizes data transfer as much as possible. Specifically, the architecture pattern *embedded artificial intelligence* is defined, which adheres to the aforementioned golden rule as its key paradigm.

7.2   Solution Architecture

In this chapter, we focus on the solution architecture and conceptual foundations regarding embedding artificial intelligence into ERP software. The proposed approach basically resolves the required ERP qualities for artificial intelligence and the deducted artificial intelligence application patterns, which both were explained in Chap. 6. To have a general valid solution, the architecture is founded on the ERP reference processes from Chap. 3, ERP reference architecture from Chap. 4, and the ERP reference artificial intelligence technology from Chap. 5. A lot of the ERP qualities (e.g., commercialization, backup, recovery) are resolved by the existing concepts and infrastructure of ERP systems. This elaboration focuses only on the concepts and techniques that we newly invented for artificial intelligence. Thus, the focus is on those challenges that are artificial intelligence specific and require new concepts and implementation framework. Challenges that can be resolved with existing concepts and technology we take as granted and won't explain them further.

Enhanced computational capabilities, more advanced algorithms, and the accessibility of vast amounts of data are enabling the incorporation of artificial intelligence features in ERP software. Moreover, the in-memory database systems that underpin modern ERP products accelerate processing, combine analytical and transactional data, and foster innovation through integrated artificial intelligence libraries. AI technology platforms allow for the addition of new capabilities to ERP solutions, spanning the entire range from simply utilizing intelligent services to training and deploying custom artificial intelligence models.

Basic tasks such as ranking, categorization, and forecasting can be addressed using traditional algorithms like classification, clustering, regression, or time series analysis. These algorithms typically consume minimal memory and CPU resources, allowing them to be implemented directly within the ERP platform where both the application data for model training and the artificial intelligence-driven business processes reside. This architectural approach we call as *embedded artificial intelligence*, which offers low total cost of ownership (TCO) and low total cost of development (TCD) since it eliminates the need for data transfers and additional software. As depicted in Fig. 7.2, the embedded artificial intelligence architecture relies on artificial intelligence libraries supplied by the database system. Consequently, data scientists identify the appropriate algorithms and required application data for model training to address a specific artificial intelligence problem during the exploration phase. Developers then create the necessary pipelines to train the algorithms using the relevant application data and integrate the resulting inferences into business processes or user interfaces.

More complex tasks, such as image recognition, sentiment analysis, and natural language processing, necessitate deep learning algorithms based on neural networks. These algorithms typically require large volumes of data and extensive GPU processing for model training. To minimize the impact on the transactional ERP system and prevent performance degradation for business processes, we recommend

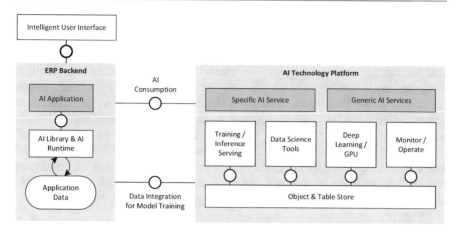

Fig. 7.2   Solution architecture for artificial intelligence

offloading such scenarios to AI technology platforms. This architectural pattern we refer to is *side-by-side artificial intelligence*. In most cases, the data needed for these scenarios—such as images, audio, text documents, historical data, and application logs—are stored not in ERP systems but in business data lakes. Generally, the utilization of a trained model relies on remote interfaces integrated into business processes and user interfaces. However, for large-scale processing, these interfaces must either support bulk operations or offer local deployment of inference models.

Our objective is to deliver inference results to the right person, in the right place, and at the right time (built-in artificial intelligence). Ideally, users should not even have to be aware of whether a feature relies on artificial intelligence. ERP users are usually business professionals with limited understanding of data science and statistical techniques. As a result, concealing these mathematical elements and converting the inference findings into the business vernacular of the ERP user is crucial for the effective utilization and adoption of artificial intelligence-based business applications. In the past, customers have implemented artificial intelligence scenarios, such as in the insurance sector. However, these models were controlled by obscure infrastructure that could only be accessed by a select few data science specialists. As a result, the outcomes were seldom used, adoption rates were low, and the potential of artificial intelligence remained untapped. Consequently, designing intelligent systems with ease of consumption in mind is essential. Specifically, artificial intelligence requires additional visualization features on the user interface, like illustrating confidence intervals or forecasting graphs. Therefore, incorporating artificial intelligence capabilities into user interfaces necessitates the inclusion of additional UI components.

In the subsequent sections, we will delve deeper into embedded and side-by-side artificial intelligence architecture. The emphasis here is on the development architecture, as the data science tasks have already been discussed in earlier sections.

7.3   Embedded Artificial Intelligence

We propose utilizing embedded artificial intelligence for applications such as ranking, categorization, and prediction, where traditional techniques like classification, clustering, or regression are adequate for execution. Generally, ERP systems include artificial intelligence libraries and runtimes that enable the creation of embedded artificial intelligence scenarios without transferring application data. To address a specific problem using artificial intelligence, data scientists conduct experiments and investigations to identify the necessary algorithms and data attributes for model training. This information serves as the foundation for developing the artificial intelligence use case, which is the central focus of this section. As depicted in Fig. 7.3, the solution relies on two primary architectural choices:

1. Leveraging the artificial intelligence runtime and libraries offered by the database system
2. Using views as a component of the core data model to access training data and consume inference outcomes.

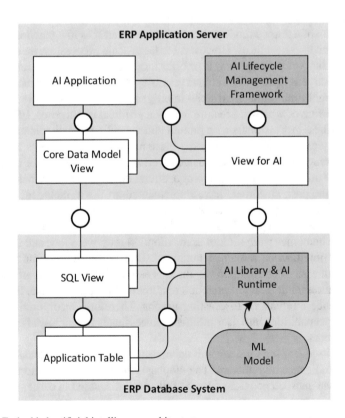

Fig. 7.3 Embedded artificial intelligence architecture

In the past, database management systems were developed to optimize performance on hardware with limited main memory, focusing on enhancing disk access, such as minimizing the number of disk pages read into main memory during query processing. However, today's computer architectures have evolved, featuring multi-core processors that enable parallel processing and faster communication between processor cores. Additionally, large main memory configurations have become more accessible and affordable, with server setups boasting hundreds of cores and multiple terabytes of main memory. These modern computer architectures present new opportunities and challenges. Since all relevant data can now be stored in memory, disk access is no longer a performance bottleneck. As the number of cores increases, CPUs can process significantly more data within a given time frame, shifting the performance bottleneck to the I/O between the CPU cache and main memory. Modern ERP products typically utilize database management systems based on in-memory technology, which takes advantage of the main memory and processing engines offered by contemporary hardware. In-memory database systems store all relevant data in main memory, allowing all operations to run there. They are also designed to leverage multi-core CPUs through parallel execution. These systems include a relational database management system where individual tables can be stored in memory either column based or row based and column based on disk. Conceptually, a database table is a two-dimensional data structure composed of cells organized in rows and columns, but memory is structured linearly. To store a table in linear memory, there are two options: a row store, which stores a sequence of data records containing the fields of one row, and a column store, where the data of a column is saved in consecutive memory locations. To enable fast searching, ad hoc reporting, and on-the-fly aggregations and to benefit from compression, transaction data in modern ERP systems is typically stored in column tables, as is master data. Master data is frequently searched and often has columns with few distinct values. It is commonly joined with transactional data for analytical queries and aggregations, which is most efficiently done using the analytical processing capabilities of the column store provided by in-memory database systems. The row store is used for metadata, application server system tables, and configuration data. Application developers may also choose to store business data in the row store if it meets certain criteria. The goal of keeping all relevant data in main memory can be achieved through data compression. Columnar storage allows for high compression rates without the need for complex algorithms, as each column contains records with identical data types, making it easy to apply standard compression procedures like length encoding or cluster encoding. This is particularly efficient for ERP systems, as most columns have few distinct entries compared to the number of rows. In contrast, row-based storage contains data from different columns, resulting in lower data fragmentation and corresponding compression rates. Column-oriented storage typically achieves a compression factor of 5–10 compared to traditional row storage database systems, although this may vary depending on the data's characteristics. Column-based storage is particularly efficient for storing columns with only one distinct value, which can be stored using minimal metadata and the single value. Since column-oriented data is stored in consecutive blocks, there is no need for complex algorithms to locate, identify, and compress the data, resulting in significant data size reduction. Moreover, column storage enables parallel execution across multiple processor cores, as data in a column store is inherently vertically partitioned, allowing operations on different columns to be processed in parallel. In-memory database systems offer high performance for both read and write operations, supporting transactional and analytical use cases. These capabilities are further enhanced with features such as text analysis and search, geospatial processing, time series analysis, streaming, and spatial processing. In-memory database management systems also provide artificial intelligence libraries and runtime, which are utilized in the context of embedded artificial intelligence architecture as shown in Fig. 7.3.

As previously discussed, the fundamental data model is realized through the use of views, which assist developers in constructing semantically rich data models. By extending SQL, views enable the definition and consumption of these data models in applications, resulting in enhanced productivity, usability, performance, and interoperability. Views are built on a collection of domain-specific languages and services designed to define and consume semantically enriched data models:

- Data Definition Language (DDL) is used to define semantically rich domain data models and retrieve them, extending native SQL for increased productivity
- Query Language (QL) is used for consuming view entities through platform-embedded SQL and reading data
- Data Control Language (DCL) establishes authorizations for views and manages data access, integrating with authorization concepts
- Data Manipulation Language (DML) is utilized for writing data

Core data models are defined and consumed at the database level rather than the application level, providing capabilities that surpass conventional data modeling tools. This approach supports SQL-compliant view definitions, allowing developers to use SQL features like *JOIN*, *UNION*, and *WHERE* clauses. Associations can be used to model relationships between views, while aliases can rename tables with more understandable names. Views also support annotations for defining metadata, such as specifying that a *DateTime* field contains the creation or last update time. Other core data model capabilities include parameters, view extensions, easy exposure as OData services, and anchors for behavior definitions. Annotations allow for the classification of entities based on their permissible reuse options and provided content.

The top-down approach utilizes the *Code Pushdown* technique, which means calculations are executed on the database system rather than the application server. This technique only pushes down calculations when it makes sense. For instance, to calculate the total amount of all invoice positions, an aggregation function [e.g., SUM()] could be used on the database instead of computing the sum in a loop on the ERP application server. This results in faster data retrieval and improved application performance and response time. Traditional ERP systems supported various database systems, necessitating a corresponding data access abstraction. Consequently, more data was exchanged between the database and application server than necessary. Additionally, data-intensive operations were performed on the application server rather than the database for better performance. However, modern ERP products supporting in-memory database systems have enabled significant optimization. As depicted in Fig. 7.3, an SQL view on the database system is generated for each view defined at the application server level. All SQL statements applied to the views are pushed down to the SQL view and executed at the database level for optimal performance. For example, authorization checks, which were previously performed on the ERP application server, are now pushed down to the database system by automatically enhancing SQL statements with a WHERE clause. Core data models consist of thousands of views, as all business processes use them to access application data. As a result, the performance of all these business processes can be systematically improved, as all data access is pushed down to the database system. Views can be defined with SQL statements or coded with SQLScript, typically using the classes of the underlying programming language of the application server. During runtime, the SQLScript code is pushed down to the database for optimal performance. When the view logic is too complex to be expressed by SQL statements, the scripted approach is facilitated. From a consumption standpoint, there is no difference between views based on SQL declarations or SQLScript coding.

Embedded artificial intelligence algorithms can be performance-intensive, as they must process high volumes of application data. For performance optimization, we recommend that these algorithms be processed close to the application data. As previously mentioned, in-memory databases provide libraries for statistical and data mining algorithms, which can be further enhanced with additional methods if needed. As shown in Fig. 7.3, these algorithms are invoked and orchestrated by the AI life cycle management framework, which we explain below. The algorithms require application data as input for model training, and the core data model views, with their database SQL views and application tables, can be reused for this purpose. In accordance with the data scientist's specifications, a core data model view is defined, or an existing one is reused by the developer. This view comprises all the necessary application data for training the algorithm of the specified artificial intelligence application. The corresponding SQL view generated from the core data model view operates at the database level, serving as data input for algorithm training. Once the algorithm is trained, the resulting model is saved in the database and presented as a core data model view for consumption. Typically, this generated view relies on SQLScript coding and includes columns calculated using the underlying artificial intelligence algorithm. This view is then integrated into business processes and user interfaces, referred to as the artificial intelligence application in Fig. 7.3. In this manner, trained models are made accessible to business processes through view wrapping. These artificial intelligence views can be combined with other core data model views and subsequently exposed to consumers. By utilizing artificial intelligence models through core data model views, existing content (such as views for business processes) and concepts (like authorization, extensibility, and user interface integration) can be reused. This leads to a straightforward and powerful solution architecture. The AI life cycle management framework, as depicted in Fig. 7.4,

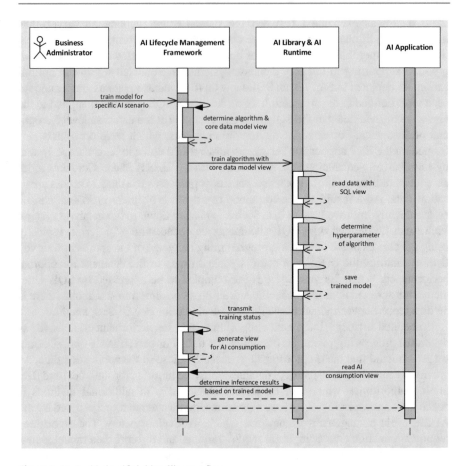

Fig. 7.4 Embedded artificial intelligence flow

supervises the entire orchestration of the described steps. This framework aims to offer a unified interface for the implementation, operation, and consumption of artificial intelligence models, regardless of the underlying technology engines. The goal is to standardize the handling of artificial intelligence models and provide a simple, common interface that enables applications to interact with various supported artificial intelligence libraries without necessitating engine-specific code development. Consumer applications only interact with APIs and avoid direct engagement with low-level artificial intelligence libraries, which facilitates also changing the underlying technology. The proposed framework supplies a repository for artificial intelligence models, containing information about model types (e.g., regression, classification, time series, and deep learning), model data sources, model training data, and model quality metrics to facilitate validation and model comparison. Additionally, the framework supports the life cycle management of associated artifacts in terms of transport within the system landscape, delivery, and upgrade mechanisms. It also shall offer configuration capabilities for model training based on customer data in their development landscape.

The proposed solution architecture offers numerous beneficial qualities. It is smoothly incorporated into the ERP programming model, which minimizes the need for developer training. This also promotes the utilization of existing ERP concepts (e.g., authorization, user interface integration), core data model components, and tools. Moreover, the architecture addresses the intricate demand for extensibility from the beginning by leveraging enhancement points from the ERP programming model. Breakouts, such as the orchestration of multiple algorithms or data transformations, are inherently supported. Life cycle management and operations are facilitated by the foundational ERP tools and concepts. Legal compliance is inherently achieved since no application data is transferred outside the ERP system, and the already compliant data access mechanisms of the underlying ERP are used. The rich set of algorithms in the in-memory database system can be used right away. As the proposed solution is deployment-agnostic, it is compatible with public cloud, on-premise, and privately managed installations.

7.4   Side-by-Side Artificial Intelligence

While embedded artificial intelligence focuses on situations where the business and artificial intelligence logic reside within the ERP platform, we propose utilizing side-by-side artificial intelligence for the following types of artificial intelligence applications:

- Artificial intelligence applications based on AI technology platforms: These applications, along with their corresponding business logic and data, are built on AI technology platforms deployed as sidecars to the ERP platform, as illustrated in Fig. 7.2. Typically, these are extension applications that expand the core ERP's functionality on the sidecar. They are loosely connected to the core ERP and have their own life cycle. Such artificial intelligence applications directly access the necessary artificial intelligence services from the AI technology platform, adhering to the principle of bringing algorithms to the data.
- Artificial intelligence applications based on ERP platforms: These applications and their associated business logic and data are built on the ERP platform, as depicted in Fig. 7.2. However, the required artificial intelligence algorithms are not supplied by the ERP platform. Additionally, the artificial intelligence logic demands advanced hardware (e.g., GPU) and data management capabilities not provided by the ERP platform. As a result, only the artificial intelligence logic is implemented on the AI technology platform and accessed remotely from the ERP platform.

Side-by-side artificial intelligence is suitable for use cases such as image recognition, sentiment analysis, and natural language processing, which require deep learning algorithms based on neural networks. These algorithms are resource-intensive, often requiring vast amounts of data and GPU time for model training. To minimize the load on the transactional ERP system and maintain acceptable response times for business processes, side-by-side artificial intelligence scenarios are scaled out to the AI technology platform, as shown in Fig. 7.2. AI technology platforms are provided by companies like Amazon, Google, Microsoft, SAP, and start-ups. This infrastructure also supplements the overall solution when specific algorithms are not available on the ERP platform, traditional methods (e.g., regression, classification) consume too many resources of the transactional system, or large volumes of external data (e.g., Facebook, Twitter) are needed for model training. In particular, ERP extension applications should leverage the AI technology platform's capabilities because the application data and business processes are typically based on the AI technology platform. This approach adheres to the golden rule of bringing algorithms to the data. As side-by-side artificial intelligence scenarios rely on AI technology platforms, the question arises: How do we integrate this technology into ERP for model training and inference? We will address this question in the subsequent sections.

The AI technology platform serves as a crucial element in the side-by-side artificial intelligence architecture. Typically designed for cloud environments, it can be deployed in any cloud, hybrid, or on-premise setting, addressing the complete end-to-end life cycle for deriving value from data. By combining artificial intelligence with information management, the platforms empower businesses to effectively implement artificial intelligence and data science in complex and real-world enterprise scenarios. The AI technology platform manages the process of helping customers discover, refine, govern, orchestrate, and scale their development efforts in extracting valuable insights from their data assets. This encompasses all data management use cases dealing with various types of data (structured, unstructured, streaming), integration approaches (batch, real time, near real time), and processing patterns (offline, online, lambda). The AI technology platform's key capabilities include typically:

- Data connectivity and orchestration: Utilize central connection management to connect to data wherever it is located on-premise or in the cloud and regardless of the data type, structured, unstructured, streaming, and integrate it with flexible data pipelines. Orchestrate data processing across highly distributed and heterogeneous landscapes, executing any ERP or non-ERP processing engines close to the data sources to minimize the amount of data to be moved or replicated.
- Data governance and cataloging: Access an advanced metadata management system/catalog, enabling data lineage, data quality, profiling, data discovery, and searching of datasets to ensure auditability and governance. This provides IT team members with the flexibility and control they need to ensure trusted and accurate data is easily discoverable by the teams that need it, all integrated within a single solution.
- End-to-end life cycle management of artificial intelligence models: Streamline data science and artificial intelligence projects, from modeling and development to operations, across all enterprise data assets to manage the end-to-end life cycle; support data discovery, access and preparation, and experimentation in Jupyter Notebook; leverage a library of pretrained models for the most common functional services; and support deployment, (re)training, serving, and monitoring of all models; and access ready-to-use, adaptable business content in terms of

operators and templates. Central repository enables versioning and a tailored life cycle management process for artificial intelligence projects. Finally, the AI technology platform provides an environment for model deployment and operation, a means to integrate results back into an application or used delayed consumption, and continuous testing and maintenance of all models in production.

- One integrated solution: The AI technology platform includes data pipelining, orchestration, artificial intelligence, and metadata cataloging in a single solution. This is very valuable: all hyperscalers have different services for these functionalities, which have to be integrated, while the main pure players and niche players focus only on a subset of these areas.
- Hybrid and multicloud deployment: The AI technology platform is available both as a service in the cloud and as a bring-your-own-license product. It is usually built on Kubernetes, allowing it to deploy the very same solution in any private cloud or on-premise data center.
- Native integration capabilities: Besides reusing all relevant open-source technologies and open standards, the AI technology platform is also capable of integrating and reusing ERP data sources and engines. The AI technology platform pipelines can natively integrate into ERP applications, orchestrate process chains and jobs, and execute streaming analytics scenarios.

Many of these capabilities may exist today in a customer's information management landscape, but they are typically offered in a myriad of different ways across several disparate toolsets that require different skills and different frameworks, whereas the AI technology platform provides a single, comprehensive way to manage all data types cohesively and intelligently. The AI technology platform is usually designed to be used by different user profiles throughout the enterprise. From a business user with technical affinity to developers and data scientists, there are modules, services, and tools for all levels. The typical life cycle the AI technology platform supports comprises the following phases:

1. Data management: A comprehensive suite of intelligent information management capabilities enables the handling of data that implies the entire artificial intelligence process. This allows IT enterprise architects, data engineers, and data management experts to eliminate data silos and guarantee that data science teams have access to the necessary data in a governed manner. By utilizing tools for profiling, preparing, and merging data, data science teams can quickly obtain the datasets they need to advance to the next stage.
2. Experimentation: The AI technology platform equips data scientists with familiar tools, such as Jupyter Notebook, and essential frameworks like R, Python, or TensorFlow. Once set up, data science teams can use a Jupyter Notebook environment to develop models employing open-source frameworks, pretrained services, and visual pipelines for orchestrating data ingestion, training steps, or multiple models. Experiments addressing specific business problems are version-controlled, enabling teams to explore various potential solutions and models, and effortlessly test and iterate until they settle on a model suitable for production.

3. Productization: Models can be rapidly deployed into production by bundling the necessary assets, such as pipelines and model assets, into an artificial intelligence scenario. In production, an artificial intelligence operations team can easily take over, connecting production data to the new scenario, (re)training, deploying models to model servers, integrating with business applications, and generating insights. Once in production, models can be centrally managed from a single cockpit, where ongoing testing, retraining, and quality monitoring can be conducted.

Models and pipelines can be reused, recombined, and traced throughout the entire process and applied to new scenarios, including dataset reuse. Data scientists directly use the artificial intelligence functionality through a set of tools run as Web applications, either within the AI technology platform or indirectly via applications that call REST APIs. Both tools and backends providing REST APIs are based on the system application server, which assists in delegating aspects like user authentication and authorization to the platform. As depicted in Fig. 7.5, the AI technology platform offers a data lake for business data, allowing application data to be extracted from the ERP system for training artificial intelligence models.

The pipeline engine facilitates pre- and post-processing of application data by providing a graphical programming model for constructing pipelines. These pipelines manage data ingestion, training, and inference tasks and are composed of operators and data flows that connect them. Operators can be pre-built connectors for integration with data sources using ERP platforms, customizable options like Python operators, or serving operators that expose a REST endpoint. Specialized artificial intelligence operators are available for calling functional services, such as image classification, or core services for model training and serving. The operator concept is compatible with third-party frameworks that data scientists prefer to use. Built on a scalable Kubernetes infrastructure, the pipeline engine orchestrates intricate data flow pipelines, supports diverse execution runtimes (e.g., R, Python, Spark AI), and enables connectivity to ERP systems. Data scientists perform exploration and feature engineering on application data to define artificial intelligence models,

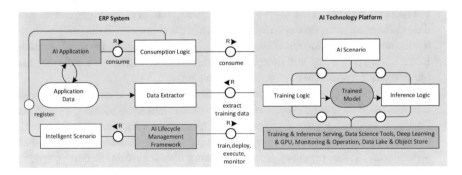

Fig. 7.5 Side-by-side artificial intelligence architecture

using common data science tools like Jupyter Notebook and Python. Typically, a framework is provided for deep learning scenarios that allows training on GPU infrastructure. To implement artificial intelligence use cases, application teams must establish artificial intelligence scenarios and model pipelines. The AI technology platform organizes each artificial intelligence use case through the artificial intelligence scenario artifact, which bundles all design-time entities needed to address an artificial intelligence business question. This artifact also keeps track of consumed and produced artifacts, such as datasets and artificial intelligence models, as well as the metrics reported by them, serving as the foundation for artificial intelligence scenario life cycle management.

Inference and training processes are developed as pipelines consisting of sequential and parallel tasks. For each artificial intelligence scenario, a training pipeline is provided that processes training data from the ERP system to train algorithms for specific use cases. Structured data is managed by a tabular operator and stored in a data lake, while unstructured data is handled by an object store and big data storage. Application data is often deleted after a training run, but in cases with frequent retraining, deltas must be periodically received and stored for subsequent training runs. Application data can be persisted or streamed based on continuous data transfer without persistency. Training and inference pipelines are exposed through REST services, which are invoked remotely by artificial intelligence applications and integrated into business processes and user interfaces. This ensures that artificial intelligence capabilities are delivered as built-in functionality to the appropriate person, location, and time. The operation and monitoring of artificial intelligence models are managed through various administration applications:

- An artificial intelligence operations cockpit displays deployed models, their runtime KPIs, and produced artifacts. It enables manual activation of artificial intelligence scenarios and pipeline calls, as well as landscape management, model configuration, and artificial intelligence scenario provisioning to other tenants.
- Scenario scheduling enables automated calls to the pipeline API.
- A debrief cockpit provides data scientists with KPIs for the created inference pipelines/models during exploration and retraining phases.

As depicted in Fig. 7.5, within the ERP framework, an intelligent scenario corresponds to the artificial intelligence scenario on the AI technology platform. An intelligent scenario is a design-time artifact representing an artificial intelligence use case, containing metadata such as the use case's name and description. It includes the coded class responsible for implementing the artificial intelligence model's consumption logic. In the AI technology platform, a model training and inference pipeline are provided for each artificial intelligence use case. The training pipeline accesses the necessary application data based on the data extractor, typically a core data model view offered by the ERP application. These pipelines are accessible through REST services and can be invoked from the ERP system. The AI life cycle management framework generically calls the training REST service, which has a standardized signature. This component manages the artificial intelligence models' life cycle and offers capabilities like scheduling training jobs and monitoring. The REST services' signature for model consumption is scenario-specific (e.g., forecasting sales order revenue or predicting debt default risk) and is managed by the consumption logic coding class, as illustrated in Fig. 7.5. This class essentially encapsulates the REST service into an ERP API, allowing artificial intelligence applications to integrate inference results into business processes and user interfaces. Optionally, inference results can be cached for scenarios requiring performance optimization. The consumption logic coding class is registered to an intelligent scenario within the ERP framework. To maintain a consistent programming model across all artificial intelligence use cases, the class is standardized by implementing interfaces. Side-by-side artificial intelligence scenarios must register the consumption logic class in the AI life cycle management framework through an intelligent scenario. During development, changes to the intelligent scenario are anticipated, so the artifact is initially saved as a draft. The draft status governs the transportation of the scenario registration content within the AI life cycle management framework. ERP customers often struggle to comprehend the technical and business prerequisites needed to train and consume artificial intelligence scenarios. For instance, an adequate data volume is necessary for training artificial intelligence algorithms, and underlying business processes must be activated and configured to provide a meaningful foundation for the training process. As the number of artificial intelligence scenarios grows, manual evaluation by ERP customers becomes unfeasible due to high total cost of ownership (TCO) and significant complexity. Consequently, an automatic prerequisite check capability is needed to validate whether the necessary prerequisites for training and consumption are met for each artificial intelligence scenario. Intelligent scenarios facilitate these prerequisite checks by implementing a consistent interface. This allows for the assessment of the artificial intelligence use case's readiness and consistency, such as determining if sufficient data is available for model training. The AI life cycle management framework performs these checks to evaluate whether the prerequisites for model training are met. To enable customer extension of the coded classes, enhancement spots should be incorporated, allowing customers to augment the consumption logic or add specific transformations, for example.

As previously mentioned, on the AI technology platform side, the artificial intelligence scenario and pipeline artifacts must be defined. The training and inference pipelines encompass the necessary artificial intelligence logic and are modeled graphically based on operators for transformation, validation, or algorithm integration. The artificial intelligence scenario serves as a link among all development artifacts in the AI technology platform to address life cycle management. The training and inference pipelines are exposed to the ERP platform via REST services. The consumption logic class is needed to wrap these REST services and make them accessible through ERP methods. Figure 7.6 illustrates the basic steps for the training and inference pipelines, which can vary per use case.

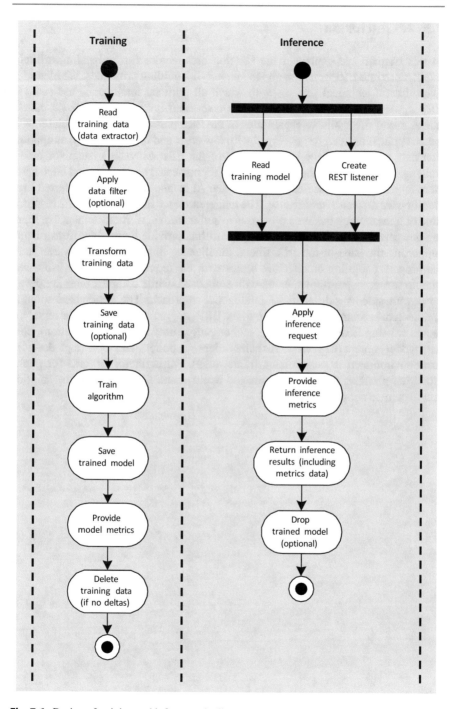

Fig. 7.6 Design of training and inference pipelines

7.5   Conclusion

In this chapter, we explained the solution architecture for embedding artificial intelligence into ERP software and the underlying guiding principles. We identified two different technical patterns with which all artificial intelligence use cases in ERP systems can be implemented. The *embedded artificial intelligence* pattern makes use of the available capabilities of the ERP platform. Thus, artificial intelligence applications can be developed with low costs and high efficiency, as application data must not be replicated outside of the ERP database system for model training. However, advanced scenario with sophisticated algorithms and huge hardware requirements are scaled out to a sidecar AI technology platform referred to as *side-by-side artificial intelligence*. The main reason for this is to avoid the response time of transactional business processes to suffer from performance intensive training and inference jobs. AI technology platforms provide a scalable infrastructure supporting the state-of-the-art artificial intelligence libraries and hardware. Thus, the proposed solution architecture scales with the requirements of the use cases. Simple scenarios are implemented with embedded, while complex ones are developed with side-by-side artificial intelligence approach. The anticipated solution architecture is seamless integrated into the ERP programming model. Conversely, it reuses existing ERP concepts (e.g., authorization, user interface integration), core data model content (e.g., views for sales order or supplier), and tools (e.g., development environment or customizing frameworks). Furthermore, it works for public cloud, on-premise, and private managed deployment. Consequently, the solution architecture is simple but powerful.

Life Cycle Management

8

In this chapter, we specify the business requirements and propose the solution concept for life cycle management. In the context of artificial intelligence, new artifacts and processes are introduced that must be considered from the life cycle management perspective. For example, artificial intelligence models must be trained, deployed, activated, and monitored. Those aspects are not covered by classic life cycle management tools and concepts. ERP systems have a very complex life cycle as they are long-lasting, rich in functionality, and available in different deployments (e.g., on-premise and in the cloud). Artificial intelligence artifacts must be seamlessly integrated in the overall ERP life cycle management.

8.1   Problem Statement

In the realm of artificial intelligence, novel elements must be taken into account in life cycle management to deliver the operational qualities that customers anticipate from an intelligent ERP system. This section concentrates on the stage where a customer investigates an artificial intelligence scenario within the ERP system to comprehend its value, prerequisites, and the necessary infrastructure for its utilization. We outline the requirements in relation to the steps customers need to undertake to use and manage artificial intelligence scenarios: check, setup, train, deploy, and monitor. The emphasis lies on the artificial intelligence specific aspects, while existing solution approaches for life cycle management, such as delivery or support processes, are assumed. Let's examine these steps and the role of artificial intelligence in each of them:

- **Check**
  Customers often find it challenging to determine the technical and business prerequisites needed to train and utilize artificial intelligence scenarios. For instance, an adequate data volume is essential for training artificial intelligence algorithms,

© The Author(s), under exclusive license to Springer Nature
Switzerland AG 2024
S. Sarferaz, *Embedding Artificial Intelligence into ERP Software*,
https://doi.org/10.1007/978-3-031-54249-7_8

and underlying business processes must be activated and configured to establish a meaningful basis for the training process. As the number of artificial intelligence scenarios grows, manual evaluations become impractical due to high total cost of ownership (TCO) and immense complexity. Consequently, an automatic prerequisite check capability is necessary to validate whether the required prerequisites for training and consumption are met for each artificial intelligence scenario.

- **Setup**
  Before customers can begin using side-by-side artificial intelligence scenarios, connectivity to the AI technology platform must be established. During this onboarding process, a customer account with service entitlement and a service key is generated. The service key's content provides the information for the initial communication configuration on the ERP platform side to access the artificial intelligence services in the AI technology platform. This operation model is manual, labor-intensive, and challenging for customers to manage. As a result, the setup process should be automated using a wizard that guides customers through the steps of provisioning and connecting the AI technology platform.

- **Train**
  Customers need to train artificial intelligence models for consumption. However, the training process is typically manual, time-consuming, and less transparent to customers. Moreover, the calculated model accuracy KPIs are not adequate for usage decisions. Thus, the training process should be offered as a self-service option for the customer for all artificial intelligence scenarios. Customers must be empowered to adjust parameters to enable successful training. Errors and warnings should be communicated in a language that non-AI experts can comprehend. Fully automated training runs based on scheduled jobs should be supported, and event-driven triggering of training jobs should be possible.

- **Deploy**
  Customers need control over the timing of deployment and activation of trained models. However, models are usually deployed in the DevOps mode, which is costly and time-consuming due to manual steps. Automating this process is beneficial, allowing customers to deploy the model as a self-service option. Simultaneous deployment of multiple models should be supported for purposes such as A/B testing before model activation. Deactivation of models should also be possible, like un-deploying models with insufficient accuracy. The history of model activation/deactivation should be documented for monitoring and auditing purposes.

- **Monitor**
  Customers want to assess the quality of productively used models at runtime. However, artificial intelligence infrastructure often only provides technical monitoring, lacking business process aspects. Monitoring should offer customers a comprehensive view of the artificial intelligence models in use, based on a central cockpit for all artificial intelligence scenarios. This should include, for example, model status, accuracy KPIs, the state of inference calls, and the volume of

processed data. In case of issues, alerts should be raised to inform administrators to take action. Solution proposals should be recommended to administrators for resolving problems. Statistics should be provided, such as the number of errors, the amount of resource consumption, or the costs incurred.

In this context, it is essential to differentiate between various roles:

- **Business Users**
  These users concentrate on managing business operations and utilize artificial intelligence features within this context, such as on user interfaces. For instance, they may modify chart layouts, date formats, or conceal table columns. These alterations are local and do not impact others. Such modifications are not exclusive to artificial intelligence and can be considered as granted.
- **Business Experts**
  These specialized key users possess extensive business and technical expertise. They handle the majority of configuration and extensibility tasks, including enhancing data sources for model training, replacing algorithms, and expanding pipelines. However, they typically require assistance from data scientists who conduct artificial intelligence explorations as a preliminary step. The changes they make affect individuals in specific business areas and the entire organization.
- **Business Administrators**
  These technical users oversee the administration of artificial intelligence applications, including training, deployment, and monitoring of artificial intelligence models. They specifically configure models and schedule training jobs for artificial intelligence scenarios. They collaborate with data scientists and implement their recommendations. The changes they make affect individuals in specific business areas and the entire organization.
- **Developers**
  These technical specialists execute complex changes by writing code. They manage breakout scenarios where artificial intelligence logic (e.g., transformations, preprocessing) cannot be graphically modeled and must be coded due to high complexity. Developers are responsible for extending coded artificial intelligence logic, with data scientists providing recommendations based on their artificial intelligence explorations. They also integrate artificial intelligence features into user interfaces and business processes. The changes they make affect individuals in specific business areas and the entire organization.

8.2 Solution Proposal

In this section, we delve into the technical execution of the business requirements outlined in the previous section. To provide the necessary background, we will first address the subsequent inquiries:

- Which artifacts, unique to artificial intelligence, demand particular attention in terms of life cycle management?
- What are the processes associated with managing the life cycle of these artifacts?
- Who initiates these processes, and in what manner are they activated?

8.2.1   Artifacts, Processes, and Roles

We have pinpointed the artificial intelligence components depicted in Fig. 8.1. The central design-time element is an intelligent scenario, encompassing all the necessary artifacts for implementing an artificial intelligence based solution. In essence, it addresses the primary problems to be tackled using artificial intelligence. Data scientists determine the required algorithms and data features for this purpose. To train the algorithm, suitable application data is needed. As a result, a core data model view is offered, which can encompass multiple application tables and carry out initial data transformations. The intelligent scenario also includes the definition of the inference API's signature during design time, enabling the integration of the inference API into consuming applications and business processes. However, the inference API only yields significant results after the underlying artificial intelligence model has been trained. Before training artificial intelligence models, prerequisite checks are conducted, which are specific to the artificial intelligence scenario and ensure that all necessary conditions for training are met, such as the availability of adequate application data or the completion of required process configurations.

Once the prerequisite checks are successfully completed, the training process is initiated. This involves utilizing the training infrastructure, which extracts the essential metadata from the relevant intelligent scenario, executes the training, and saves the trained model. The inference infrastructure supplies the consumption API tailored to the particular scenario and model, allowing the artificial intelligence functionality to be incorporated into applications and business processes.

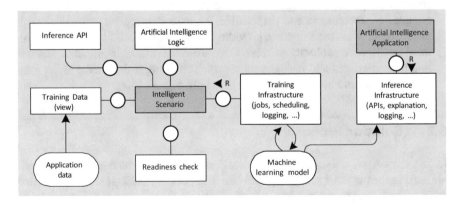

Fig. 8.1   Life cycle management artifacts

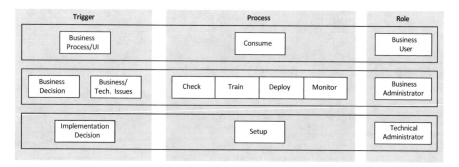

Fig. 8.2 Life cycle management triggers, processes, and roles

In Fig. 8.2, we outline the various processes, triggers, and roles associated with the mentioned artifacts, which necessitate life cycle management considerations. Business users typically utilize artificial intelligence features to carry out their daily tasks and meet their business requirements. Business administrators conduct the prerequisite assessments. These findings serve as the foundation for determining if the artificial intelligence scenario can be executed. If the decision is affirmative, technical administrators carry out the setup, while the business administrator oversees the training and deployment phases. Artificial intelligence scenarios are constantly monitored. However, business administrators generally only take into account the monitoring data when there are alerts related to business or technical problems, such as incorrect results from the inference API or excessive system resource allocation by the training job.

In managing the life cycle of an artificial intelligence application, we suggest utilizing the AI life cycle management framework. This framework aims to facilitate and standardize the execution and operation of intelligent scenarios within ERP software, with a primary emphasis on operational aspects. The framework streamlines life cycle management tasks such as prerequisite assessments, training, deployment, activation, deactivation, monitoring, and inference consumption across a variety of business domain-specific intelligent scenarios. The AI life cycle management framework offers more straightforward functionality and features, enabling individuals without expertise in artificial intelligence to carry out life cycle management operations for an intelligent scenario. The intricacies of managing intelligent scenarios across different layers, such as the ERP platform and the AI technology platform, are made more accessible through this framework. It allows business administrators to conduct life cycle management operations for intelligent scenarios as a self-service operation from a centralized control center. The framework's architecture is illustrated in Fig. 8.3.

Furthermore, the framework provides a cohesive operational experience for both embedded artificial intelligence and the side-by-side artificial intelligence approach, based on intelligent scenarios.

In side-by-side scenarios, the framework incorporates a consumption client REST API for the AI technology platform. This contains the logic necessary to call

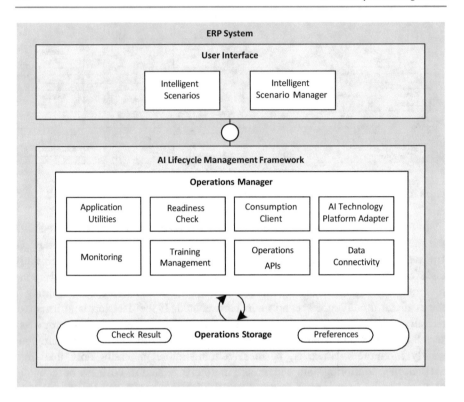

Fig. 8.3 AI life cycle management framework architecture

the platform-specific REST APIs in a native manner. The AI technology platform offers a range of REST APIs for various aspects, such as artificial intelligence scenarios, training, deployment, and metrics. The AI life cycle management framework consumes and orchestrates these APIs to present a more straightforward view for non-experts in artificial intelligence when operating side-by-side intelligent scenarios. The framework presumes that the connection between the AI technology platform and the ERP system is set up beforehand, complete with the necessary authorizations and valid authentications, for instance, exchanging data for model training or batch inference. The framework includes the following applications, as depicted in Fig. 8.3:

- **Intelligent Scenarios**
  With this application, developers can establish intelligent scenarios in the AI life cycle management framework, including basic details and a class that refers to the code for artificial intelligence logic (e.g., data transformations or consumption behavior). Customers and partners can access this application to develop their own intelligent scenarios.

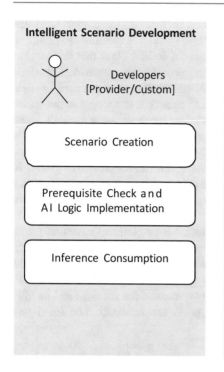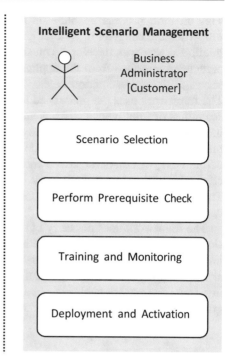

Fig. 8.4 Development and operations roles

- **Intelligent Scenario Management**
  Utilizing this application, business administrators and domain experts can carry out operations such as prerequisite checks, training, deployment, activation, and monitoring of the intelligent scenario for a specific business domain. This application is designed with a focus on non-experts in artificial intelligence, enabling them to manage intelligent scenarios.

The AI life cycle management framework encompasses the business administrator's perspective on operating an intelligent scenario. To provide a simplified operational approach, the framework necessitates the development-related artifacts and processes. Figure 8.4 demonstrates the phases to be executed by the developer during design time and the phases to be performed by the business administrator on the customer side. The technical specifics of these phases vary based on the artificial intelligence approach (embedded or side by side).

The development of an intelligent scenario is an activity that takes place during the design phase, carried out by developers as they work on the project. These intelligent scenarios, which come from various application domains within ERP system, adhere to an interface that has been pre-established by the framework.

This creation process enables the framework to thoroughly comprehend the properties and behavior of an intelligent scenario while it is running. To create an intelligent scenario, developers must implement a coding class that follows the predefined interface from the applications that provide the scenario. This class serves as the representation of the intelligent scenario within the ERP system. The framework uses the predefined interface as a marker to recognize the representations of intelligent scenarios and to associate them with the content found in the artificial intelligence technology platform during runtime, using a globally unique identifier (GUID). The predefined interface requires the implementation of the GET_SCENARIO_GUID method, which returns the scenario GUID to align with the content present in the connected AI technology platform instance. This scenario GUID is a globally unique identifier generated by the AI technology platform.

The framework does not carry out the AI technology platform's content provisioning. Figure 8.5 demonstrates the interdependencies between the framework, an intelligent scenario from the application domains, and the content GUID of the artificial intelligence technology platform. By default, the registered scenarios are in a draft state and are published once the development of the scenario and its integration with the framework's operational aspects are finalized. The intelligent

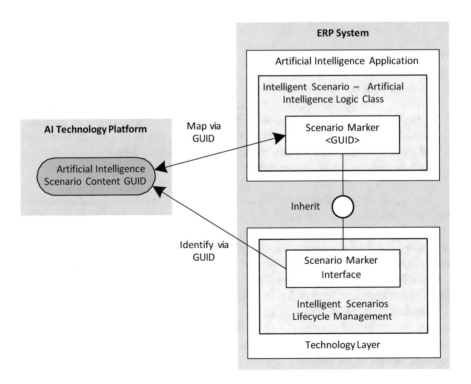

Fig. 8.5 Content mapping and identification

scenarios are registered within the framework, transported, and made accessible for customers to utilize in different releases.

8.2.2   Prerequisite Check

The AI life cycle management framework assists in conducting necessary checks for intelligent scenarios before integrating them into the system. These scenarios demand high-quality training data with a sufficient volume to achieve optimal results. In certain instances, configuring a business process in the system may be required in addition to meeting data prerequisites. The framework offers a distinctive approach to perform qualification checks for an intelligent scenario beforehand and appraise the outcomes to determine the implementation strategy. Business administrators can choose an intelligent scenario from the framework and initiate the prerequisite evaluations using the necessary parameters. The resulting information provides crucial insights into data quality, data volume, and configuration checks, enabling business administrators to either utilize the intelligent scenario or make any additional adjustments needed in the system. The framework also records historical evaluations of prerequisite conditional checks for an intelligent scenario, ensuring traceability and supportability. Typically, business data found within the ERP application area is used for these evaluations. Prerequisite checks are specific to a business domain, so they must be implemented by the intelligent scenario developer and linked to the scenario in the framework with the artificial intelligence logic class. For instance, a finance-related table needs over 10,000 records for accurate results in the intelligent scenario inference calculation related to a finance use case. Developers of these checks should adhere to the framework's design guidelines. A scenario may examine various conditions at the individual breakdown level in the system and generate a composite outcome to inform the business administrator about the feasibility of using that scenario. The framework defines the respective data structures, table types, exceptions, and interfaces for the prerequisite checks. Developers should utilize these objects when implementing the prerequisite evaluations. Business administrators have the authority to execute these checks from the business data authorization profile and maintain access control. Prerequisite checks for intelligent scenarios can be enhanced or corrected over time due to ongoing learnings and findings from customer implementation experiences. In such cases, improvements to the check logic from the intelligent scenarios can be delivered through regular updates.

8.2.3   Training

For an efficient computation of inferences related to a business problem, the intelligent scenario is consistently trained using the corresponding historical data. The business administrator initiates the training of an intelligent scenario within the AI life cycle management framework. The sequence shown in Fig. 8.6 illustrates the process for training using the side-by-side artificial intelligence approach.

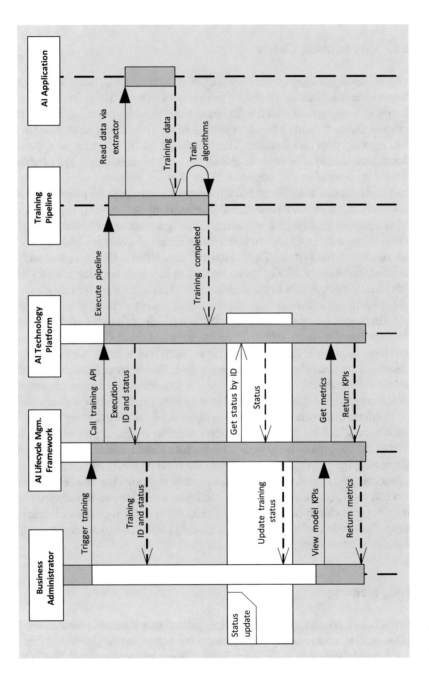

Fig. 8.6 Training process

Upon completion of a training operation within the AI technology platform, the relevant metrics, key influencers, and overall quality of the training process are supplied to the business administrator for examination and decision-making purposes. The business administrator has the ability to input various parameters for the training activity, as outlined in the intelligent scenario, and assess the outcomes of the trained models. The framework should offer a comparative perspective for the business administrator, enabling them to evaluate different training executions and determine which trained model should be utilized in the deployment process. The framework records the parameters used during a training activity to create templates for the training process. Furthermore, the framework should support regular scheduling of training jobs, notifications, and asynchronous training executions.

8.2.4   Deployment

Business applications ought to have the capability to consume trained models for inferring from a given dataset without any disruptions. It is essential that business users are not burdened with the intricacies of the process, yet they require a method to manage the consumption of trained models by their applications. The responsibility of choosing a trained model does not lie with the business user, but rather with the business administrator. The AI life cycle management framework assists in streamlining the deployment and activation process from the viewpoint of the business administrator, as demonstrated in Fig. 8.7. Deployment refers to the creation of an operational server instance using the trained models obtained from a training activity, intended for productive inference consumption. The business administrator has the flexibility to create a deployment of a trained model at any moment within the framework, without affecting the business applications. In this scenario, the application benefits from the ability to modify deployments during runtime, based on the analysis conducted by the business administrator.

In an intelligent scenario, numerous trained models and multiple deployments can coexist, but by default, only one active deployment is supported. The business

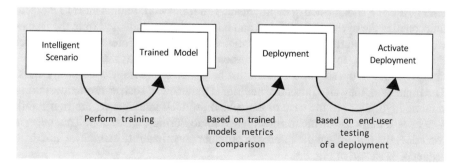

Fig. 8.7 Artificial intelligence model states

administrator selects a trained model for deployment based on metrics, key influencers, and the quality of the training models. The framework offers the ability to test a deployment from the standpoint of the business application and determine whether to activate it for productive use. The activation of a deployment is a feature within the framework that enables business administrators to successfully test deployment and the corresponding inference consumption within the business context. If the results are accurate, the business administrator can activate the deployment for consumption by all business users. This functionality within the framework allows for the integration of intelligence into the ERP business application while giving business administrators more control. The active model of an intelligent scenario is utilized by ERP business applications to consume the inference, as the framework conceals the complexity of active deployment from the applications. Business administrators also have the option to roll back an active deployment under specific circumstances and conditions. Furthermore, the framework recommends un-deploying a trained model in instances where a trained model is nonactive and has been running for an extended period.

8.2.5   Inferencing

The application of artificial intelligence takes advantage of inference values by inherently incorporating them into business procedures and user interfaces. In the case of side-by-side artificial intelligence, the applications make use of the inference outcomes by calling upon the inference REST API, which is connected to the active deployment.

Every new implementation of a trained model creates a new REST API within the artificial intelligence technology platform, which can cause issues for the stable consumption of an inference REST API by artificial intelligence applications. To address this, the framework provides a utility class that enables the stable consumption of the inference REST API. However, business applications still need to directly call the inference REST API. As a result, the AI life cycle management framework offers a generic utility, as illustrated in Fig. 8.3, to obtain the dynamic inference REST API of a specific active deployment. The framework returns an HTTP object that contains the dynamic REST API and other properties inherited from the framework. With this returned object, applications can execute the inference and interpret the response data. To identify the corresponding active deployment in the AI technology platform, the scenario GUID must be passed to the framework utility class. The framework may also introduce additional parameters, such as username, during runtime invocation. In the case of embedded artificial intelligence, the framework generates a class for artificial intelligence logic during registration. This class is used directly, rather than the inference provider generic utility class. The inference sequence is shown in Fig. 8.8.

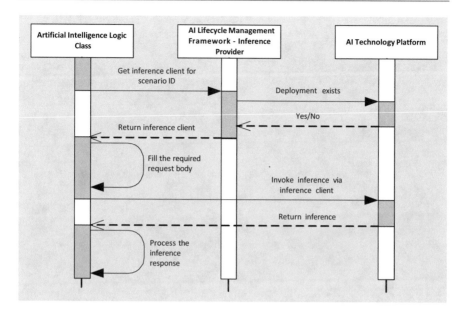

Fig. 8.8 Inference process

8.2.6 Monitoring

The AI life cycle management framework allows business administrators to constantly oversee the implementation of trained models and the progress of asynchronous training processes. This framework includes a functionality that persistently verifies the presence of a deployed trained model and alerts the business administrator if any issues arise. As discussed in the training segment, the process of data ingestion and running an artificial intelligence algorithm can be time-consuming and may be carried out asynchronously. Consequently, the framework consistently considers the training execution and informs the business administrator at consistent intervals. Additionally, the framework offers sophisticated monitoring of the decline in performance of deployed trained models and the usage of inference.

8.3 Conclusion

New artifacts and processes related to artificial intelligence are being introduced in this chapter. These must be taken into account from the perspective of life cycle management. For instance, it is necessary to train, deploy, activate, and monitor artificial intelligence models. Traditional life cycle management concepts and tools do not address those aspects. As a result, we deducted the business requirements and proposed implementation concepts for managing the life cycle of artificial intelligence. Particularly, we suggested a framework handling the entire life cycle and covering the aspects prerequisite checks, training, deployment, inferencing, and monitoring.

Data Integration 9

In this chapter, we specify the business requirements and propose the solution concept for data integration. For the side-by-side artificial intelligence approach, data integration is required because application data must be extracted from the ERP system into the AI technology platform for model training but also batch inference. While the data integration for model training is unidirectional, for batch inference, the results must be transferred back to the ERP system. Initial load but also delta handling and packing must be resolved for the data replication as ERP systems always process mass data.

9.1   Problem Statement

Data integration entails combining information from various distinct sources, which utilize different technologies, in order to present a cohesive view of the data. Within the realm of artificial intelligence, data integration becomes essential during the training phase. While data integration is not pertinent to online inference when using artificial intelligence models through APIs, it is relevant for batch inference, where predictions are generated for multiple requests simultaneously. As previously mentioned, the training process is crucial for both embedded and side-by-side artificial intelligence. However, in the case of embedded artificial intelligence, the training data is accessed locally, eliminating the need for data integration. As illustrated in Fig. 9.1, data integration is typically necessary for side-by-side artificial intelligence, where application data must be transferred from the ERP system to AI technology platform for the purpose of model training and batch inference.

Application data may be organized in a well-defined relational schema, known as structured data, or it may be unstructured, such as files or emails. Both types of data will be considered for data integration, with the primary emphasis on extracting structured data, which is the main case for ERP data.

S. Sarferaz, *Embedding Artificial Intelligence into ERP Software*,
https://doi.org/10.1007/978-3-031-54249-7_9

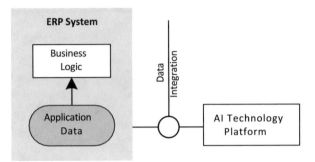

Fig. 9.1 Data integration requirement

The data integration solution should facilitate an initial load, which is the first step in transferring all records from the ERP system to the target system. Delta loads must also be supported. If a data source's overall size (the number of rows multiplied by the width of a row) is small, the data consumer can monitor changes to the data source through a full reload of the source. However, this is only recommended for customizing-like data sources (e.g., code lists) that seldom change. For other sources that change frequently (e.g., transactional data), this approach is generally not viable. To replicate such data sources, delta handling is necessary, which accomplishes the initial load by replicating changes that occurred since the last data replication. Long-running data extraction tends to become unsynchronized, meaning that the data source contains different data than the replicated version, but the synchronization process does not show an error. Possible reasons for this include:

- Lost updates during the synchronization process
- Deletion on the receiver side
- Source objects falling out of scope if source object filters are used

As a result, a resynchronization of the replicated data must be supported, either through a complete reload of the data or by comparing and resolving the differences between the source and receiver. The second approach is more complex, but a complete reload may not be feasible for large data volumes. Data replication typically increases the total cost of ownership (TCO) due to factors such as additional disk space requirements. For artificial intelligence scenarios where data replication can be avoided, a live connectivity/data streaming capability should be offered.

ERP systems deliver data for extraction in a provider-driven manner, meaning that data sources are designed to ensure comprehensive coverage of ERP data with minimal redundancy. Specific consumer scenarios may necessitate data in a particular structure or with transformations (e.g., aggregations) already executed. Some of these transformations could be achieved by creating customer- or consumer-specific data sources. Tools should be available for key users to create their own data sources or enhance existing ones, including the ability to add simple transformations. Some of these transformations may also require access to additional data in the source system that is not replicated, in which case custom data sources are the only option.

Certain transformations may necessitate access to external data or be so consumer-specific that they will not be implemented in the source system. In these cases, the data integration technology must provide the option to add transformations before delivering the data to the consumer. ERP software stores data in an internal format (e.g., internal code lists or currency-related amounts with two decimals). Some consumers may be able to consume data in the internal format (assuming that all relevant customizing settings are synchronized between the provider and consumer systems). However, most consumers are either unaware of the internal format or unable to perform the necessary conversions because they do not support the same conversion routines. Consequently, a consumer must be able to receive data in an externally understandable format. Additionally, it must be possible to map the key of the object instance during the extraction process so that sender and receiver instances with different key values/structures can be mapped to one another.

Modern ERP systems offer a comprehensive framework for data integration scenarios. They rely on core data model views as the internal layer for accessing data, and the data integration model should be built upon them. Various tools can utilize this model, offering diverse integration capabilities and qualities. For artificial intelligence applications, a data extraction solution must possess the following features:

- **Consistency**
  Data integration consistency is essential at the view level. Typically, a core data model view is composed of multiple database tables. To ensure consistency, data extraction must be aware of the view's associations with the underlying database tables and accurately replicate all changes from a single database transaction involving these tables (delta load). Additionally, a consistent method for the initial load of core data model views should be available.
- **Read access**
  In certain contexts and for specific data sources, read-access logging may be necessary to guarantee auditing of each data access in the provider system. As a result, the data extraction solution must allow read-access logging for particular data sources.
- **Data protection and privacy**
  Data in the source ERP system must comply with legal and product standards for data protection and privacy (data blocking, end-of-purpose deletions, retention period handling). Even when extracted to another storage source, data must meet these requirements. The provider system must enable the consumer to be informed about data life cycle events through an information lifecycle management solution, and the consumer must consider these events and manage the data accordingly. ERP software offers interfaces to obtain information about information lifecycle management events. The data extraction technology must provide this information to relevant consumers. If an ERP system delivers a consumer, it must ensure proper data handling, or the customer can add the handling as desired.
- **Implicit selection**
  Since the smallest selectable entity for extraction by a consumer is a core data model view, this feature requires an option to define a set of views ($1..N$) for

extraction. To simplify this selection, an option for implicitly selecting all core data model views related to a single business object should be available.

- **Consumer-defined views**

  ERP data sources are generally not designed for specific consumer applications. They are defined as provider-driven core data model views and may not be tailored for a particular customer use case. Consequently, customers must be able to create their own data sources for replication (consumer-defined views). These data sources should have the same features and functions as defined ERP data sources. A customer may use all available whitelisted artifacts to build their data source, preferably based on stable core data model views. Customer- or consumer-specific data sources may be required to replicate customer-specific data (custom business objects or fields) or to transform data to meet a specific consumer's needs.

- **Monitoring and analysis tools**

  The data integration solution must offer local tools for monitoring and error analysis to identify and resolve data integration problems. Additionally, it must support integration into ERP's central tools for monitoring and error analysis, such as cross-system monitoring and error correction.

- **Stability contracts and independent upgrades**

  Communication partners in a data integration scenario must be capable of independent upgrades without requiring downtime on one side during the other's upgrade. Therefore, data integration interfaces must adhere to specific stability contracts. Moreover, the integration technology must ensure that partners can be upgraded independently, including irregular field length extensions on the ERP system. The technology must provide a means to resume data integration at the point of disruption (e.g., network failure, consumer upgrades) without needing a complete data reload, ensuring that occasional disruptions do not affect overall data integration quality.

- **High data volume/data change support**

  The data integration technology should not impact the ERP system in a way that hinders normal, operational tasks. In particular, data integration should not necessitate planned downtime for the initial load to achieve consistency. The technology and protocols employed must support high data volumes and/or frequent data changes. The consumer should be able to receive data in defined package sizes to avoid overload. The technology and protocols must also support scenarios with low bandwidth between communication partners. In accordance with the specific requirements of a given situation, it is essential to have the ability to adjust the settings so that modifications in the data source can be reflected in the target system either almost instantaneously or within a designated time frame.

- **On-premise and cloud support**

  The data integration solution should be capable of facilitating data integration between on-premise and cloud-based ERP systems, encompassing all possible combinations and interactions with external systems.

9.2 Solution Proposal

Data Integration refers to the process of transferring ERP data through a universal mechanism for a variety of objectives, such as analytics, artificial intelligence, or the development of transactional applications. It is important to note that Data Integration does not initiate any business process steps. This section delves into the various orchestration patterns and technologies available for data integration in the context of ERP solutions. In a *consumer-driven data replication* approach, the data consumer chooses the data sources from a data provider that are required for their needs. The underlying technology then replicates the data from these sources to the data consumer, adhering to the selected quality standards. From a business standpoint, the data provider remains unaware of who is requesting the data and for what purpose. In contrast, *provider-driven data replication* involves the data provider being aware of the purpose of the data replication, defining the quality standards, and ensuring they are met. A common example of this type of replication is the transfer of master data from ERP systems to other applications. Data integration can be technically implemented using various patterns, with the primary data integration patterns in the context of ERP illustrated in Fig. 9.2. There are two primary methods for replicating data from the source to the target system. The *Push Data* method involves the source system transmitting all relevant data or changes to the target system via APIs. As a data provider, the source system monitors the data and sends any detected changes to the target system, which acts as a passive data receiver, waiting for new values.

In contrast, *Pull Data* operates at consistent intervals, extracting pertinent information from the source system. A particular logic detects alterations in the source system, extracts the data, and transfers it to the target system. The pull model is typically executed using a specific protocol, such as one for initial handshaking and package-wise data transmission. Consequently, the target system must also implement this protocol, leading to tighter coupling and increased development efforts. Additionally, the source system must open a port to allow the target system to periodically retrieve data. This presents a security risk for ERP system setup, necessitating extra protective measures. Moreover, the performance of transactional processes in ERP may be impacted if numerous target systems and a high volume of data sources are involved. The push model effectively decouples the source and target systems, but it primarily shifts the data transfer responsibility to the source system. The push and pull methods can also be combined, as seen in the *Feed and Query*

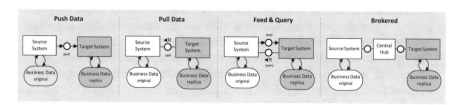

Fig. 9.2 Data integration patterns

model. In this approach, initial changes (such as employee ID, name, and email address) are pushed from the source to the destination application as notifications. If needed, an optional change feed may also be present, offering a full object representation. These minimal attributes are referred to as the feed in the diagram above. The destination acquires additional data to update its local replica of the application data based on the notification. If necessary, a query can also be used, for instance, to continue business operations or display information to the end user in user interfaces. Although the preferred method is to obtain extra data from the application layer using APIs, data integration tools can also be utilized to implement the transfer of application data from an API to a local schema. When data replication occurs, the initial data load can be accomplished by pulling data from the source system. To reduce data transfer following the initial load, only modified data should be transmitted. A suitable protocol mechanism (such as an OData delta token) enables this. The *Brokered Pattern* is facilitated for applications that necessitate advanced data transformation options not available as built-in functions within ERP data provisioning. Data consolidation, governance, and quality are also primary reasons for implementing the brokered pattern based on a central hub. The central hub typically supports both push and pull capabilities.

Data integration technologies in context of ERP systems can be categorized by organizational level and persistence handling. The organizational level takes into account whether technologies are data-centric or application-centric. The more application logic and code can or must be integrated into a given technology to create a solution, the more application-centric it becomes. Conversely, if data structures and data storage aspects dominate the data integration setup, the technology is considered data-centric. The following levels of data integration exist:

- Manual integration/common user interface: Users interact with all relevant information by accessing source systems or Web page interfaces directly. There is no unified view of the data.
- Application-centric/orchestrated integration: Integration logic shifts from applications to a middleware or central hub layer. While the integration logic is not developed within the applications, they still need to contribute to data integration partially.
- Data-centric integration: This level of integration is achieved using data-oriented technologies, including message brokers like KAFKA, RabbitMQ, Solace, and others, as well as replication solutions.
- Virtual integration/uniform data access: This method does not necessitate data replication from source systems. Instead, it establishes a set of views for providing and remotely accessing a unified view for the customer. Data is accessed remotely or virtually during runtime without being moved.
- Physical data integration/common data storage: A separate system stores a copy of the data from source systems, managing it independently from the original system. Technologies that follow the Extract-Transform-Load (ETL) paradigm are part of this level.

Data integration persistence can be divided into copying (movement, replication) and non-copying (federation) paradigms, with the following cases:

- Non-copying: No data copy is created. Queries are evaluated against live data, and only the query evaluation result is sent back to the originator.
- Transitory copy: Message brokers typically store data temporarily in the payload part of a message to ensure the desired quality of service. Replication technologies maintain changed data in shadow copies or stable devices.
- Copying: Data is duplicated and stored in another logical structure, such as within the same database in data marts.
- Moving: Unlike copying, moving involves deleting the original data in the source system after successfully completing the copy operation.

Consequently, the following data integration technology groups are identified: Application to Application, Orchestration, Stream Processing, Message Broker, Replication, Offline and Occasionally Connected, Virtualization, Extract-Transform-Load, Migrations, and Conversions.

The comprehensive solution architecture for data integration, proposed in the context of side-by-side artificial intelligence, is illustrated in Fig. 9.3. Core data model views are defined on top of application tables, representing the semantic data model of the ERP system. These views conceal the complex database models and transform them into human-understandable entities. In addition to the SQL view definition, core data model views contain domain-specific metadata, known as annotations, used for analytics, data extraction, or search. Business logic consumes the core data model views to access structured data. A view-based data extraction framework should be used extracting structured data from ERP systems for artificial intelligence training. Output management and attachment services are utilized to extract unstructured data from the ERP system. Key user tools are provided for customers to define structured and unstructured sources for data extraction.

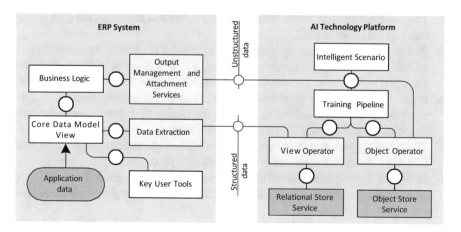

Fig. 9.3 Data integration architecture

Let's explore the technical procedures associated with integrating data using artificial intelligence methodologies.

9.2.1   Data Extraction with Views

Within the AI technology platform, each use case involving artificial intelligence is structured according to the artificial intelligence scenario artifact, as illustrated in Fig. 9.3. This artifact encompasses all the necessary development components for implementing a specific artificial intelligence use case. Both inference and training procedures are designed as pipelines consisting of sequential and parallel tasks. Notably, a training pipeline is established that obtains training data from the ERP system and processes it to train algorithms tailored to the specific scenario. Structured data is managed by a view operator and stored in a relational database, while unstructured data is overseen by the object operator and saved in an object store. In many cases, the stored application data is removed after the training is completed, although there are instances with high retraining frequency where, following an initial upload, the differences must be periodically received and stored for subsequent training runs. Data persistence is one option; alternatively, streaming the data and training the algorithm with live connectivity is a crucial capability for various artificial intelligence use cases.

For data extraction, core data model views are used within the ERP system. This method offers the benefit of extracting data based on the same semantic layer as analytical and transactional applications, ensuring high quality and consistency. Additionally, the total cost of development (TCD) is lowered since existing core data model views can be repurposed. The initial data extraction steps using core data model views are as follows:

1. During the design phase, views are enabled as outbound data interfaces through the extraction annotation for full delta extraction.
2. The metadata of these views is exposed and utilized as structures for data persistency in the target system.
3. As shown in Fig. 9.4, an operational data provider is enabled for views from a technical standpoint. This provider supports extraction and replication scenarios for target applications and enables delta mechanisms in these situations.
4. In the case of a delta procedure, data from a source as an operational data provider is automatically written to a delta queue using an update process or transferred to the delta queue via an extractor interface.
5. The target applications, known as operational data queue consumers, obtain the data from the delta queue and proceed with data processing.
6. Based on the required capabilities, the view operator is utilized for data pull scenarios, while the data integration operator is applied for data push scenarios.

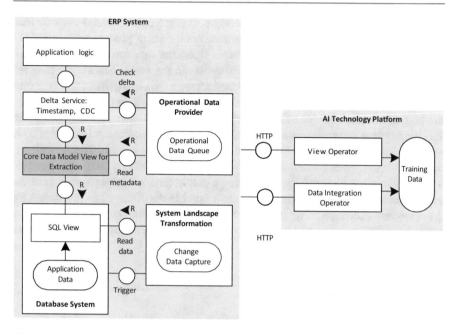

Fig. 9.4 Integration of structured data for model training

There are two methods for managing delta changes: one that relies on timestamps and another that utilizes change data capture (CDC). When dealing with core data model views that include time-related attributes, the timestamp-based technique can be used, allowing the engine to compute deltas using this information. However, for core data model views that lack timestamp attributes, change data capture is the most suitable option. This method hinges on triggers associated with the database tables involved in a view. By analyzing the modifications made to the table, the subsequent alterations in the relevant data extraction views can be determined and saved in the operational data queue for any extraction consumer. While this approach does not require a specific field like a timestamp to calculate the delta, there are certain restrictions concerning the view structure. To determine the altered view rows from the modified table entries, the view must include the key fields of the underlying tables. Furthermore, any component that needs functionality based on database triggers can consume the change data capture.

9.2.2   Pipelines and Operators

The AI technology platform uses pipelines for algorithm training, as illustrated in Fig. 9.3. These pipelines embody process logic rooted in a graphical programming paradigm, facilitating data flow with transformations and persistence. A corresponding runtime component enables pipeline execution within a containerized environment, typically running on Kubernetes. Pipelines are composed of process steps known as operators, which serve as vertices in a graph. Operators function as reactive components, responding solely to environmental events in the form of messages received through their input ports. They can also interact with the environment via their output ports. Importantly, operators remain oblivious to the graph they are part of and the origins and destinations of their connections. To function, operators necessitate specific runtime environments. For instance, an operator executing JavaScript code would require an environment equipped with a JavaScript engine. The AI technology platform supplies predefined environments for operators, which are accessible to users through a library. When executing a graph, the tool converts each operator into processes and searches the library for a suitable environment to instantiate for the operator's execution. Frequently, there are pre-established operators available for connecting ERP systems and converting structured or unstructured application data within the AI technology platform.

9.2.3   Output Management

Ordinarily, the primary access point for functions like printing, sending emails, or managing form templates in an ERP system is output control, as depicted in Fig. 9.5. This crucial component forms the backbone of ERP's output management, which encompasses all functions and processes related to document output. By structuring output management functionality, output control enables its reusability across all business functions that have implemented it. Output management generates documents using templates and application data, with templates stored in a template repository and authored by both ERP developers and key users. Print forms, which are specifically designed for precise print output, represent a unique document category and are produced using forms technology. The document output component is responsible for managing document output through the user interface (frontend output), backend printing, and backend email. The attachment service, a reusable UI component, can be utilized by ERP applications to attach documents, which are then stored on content management servers.

This reusable element relies on user interface control and allows attachments to be connected to business objects through document management or generic object services. The attachment service offers fundamental capabilities such as uploading, downloading, renaming, and removing an attachment within the primary application. It also embraces the notion of drafts for adding a new attachment, modifying the attachment's name, and eliminating an attachment, with changes being saved only when the user executes a deliberate save action. The creation of attachments necessitates a consuming application object. In the realm of artificial intelligence, this versatile component facilitates the training pipeline's access to unstructured data generated by output management and attachment services.

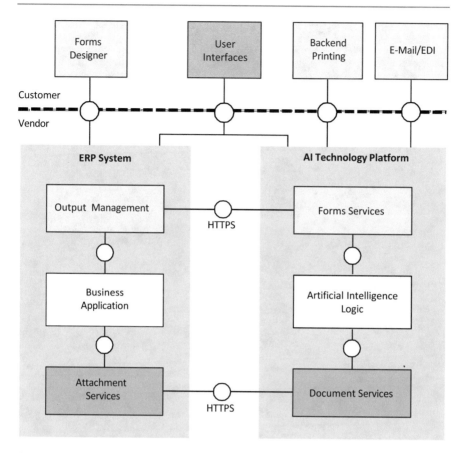

Fig. 9.5 Integration of unstructured data for model training

9.3 Conclusion

For side-by-side artificial intelligence, data integration is required because application data must be extracted from ERP system into AI technology platform for model training and batch inference. In this section, we deducted the business requirements and proposed implementation concepts for data integration regarding artificial intelligence. The solution architecture for data integration that we suggest is based on core data model views that represent the semantic data model of the ERP system and is defined on top of the application tables. The core data model views also include domain-specific metadata, which are used for data extraction. This method has the advantage of providing high-quality and consistent data because the extracted data is based on the same semantic layer as analytical and transactional applications. We proposed two solutions for handling deltas, namely, timestamp and change data capture based. To extract unstructured data from the ERP system, we suggested to use output management and attachment services. Customers can define structured and unstructured sources for data extraction using key user tools.

Data Protection and Data Privacy

10

In this chapter, we specify the business requirements and propose the solution concept for data protection and data privacy. ERP systems must fulfill legal requirements. Thus, processing of artificial intelligence must be compliant with data protection and data privacy legislations. For example, the training job must only consider personal data for which consent is given. Compliance must be ensured for all aspects of General Data Protection Regulation (GDPR). Authorization concept must ensure that only permitted user apply inference calls and consume the results.

10.1 Problem Statement

Over the years, the subjects of data-sharing standards and personal data protection have evolved, driven by the growth of information technology. The first legislation addressing these issues have been introduced in 1970 in the German federal state of Hessen. This law aimed to regulate data sharing within Germany but did not cover international data transfers. Consequently, data was processed and stored in other locations and jurisdictions with less stringent regulations. Regulators had to address this problem and implement restrictions on international data transfers. The ultimate goal was to harmonize effective data protection across jurisdictions, allowing for the removal of transfer restrictions across national borders. The initial two data protection frameworks were the Organization for Economic Co-operation and Development Privacy Guidelines (OECD) in 1980 and the Council of Europe Convention for the protection of individuals concerning the automatic processing of personal data in 1981, also known as Convention 108. These regulations permitted data transfers to other participating states and even prohibited some transfer restrictions for privacy reasons between participating states. A more recent approach to regulating data sharing and data protection was introduced by the European Union's Data Protection Directive in 1995, which led to the introduction of its successor in 2016: The General Data Protection Regulation took effect on May 25, 2018. Data

© The Author(s), under exclusive license to Springer Nature
Switzerland AG 2024
S. Sarferaz, *Embedding Artificial Intelligence into ERP Software*,
https://doi.org/10.1007/978-3-031-54249-7_10

protection and privacy have been significant concerns for decades and have grown in importance in recent years. Regulations like the General Data Protection Regulation (GDPR) and Organization for Economic Co-operation and Development Privacy Guidelines (OECD) significantly impact how personal data is managed and stored. ERP vendors must help their customers comply with all requirements using their products. Two aspects must be considered when working with personal data: data protection and data privacy. Data protection involves safeguarding information against unauthorized access through computing environments. For instance, it is crucial to ensure that unauthorized users cannot read or edit data. In the worst-case scenario, data could be lost, deleted, or misused, leading to further consequences. The information security officer is responsible for ensuring that all requirements in this area are met. Data privacy focuses on protecting individuals concerning the processing of personal data. Ignoring this issue could result in the violation of personal rights, leading to substantial monetary penalties. The data privacy officer is responsible for ensuring that all requirements in this area are met. To meet data protection and privacy requirements, technical and organizational measures (TOMs) must be implemented. These measures ensure a level of security appropriate to the risks described.

10.1.1 General Data Protection Regulation

As previously noted, the European Union introduced the General Data Protection Regulation (GDPR 2023) in 2016 as a follow-up to the initial attempt made by the European Union's Data Protection Directive in 1995. The GDPR became effective on May 25, 2018. While there were no significant technical alterations compared to the 1995 approach, the GDPR raised penalties to as much as 4% of a company's annual revenue, prompting many businesses to pay closer attention to compliance with the regulations. As of April 2020, the largest fine imposed was nearly 205 million euros. The GDPR mandates that any transfer to a country outside the European Union must be carried out in accordance with a transfer justification, which must be approved beforehand by the European Commission.

The GDPR establishes various definitions and principles. Personal data is defined as information related to an identified or identifiable natural person (the *data subject*) who can be identified either directly or indirectly, particularly by reference to an identifier or one or more factors specific to the individual's physical, physiological, genetic, mental, economic, cultural, or social identity. Consequently, personal data encompasses all information that directly identifies a person or can lead to their indirect identification. Direct identifiers include names, postal addresses, phone numbers, and email addresses, while indirect identifiers include bank account numbers, IP addresses, MAC addresses, membership numbers, and license plate numbers. To enhance data privacy standards, the GDPR outlines several principles for processing data in accordance with its requirements, such as lawfulness, fairness, transparency, purpose limitation, data minimization, accuracy, storage limitation, integrity, and confidentiality. As a result, processing personal data is prohibited unless there is a valid and justifiable reason. The purpose of data processing must be documented at every stage, applying to entire sets of personal data and business partner records as well as individual data pieces. Justifiable reasons for processing personal data include:

- The data subject's consent
- The necessity for contract processing
- The need to fulfill legal obligations
- The requirement in the public interest
- The need to protect a vital interest
- The basis on a legitimate interest

Consent is characterized as a freely given, specific, informed, and unambiguous indication of the data subject's desires, signifying their agreement to the processing of their personal data through a statement or clear affirmative action. Data processing is necessary for contract performance when it is essential or intended for entering into a contract. Examples of legal obligations include tax reporting, income tax reporting, or social insurance reporting in ERP software. Public interest exists when processing is necessary for performing a task in the public interest or exercising official authority, and it should be based on Union or Member State law. Vital interest refers to situations where data processing is crucial for the life of the data subject or another natural person. Legitimate interests pertain to the fundamental rights and freedoms of the data subject.

10.1.2 California Consumer Privacy Act

The California Consumer Privacy Act (CCPA 2023) is a legislation akin to the European Union's General Data Protection Regulation (GDPR), enacted by the California Department of Justice in 2018. This law empowers individuals with greater authority over their personal data collected by companies. It establishes privacy protections for consumers in California, encompassing rights such as:

- Understanding the nature of personal data collected by businesses, as well as its usage and distribution
- Requesting the deletion of collected personal information, subject to certain limitations
- Choosing to prohibit the sale of their personal data
- Ensuring fair treatment (non-discrimination) when exercising their CCPA rights

10.1.3 Requirements for Artificial Intelligence

The General Data Protection Regulation (GDPR) and the California Consumer Privacy Act (CCPA) encompass a multitude of legal obligations and privacy considerations. Beyond adhering to general data protection laws, compliance with industry-specific regulations in various countries is also crucial. But how do these legislations impact artificial intelligence? Naturally, artificial intelligence within the context of ERP must abide by these legal and data protection guidelines. However, what specific aspects should be taken into account for artificial intelligence? In this section, we will extract the key technical requirements for incorporating artificial intelligence into ERP software from the aforementioned laws. The concept of personal data is outlined in numerous regulations, standards, and guidelines, with most definitions being as comprehensive as possible to ensure maximum protection for individuals. The common thread among these definitions is that personal data refers to any information connected to an identified or identifiable natural person. One primary legal requirement is that processing personal data is prohibited unless a valid reason is provided, such as a contract, other legal grounds permitting the processing, or explicit consent from the data subject. Basic data protection requirements are often categorized as technical and organizational measures, including authentication, authorization, communication security, secure system landscape and operation, read access logging, information retrieval, encryption and decryption of sensitive data, input control change logging, separation by purpose, and masking or anonymization. The implementation of these requirements is well established and not specific to artificial intelligence, so they will not be discussed further in this section.

In the context of artificial intelligence, the following legal requirements must be taken into account:

- **Deletion**
  In some countries, personal data must be erased once the specified, explicit, and legitimate purpose of the processing has concluded, provided that no other retention periods are outlined in legislation, such as those for financial documents. In certain cases, personal data may also encompass referenced data. Consequently, the challenge for deletion lies in managing referenced data first, followed by data like business partner information. Artificial intelligence training and inference must be capable of handling the deletion of personal data.
- **Blocking**
  Legal requirements in specific scenarios or countries may also necessitate blocking data, limiting further processing or usage when the specified, explicit, and legitimate purposes of the processing have concluded but the data remains in the database due to other legally defined retention periods. Artificial intelligence training and inference must not process blocked data.
- **Consent**
  A legal basis is needed to process personal data. GDPR identifies six legal options for processing personal data, one of which is consent. Other legal grounds include contracts, legal obligation, protection of vital interest, public interest, and legitimate interest. If none of the other legal grounds apply, the individual's consent for the intended processing of personal data is necessary. Artificial intelligence training must not process data without the required consent. This is only relevant for artificial intelligence scenarios that necessitate consent.

- **Automated decision-making**
  The controller must inform the data subject about the existence of automated decision-making and provide meaningful information about the logic involved, as well as the significance and the anticipated consequences of such processing for the data subject. An explanation of artificial intelligence for automated decision-making and its consequences is required.

Moreover, it is essential to avoid bias and discrimination against individuals in artificial intelligence applications. The performance of these models should be consistent for all users, regardless of their group affiliation, based on as many factors as possible. Artificial intelligence developers must guarantee fairness at the individual level, ensuring that similar people receive similar results. To prevent biased outcomes, it is crucial to assess any discrepancies in accuracy across different groups. The use of sensitive personal information should be carefully considered and used only when absolutely necessary for the intended purpose. This processing must not lead to direct or indirect discrimination against any specific group of people. For the bias and discrimination, various frameworks are available in the market and therefore not further considered.

10.2 Solution Proposal

In this section, we propose how to resolve the previous explained legal requirements. Addressing these requirements, which include deletion, blocking, and consent, relies on both embedded and side-by-side artificial intelligence variants. However, automated decision-making can be contemplated for both variants collectively and is discussed in a shared segment. We will explore the diverse solutions that aid in meeting legal requirements, as well as the implementation of these requirements in embedded and artificial intelligence systems.

10.2.1 Blocking, Deleting, and Consent

Simplified blocking and deletion refer to the systematic and integrated methods for blocking and deleting personal data. These techniques enhance the functions for erasing data across distinct archiving processes and blocking data through authorization-based grouping by modeling and applying blocking and deletion rules in ERP systems. These methods are grounded in Information Lifecycle Management within ERP systems. The technical aspects of Information Lifecycle Management are depicted in Fig. 10.1 and will be explored in the subsequent sections.

To utilize blocking effectively, residence and retention periods for specific objectives are established in Information Lifecycle Management. Various purposes necessitate different residence and retention periods. For instance, trading peppermint oil serves different purposes than trading cough syrup. The system identifies the data processing purposes by examining the following technical attributes:

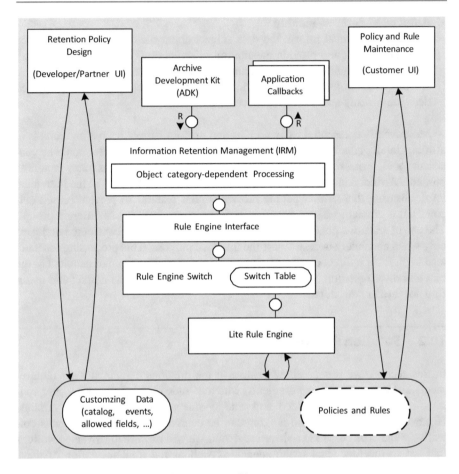

Fig. 10.1 Information Lifecycle Management architecture

- Line organizational attributes signify the data controller, such as the company code.
- Process organizational attributes aid in distinguishing between business processes. For example, by allocating specific order types, processes like the peppermint oil trade and the cough syrup trade can be differentiated.

When a document has fulfilled its intended purpose, the Information Lifecycle Management framework is used to archive and block the document within the system. To block central master data, such as business partners, customers, or vendors, an end-of-purpose check first ascertains if any applications, like sales and distribution or financials, continue to utilize the pertinent master data in accordance with its original purpose. If not, the system designates the data as blocked, thereby preventing any further legally compliant processing. Consequently, transactional data is blocked through Information Lifecycle Management, while master data is blocked using a central blocking indicator. An authorization framework governs both blocking methods, ensuring that only authorized individuals, such as auditors, can access the blocked data. Following the conclusion of the retention period, both transactional and central master data must be erased.

If no other legal grounds exist for the lawful processing of personal data, consent from the data subject is required to utilize their personal information. Consent management framework allows for the storage, search, and display of consent data, as depicted in Fig. 10.2. The importation of consent records as duplicates from a file or through the consent repository service is also supported. Consent management aids in demonstrating the legality of personal data processing and guarantees the accurate processing of personal data in line with the purpose for which consent was granted.

Consent management harmonizes consent operations and data structures throughout various applications and products. This serves as the foundation for consent scenarios that extend beyond the upkeep of consent information within a single application or system. A local API, functioning as a consent facade or proxy, enables access to consent data. Generic user interfaces are available for searching and displaying this data. Moreover, this application lays the groundwork for centralizing consent data on an AI technology platform, where front-office applications gather consent documents and back-office applications utilize them for further processing. This establishes the framework for engaging with third parties to exchange not only personal data but also associated consent details. Furthermore, it offers transparency

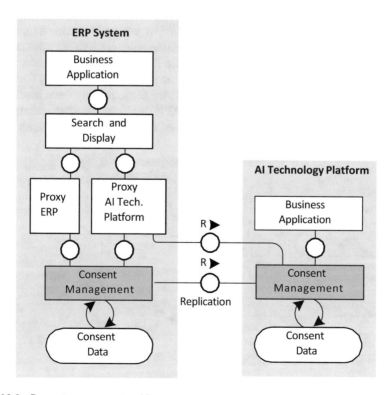

Fig. 10.2 Consent management architecture

and evidence of the specific personal data and processes or purposes for which consent was granted.

10.2.2 Embedded Artificial intelligence

Illustrated in Fig. 10.3, the resolution of deletion, blocking, and consent requirements for embedded artificial intelligence is demonstrated. The application data, which is stored in database tables, is encapsulated through core data model views and subsequently processed by artificial intelligence algorithms to facilitate model training. These trained models are then made accessible through APIs, allowing seamless integration with artificial intelligence applications and various business operations.

As depicted in section ❶ of Fig. 10.3, training data is read via core data model views. In the training phase, data is typically accessed without any authorization checks. As previously mentioned, deletion and blocking are carried out according to Information Lifecycle Management principles. As a result, personal information that needs to be deleted or blocked is transferred from the online database to archive storage by Information Lifecycle Management, making it inaccessible through core data model views. This ensures that such records are not included in the artificial intelligence training process, which inherently complies with GDPR deletion and blocking requirements. However, there are certain exceptions, such as business partners or vendors, where blocking can be achieved by setting a blocking flag. In these instances, the core data model view for artificial intelligence training must take into account the blocking flag as a filtering condition in the SQL where clause. As shown in section ❷ of Fig. 10.3, the trained models are stored in the database. Ordinarily, these models are preserved in a secure, encrypted form, making them inaccessible directly and only available through regulated APIs that include authorization checks. As a result, it is generally believed that trained models do not necessitate special

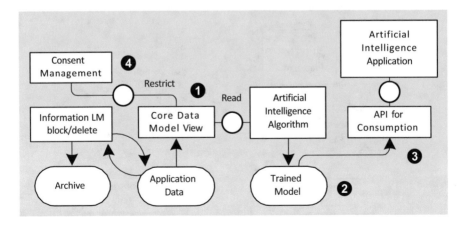

Fig. 10.3 Legal fulfillment for embedded artificial intelligence

handling concerning GDPR compliance. However, if the model retains personal information, periodic retraining is essential to remove blocked or erased records from the model. This retraining process can also be initiated automatically in response to blocking and deletion events generated by Information Lifecycle Management.

As outlined in section ❷ of Fig. 10.3, the trained models are exposed via APIs for consumption by artificial intelligence applications. There is no aspect of artificial intelligence that is specific to the utilization of APIs, which means that established techniques for ensuring GDPR compliance can be effectively used. Artificial intelligence applications that must ensure the legal consent requirement must restrict the access to application data as shown in section ❶ of Fig. 10.3. Processing data for artificial intelligence model training is only permissible when there is existing consent. To accomplish this, it is necessary to merge core data model views for accessing application data with consent data, thereby implementing the necessary restrictions. A connection between consent records and application data must be established, which requires defining the following attributes:

- An attribute that holds the data subject and type of consent. For instance, if I_SALESORDER.SoldToParty represents a customer, then DataSubjectId = SoldToParty and DataSubjectIdType = 3 signify the data subject and type.
- An attribute that contains the data controller and type of consent. For example, if I_SALESORDER.SalesOrganization is a sales organization code, then ControllerName = SalesOrganization and ControllerType = 2 indicate the controller and type.

To align with the intended consent purpose, the following characteristics must be ensured:

- Application-specific functional attributes should represent the purpose. For instance, "I agree that the ERP vendor can use order data from the past four years to create a profile of my product preferences." In this case, the term order data corresponds only to orders, so purpose X is defined by I_SALESORDER. SalesOrderType = 'OR' (OR = ORDER).
- Consent-specific functional attributes should represent the purpose. For example, "I agree that the ERP vendor can use payment data from the past quarter to calculate a risk profile of my payment behavior." The terms profile/profiling and product preferences must be represented by attributes of the purpose: Purpose. Action = 'Profiling' and Purpose.Aspect = 'Payment'.

Consent management data is stored in database tables. Figure 10.4 illustrates the static SQL statement used to join application and consent data, ensuring that only records with given consent are considered for artificial intelligence model training.

Nonetheless, due to the necessity for consent management data to be adaptable and customizable, a static SQL statement is inadequate. A more dynamic method is required, as demonstrated in Fig. 10.5. The primary distinction is that this technique

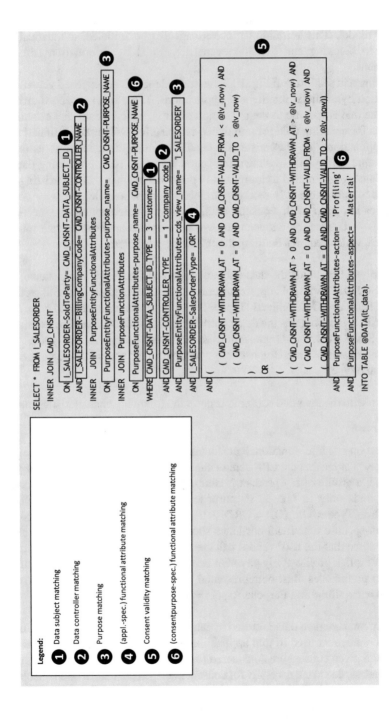

Fig. 10.4 Static SQL statement for considering consent data

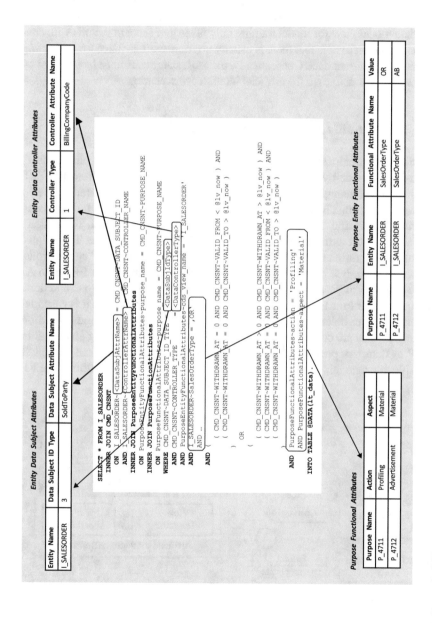

Fig. 10.5 Dynamic SQL statement for considering consent data

is universal and can be used in various use cases. However, this dynamic functionality also necessitates the use of generic database tables to store consent information. The organization of these database tables is depicted as boxes in Fig. 10.5. Using these table definitions, the SQL statement for merging application data with consent details can be dynamically established, as shown in the code in Fig. 10.5. As a result, the central data model view for model training only takes into account records with consent. It is important to note that there is usually no framework in place for integrating application and consent data. Consequently, the SQL statements must be supplied by the developer responsible for the artificial intelligence scenario.

10.2.3 Side-by-Side Artificial intelligence

Illustration 10.6 demonstrates the resolution of deletion, blocking, and consent prerequisites for side-by-side artificial intelligence systems. Data from the ERP system is obtained using core data model views and subsequently stored on the AI technology platform. The artificial intelligence algorithms are then trained using this extracted data, and the resulting models are preserved as needed. To facilitate the utilization of these trained models, a REST API is made available. This allows for seamless integration of artificial intelligence capabilities into ERP applications. As shown in section ❶ of Fig. 10.6, training data is extracted from ERP into AI technology platform based on view operators covering the initial upload and delta handling. In order to maintain legal compliance for duplicated data, it is essential to guarantee proper deletion and blocking procedures. The removal and restriction of application data are contingent upon the business operations taking place within the ERP system. As previously outlined, Information Lifecycle Management is responsible for managing these deletion and blocking processes within the ERP

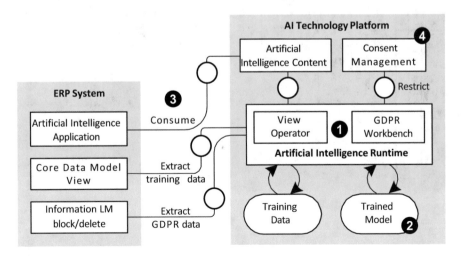

Fig. 10.6 Legal fulfilment for side-by-side artificial intelligence

system. Consequently, Information Lifecycle Management possesses all pertinent information about deleted or blocked records and makes this information available through an extraction API to the AI technology platform. A GDPR workbench that aligns with these requirements is necessary, which obtains deletion and blocking data from the extraction API and subsequently deletes or blocks the impacted records on the AI technology platform.

This article discusses how legal requirements for deletion and blocking can be addressed in the context of parallel artificial intelligence systems. Figure 10.7 provides a detailed illustration of the process. A notification API is made available for applications to invoke their deletion programs, which in turn inform users about the removal of their personal data. This API call is incorporated into the Archive Development Kit framework of Information Lifecycle Management, ensuring automatic activation during each archiving session. Notifications are dispatched to recipients who previously obtained the personal data, using either the same or distinct channels as configured in the standard integration channels. A filtering mechanism is set up to ensure that the information reaches the appropriate recipients. The notifications include business objects, so a mapping from Information Lifecycle Management objects is provided. It is essential to verify if a recipient may need additional context information. Key mapping is necessary and can only be performed while the relevant data remains in the database. Proper user permissions are needed for the data controller to view and send notifications based on purpose and other attributes. Moreover, deletion notifications and their statuses are recorded. In the AI technology platform, a GDPR workbench is necessary to periodically extract Information Lifecycle Management data protection and privacy information from the ERP system and subsequently delete or block the affected records as needed.

As shown previously in section ❷ of Fig. 10.6, trained models are stored in an encrypted format without identifiable information and can be accessed not directly, but only based on controlled APIs with authorization checks. As a result, there is no need for distinct actions to address GDPR concerns. However, if the model includes personal information, it is essential to conduct ongoing retraining to remove any restricted or erased data. This procedure can be entirely automated through event-driven retraining, as Information Lifecycle Management can generate the necessary

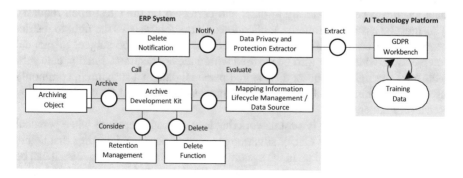

Fig. 10.7 Information Lifecycle Management integration for side-by-side artificial intelligence

blocking and deletion events. As illustrated previously in section ❸ of Fig. 10.6, the trained models are exposed via APIs for consumption by artificial intelligence applications. There is no specific aspect related to artificial intelligence when it comes to utilizing APIs for consumption, thus traditional approaches for ensuring legal compliance can be used. The necessity for obtaining consent in the legal context does not pertain to every artificial intelligence application; for instance, in cases where the training data does not include any personal details, this requirement becomes inapplicable. However, if consent handling is requested, section ❹ in Fig. 10.6 shows that the training dataset must be restricted only to the records for which consent is given. In this context, several inquiries emerge: What methods can we use to create a linkage between consent records and the data used in applications? How can we accurately align the intended purpose of consent? To address these issues, we repurpose the concept previously demonstrated for embedded artificial intelligence in Figs. 10.4 and 10.5.

10.2.4 Additional Frameworks

The GDPR outlines a series of rights that can be exercised by the individual (data subject). These rights include the following:

Before processing begins, the data subject must be informed about the type of data being processed and stored, the purpose of the processing, and the duration of storage. Data protection has long been a crucial aspect of ERP product design, and as mentioned earlier, there are various features in ERP systems that help customers comply with legislation. These features provide a centralized solution to data privacy challenges, reducing the effort required for all ERP applications. The right to prior information is addressed by the Information Retrieval Framework in ERP systems. Additionally, the GDPR mandates that data subjects have the right to request information about the data being processed, which is also covered by the Information Retrieval Framework. Furthermore, data subjects have the right to request the deletion of personal data. Data must be deleted once all retention periods have passed or blocked when the primary purpose has expired, and the residence time has elapsed. The life cycle of personal data in ERP systems must address this issue. Personal data must also be accurate, up to date, and corrected (at the latest upon request). This must be ensured within the applications. Data subjects have the right to restrict processing in certain cases, and automated decisions may be subject to manual intervention, which must also be ensured within the applications. Finally, data subjects have the right to request their stored personal data in a structured, commonly used, and machine-readable format. This process is supported by the Information Retrieval Framework.

Read Access Logging is a framework that logs all read operations when personal data is accessed. It helps clarify situations in case of abuse and ensures that actors who may have access to data in the system but were not supposed to access it can be held accountable for potential consequences. Read Access Logging is often necessary to comply with legal regulations or public standards, such as data protection and privacy, in industries like banking or healthcare. Data protection and privacy involve safeguarding and limiting access to personal information. Some countries' data protection and privacy laws even require reporting access to specific personal data. Companies and government agencies may also want to monitor access to classified or sensitive data for their own reasons. Without a trace or log of data access, it is challenging to identify the person responsible for any data leaks. Read Access Logging provides this information. The framework is based on a logging purpose that is defined according to an organization's needs (e.g., data protection and privacy) and assigned as an attribute to each log entry, allowing log data to be classified and organized based on the logging purpose. Archiving rules or reporting can be created based on logging purposes. Thus, the Read Access Logging framework can be used to comply with legal or other regulations, detect fraud or data theft, conduct audits, or for any other internal purpose.

Change documents are used to track all attribute changes to objects with this feature enabled. Parameters such as date, time, old value, new value, initiator, and more are logged. The framework offers various applications that can be used to view changes made to different objects. Many business objects are frequently changed, and it is often useful or necessary to trace these changes. If changes are logged, customers can always determine what was changed, when it was changed, and how it was changed, which can help in error analysis. Change documents are used to support auditing in financial accounting, for example. A change document records modifications to a business object, created independently of any changes to the database.

10.3 Conclusion

Processing of artificial intelligence must be compliant with data protection and privacy legislations. For example, the training job should only consider personal data for which consent is given. In this section, we determined the business requirements and the necessary technical implementation for general data protection regulation in the context of artificial intelligence. We transferred the legal regulations into technical requirements of blocking, deletion, consent, and automated decision-making. Thus, we built the foundation to implement those legal requirements in ERP software for embedding artificial intelligence. We proposed specific solutions for embedded and side-by-side artificial intelligence. In this chapter, we concluded with additional frameworks that are typically available in ERP systems to resolve legal requirements and are also reused in the context of artificial intelligence.

Configuration

11

In this chapter, we specify the business requirements and propose the solution concept for configuration. ERP software contains predefined artificial intelligence scenarios. This means that for a business question solved by artificial intelligence, all the needed development is provisioned. This includes integration to business processes and user interfaces, defining the data source for training, implementing transformations, and delivering predefined models. However, ERP customers or partners require adapting this artificial content to their specific needs based on configuration. The focus is on artificial intelligence-specific configuration while general concepts are taken as granted, such as configuration of user interfaces, forms, or analytics.

11.1 Problem Statement

Configuration is the process of setting up or adjusting systems at a customer's location to adopt the provided functions with the customer's business needs. This process, also known as customization, is carried out by using the predefined variability of the underlying models. ERP products have always excelled in offering a high degree of flexibility and a broad array of customization options. This allows the standard definition of business software to be adjusted and expanded to address the requirements of each individual user. Presently, ERP systems provide thousands of unique settings for tailoring an installation to suit specific company's needs. However, it is crucial to determine which configuration combinations are semantically correct, which ones result in a reliable business process, and which ones strike the ideal balance between diversification and efficiency. For over a decade, ERP products have supplied reference content, enabling customers to equip their solutions with a consistent and reliable pre-configuration of all relevant business processes and supporting features. This pre-configuration fulfills three key criteria:

© The Author(s), under exclusive license to Springer Nature Switzerland AG 2024
S. Sarferaz, *Embedding Artificial Intelligence into ERP Software*,
https://doi.org/10.1007/978-3-031-54249-7_11

- Quick implementation: Pre-configuration allows for the initiation of ERP system implementation with a basic, consistent set of configurations. In many business domains, customers can start by accepting standard settings as the default and then defining custom settings in focus areas. This approach enables customers to quickly launch a fully functional solution and further customize the application later, reducing the initial total cost of implementation (TCI) and leading to faster deployment and go live.
- Best practices-based approach: ERP vendors draw on their extensive experience to offer a best-of-breed solution for an enterprise's core business processes. Best-practice content achieves a balance between high performance, robust flexibility, and country-specific nuances. This reference content is not inflexible; it can be adjusted and extended at various points. On the other hand, the reference content serves as a de facto standard that allows for a reliable and quick implementation.
- Life cycle compatibility: The business world and the reference content are constantly evolving. The speed at which innovations are adopted in ERP software is a crucial differentiator. New innovations must be easily accessible, simple to use, and highly reliable in terms of quality and performance. Consequently, ERP vendors integrate these changes into the reference content and regularly update the affected installations. However, these updates must not compromise the stability of customers' operational environments. Therefore, the reference content is enriched with life cycle-relevant metadata to manage how changes in existing implementations should be addressed during the upgrade. This enables a secure, automated upgrade process, which is an essential quality. Incompatible changes with the software and its content's life cycle are avoided.

A significant portion of a company's required business functionality is determined by the function of its organizational unit. The unit's purpose must be considered, such as whether it is a sales office, a legal entity, or merely a division of the company. Configuration must accommodate multiple organizational units within a single tenant and separate them using dedicated company codes. Consequently, the configuration and related content must incorporate the appropriate company code for the customizing settings to distinguish between the units. Additionally, the scope varies depending on the purpose of the organizational unit. An organizational unit is usually linked to a physical installation and, therefore, assigned to a legal space. The legal space also influences the selection of correct configuration settings, as country-specific settings that either support legal compliance or represent regional best practices must be chosen over global or general ones.

In the context of artificial intelligence, it is crucial to take into account the following use cases for configuration:

- **Support for multiple models:** For the same scenario, it is essential to have active artificial intelligence models for each data segment. This approach, as opposed to using a single model, can enhance prediction accuracy. For instance, a sales revenue prediction model for all countries may not be as accurate as individual models for each country that take into account specific country characteristics. The artificial intelligence application consuming these models should not manage them individually but rather through a single, stable API. The artificial intelligence infrastructure should automatically determine the appropriate model for a given inference request.

- **Model hyperparameters:** When an artificial intelligence algorithm is tailored for a specific data environment, the model's hyperparameters are configured. These hyperparameters are determined without using actual observed data. Examples include the number of clusters in K-means clustering, the number of leaves in a tree, or the number of hidden layers in a deep neural network. There is a need for mechanisms and tools to maintain, deliver, and apply these hyperparameters.

- **Configuration life cycle management:** User interfaces are necessary for customers to maintain configuration data. It should be possible to manage this data in a test system and securely transfer it to a production system. Configuration data must be stored separately from system and application data. Mechanisms and tools are needed to deliver and apply configurations. Only configuration actions that align with customers' activated ERP business scopes should be suggested. All configurations provided to customers must continue to work after patches and upgrades without manual intervention. Changes to core ERP software must not compromise customer configurations, and extension mechanisms must not jeopardize the ERP system's integrity. Additionally, time-consuming activities before and after upgrades should be minimized.

- **Model training and validation:** For artificial intelligence model training, jobs must be scheduled, either as regular jobs or events. Customers must explicitly activate and deploy trained models for use. Before doing so, they should be able to validate the models. When model accuracy declines, automated retraining should be facilitated to address model degradation. Suitable mechanisms and tools are needed for these activities.

While configuration life cycle management and model training and validation are specific to artificial intelligence, they do not require further investigation here, as they are covered by artificial intelligence life cycle management and tools discussed in the previous life cycle management chapter. However, solutions are needed for multiple model support and model hyperparameters, which are considered in this section.

11.2 Solution Proposal

In this section, we present our proposed solution for configuring and extensibility the use cases of artificial intelligence. Figure 11.1 demonstrates the unique aspects of artificial intelligence that need special attention for configuration and extensibility, which we will explore further in the following chapter. The central design-time component that encompasses all necessary elements for implementing an artificial intelligence scenario is called an intelligent scenario. In essence, it represents the

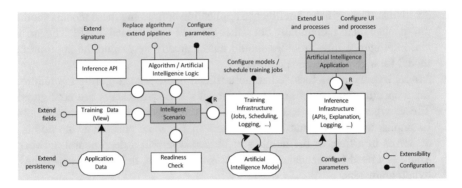

Fig. 11.1 Artificial intelligence artifacts: configuration and extensibility

primary problem being addressed using artificial intelligence. To achieve this, data scientists determine the necessary algorithm and data features.

Application data is required for training the algorithm. As a result, a view is offered that can encompass multiple application tables and carry out initial data transformations. From an extensibility perspective, both the training data view and the underlying persistence can be expanded. Additionally, the algorithm can be replaced, and the hyperparameters can be reconfigured. The artificial intelligence logic, in terms of data transformations and feature engineering, can be adapted to suit a specific customer situation. The inference API's signature is also established during design time as part of the intelligent scenario. As a result, consuming applications and business processes can integrate the inference API during design time. However, the inference API only provides meaningful results once the underlying artificial intelligence model has been trained. The consumption API's signature can be extended with optional fields. Before training any artificial intelligence models, certain readiness checks must be carried out. These evaluations are tailored to the specific artificial intelligence scenario and ensure that all necessary conditions for training have been met, such as the availability of adequate application data or the completion of required process configurations. Once these readiness checks have been successfully completed, the training process can begin. To initiate training, the training infrastructure is employed. This system retrieves the essential metadata from the relevant intelligent scenario, conducts the training, and saves the resulting trained model. The configuration encompasses both the scheduling of training tasks and the activation of artificial intelligence models. The inference infrastructure supplies the consumption API for the particular scenario and model, allowing the artificial intelligence capabilities to be incorporated into applications and business processes. The configuration and adaptability of user interfaces and business processes within the artificial intelligence application are addressed using already-established concepts and frameworks. Since these aspects are not specific to artificial intelligence, they are not discussed in this context.

As previously noted, the primary focus of the configuration implementation lies in supporting multiple models and managing model hyperparameters. Additional requirements are handled by artificial intelligence life cycle management and do not necessitate further exploration in this section.

11.2.1 Multiple Model Support Configuration

Figure 11.2 illustrates the solution framework for supporting multiple models. In some cases, relying on a single, coarse-grained model for an artificial intelligence scenario can lead to suboptimal accuracy and lengthy training processes. To enhance the predictive power of these models, it is essential to run several models concurrently for the same scenario, each based on distinct data segments. To achieve this, both the training infrastructure and runtime need to be adapted for configuration purposes. The design-time artifact for the intelligent scenario contains metadata about the view used to access training data and the consumption application programming interface (API). The collection of intelligent scenarios serves as a starting point for business administrators to schedule training tasks. In this setting, filters are established to divide the training data into segments. During runtime, the training process uses these filter criteria and develops models for each segment. A crucial limitation is that the filter criteria must rely solely on the attributes of the API inference request structure. Once the fine-grained models have been trained, the next hurdle is identifying the relevant model for consumption. This is where the model dispatcher component becomes crucial. When the artificial intelligence application invokes the inference API for consumption, the underlying request is directed to the model dispatcher. By matching the request to the specified filter criteria, the dispatcher forwards the request to the appropriate segment model. This is feasible because both the request and the filter are based on the same set of attributes. For instance, if a sales organization is included in the API inference request signature, it can be used to segment the training data and generate artificial intelligence models tailored to different sales organizations.

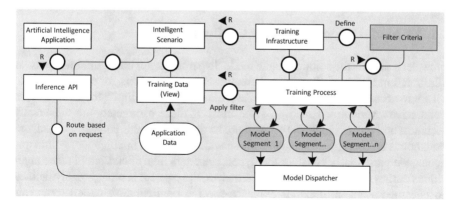

Fig. 11.2 Multiple-model support

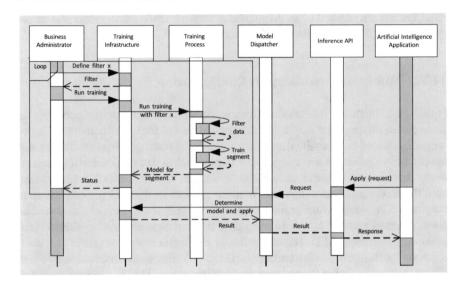

Fig. 11.3 Multiple-model processing

The interaction of these components can be seen in Fig. 11.3. As previously mentioned, the training tasks are organized by the business administrator. For each section, the business administrator must establish the filtering parameters and execute the appropriate training task, leading to highly detailed models. These precise models allow for better coordination of system resource usage, such as memory and CPU time, compared to using a single model for all sections. When it comes to utilizing the models, the right one must be identified. This responsibility falls on the model dispatcher, which directs the inference requests from the artificial intelligence application to the pertinent model. The required association occurs based on the request structure's attributes, which are also used for model segmentation.

11.2.2 Model Hyperparameter Configuration

Now, let's discuss the solution to the model hyperparameter configuration needs, as illustrated in Fig. 11.4. Typically, there are several parameters for configuration to take into account, such as country codes, sales order types, limits for CPU time, or connectivity variables. However, since most of these parameters are universally technical and process related, they will not be discussed in this context. Instead, our attention is on configuration parameters specific to artificial intelligence. Within this scope, we particularly consider the hyperparameters of artificial intelligence algorithms during the training phase. Nevertheless, the concept is more broadly defined to encompass any artificial intelligence-specific configuration parameters. This especially includes configuration parameters necessary for the inference process.

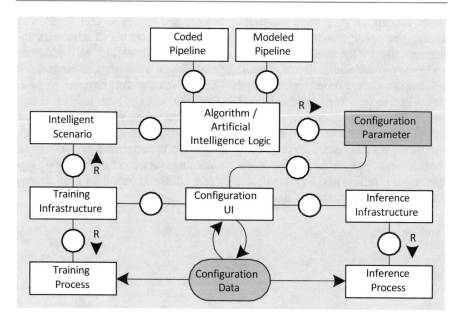

Fig. 11.4 Configuration parameter

The logic behind artificial intelligence involves transforming data, engineering features, initiating algorithms, and executing postprocessing steps. To ensure adaptability, parameters are incorporated into the artificial intelligence logic rather than using fixed values. As a result, various values can be assigned to these parameters during the configuration process. This is particularly true for hyperparameters within the artificial intelligence algorithms, which are adjusted to suit specific customer scenarios, thereby enhancing model precision. Depending on the needs of the particular use case, the artificial intelligence logic can be either programmed or visually represented. While coding offers greater expressiveness, graphical models provide a more comprehensive view. In instances where the artificial intelligence logic requires adaptable configurations, relevant parameters are implemented. Specific values for these parameters can be managed through a universal configuration user interface composed of key-value pairs.

11.3 Conclusion

ERP systems deliver predefined artificial intelligence scenarios. This means that for a business question solved by artificial intelligence, all the needed development is provisioned: integration to business processes and user interfaces, defining the data source for training, and delivering predefined models. However, customers or partners might require adapting this artificial intelligence content to their specific needs based on configuration and extensibility. We focused in this section on artificial intelligence-specific configuration, which is the process by which customers and partners adopt ERP functionality based on predefined variability. ERP products' ability to provide a high degree of flexibility and thus a wide range of customizing options has always been a core strength. This enables standard business software definitions to be adjusted and extended to meet the needs of each individual consumer. We identified the configuration requirements of multiple model support, model hyper-parameterization and the life cycle management of configuration data. For those, we proposed a corresponding solution so that, for example, concurrent models can be run for the same scenario considering specifics of different data segments and resulting into improved accuracy (e.g., different model for each country instead of a global model for all countries).

Extensibility

12

In this chapter, we specify the business requirements and propose the solution concept for extensibility. ERP software includes predefined artificial intelligence scenarios. However, customers or partners might require adopting this artificial intelligence-related content to their specific needs based on extensibility. This might be also necessary for use cases ERP customers or partners develop by themselves. Thus, technical solution is required, which allows enhancements of existing use cases while those extensions are protected from upgrades to avoid been overwritten.

12.1 Problem Statement

The following definition of extensibility serves as a foundation for all extensibility use cases: Extensibility refers to the adaptation of standard software by partners, customers, or ERP vendors, as well as the associated integration into system landscapes. The objective is to provide additional functionality for individual or industry-specific requirements that cannot or should not be addressed by the standard software. Its primary responsibility is to empower business experts to develop simple enhancements independently. Each customer has additional use cases for enhancing the functionality of their ERP implementation. With extensibility for every specific use case, an expert or even individuals without technical expertise can create their own enhancements. These must be suitable for both cloud and on-premise ERP solutions. ERP systems undergo regular patching and upgrading to eliminate security vulnerabilities, fix bugs, and enhance the user experience by introducing valuable new features. As a result, innovations are also delivered through patches and upgrades. However, providing upgrades can take a long time and may not meet specific customer needs, necessitating the constant availability of extensibility mechanisms. Customers typically expand artificial intelligence use cases to increase the accuracy of their artificial intelligence models. Several methods can be used to achieve better models, as detailed in the list of requirements:

© The Author(s), under exclusive license to Springer Nature
Switzerland AG 2024
S. Sarferaz, *Embedding Artificial Intelligence into ERP Software*,
https://doi.org/10.1007/978-3-031-54249-7_12

- **Training data source extension:** The accuracy of artificial intelligence models can be enhanced by incorporating more attributes. Customers should be able to extend the ERP-delivered core data model view for model training with additional fields. Various options must be supported, such as adding fields from extended applications, lower-level core data model views, new core data model views, and external datasets.

- **Algorithm exchange:** The predictive power of artificial intelligence models can be improved by altering the algorithm. Customers should be able to replace the predefined algorithm with a new one of the same type, such as switching from linear regression to exponential regression. To accomplish this, a customer's data scientists must conduct explorations and experiments to identify the best algorithm for their specific situation and data environment.

- **Artificial intelligence logic extension:** Artificial intelligence logic encompasses aspects like data preparation, feature engineering, and transformations. By extending the predefined pipelines of artificial intelligence logic, model accuracy can be improved. Customers must be able to extend the predefined artificial intelligence logic, with data scientists conducting explorations and experiments to determine the best approach for their specific situation and data environment.

- **Consumption API extension:** The consumption API encapsulates the artificial intelligence model and makes it available for integration into applications and business processes. This API includes the necessary request-and-response signature for interacting with the trained model. To prevent disruptions to consuming applications and business processes, the API must remain stable and be extended compatibly. Customers should be able to extend the consumption API with optional fields, such as statistical KPIs to explain prediction results.

- **New artificial intelligence application:** Customers and partners should have the ability to create a new artificial intelligence application from the ground up. This involves modeling core data model views for training, creating intelligent scenarios, defining consumption APIs, and integrating them into business logic. Subsequent development activities are not specific to artificial intelligence, so ERP concepts and tools can be reused.

- **Extensibility life cycle management:** All extensibility capabilities provided to customers must continue to function after patches and upgrades without manual intervention. Extensibility should adhere to the whitelisting approach and only offer measures or objects for extensibility that are designed for those purposes. Changes to the core ERP software must not compromise customer extensions. There should be a clear distinction between standard functionality and extensions, such as through a namespace concept. Extension mechanisms must not compromise the system's integrity, and time-consuming activities before and after upgrades should be avoided. All extensions are created and transported across the system landscape using standard ERP mechanisms, ensuring that a transport contains a complete extension without the need for additional activities and tools.

12.2 Solution Proposal

In this chapter, we resolve the extensibility requirements identified in the previous section.

12.2.1 Training Data Source Extension

The need to expand the training data source involves incorporating more fields to enhance the predictive capabilities of the artificial intelligence model. The choice of additional data fields determines the suitable extensibility method, which may also be combined if needed:

- Custom field extensions involve adding fields from extended applications.
- Data source extensions incorporate fields from fundamental core data model views.
- Custom core data model views that join other ERP views or include fields from new customer core data model views.
- Custom core data model views that connect custom business objects and incorporate fields from external datasets.

Custom field extensions enable the addition of customer-specific fields to an application's business context in a one-to-one relationship or the inclusion of ERP fields found in the application's tables and structures. This method relies on extension includes, which are nearly empty includes with a placeholder field in the ERP system's data dictionary. These extension includes serve as anchor points for enhancements and are part of all necessary structures, such as databases, API structures, or service implementations. Enhancement fields are part of data dictionary appends, a modification-free extensibility approach. Custom field extensions are based on extension includes, which must be explicitly prepared by the application. In this scenario, database tables and data dictionary structures must be integrated as extension includes to establish a stable anchor point for data dictionary appends. Custom fields are then added via data dictionary appends, and the application's coding must generically transfer extension fields between structures/internal tables using move-corresponding techniques. For training data, extensible core data model views must offer an extension include association to an extension include view. This extension include view is based on the database table containing only key fields and, later, custom fields from the extension include. The extension include view serves as a stable anchor point for view extensions and makes extension fields accessible on extensible views through the extension include association. Custom fields are added to the extension include view as soon as they are incorporated into the persistency. Extensible views are extended when selected in the custom field UI dialog because not all consumers can traverse the extension include association to access custom fields (refer to Fig. 12.1).

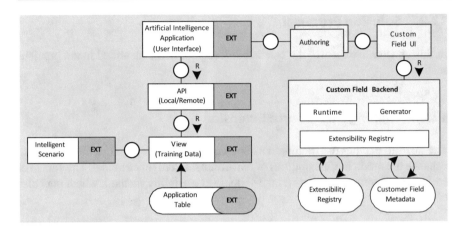

Fig. 12.1   Core data model view: customer field extension

The structural definition of local and remote application programming interfaces must include the extension as well. Based on the specific implementation, manually written sections in the application programming interface's implementation need to be deliberately designed for expandability by invoking extensibility function modules, such as those that improve metadata or transfer extension data between internal and external structures. At a client location, a key user initiates the custom field user interface, which enables the user to define the technical aspects of a custom field (e.g., label, type, length) and offers a list of where the field is used. This tool can be used independently or, ideally, incorporated into the user interface's runtime authoring. The list of where the field is used relies on the extensibility registry, which recognizes all application programming interfaces and core data model views and reveals the extended persistence. When choosing an entry in the list of where the field is used, the underlying application programming interface and core data model view are expanded. As a result, the relevant consumers have access to the extension field in their field catalog, and they can use it like any standard field provided by the enterprise resource planning solution. Following that, the data source extension enables customers to incorporate new enterprise resource planning standard fields from the underlying core data model views. The core data model view for model training is typically constructed on top of basic core data model views. These basic views may contain fields that could be integrated into the training process to enhance the predictive capabilities of the artificial intelligence model.

Figure 12.2 demonstrates the fundamental concept of extending data sources. The core data model, referred to as View 1, which is to be improved, must be made available in the extensibility registry. Additional fields can be chosen from the View 2.1 (Field1) subview or from the View 2.2 (Field2)/View 2.3 (Field3) views, which can be accessed through 0..1 associations. From the perspective of a key user, the data source for the extension must be selected and enhanced within the custom field

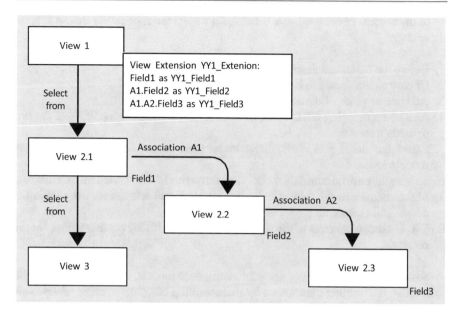

Fig. 12.2 Core data model view: data source extension

application. Including extra standard fields may allow end users to access restricted data in the expanded data source without the necessary authorization. Moreover, depending on the field path and the nature of the chosen fields, data retrieval might become slower after a data source extension has been implemented. If the previously mentioned methods of customer field and data source extension are insufficient or inapplicable, new core data model view modeling is necessary. Situations where this may occur include needing fields from core data model views of other view hierarchies or when the training core data model view is not registered for data source extension. A new training core data model view can be established to combine fields from other core data model view hierarchies, access different data tables, or reduce the fields of existing training core data model views using SQL projection. We suggest introducing a Custom Core Data Model View app, which allows key users to model customer-specific data access on top of public core data model views. Additionally, previously created custom core data model views should serve as a foundation for new custom core data model views. The Custom Core Data Model View application should offer the following features:

- Display a list of all ERP-delivered data sources and existing custom data sources, including personal custom core data model views
- Show details of available data sources and custom core data model views
- Search for a specific data source or custom core data model view
- Filter by data source name, label, type, and the user who last published the view
- Create a core data model view

In the context of creating core data model views, the application should support these steps:

1. Define the name and description of the new custom view.
2. Choose a data source to be used as the primary data source.
3. Add one or more associated data sources.
4. Assign the mapping fields of the associated data sources to the fields of the primary data source.
5. Select the fields and associations to be used in the new custom core data model view.
6. Expose the custom core data model view through a REST service for external use.
7. Make changes to the semantics of the selected data sources for use within the new custom core data model view.
8. Display the parameters of the selected data sources if they contain a filter for the result set.

To enhance the precision of artificial intelligence models, it may also be essential to broaden the training data source by incorporating customer-specific tables. This concept of table extensibility refers to the ability to add fields unique to a customer within the business context of an application, either in a one-to-one or one-to-many relationship. New tables tailored to the customer are generated in the database and paired with core data model views. These core data model views can be merged with the provided core data model view for model training, resulting in a new data source. In the context of customer-specific tables, there are two types of enhancements that can be identified:

- New independent custom tables that are not sub-tables of ERP tables are populated through a user interface or data import from other customer systems. These independent tables may serve as code lists, process control tools, or facts or dimensions for transactional and analytical purposes. An additional enhancement could involve grouping several independent custom tables into a hierarchy, forming a new application with basic business logic. This feature is accessible as a custom business object.
- Custom tables are used to introduce fields to ERP business contexts in a one-to-many relationship (e.g., a customer's hobbies) or to address the technical limitations of field extensibility in the case of one-to-one relationship extensions. In this scenario, the custom data behaves similarly to standard ERP data (for instance, inheriting authorization from the ERP parent), and custom data is removed when the parent is deleted. This use case necessitates that ERP applications be designed for this type of extensibility, which is typically not the case.

We propose developing a Custom Business Object application that allows customers to create and manage business objects. A custom business object is a hierarchical collection of database tables with an API for creating, retrieving, updating, and deleting data. Business logic can be supplied in a Web editor using code. The Custom Business Object application should support the following features:

- Create business objects and their corresponding database tables
- Add fields to business objects
- Remove fields and business objects that have not yet been transferred to the production system
- Create core data model views, REST services, and a user interface for data entry or importing data from other customer systems
- Establish multiple sub-nodes for a single business object
- Define fields of association type to other custom business objects and standard ERP business objects
- Implement custom logic at the node level
- Write to custom business objects from custom logic
- Publish business objects
- Modify published business objects
- Revert business objects to their most recent published version
- Copy or delete an existing custom business object
- Conduct a trace

The intelligent scenario automatically reflects the data source extension, depending on how it is expanded, as it only maintains a reference to the core data model view. Specifically, the data source extension must not result in an incompatible change to the consumption API.

12.2.2 Algorithm Exchange and Artificial intelligence Logic Extension

Now, let us discuss the exchange of algorithms and the expansion of artificial intelligence logic. The term *artificial intelligence logic* pertains to the implementation of necessary steps for the processing of training and inference. These steps encompass data validation, statistical calculations, transformations, feature reduction, and the computation of model accuracy metrics. The artificial intelligence logic for training and inference is tailored to specific scenarios. Expanding artificial intelligence logic involves adapting the ERP standard-delivered content with customer enhancements that can withstand upgrades. In the context of training logic, algorithms can be primarily exchanged to enhance the predictive power of the model. However, it is typically meaningful to replace an algorithm with another of the same type, such as substituting linear regression with robust linear regression. To augment artificial intelligence logic, different approaches are needed based on the underlying technology:

- **Automated Library**
- The artificial intelligence logic for training and inference is integrated into the library implementation itself. Consequently, the required artificial intelligence logic is supplied automatically by the library. Enhancements are driven by metadata and are also provided without explicit development activities. Various AutoML libraries in the community operate in this manner.

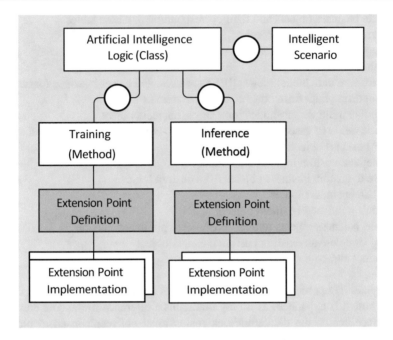

Fig. 12.3 Service library extensibility

- **Service Library**
- This library is used for breakout scenarios, which are generally more complex compared to automated-based ones. The artificial intelligence logic for training and inference is implemented as a coded class with interfaces, as illustrated in Fig. 12.3. The extensibility of the coded class relies on extension point definitions, which serve as the foundation for object plug-ins that enhance functions in coding without necessitating modifications. Extension point definitions facilitate the creation of enhancement options in the form of interfaces that can be suitably implemented later in the same system or an external system by customers. Upgrades of the original business function can be applied without losing customer-specific enhancements and without merging changes. The two code lines (the original and customer-specific coding) are strictly separated yet integrated.
- Extension points should differentiate between the definition and individual implementations. The ERP vendor typically creates the definition of an extension point, and along with its calling points in coding, it constitutes an explicit enhancement option in such programs. The definition of an enhancement point includes an interface, a set of selection filters, and some settings that influence runtime behavior later. An extension point interface constitutes the entire interface or part of the interface of an object plug-in. The term *extension point implementation* refers to an enhancement implementation element, consisting of an

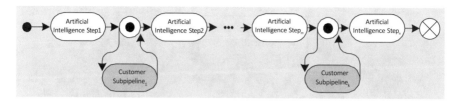

Fig. 12.4 Pipeline extensibility

extension point implementation class that implements the extension point interface and a condition imposed on the filters specified in the extension point definition. These can be utilized to select the extension point implementation. The calling points of an extension are determined through corresponding methods, which form the enhancement calls.

- **AI Technology Platform**
  For advanced scenarios, such as image recognition or natural language processing, which necessitate the use of neural networks, graphics processing units (GPUs), and external data, AI technology platforms come into play. In this context typically, the logic for training and inference in artificial intelligence is visually modeled through pipelines. Furthermore, core data model extraction views can be integrated into these pipelines to access training data. As shown in Fig. 12.4, enhancement points must be incorporated into the pipelines by ERP development to allow for customer-specific customization. Naturally, the enhancements should be positioned where they are semantically meaningful, such as after the provided data validation steps, so that additional validations can be included. Customers implement these extensions as sub-pipelines, which should remain stable after upgrading the ERP-provided portions of the pipelines. The pipelines are made available to the ERP system for consumption through REST APIs. As a result, it is crucial that the pipeline extensibility leads to stable and compatible REST APIs.

12.2.3 Consumption API Extensibility

Moving forward, we delve into the topic of extensibility in consumption application programming interfaces. When it comes to applying artificial intelligence, a variety of APIs are set up and utilized, as depicted in Fig. 12.5. The choice between remote or local APIs depends on how the artificial intelligence scenario is executed. Local APIs are invoked within the ERP system, whereas remote APIs venture beyond the system's boundaries and toward the AI technology platform.

The artificial intelligence application utilizes a consumption API for integration into business operations and user interfaces. The consumption can be either local or

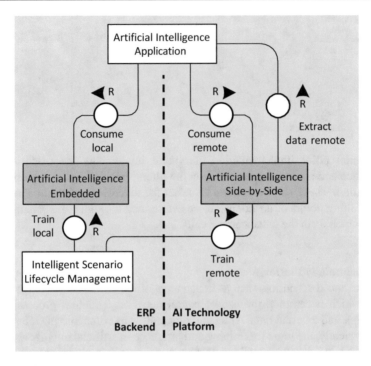

Fig. 12.5 Consumption API extensibility

remote, depending on whether the use case is implemented in an embedded or side-by-side mode. To train the models for artificial intelligence, a training API is available, which can also be local or remote based on the implementation approach. The Intelligent Scenario Lifecycle Management framework oversees the orchestration of these training APIs and is responsible for managing the life cycle of the artificial intelligence models (refer to the life cycle management chapter). For embedded artificial intelligence, training data can be accessed locally via the ERP platform. However, this is not feasible for side-by-side artificial intelligence. As a result, an API for transferring application data from the ERP to the artificial intelligence technology platform must be supplied. Various tools are available for implementing these APIs, depending on the underlying technology. It is crucial from an extensibility standpoint that all mentioned APIs are enhanced for compatibility, ensuring that the API consumer does not break after extensibility. This is particularly important for consumption APIs integrated into artificial intelligence applications and business processes. Consequently, both local and remote consumption APIs should only be extended with optional fields, and existing fields in the signature should remain unchanged, not deleted, or renamed or have their data types replaced. To guarantee stability and compatibility, governance measures and automatic checks are necessary. Since the Intelligent Scenario Lifecycle Management framework orchestrates the training APIs, there is more flexibility regarding extensibility. However, to enable generic handling, the signatures of training APIs are uniform and do not include any business process-related parameters. As a result, there is no use case for extensibility concerning the training APIs. The situation differs for data extraction APIs, which can be extended as additional fields will be taken into account for model training. Data extraction APIs are built on core data model views for data extraction. To extend such an API, the underlying core data model view must be extended first. As the core data model view extraction is based on generic data integration technology (refer to the data integration chapter), extending the core data model view automatically adapts the API and the consuming artificial intelligence technology platform functionality. This allows the consumer to access the extended fields while the data integration processes continue to function, ensuring the extensibility of the data extraction API.

12.2.4 New Artificial Intelligence App

The latest requirement for extending artificial intelligence applications aims to empower customers and partners to develop an artificial intelligence application from beginning to end. As depicted in Fig. 12.6, this necessitates that the customer can generate all essential design-time components. The assumption is that data scientists have already completed the exploration phase, allowing the focus to be placed on the development objects.

The initial step involves working with application data. In most cases, the standard ERP tables are adequate and can be repurposed. If there is a need for custom

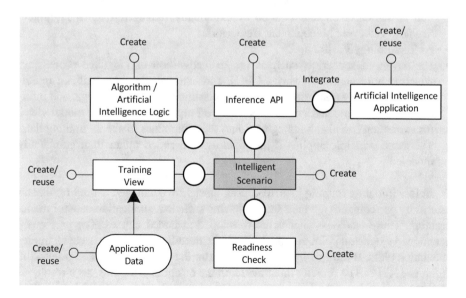

Fig. 12.6 New artificial intelligence application

tables, the Customer Business Object application, as previously mentioned, can be used. New core data model views can be built on top of the application tables using the recommended Custom Core Data Model Views app. In this context, existing core data model views can be reused. Intelligent scenarios serve as the central element for managing the life cycle of all development objects. The Intelligent Scenario Lifecycle Management framework can be used to create this artifact. Since an intelligent scenario always represents a single use case for artificial intelligence, existing intelligent scenarios cannot be reused. The way the artificial intelligence logic (e.g., data transformations, feature reduction) and inference API are provided varies based on the underlying library:

- **Automated Library**
- In the context of the intelligent scenario, the inference API is defined and generated during the activation step. The Intelligent Scenario Lifecycle Management framework provisions the core data model view and a corresponding coding class as a result of the generation. Therefore, no custom coding is necessary. This also applies to the artificial intelligence logic related to transformation or feature reduction, as automated libraries (e.g., AutoML) integrate these data science activities into the library implementation itself.
- **Service Library**
- This library is used for more complex breakout scenarios than those based on automated libraries. The artificial intelligence logic and inference API are implemented as a coding class with a specified interface. As a result, developers can extend or replace data transformations or post-processing according to the data scientists' specifications. The predefined interfaces ensure that the implementation is standardized and can be systematically managed by the Intelligent Scenario Lifecycle Management framework.
- **AI Technology Platform**
- For advanced scenarios, such as image recognition or language processing, which require neural networks, GPUs, and external data, the artificial intelligence technology platform is utilized. The artificial intelligence logic and inference APIs are modeled graphically based on pipelines. Core data model views for extraction can also be integrated into these pipelines to access training data. The same principle applies if the pipelines are coded rather than graphically modeled.

Before initiating training jobs, readiness checks are conducted to confirm that all necessary prerequisites are met, such as having sufficient application data for model training. These readiness checks are developed as coded classes. The previously mentioned extension point approach should be used for the readiness check implementation class. If the existing applications offer the required extension points, the inference API can be directly integrated into the business processes. As a result, all design-time artifacts can be implemented to support a new artificial intelligence application by customers and partners.

12.2.5 Extensibility Life Cycle Management

Extensibility life cycle management falls under the umbrella of solutions and tools designed for general life cycle management. There are no specific concerns related to artificial intelligence that need to be addressed. As such, we will only provide a few general observations in this context. All essential user extensibility components should adhere to the principles of decoupled extensions:

- Customers must be able to use all extensibility features without manual intervention after an ERP software update; this means that ERP software updates are not dependent on customer adaptations.
- Extensibility objects should never block an update of the core ERP software.

To uphold these fundamental principles, custom artifacts must conform to the following guidelines:

- Custom artifacts should be technically free of modifications; they are created as own objects that reference the base object.
- Custom artifacts should be technically conflict-free. Additionally, extensions should not conflict with parts of the core ERP objects added later, nor should they conflict with extensions from different extending parties. This requirement is met by using a unique namespace that is taken into account at every level of the architecture.
- Custom artifacts should only utilize released, stable ERP extension points and APIs. This can be ensured through object/code checks. On the ERP side, checks prevent incompatible changes to objects marked as released/extensible and previously delivered. A deprecation mechanism is necessary since, over time, incompatible changes may be needed for the API, such as due to changes in underlying business processes or database tables. Since such incompatible changes disrupt existing applications, they must be notified in advance that the current API will be deprecated and replaced with a new one. This allows consumers ample time to react to the incompatible changes.

For business-critical applications, extensions are usually developed and tested before being activated for all users in the production environment. In cloud deployment, the key user transports extensibility objects from the test to the production system without interacting with the service provider and outside the service provider's maintenance window. In an on-premise environment, customers have much more flexibility in development and system landscape setup, as well as quality assurance processes. As a result, customers can manage ERP updates and customer transports for key user extensibility using traditional transport tools. Extensions created with key user tools can be combined with transports featuring custom development done with classic development tools.

12.3   Conclusion

Extensibility plays an important role in the context of business applications. The software is supposed to be dynamically adjustable to the present businesses needs and the future ones too. Another benefit of extensibility is that software can be even more function rich, because add-ons could target a very specific or unique problem without bloating the core software. It is important to distinguish at least two roles within the extensibility process: the line-of-business (LOB) expert and the developer (or sufficiently skilled IT expert). Extension projects are triggered and driven by business experts. Therefore, it is essential to incorporate them by providing suitable, non-technical extensibility tools. Still, certain tasks require the involvement of the IT expert/developer. Key requirements concerning extensibility are:

- Ensure stability after upgrades: Customers and partners extension must continue to work after patches and upgrades, without any manual or automated after-import activities.
- Enable multilayer extensibility: Multilayer extensions shall be supported in terms of allowing customer extensions on top of industry extensions.
- Avoid changing ERP delivered artifacts: Modification of ERP standard objects can be overwritten after updates and upgrades. Modifications of the ERP functionality discontinuous the customers from new innovations provided with updates and upgrades.

ERP software includes predefined artificial intelligence scenarios. However, customers or partners might require adopting this artificial intelligence content to their specific needs based on extensibility. This might be also necessary for use cases that customers and partners develop by themselves. Therefore, in this section, we identified the business requirements and the proposed necessary technical implementation for extensibility in the context of artificial intelligence.

Model Degradation

13

In this chapter, we specify the business requirements and propose the solution concept for model degradation. Over the course of time, the prediction power of artificial intelligence models decreases due to changes in the data environment. Determining this time point and triggering retraining is the objective of model degradation. However, this is a challenging task as in addition to statistical techniques, feedback of the users is required and also the ability to parallelly run models in ERP systems. Our focus is less on the data science methods for model degradation but on the integration aspects regarding ERP software.

13.1 Problem Statement

In the process of creating an intelligent ERP system that utilizes algorithms derived from artificial intelligence, the life cycle is usually not static. The model, after its initial training with a specific dataset, requires continuous retraining as it encounters new data during its operation, as depicted in Fig. 13.1. This new data also encompasses feedback and inputs from the system's end users.

The act of retraining is a distinguishing feature that separates artificial intelligence systems from traditional ones. This ongoing process imposes specific requirements on the user experience and, based on the feedback loop's structure, necessitates the inclusion of new roles like data scientists and specialized user interfaces for tracking and data examination. Notably, as the surrounding environment changes over time, the predictive accuracy of artificial intelligence models tends to diminish, necessitating periodic retraining or even complete remodeling. This phenomenon is referred to as model degradation. Model degradation is the gradual decline in a model's performance over time. This decline can be attributed to several factors, including data drift, overfitting, and suboptimal hyperparameter tuning. Data drift is a situation where the data distribution changes over time, which in turn reduces the model's accuracy. Overfitting happens when the model is overly complex and learns

S. Sarferaz, *Embedding Artificial Intelligence into ERP Software*, https://doi.org/10.1007/978-3-031-54249-7_13

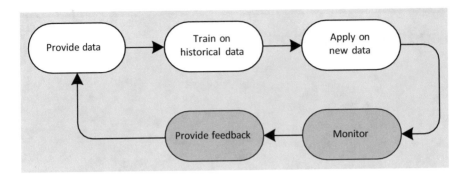

Fig. 13.1 Artificial intelligence model life cycle

the training data too well, which reduces its accuracy when applied to new data. Suboptimal hyperparameter tuning happens when the model is not fully optimized, leading to a drop in performance. The crucial issue that needs to be addressed is: What are the ways to identify and rectify model degradation?

13.2 Solution Proposal

In order to effectively address the issue of model degradation, it's crucial to consistently monitor the precision of the artificial intelligence model. It's necessary to include feedback mechanisms, and the artificial intelligence models should be validated using data sets that mirror environmental changes. If there's a decline in the model's performance, specifically in its predictive accuracy, then it becomes necessary to initiate retraining or even a complete overhaul of the model. The following sections will outline chosen strategies to identify model degradation. Notably, there are a variety of statistical techniques that can be used to mathematically tackle model degradation. However, this viewpoint from data science is assumed as a given and is not the focus of this discussion. Our deliberations are centered on the integration aspects of model degradation that are related to ERP.

13.2.1 Accuracy KPIs

Determining the precision of an artificial intelligence model is crucial in assessing the model's deterioration. An artificial intelligence model is essentially a function that correlates a specific set of values for the input variables to the appropriate corresponding values for the output variable. The process of identifying such a function for a specific dataset is referred to as model training. Effective models not only minimize errors for known input values but also generate predictions for scenarios that are only somewhat analogous to the situations already recorded in the existing data table. For all artificial intelligence techniques, it's critical to understand the performance of the artificial intelligence model, whether it's a decision tree or a deep learning model. So, how do we determine the precision of an artificial intelligence model? The fundamental concept is to train an artificial intelligence model on a specific dataset and then apply that underlying function to data points for which the output value is already known. This leads to two output values: the actual one and the prediction from the artificial intelligence model. It's then relatively straightforward to calculate how often the predictions are incorrect by comparing the predictions with the actual values. This forms the basis of various static methods to calculate accuracy key performance indicators (KPIs). For instance, for classification, regression, or clustering models, the predictive power and prediction confidence can be evaluated. The *predictive power* assesses the artificial intelligence model's ability to predict the target variable's values using input variables present in the input dataset. The predictive power indicator ranges from 0% to 100%. Ideally, this value should be as close to 100% as possible, without being exactly 100%. A predictive power of 1 represents a theoretically perfect model, where the input variables can account for 100% of the information in the target variable. However, in practice, this usually suggests that an input variable that is 100% correlated with the target variable was not removed from the dataset analyzed. A predictive power of 0 represents a completely random model with no predictive strength. To enhance a model's predictive power, consider adding new variables to the training dataset and combining input variables. For instance, a model with a predictive power of 79% can account for 79% of the variation in the target variable using the input variables in the analyzed dataset. There is no precise threshold to distinguish a good model from a poor predictive model in terms of predictive power, as this depends on the business case. The *prediction confidence* reflects the model's robustness to achieve the same performance when applied to a new dataset that shares the same characteristics as the training dataset. The prediction confidence indicator also ranges from 0% to 100%. A model with a prediction confidence of 95% or higher is considered robust and has a strong generalization capacity. A prediction confidence below 95% should be treated with caution, as there is a risk of producing unreliable results if the model is applied to a new dataset. To enhance the prediction confidence, typically, more observation rows are added to the training dataset. The accuracy KPIs need to be constantly monitored. If, for instance, the predictive power and/or the prediction confidence of the model on the control dataset are significantly low, it implies that the relationship between the input variables and the target variable has changed. When this occurs, it is advisable to retrain the artificial intelligence model using new data.

13.2.2 Drift and Skew Detection

The strategy of accuracy key performance indicators (KPIs) that was previously discussed is designed to keep track of the relationship between the input variables and the predicted target variable. However, the detection of drift and skew is more concerned with managing the distribution of the input and prediction variables. The detection of drift and skew is a method that identifies shifts in a dataset's data distribution over time. This method is used when a dataset appears to have deviated from its initial distribution or when the data seems to have become disproportionately skewed in a particular direction. This method can be used to identify anomalies in the data, such as outliers or changes in the data distribution. It can also be used to detect changes in the underlying data generating process, such as changes in the underlying parameters or assumptions. In the case of live data, the predictions made by the artificial intelligence model are monitored. If the distribution of these predictions begins to change, it could indicate that the model is degrading, or at the very least, it could be worth investigating. For example, if the model is being used to classify images as either urban or nature, and for the first month, it was predicting urban for 50% of the images and nature for the rest and then, in the following month, the distribution suddenly shifted to 90% urban, this could be a sign of model degradation. Similarly, the distribution of the input can also be monitored. For instance, if we have a model that classifies texts and we suddenly start receiving text documents with new words or the frequency of certain words begins to increase, then it suggests that the data distribution has shifted and the model has likely deteriorated.

13.2.3 Feedback Loops

The input from a final user is a crucial element in strengthening the foundational data model. If the feedback is negative, it suggests that the performance of the model is declining, which may necessitate a retraining or even a complete remodeling. As depicted in Fig. 13.2, there are various forms of feedback that can be identified.

Implicit feedback ❶ is obtained by monitoring the actions of the user. This includes tracking the user's navigation routes and search inquiries, as well as interactions related to business processes, such as overruling predictions, as demonstrated in Fig. 13.2. The user has the ability to change the classification outcome by moving the SUBJECT into different categories using implicit feedback. The collection of implicit feedback generates a wealth of data, which is typically consolidated for user groups. Implicit feedback is more indicative of user behavior than explicit

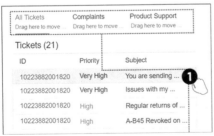

Fig. 13.2 Types of feedback

feedback because it reflects the actions users actually take. This type of feedback can be collected unobtrusively, without interrupting the user's experience. However, this also implies that the user is not aware of the process. One of the drawbacks of implicit feedback is its weak correlation with the user's long-term behavior. We suggest using methods of implicit feedback under the following conditions:

- If the collection of appropriate feedback is essential for regularly retraining the model and explicit feedback methods are not sufficient
- If users are not likely to accurately record their feedback using explicit feedback methods
- If the user's primary task involves making the decisions that are being monitored

Explicit feedback ❷ comes from direct engagement with the user, such as through ranking systems, voting, flagging, polling, or commenting. However, this type of feedback can be more prone to bias, particularly if it's not limited to users with expertise. The nature of explicit feedback is subjective, as it depends on the user's personal views, which may not always align with their actual behavior. While explicit feedback is clear to the user, it can also be disruptive and negatively affect the user experience, posing a significant design challenge. Despite this, it is a crucial source of information for refining long-term strategies. In certain situations, explicit feedback can also lessen the work needed to retrain models. We suggest using methods of explicit feedback when:

- The user has the option to provide feedback but it's not a requirement
- The process of giving feedback doesn't require a significant amount of mental effort
- The act of providing feedback doesn't distract users from their main tasks

Delayed feedback is a method of collecting explicit feedback from users without interrupting their workflow. If the system requires feedback from the user, for instance, to understand why an approved amount surpasses the system's recommendation, it doesn't disrupt the user with a feedback form. Instead, the user is simply informed that feedback is needed and can decide whether to respond immediately or continue working and provide feedback later. The user can access a list of all pending feedback questions that need responses and address them at their convenience. The primary design challenge with the delayed feedback system is recreating the context of the user's decision when the user provides feedback to the system at a later time. To tackle common feedback problems, feedback data might need extra processing before it can be used for model degradation. For instance, implicit feedback could be influenced by event-related bias, or explicit feedback might only represent the views of a specific user group. In these situations, the feedback might first need to be evaluated by a user in a different role, such as a data scientist, using a separate user interface.

Choosing the right input control requires considering various ways of asking for feedback and how effectively we can use the insights gained. The method and format of feedback collection determine the quality of the feedback. We distinguish between structured user input and unstructured user input. Structured user input allows us to gather very specific feedback by asking a closed question with a set of given options. The user can only respond in the predefined format and cannot freely provide feedback. Structured feedback typically involves focused questions that can be answered with a simple yes or no, and the feedback usually pertains to the quality of recommendations. Unstructured user input, on the other hand, allows us to collect unrestricted feedback by asking open-ended questions. This enables the user to provide complex responses and offer feedback on aspects we may not have considered. This method allows for the collection of insights on external real-world factors that are not part of the ERP system. Unstructured feedback typically involves open-ended questions that invite unlimited responses. The feedback is collected to gain information on the quality and performance of intelligence services. Additional characteristics include collecting feedback to understand user behavior on the user interface while performing a task and that processing feedback requires time and detailed investigation for accurate interpretation.

13.2.4 Solution Architecture

The strategies for managing the degradation of model accuracy, such as key performance indicators, detection of drift and skew, and feedback loops, can be effectively put into practice with the solution we suggest in Fig. 13.3.

The artifact of an artificial intelligence scenario represents an application of artificial intelligence. The idea of artificial intelligence scenarios ensures a consistent

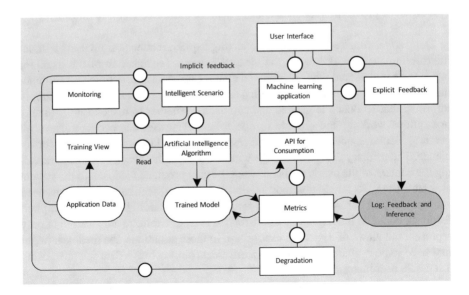

Fig. 13.3 Model degradation solution

management throughout the life cycle and facilitates monitoring at the level of business processes. Above the application tables, we define views of the core data model, which embody the semantic data model of the ERP system. These core data model views conceal the encrypted database models and encapsulate them into entities that are understandable to humans. In addition to the SQL view definition, these core data model views include domain-specific metadata, referred to as annotations. For applications of artificial intelligence, a specific view of the core data model is provided for model training. During the training process, artificial intelligence algorithms access the application data. The artificial intelligence model, once trained, is stored in the database system.

To make it accessible for use, the fully trained model of artificial intelligence is encapsulated within an application programming interface (API). This allows the capabilities of artificial intelligence to be seamlessly incorporated into business operations and their corresponding user interfaces. The component responsible for metrics calculates key performance indicators (KPIs) of accuracy during the training phase by partitioning the data from the application into training and validation sets. The validation sets serve as a basis to measure the performance of the trained model. The component that handles degradation interprets the accuracy KPIs and offers suggestions to the monitoring module, such as the need for retraining with a larger dataset or adjusting the model's definition. The metrics component can also provide drift and skew detection as it can continuously analyze the stream of inference calls in terms of input and prediction. Depending on the method used for drift and skew detection, the data from the inference could either be temporarily stored or processed in real time, eliminating the need for data persistence. Implicit feedback is typically stored as part of the application data and is reflected in the training process as per the metrics component, as depicted in Fig. 13.3. The management of explicit feedback is generally more intricate and is not automatically included in the design of the application table. Hence, we recommend having a universal persistency for the explicit feedback to minimize the total cost of development (TCD) for application development. With the explicit feedback and the associated inference data in terms of input and predictions, the degradation component can easily generate evidence for the performance of the artificial intelligence model. Since the provision of explicit feedback occurs after the execution of the related inference call, establishing a correlation between the two is usually a challenging task.

In the diagram labeled as Fig. 13.4, we propose a method to identify the deterioration of a model based on implicit feedback, eliminating the need for additional exploration of the impacted artificial intelligence application. This is achievable because such implicit feedback is preserved within the application's data and is made accessible through core data model views for model training.

The ticketing scenario previously depicted in diagram 13.2 exemplifies this: the user has the ability to overrule the ticket priority suggested by the artificial intelligence model. This priority adjustment is recorded and can be interpreted as implicit feedback. If the artificial intelligence's recommendation is frequently overridden, it could signal a decline in the model's precision. The ticket priority embodies the target variable and is thus included in the core data model view for model training.

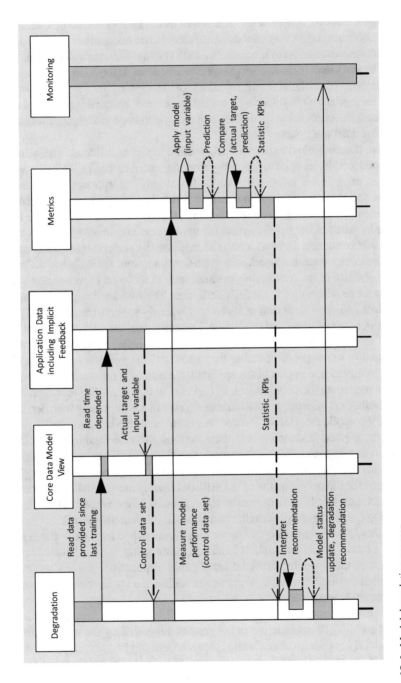

Fig. 13.4 Model degradation process

These core data model views are typically time-dependent, containing fields for selecting data records for a specific time frame. To evaluate the performance of the artificial intelligence model, the degradation component utilizes the view for model training to access new data that has become available since the last training session. Since implicit feedback is incorporated into the application data, this control dataset includes the actual values for the target variables and the value of the input parameters. The current version of the trained model is used to compute the predictions based on the input values. This is the responsibility of the metrics component, which also compares the actual and predicted values to compute static key performance indicators (KPIs). The degradation component interprets these KPIs and suggests corresponding actions (for instance, retraining or remodeling), which are presented in the monitoring view.

13.3 Conclusion

In the course of time, the prediction power of artificial intelligence models decreases due to changes in the data environment. Determining this time point and triggering retraining is the objective of model degradation. It is essential to anticipate how data will evolve over time in all artificial intelligence projects. In fact, before we use a model, its accuracy is at its highest. Model degradation is a phenomenon that has been extensively researched in academics for the past 20 years, although industry best practices still frequently overlook it. Thus, it is important to regularly assess model performance on new data sets. To know when to take action, these performance traces should be periodically compared and shown. There are many KPIs available to evaluate model performance. Without a strategy for routinely evaluating performance measurements and initiating model retraining or rebuilding, we are able to detect performance loss but lack a system for addressing it. Explicit and implicit feedback must be also taken into account, which are, in the context of ERP systems, complex to resolve. In this section, we deducted the business requirements and the necessary technical implementation for model degradation regarding ERP software. We proposed, for example, feedback loops as an important technique for resolving model degradation. Implicit, explicit, and delayed feedback loops were depicted.

Explanation of Results

14

In this chapter, we specify the business requirements and propose the solution concept for explainability. To build trust between human and machine, it's important to explain the results provided by artificial intelligence models. Transparency and traceability of artificial intelligence models are also needed for statutory reasons. However, depending on the underlying artificial intelligence techniques, this can be very challenging, for example, neuronal networks are hard to explain. In the context of ERP systems, additionally, the explanation must be transferred into a business language. Thus, user interface designers must investigate long time, for each use case translates the statistical numbers into the end user's business domain.

14.1 Problem Statement

When an algorithm's underlying model is adequately explained, and the rationale behind its results is made clear, a foundation of trust is established between humans and machines. Assessing trust is a crucial factor for humans to act based on a prediction. This element becomes even more significant in the context of ERP business applications, where users are legally responsible for every decision they make. The concept of explainable artificial intelligence implies that the logic behind the suggestions of an intelligent system can be elucidated in a timely and contextual manner. This approach facilitates the building of trust and allows for the anticipation of legal requirements related to automated decision-making. The need for explanations from artificial intelligence should be considered under one or more of the following circumstances:

- **Criticality**
  When there is a substantial risk linked to making an incorrect decision and the actions taken are difficult to undo, an explanation for the system's suggestion

shall be necessary. Conversely, if the risk is minimal and actions can be easily reversed, users may not require an explanation.

- **Complexity**
  When users find it challenging to immediately evaluate the impact and quality of their decisions, they may need additional input. On the other hand, if users can readily determine whether a suggestion is suitable without any training, they may not need further information.
- **Transparency**
  When a business process is subject to rigorous auditing requirements, auditors must be able to trace transactions back and understand the reasoning behind each step of execution. However, if there are no auditing requirements, explanations may not be necessary, assuming they are also not required by end users.
- **Volatility**
  When the artificial intelligence application needs to adjust to shifting conditions or requirements, it relies on continuous feedback. Conversely, if the feedback has little or no impact on the algorithm's output or the user experience, providing an additional explanation may be more of a distraction than a help.

14.2   Solution Proposal

When considering ERP software, we are faced with two primary inquiries related to explainable artificial intelligence:

- What design principles should we use to incorporate explainable artificial intelligence into the user interfaces?
- What elements need to be incorporated into the ERP backend to facilitate explainable artificial intelligence?

This chapter will not delve into the techniques used to generate explanations for specific artificial intelligence algorithms. These methods are well-known in the data science community and taken as granted. Therefore, this discussion will focus solely on aspects specific to ERP, as guided by the aforementioned questions.

14.2.1 User Interface

The level of information that individuals require to comprehend a system proposal can fluctuate. This variation is influenced by the specific technique of artificial intelligence being used, the context in which it is used, the task the user is performing, and the role of the user. We can distinguish between three levels of explanation:

1. **Indicator (What?)**
   This represents the most basic level of explanation. An indicator becomes necessary whenever there is an output from the artificial intelligence system. This indicator also serves as the entry point to the subsequent level of explanation.

2. **Abstract (Why?)**

This offers a summarized perspective of the pertinent characteristics, quantities, and contextual data. An abstract helps users in gaining a better understanding of the suggestions made by the artificial intelligence system. It may also include links to the final and most comprehensive level of explanation.

3. **Detail (How?)**

This is a comprehensive report designed specifically for users with advanced knowledge. It encompasses all aspects processed by the intelligent system, the performance of the artificial intelligence, and any additional context and conditions that aid users in overseeing the operations of the artificial intelligence.

Different user interface techniques can be used to provide these explanations, ranging from simple text-based information to engaging with users in natural language through a digital assistant. Figure 14.1 provides an example of how an application can explain the ranking of suppliers for a specific material, based on artificial intelligence. At the individual item level, the user has the ability to understand how the system determined the score for a specific object. The explanations can encompass several components:

- A brief explanation in natural language as a trigger for navigation to explanation details
- The ability to interact with the digital assistant in the context of this explanation
- Potentially, a compilation of the most significant parameters that influenced the explained results
- Potentially, a comparison of the results with the average outcomes for other objects

Fig. 14.1 Example for explanation

We suggest using the method of progressive disclosure to prevent overwhelming the user with an excess of information all at once. The most frequently accessed information is presented in a succinct format on the primary screen, as depicted in Fig. 14.2, with the choice to drill down into more comprehensive information on secondary screens. The advantage of this strategy is that it provides users with a more streamlined and condensed user interface, and they only need to delve into the specifics if they are actually required.

Let's break down the different layers of the user interface as depicted in Fig. 14.2:

- The first level provides a concise explanation without the possibility of obtaining more comprehensive details. This is applicable in straightforward scenarios where a brief explanation is sufficient to clarify the matter. The user doesn't need to have an in-depth understanding. They are directed by the quality indicator on how to process the given information, what is significant, and at what level.
- The second level offers more comprehensive information, including tables, graphs, and other user interface components that provide a deeper understanding of the issue. At this level, the current situation is contextualized and put into perspective. The user can see the criteria that the prediction is based on and the influence these criteria have had on the prediction. To interpret this information correctly, the user needs a solid understanding of the domain and business, but no additional skills beyond that.
- The third level isn't exactly part of the explanation, but it allows the user to interact with a digital assistant for more information (through speech or chat field). This level demands a robust knowledge and a profound understanding of the technology to handle the provided information. The user must be trained to make informed decisions and take action.

Figure 14.3 demonstrates, using a linear regression model as an example, how an explanation for results produced by artificial intelligence can be computed.

The forecast is essentially a blend of the values of the features, each one adjusted by the coefficients of the model. In reality, these coefficients signify the extent of their contribution to the forecast and offer an understanding of how the prediction is

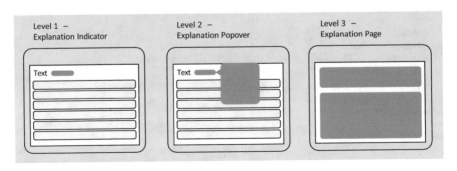

Fig. 14.2 Explanation User Interface Illustration

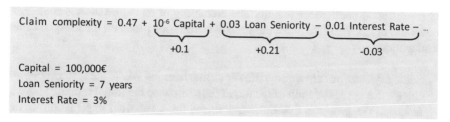

Fig. 14.3 Example of explanation for regression algorithm

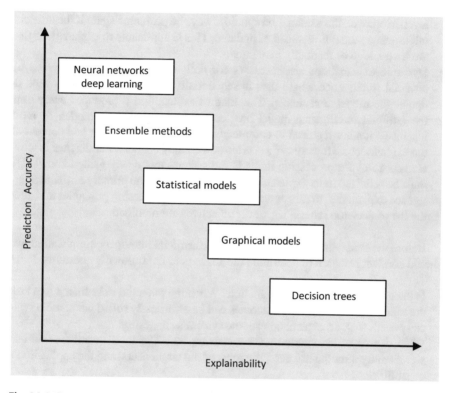

Fig. 14.4 Degree of explanation of artificial intelligence algorithms

made. However, as depicted in Fig. 14.4, the most precise results are frequently obtained from intricate models based on artificial intelligence. These models are so complex that even specialists find it challenging to interpret them.

We should only display explanatory components when the service powered by artificial intelligence can offer predictions with a satisfactory level of confidence and precision. The acceptable quality level for predictions should be determined individually, depending on the specific use case and the capabilities of the artificial intelligence. However, we advise against revealing any predictions that are only of low reliability. Untrustworthy results can erode user trust and obstruct the adoption of the artificial intelligence feature. The credibility of an explanation is contingent on its life cycle. We distinguish between two scenarios based on the lifespan of the explanation:

- Static explanations are appropriate for offline learning where the system does not change the approximation of the target function once the initial training phase is finished. We presume that the requirement for a repeated explanation of the model may reduce or even vanish over time as the user becomes more familiar with the system. Once the user comprehends the main principle of the underlying service (algorithm), it should be considered to omit explanations at the model level. Moreover, the explanation should always be presented again if the artificial intelligence model is changed or updated. This is applicable to explanations that are hard-coded or manually maintained.
- Dynamic explanations are necessary for online learning services powered by artificial intelligence where data is sequentially made available and is used to update the model at each step. This kind of explanation is produced every time the artificial intelligence model has learned and adjusted its model. In most instances, it's not required to completely change the appearance and content of the explanations. However, if a service powered by artificial intelligence discovers new rules for processing items in the system, this newly gained knowledge must be reflected in its explanations. We should adapt the primary artificial intelligence explanation to mirror newly implemented processing principles and alter the list of decision criteria whenever objectives are modified.

Before we commence with the design of the artificial intelligence application, we should conduct research to determine the answers to the following questions:

- Is the user anticipating an explanation? When the potential risks linked to a task are relatively minor and the outcomes can be effortlessly rolled back, users typically don't seek an explanation for the system's suggestion.
- What degree of automation are we striving for? The level of automation can significantly alter the use case, the roles of the target users, and the application's capabilities.
- Besides the intended business user, what other roles participate in the experience? The interaction with artificial intelligence systems also includes technical roles that are not business-related. We should also take into account roles that contribute to development, support, or maintenance.
- How transparent or trackable does the artificial intelligence service needs to be? Some use cases are more sensitive than others. Enterprise applications, for instance, often face stricter auditing requirements due to legal and regulatory mandates, compared to consumer software.
- Can users generally comprehend the displayed information and data, and can they deduce the subsequent actions and their effects? While artificial intelligence can aid in enhancing even the simplest tasks, it may be overengineered to offer artificial intelligence explanations when the user already comprehends the outcomes and their implications.

- What is the potential damage to the customer's business if data is processed incorrectly? Some tasks in processes are inherently critical and can lead to severe consequences. Artificial intelligence explanations must protect against such scenarios and assist in preventing any harm or disruption.
- How simple or complex is it to undo changes made to the system or process? In situations where the user is up against deadlines, end-of-period closing, or other tasks that must be successful on the first attempt, providing supportive information to the user is vital. However, explanations may not be necessary if it's feasible to instantly reverse everything in the event of a failure.

Does the business case necessitate constant adaptation? We presume that as the user becomes more experienced, the need for a repeated (static) explanation of the model may decrease or even vanish. However, if the algorithm powered by artificial intelligence learns dynamically, users must always be kept informed of changing conditions (dynamic explanations).

14.2.2 Backend Processes

The concept of explainability can be realized by either limiting the intricacy of the artificial intelligence model, which is an intrinsic approach, or by implementing techniques that scrutinize the model after its training phase, known as the post hoc method. Intrinsic interpretability is associated with artificial intelligence models that are deemed explainable due to their uncomplicated structure, such as concise decision trees or sparse linear models. It's worth noting that there are established explanation methods for artificial intelligence algorithms that are widely recognized within the data scientist community, but these are not the primary focus of this discussion. In the context of business applications, it's crucial to select methods that elucidate both the individual prediction and the overall behavior of the model.

The proposed comprehensive artificial intelligence solution is depicted in Fig. 14.5. During the training phase of the artificial intelligence, basic explanation data is computed and preserved alongside the trained model. This data includes statistical values for the overall precision of the artificial intelligence model, which are termed as the global explanation. For incoming inference requests, individual explanation figures are calculated, which are termed as local explanation. The explanation component supplies the global/local explanations and enhances the inference outcomes with these values, which are then made available to the business logic that utilizes them. To display explanation data, user interface controls are necessary, as previously specified.

The explanations that are both global and local in nature often take the form of statistical metrics. These metrics need to be converted into the specific language of the end user's domain. The explanation component aids in this process technically through its ability to map these metrics accordingly. This presents a significant challenge for those designing the user interface.

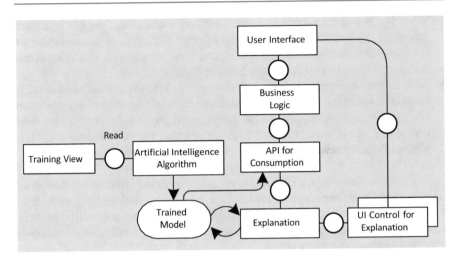

Fig. 14.5 Explanation solution

Delving one level deeper into the solution, as illustrated in Fig. 14.6, for a specific use case, the appropriate artificial intelligence algorithm and the necessary data for training are identified by data scientists once the exploration phase is completed. The training job then uses this application data to train the chosen artificial intelligence algorithm and to save the trained model for future use. During the training job, global explanations are also generated by providing accuracy measures based on a specific method of explanation. The process of determining the accuracy of an artificial intelligence model assists in explaining the model.

What is the method for determining the precision of a model developed through artificial intelligence? To recap, the fundamental concept involves training an artificial intelligence model using a specific dataset, and then applying the derived function to data points where the y-value is already established. This process results into two y-values: the actual one and the prediction made by the artificial intelligence model. It then becomes relatively straightforward to determine the frequency of incorrect predictions by comparing these predictions to the actual values. This comparison forms the basis for several static methods used to compute accuracy key performance indicators (KPIs) for global explanations. The model, once trained, is made accessible to artificial intelligence applications through consumption application programming interfaces (APIs). The consumption request is utilized to generate a local explanation based on a chosen explanation method. For legal audit purposes, it is necessary to store the local explanation in the database, just as it is for the global explanation. The consumption view forms the basis for the consumption API. It identifies the inference results and supplements them with local and global explanations. These explanations are included in the response structure provided to the artificial intelligence application and can be shown in the user interface as recommended in the preceding section. This interaction is depicted in Fig. 14.7.

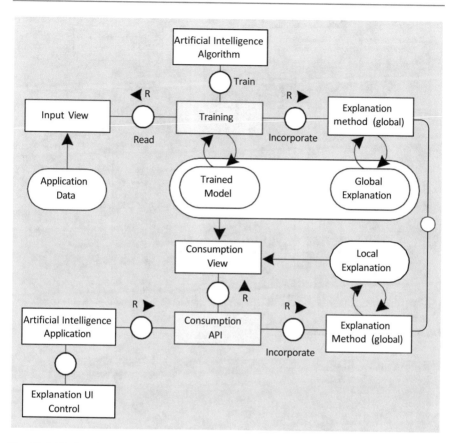

Fig. 14.6 Explanation solution detailed

The explanation of artificial intelligence models is typically tailored to the specific use case, making it challenging to establish a generic framework. Nevertheless, the suggested method aids those who are developing applications based on artificial intelligence in overcoming this hurdle. The implementation of this solution is illustrated through an example that involves predicting the delivery time for products. In this case, regression is used as the foundational model for artificial intelligence. As shown in Fig. 14.8, the global explanation involves computing the predictive power and prediction confidence, while the local explanation calculates the variable contributions of the inference calls. In the local explanation, a method for determining variable contributions is utilized, which reveals the relative significance of each variable incorporated in the model or the influence of a category. The influence of a category is an examination of how different categories of a variable impact the target, derived from fundamental information. The larger the absolute value of the influence, the more potent the influence of the category. Categories with values equal to or near zero have no impact on the target. The influence of a category can be either positive or negative:

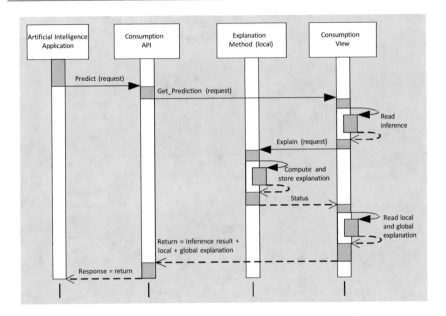

Fig. 14.7 Explanation process

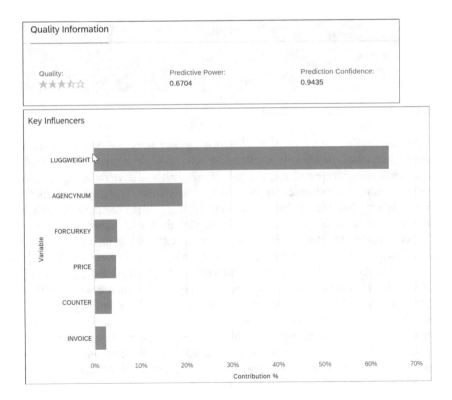

Fig. 14.8 Example implementation for local and global explanations

- Categories with positive values are those where observations are more likely to fall into the positive category of the target. The proportion of positive targets within such a category exceeds the proportion of positive targets in the entire dataset.

14.3 Conclusion

To build trust between human and machine, it's important to explain the results provided by artificial intelligence models: transparency and traceability of artificial intelligence models When artificial intelligence is introduced into business applications, systems originally designed to *react* can become active players that propose, change, or create elements in the interface. Objects, actions, or attributes are manipulated not only by humans but also by artificial intelligence algorithms. To avoid confusion and loss of control, users need to be aware of the working principles, actions, and consequences of artificial intelligence at any point in time. When designing artificial intelligence, services are also needed for statutory reasons. Therefore, in this section, we deducted the business requirements and proposed the necessary technical implementation for explanation of results computed by artificial intelligence. We suggested techniques for user interface design for considering explainability. Furthermore, we proposed a solution architecture regarding implementation and preparing of explainability in the ERP backend.

Workload Management and Performance

15

In this chapter, we specify the business requirements and propose the solution concept for workload management and performance. Depending on the underlying algorithms, training of artificial intelligence models can have high requirements for hardware. Inference calls must have very short response times. Thus, measures must be put in place to resolve those challenges. Especially, consumption of computing resources for artificial intelligence must not slow down the transactional processes in ERP systems as they are critical of running the enterprise. Consequently, in additional to the already proposed solution architecture, which scales from embedded to side-by-side artificial intelligence approach, we suggest further performance optimization techniques.

15.1   Problem Statement

The reliability of processes infused with artificial intelligence outlined in a company's ERP system is of utmost importance. As we move further into the digital age, an increasing number of processes are being digitized or semi-digitized and incorporated into ERP systems from a variety of vendors. To maintain consistent service quality, companies must depend on the availability and performance of artificial intelligence based processes. This need extends to the IT systems that execute and manage these processes. The primary goal of ERP systems, in addition to offering necessary functionalities, should be to ensure that systems of any size can complete tasks within a reasonable timeframe. Whether a company is transitioning from an older ERP system or constructing their first ERP system from scratch, it's crucial to plan the hardware optimally. This planning encompasses everything from storage and computing power to other considerations like hosting and tariff options. The term "sizing" is used to encapsulate the answers to these questions. Insufficient resources typically result in poor system performance. Conversely, an overly large system can be a financial drain and contribute to environmental pollution through

S. Sarferaz, *Embedding Artificial Intelligence into ERP Software*, https://doi.org/10.1007/978-3-031-54249-7_15

increased power usage, without providing any additional value to the company or society. The term *clean-up* refers to various activities associated with the life cycle of data and storage media. This includes routine tasks like defragmenting file systems and deleting temporary data, which are designed to maintain IT system performance. It also includes archiving unnecessary data. Another significant consideration is the network. The use of cloud systems or other distributed systems not operated within an intranet increases the amount of data that must be transported through public local area network (LAN) or wide area network (WAN) lines from the server to the user. As public Internet lines are not under the control of individual software service providers, no optimizations can be made in this area. However, there are methods to reduce a system's network traffic, such as avoiding the transmission of unnecessary data or separating historical and current data, which is typically needed more frequently. Finally, the hardware used is also a significant factor. It's reasonable to expect that a system's performance requirements will change over time. Given the high cost of computing power, it's in a company's best interest to keep hardware costs as low as possible and minimize resource waste. Therefore, it's crucial to design an ERP system that can dynamically manage changing loads and allow for scaling measures, including the addition and removal of hardware components like CPUs or RAM.

Within the context of artificial intelligence, the process of training a model necessitates supplying the algorithm with training data from which it can glean knowledge. This training data must include the correct response, often referred to as a target or target attribute. The learning algorithm identifies patterns within the training data that link the input data attributes to the target and subsequently produces an artificial intelligence model that encapsulates these patterns. The training of artificial intelligence is an asynchronous process typically carried out on a yearly, monthly, or weekly basis. As such, performance isn't the primary concern, but the allocation of memory, CPU time, and disk space is. Here, performance is defined as the overall efficiency of a system, encompassing throughput, individual response time, and availability.

Inference, on the other hand, is the procedure of using the artificial intelligence model to generate predictions on fresh data where the target is unknown. For instance, consider an artificial intelligence model that has been trained to determine whether an email is spam or not. In this scenario, the AI technology platform would be supplied with training data comprising emails for which the target is known (i.e., a label indicating whether an email is spam or not). The AI technology platform would then train an artificial intelligence model using this data, resulting in a model that strives to predict whether incoming emails will be spam or not. For inference calls on top of the trained model, typically, fast response time, respectively, high performance is required. Usually, inference is based on synchronous calls by end user who are expecting prompt results.

Thus, the training and inference of artificial intelligence can potentially have negative impacts on the transactional processes of the ERP system. This is because inferences typically prioritize performance, while aspects like memory, CPU time, and disk space are often neglected. It's crucial to prevent such negative

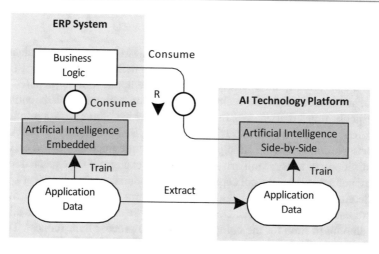

Fig. 15.1 Workload required for training and performance for inference

implications. However, as depicted in Figure 15.1, these implications are contingent on the artificial intelligence infrastructure used, the necessary artificial intelligence algorithms, and the underlying programming model.

As previously discussed, scenarios that require algorithms with minimal memory and CPU time are implemented directly into the ERP platform, while more demanding algorithms such as deep learning are delegated to the AI technology platform. However, it's important to note that even embedded artificial intelligence can potentially cause a slowdown in ERP business processes. Therefore, the following considerations must be taken into account:

- The total response time for utilizing an artificial intelligence model should not exceed 1 second. This is because artificial intelligence functionalities are incorporated into large-scale transactional processes and user interfaces.
- The process of training artificial intelligence should not negatively affect the performance of transactional operations due to improper allocation of memory, CPU time, and disk space.

When it comes to side-by-side artificial intelligence, the training of the model takes place on the AI technology platform. This platform is both scalable and distributed, so it's not expected to have any adverse effects. However, when it comes to using the model, the associated key performance indicator (KPI) must be taken into account, especially since large-scale transactional processes on the ERP side are involved.

15.2   Solution Proposal

The performance of a system can be evaluated from two angles: the technical aspect and the user's viewpoint. The term *response time* is defined as the duration from the moment a user initiates an interaction to when the application is prepared for the subsequent interaction. In the realm of information technology, it is common to have response times that are less than a second, which aligns with the findings of performance perception studies carried out by, e.g., SAP's usability teams. An interesting observation is that the anticipated response time fluctuates based on the perceived difficulty of a task. Similarly, user behavior changes if the expected response times are not achieved. This concept is easier to understand than it appears, and it's worth delving into further. To begin with, users form expectations about the complexity of each of their requests. Depending on these expectations, users allocate a certain amount of time for the computer system to process their request. The time users allot for the ERP system is heavily influenced by their perception of the task's complexity. So, how can we define the complexity of tasks? The tasks that ERP systems most commonly deal with can be broadly classified into three categories: acknowledging user input, displaying the results of a simple task, and displaying the results of a complex task. An acknowledgment of user input provides the user with visual or auditory confirmation that their input has been received. For instance, consider a numeric input field: when the user shifts focus or hits the enter key after entering a value, the system verifies the syntax of the input value, and either produces an error or reformats the input value to the standard number format. So, what constitutes a simple task? A simple task could be adding a new line item to a sales order or progressing to the next step in a business process wizard. On the other hand, complex tasks involve navigating to another work center or initially logging into the system. To improve the performance of an artificial intelligence application, these factors must be considered.

As discussed in the previous section, for training artificial intelligence, it's crucial to manage and optimize the use of memory, CPU time, and disk space. To meet this requirement, it's necessary to implement workload and quota management.

Workload and quota management involve optimizing infrastructure resources (memory, CPU time, disk space) to maintain or improve performance or throughput. These actions can include rescheduling, moving, technically virtualizing, or limiting a specific service or workload. For instance, an administrator can set limits for jobs regarding CPU time and memory usage. From our viewpoint, successful workload and quota management requires continuous, diligent monitoring. In the context of artificial intelligence, quota management is typically not relevant for the following reasons:

- During embedded artificial intelligence training, the application data is accessed in real time from the ERP database.
- For side-by-side artificial intelligence, the application data for training is replicated from the ERP system to the AI technology platform but is usually deleted after the training run.

However, we believe that the read access of training data should be optimized using packing and pipelining mechanisms. This means that the training data is not read all at once, which could lead to out-of-memory problems, but is processed in batches by the training process. As highlighted in the previous section, for artificial intelligence inference, the primary requirement is optimal performance in terms of response time. In addition to the well-known methods of improving API performance, we suggest caching and bulking inference results to meet this requirement.

Let's discuss how the implementation techniques for workload and performance management vary depending on artificial intelligence approach.

15.2.1 Embedded Artificial Intelligence

The manner in which we have structured the embedded artificial intelligence ensures that inference requests are handled locally in real time. Therefore, from a standpoint of performance, this is already the best possible solution, and there is no need for further exploration. Since training is an intermittent background process, there is no need to take into account any extraordinary performance KPIs. Specifically, our measurements of training for embedded artificial intelligence algorithms showed that the response time is less than 5 minutes, which exceeds by far the necessary performance KPIs. Let's examine some representative results from measurements for SAP ERP. Table 15.1 displays performance measurements for logistic regression. For this, tables with varying numbers of columns and rows were used as input for training. The durations of the training runs, in seconds, are listed in the table, including a dataset with 700 columns and 300,000 rows that resulted in a training time of 25,740 seconds.

In another perspective, Table 15.2 shows an evaluation of the performance for K-means algorithms. This assessment takes into account a variety of datasets as well.

The circumstances vary when it comes to training procedures that are focused on the usage of system resources, as these could potentially have a detrimental effect on the business processes of the ERP system. To address this, we suggest implementing strategies for managing the workload, as depicted in Fig. 15.2.

Table 15.1 Logistic regression

	50 Columns	100 Columns	200 Columns	500 Columns	700 Columns
10,000 rows	0.159	0.259	0.308	0.968	1.278
50,000 rows	0.367	0.840	1.673	4.085	5.475
150,000 rows	0.925	1.669	3.953	9.819	13.494
300,000 rows	1.155	3.380	7.317	17.868	25.740

Table 15.2 K-Means

	50 Columns	100 Columns	200 Columns	500 Columns	700 Columns
10,000 rows	0.2476	0.327	0.4814	0.9158	1.2896
50,000 rows	0.407	0.6458	1.9714	3.1444	3.6752
150,000 rows	0.7828	1.9548	3.4436	9.8342	9.201
300,000 rows	1.453	4.083	7.0614	19.748	28.9356

Fig. 15.2 Workload management measures for embedded artificial intelligence

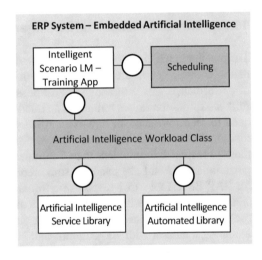

Scheduling is a process that enables the automatic execution of training at predetermined times. To set up a schedule for training, one must provide patterns of recurrence, such as every Monday weekly or on the first day of each month. This allows for the precise control of when and how frequently the training should be executed. When a training schedule is set up, the system generates a scheduled instance that only includes object and schedule details, but no data. When the system executes the training, it produces models of artificial intelligence as a result. Event-based scheduling offers an extra feature that allows for the initiation of training runs. For instance, if the accuracy of a model drops below 60%, a retraining process is triggered. To prevent excessive resource usage, we suggest processing scheduled training runs as background tasks and restricting the number of concurrent background tasks. For example, the total number of tasks should not exceed five. The scheduling process should be incorporated into the previously proposed Intelligent Scenario Lifecycle Management framework, which offers a training application.

From our viewpoint, the second method of preventing excessive resource usage is to restrict the memory and CPU time used by the algorithms of artificial intelligence, as shown in Fig. 15.3. We propose implementing this using workload class

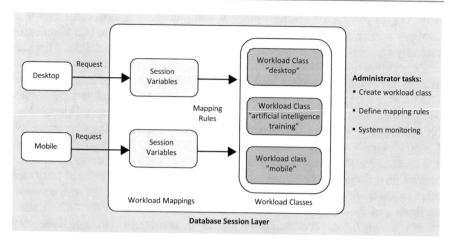

Fig. 15.3 Workload classes for embedded artificial intelligence

and mapping technology. The aim of workload class and mapping is to prevent the overuse of system resources like CPU time and memory by applying predefined mapping rules. This process generally involves the following steps:

1. The administrator sets up a workload class, which outlines the quantity of system resources that a group of applications can use, and a workload mapping, which details how to align an application workload with a workload class.
2. When an application sends a request to the session layer of the ERP's database system, the relevant workload class is identified based on the session context information, such as the application name, application username, and database username.
3. Once the relevant workload class has been identified, the application request can have its resources managed according to the definition of the workload class.

The workload class should support at least three types of resource properties for regulation:

- Statement thread limit: This represents the highest number of parallel threads that can execute a statement.
- Statement memory limit: This represents the maximum memory allocation per statement.
- Statement priority: This represents the priority level for a statement to be executed in the job execution framework.

15.2.2 Side-by-Side Artificial Intelligence

The workload management looks different for side-by-side artificial intelligence using AI technology platform as it offers enhanced scalability features. Scalability is the degree to which a business process, component, or system can increase or decrease in size, volume, or the number of users it serves while still functioning correctly and predictably. Essentially, scalability is about how a software application's resource usage changes predictably under varying system loads, such as an increase in multiuser or parallel load, while maintaining a reasonable response time. The AI technology platform typically offers a scalable infrastructure for inference and training, built on Kubernetes technology. We suggest utilizing this technology for workload management and performance of artificial intelligence scenarios. Kubernetes automates the processes of deploying, scaling, maintaining, scheduling, and operating multiple application containers across clusters of nodes. Containers operate on a shared operating system on host machines but are isolated from each other unless a user decides to connect them. Kubernetes can be used with container runtimes and the container runtime interface. It includes tools for orchestration, secrets management, service discovery, scaling, and load balancing. Kubernetes technology also includes automatic bin packing to optimally allocate resources for containers, and it applies configurations through configuration management features. It safeguards container workloads by implementing or reversing changes and provides availability and quality checks for containers. In Kubernetes, containers operate in pods, which are the basic scheduling unit for Kubernetes and add an abstraction layer to containers. Pods consist of one or more containers located on a host machine, and they can share resources. Kubernetes identifies a machine with sufficient free compute capacity for a specific pod and launches the associated containers. To prevent conflicts, each pod is assigned a unique IP address, allowing applications to use ports. A node agent, known as a kubelet, manages the pods, their containers, and their images. A node, also referred to as a minion, is a worker machine in Kubernetes. It can be a physical machine or a virtual machine. Nodes contain the necessary services to run pods and receive management instructions from master components. Services found on nodes include Docker, kube-proxy, and kubelet. Tenant namespaces and content are respectively deployed and deleted as Helm releases. A release is an instance of a chart running in a Kubernetes cluster. One chart can often be installed many times in the same cluster. The Helm tool installs charts into Kubernetes, creating a new release for each installation. The tenant ID and related configuration are also easily injected by Helm. With the correct template logic, such as feature flags or a cloud provider, differences are managed. Upgrading tenants with new releases is also supported. Templating is also provided for creating Kubernetes job specifications. Additionally, the mounting of tenant data and access to GPUs are enabled.

The performance of remote artificial intelligence consumption must be high as there are (mass) transactional processes involved on the ERP side. Therefore, steps must be taken depending on the specific requirements of a particular artificial intelligence use case, as shown in Fig. 15.4. We suggest caching inference results on the server side to improve response time. However, this might be applicable for a small number of scenarios. Therefore, we recommend bulking of inference calls, which involves combining multiple requests into one inference call.

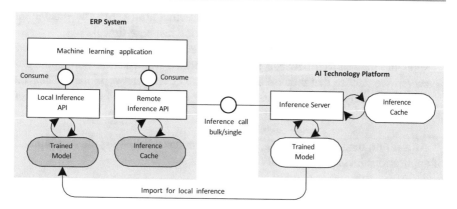

Fig. 15.4 Performance improvement for inference calls

In addition, we recommend that within the ERP system, the outcomes of inferences are stored by utilizing batch processing, thereby making these results readily accessible for local use. We also put forward the idea that specific types of side-by-side trained models should be imported into the ERP system and consumed locally. This approach would significantly enhance the speed of inference calls, given that local application programming interfaces (APIs) are typically 10 to 100 times faster than their remote counterparts. A technology that aids in the export and import of models is the Open Neural Network Exchange (ONNX). For both deep learning models and traditional models of machine-based intelligence, ONNX provides an open-source format. It also establishes built-in operators and common data types, along with a computation graph model that can be expanded. There are a multitude of hardware, software, and frameworks that support ONNX. The transition from research to production can be made more efficient and compatible across different frameworks, thereby fostering innovation in the field of machine-based intelligence.

15.2.3 Performance-Optimized Programming

From our viewpoint, the primary factor in optimizing the performance of an ERP system lies in the programming. Various implementation methods can be discovered under the term Performance-Optimized Programming. In relation to network and data, the following KPIs can be defined:

- Count of network roundtrips for each user interaction step: The duration of a roundtrip is contingent on the number of network hops, essentially the count of intermediary devices that data must traverse from source to destination, and latency, which is the time it takes for a packet to be sent from the source and received at the destination. When data is transmitted over wide area networks (WAN) or global area networks (GAN), latency makes up the majority of the roundtrip time. Ultimately, our deduction is straightforward: The greater the number of roundtrips, the poorer the application response time.

- Amount of data transferred for each user interaction step: This essentially measures the data moved between the user interface frontend and the application server. We deduce that the less data transported over a network, the quicker the transfer is completed and the sooner the user can engage in the next interaction with the user interface.

As a result, the following design principles are established for the development of applications involving artificial intelligence:

- An application involving artificial intelligence initiates a minimal count of sequential round trips and only transfers necessary data to the frontend. The conclusion is clear: the more roundtrips, the greater the effect on network performance and the poorer the application's end-to-end response time.
- An application involving artificial intelligence transfers no more than 10 KB to 20 KB of data for each user interaction step.
- Key strategies to enhance network performance include compression and frontend caching, both of which should be incorporated as part of applications involving artificial intelligence.

In our view, another critical aspect of performance-optimized programming is the database. Frequently, poor performance of applications involving artificial intelligence is due to databases, which are the bottleneck that needs to be expanded. To address this issue, other factors must be taken into account in addition to the choice of database technology. An initial step, for instance, is the creation of replicas. A replica is a duplicate of a database or document that is updated regularly and thus kept synchronized. There is a database for all write operations, also known as primary. All these actions are then transferred to the replicas. This benefits availability because if a primary node fails, a replica simply becomes the new primary node. Additionally, it has the advantage that read queries, which constitute the majority in an ERP system, can be executed on all nodes, whether they are primary or replica. This distribution of the load results in significant performance improvements. Another step is multi-temperature storage. Here, different storage technologies are used based on the type of data. For instance, data that is frequently used is stored on especially fast cache memories so that it can be processed and sent within a very short time. Since this type of memory is very costly, not all information can be stored on it. For this reason, other types of storage are used, and decisions are made, for example, based on the criticality and access frequency of the data as to where it is stored.

Performance-optimized programming must take into account a crucial aspect: the system footprint, with a particular focus on the memory footprint. One way to minimize this is by transferring application data from the cache to less expensive, less powerful memory options. Distributing data efficiently across databases and tables can also help decrease the footprint of applications that utilize artificial intelligence. The management of old data is of primary importance. In an ERP system, data accumulates significantly over time. Ideally, a system should be able to scale massively without requiring additional intervention. However, this can lead to substantial costs, which may not be justified by the resulting value. It's important to differentiate between various types and states of data. Data can vary in age and undergoes a life cycle. Each stage of this life cycle impacts the data's relevance and availability differently. For instance, data in the Legal Hold section is typically accessed less frequently. Therefore, it doesn't need to be stored in high-performance cache memory. Instead, it can be archived in a compressed format on durable, affordable, and slightly slower memory, as access speed isn't a crucial performance indicator for this data. Other performance indicators and measures can be developed for other life cycle stages to enhance storage efficiency, indirectly reducing costs and improving performance, thereby minimizing a system's footprint.

Lastly, we suggest the use of code-pushdown for performance-optimized programming. Data processing requires transfer between the application server and the ERP system's database via a network. This transfer is considerably slower than the internal server transfer between the main memory and various caches. The difference is even more extreme when hard disk accesses or other mechanical steps are involved. To mitigate the network connection's bottleneck effect, the programming paradigm of code-pushdown can be used. Traditionally, the database is accessed for data needed for processing and calculations. This data is then sent to the application server for processing, a principle known as data to code. However, this requires the data request to be sent to the database first, and then the entire data set must be transferred from the database to the application server via a network. To conserve bandwidth and enhance performance, this principle has been inverted. Following the code to data motto, calculations are performed locally within the database management system. This shifts some of the workload to the database server. Consequently, performance-intensive logic, such as the training of artificial intelligence algorithms, can be executed almost entirely on the database rather than on the application server.

15.3 Conclusion

Depending on the underlying algorithms, training of artificial intelligence models can have high requirements for hardware. Inference calls must have very short response times. Thus, measures must be put in place to resolve those challenges. In this section, we deducted the business requirements and proposed the necessary technical implementation for workload management and performance in the context of artificial intelligence. High performance is required for inference calls as typically end users consuming the results on the user interface and expect fast response time. Training jobs are usually asynchronous and can take long time without being an issue. However, workload management must be established for training jobs as they absorb too many hardware resources from which the ERP business processes otherwise would suffer. We proposed solutions for embedded and side-by-side artificial intelligence and suggested techniques for performance-optimized programming.

Legal Auditing

16

In this chapter, we specify the business requirements and propose the solution concept for legal auditing. Artificial intelligence training and inference processes must be traceable. For this, proper logging is necessary. These logs are also the basis of auditing of artificial intelligence, which is a legal obligation. Thus, artificial intelligence applications must be integrated into the auditing infrastructure of ERP systems and facilitate auditors performing all their tasks including generating audit reports. In particular, we determine the artifacts that should be in the scope of legal auditing. Furthermore, we also define the necessary tasks and processes regarding legal auditing in context of ERP software infusing artificial intelligence.

16.1 Problem Statement

Logging in the context of ERP systems refers to the process of recording activities, events, or operations that occur within the system. This can include user actions, system errors, data modifications, access times, and other significant events. Here are some key points about logging in ERP systems:

1. Audit trail: Logging provides an audit trail that can be used to trace and review actions. This is particularly important in ERP systems, which often handle sensitive business data. If something goes wrong, logs can help identify what happened and who was involved.
2. Security: Logs can be used to detect unauthorized access or other security incidents. For example, if an account is logging in at unusual times or performing unexpected actions, this could be a sign of a security breach.
3. Performance monitoring: Logs can also be used to monitor the performance of the ERP system. For example, if certain operations are taking longer than expected, this could be a sign of a performance issue that needs to be addressed.

© The Author(s), under exclusive license to Springer Nature
Switzerland AG 2024
S. Sarferaz, *Embedding Artificial Intelligence into ERP Software*,
https://doi.org/10.1007/978-3-031-54249-7_16

4. Compliance: In many industries, companies are required to keep detailed logs to demonstrate compliance with various regulations. For example, regulations may require companies to show who has accessed certain data and when.
5. Debugging and troubleshooting: Logs are crucial for debugging and trouble-shooting. If a user reports an issue, logs can be used to understand what the user was doing when the issue occurred.
6. System optimization: By analyzing logs, you can identify patterns and trends that can help optimize the system. For example, you might identify peak usage times and plan system maintenance during off-peak hours.

Thus, logging is a critical aspect of managing and maintaining ERP systems. It provides a way to monitor system activity, ensure security, demonstrate compliance, troubleshoot issues, and optimize system performance. Application logs are used to trace and recreate the steps of business operations. For instance, a sales order numbered 4711, placed by Mr. Smith on July 3 in an approved status, would be tracked in an application log.

Legal auditing in the context of ERP systems refers to the process of reviewing and verifying the legal compliance of the ERP system. This can include a wide range of legal requirements, such as data privacy laws, financial reporting regulations, industry-specific regulations, and more. Here are some key aspects of legal auditing in ERP systems:

1. Data privacy and security: ERP systems often handle sensitive data, including personal information of employees and customers, financial data, and proprietary business information. Legal auditing ensures that the ERP system complies with relevant data privacy and security laws, such as GDPR in Europe or CCPA in California.
2. Financial reporting: ERP systems are often used to manage financial data and generate financial reports. Legal auditing can ensure that these processes comply with financial reporting regulations, such as Sarbanes-Oxley Act in the USA.
3. Industry-specific regulations: Depending on the industry, there may be specific regulations that apply to the data and processes managed by the ERP system. For example, in the healthcare industry, an ERP system would need to comply with HIPAA regulations.
4. Contractual obligations: The ERP system must also comply with any contractual obligations the company has with its customers, suppliers, or other third parties. This can include service-level agreements, data handling agreements, and more.
5. Audit trails: ERP systems should have robust audit trails that record who has accessed the system, what changes they made, and when. This is not only a good practice for security and accountability, but it's often a legal requirement as well.
6. Access controls: Legal auditing can also review the ERP system's access controls to ensure that only authorized individuals have access to sensitive data and critical system functions.

The goal of a legal audit is to identify any areas where the ERP system may not be in compliance with legal requirements and to recommend changes or improvements to ensure compliance. This can help mitigate legal risks and avoid potential fines or penalties. This process is typically conducted by a lawyer or a team of lawyers using logs and auditing tools of ERP systems.

Artificial intelligence shifts how additional automatization and optimization is incorporated into business applications. This shift involves the creation of additional components, such as artificial intelligence models or accuracy metrics. When it comes to auditing and logging, several factors need to be considered: What needs to be logged? Who is the intended audience for these logs? Where should these logs be stored? How should the auditing process be conducted? These questions will be addressed in the following section. However, the emphasis will be on the specifics of artificial intelligence, assuming that existing solutions for auditing and logging are taken as granted.

16.2 Solution Proposal

The underlying ERP infrastructure typically handles system and security logs, so we won't delve into those details in this discussion. Instead, we'll focus on the aspects of logging and auditing that are specific to artificial intelligence. The first step in this process is to identify what needs to be logged. As shown in Fig. 16.1, we categorize these logging and auditing entities into two main groups: data and actions.

The process of making an inference call involves two parts: the request and the response. The request is where the inquiry for the artificial intelligence system is posed, such as asking for a sales forecast for a particular product in a specific month. The response, on the other hand, is the answer provided by the artificial intelligence system, like a prediction of 5 million euros in sales revenue for bicycle sales in June. It's crucial for the sake of transparency that the end user understands how the

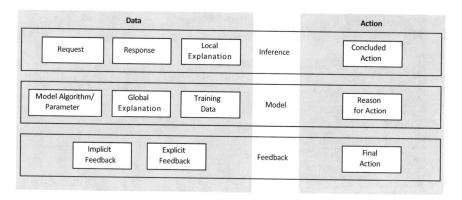

Fig. 16.1 Entities for logging and auditing

artificial intelligence system determined at its conclusion and how confident it is in its prediction. The user then decides whether to accept or disregard the prediction or suggestion and takes action accordingly. For instance, they might initiate a marketing campaign to boost bicycle sales in June.

Artificial intelligence models are created by training an algorithm using data and setting certain parameters. As part of the training process for the artificial intelligence, basic explanations are computed and stored alongside the trained model. These explanations are statistical measures of the overall accuracy of the artificial intelligence model and are known as the global explanation. It's also important to record why a particular action was taken. Feedback from end users is a valuable resource for improving the underlying data model. Negative feedback can signal a decline in the performance of the model, which might necessitate retraining or even a complete overhaul of the model. Once the content for logging artificial intelligence scenarios has been defined, the next step is to discuss the parties involved who will be using the logs. Table 16.1 provides a summary of the relevant parties and the log information they require. The primary uses for the artificial intelligence logs are to ensure legal compliance by auditors, to maintain transparency for end users, and to troubleshoot any issues that arise.

Table 16.1 Information required by actors

	Auditor	Support	End User	Developer	Key User
Request	X	X	X	X	
Response	X	X	X	X	
Local explanation	X	X	X	X	
Model algorithm	X	X		X	X
Model Parameter	X	X		X	X
Global explanation	X	X	X	X	X
Training data	O	O		O	
Concluded action	X	X	X	X	
Reason for action	X	X	X	X	
Final action	X	X	X	X	
Implicit feedback	X	X		X	
Explicit feedback	X	X		X	

X = Access restricted with authorization; O = Access depends on availability

An auditor is an individual who carries out an audit. To serve as an external auditor for a company, one typically needs a practice certificate from a regulatory authority. This auditor is granted access to all the logging entities that are specific to artificial intelligence, as mentioned earlier. However, this access is controlled through authorization checks; for instance, only data relevant to the audit period can be viewed in read mode. A snapshot of the data used for training could be saved with additional metadata, such as a timestamp or the artificial intelligence scenario, for logging purposes. Given that the data volume of these snapshots could rapidly increase, it's important to strike a balance between disk space and the total cost of ownership (TCO), keeping logging requirements in mind. It is suggested that the logging of training data be made configurable, allowing customers to choose based on their needs whether no snapshot, only the most recent snapshot, or snapshots for a specified duration will be captured. Logging should be enabled by default for models that contain sensitive data. Sensitive personal data should be used wisely, only if it's absolutely necessary to achieve the processing objective. Such processing should not result in discrimination against a group of people, either directly or indirectly.

An end user is an individual who uses the artificial intelligence application to execute a business task, not for administrative or developer tasks; end users could be buyers, salespeople, or product planners. End users only need access to the logging data necessary for understanding, tracking, and reproducing the business processes. A developer is an individual who codes the artificial intelligence application to address business issues. Like support staff, developers are involved in situations of failure. These individuals need access to all logs as they are usually relevant for problem resolution. However, access to the log data should be safeguarded with authorizations. As key users schedule and carry out training jobs, access to the logging data for this purpose should be granted. Once again, access must be limited based on authorizations.

In Fig. 16.2, we propose a method for the provision and utilization of logs related to artificial intelligence. Prior to the execution of inference calls by the artificial intelligence application, a training job must supply the underlying artificial intelligence model. During the training process, as we see it, the training infrastructure can automatically capture the following log entities:

- The model's algorithms and parameters
- A global explanation
- The training data

It's important to note that the storage of training data snapshots is dependent on the configurations set by the customers. The infrastructure for inference can generally gather the following log information:

- The request
- The response
- A local explanation

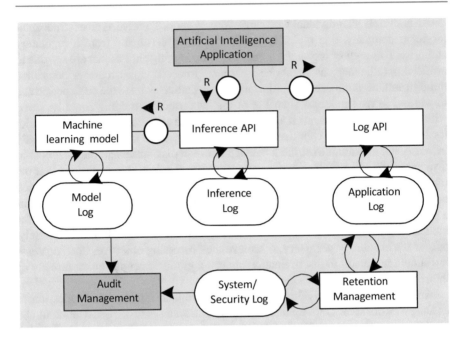

Fig. 16.2 Artificial intelligence logs provisioning and consumption

- The reason for the action

There's no need to store the response as it can be recalculated using the artificial intelligence model and the request data, both of which are already logged. Logging by the artificial intelligence application is crucial for recording the business process. This is specific to each scenario and must be considered by all artificial intelligence applications. In this context, the final action should be logged, and at the very least, references to the inference logs (e.g., local explanation) and model logs (e.g., global explanation) should be provided. Both implicit and explicit feedbacks are addressed with a proficient management solution. For system, security, and artificial intelligence logs, integration with the retention management of the ERP system is necessary. This allows for the periodic deletion or archiving of logs from the system, reducing the memory footprint and ensuring compliance with legal regulations.

Typically, the ERP's audit management consumes the artificial intelligence logs. This is a comprehensive audit management solution. The audit department can utilize it to create audit plans, prepare for audits, analyze relevant information, document results, form an audit opinion, communicate results, and track progress. From our viewpoint, key features of such an audit management should include:

- Complete coverage of the audit process
- A single source for audits
- Integration with third-party systems like fraud or risk management

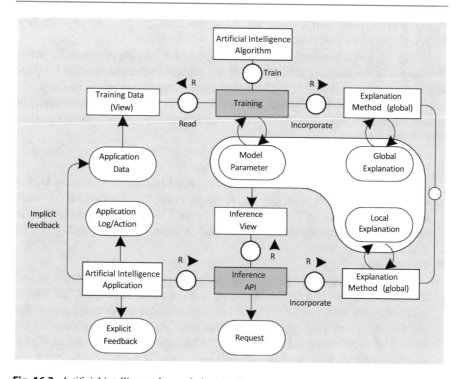

Fig. 16.3 Artificial intelligence logs solution details

- Document management integration
- Support for global monitoring
- Support for multiple devices
- Search functionality and an intuitive user interface

In Fig. 16.3, we depict the solution one level deeper. The diagram provides a detailed view of the provisioning of artificial intelligence-specific entities for logging.

The process of training involves utilizing application data to train the chosen artificial intelligence algorithm and to save the trained model for use. Throughout this training process, global explanations are calculated by offering accuracy metrics based on a specific method of explanation. This forms the groundwork for recording the model algorithm/parameter, global explanation, and training data entities. The trained model is made accessible to the artificial intelligence applications via an inference application programming interface (API). The inference request is used to compute a local explanation based on a chosen method of explanation. Both local and global explanations are supplied to the artificial intelligence application as part of the response structure and can be shown in the user interface. This forms the basis for recording the request, response, local explanation, and reason for action entities. Within the application log, the concluded and final action entities must be taken into account, which necessitates application-specific development and cannot be generically managed.

In Fig. 16.4, we demonstrate the interaction of the logging components within the context of the auditing process. While the audit management solution is operational, the logging specific to artificial intelligence must be supplied by the developer of the artificial intelligence use case based on the outlined approach. The auditor begins the process using the audit management system, which, in our view, should support the following steps:

1. **Planning**

   The planning phase of the audit is the first step in the auditing process. During this phase, the overall strategies and focus areas for the organization are established, the audit plan for the upcoming audit period is created, and audit resources are organized for the planned audits. Auditable items, audits, and audit plans are generated in this phase.

2. **Preparation**

   During the preparation phase of the audit, the auditor creates and documents the audit work program that meets the audit engagement objectives. The auditor establishes the structure of the work program, outlines the detailed procedures for the audit, and gets approval from the audit manager before initiating the audit. The audit manager receives the work program, reviews it, and decides to approve or reject it. If an audit announcement letter is needed for the audit, the auditor can also prepare audit announcement letters in this phase. Once the announcement letter is approved and distributed, the auditor proceeds with the preparation of the work program.

3. **Execution**

   The implementation phase is the stage where the actual auditing activities occur. During this stage, auditors carry out interviews, collect data, document evidence, and formulate conclusions and recommendations. In the course of the execution phase, the inspector has the opportunity to examine the applications of artificial intelligence. To do this, the logs of the application are studied as they form the foundation for comprehending and recreating the business procedures into which the capabilities of artificial intelligence are incorporated. A generic transaction with a variety of filter criteria is offered to present the application logs. Moreover, the applications of artificial intelligence may also include user interface sections to show the application logs. To facilitate the drilldown analysis from the application logs to the specifics, the logs of inference and model are connected to the application logs.

4. **Disclosure**

   Disclosure is the concluding stage of the auditing. In this stage, auditing reports are generated, reviewed, and shared with the interested parties. Auditors assess the adequacy, effectiveness, and timelines of actions undertaken by the management on reported conclusions and recommendations. In reviewing the evaluation outcomes, the auditor decides whether the management has put the recommendations into practice or acknowledged the risks of not putting them into action.

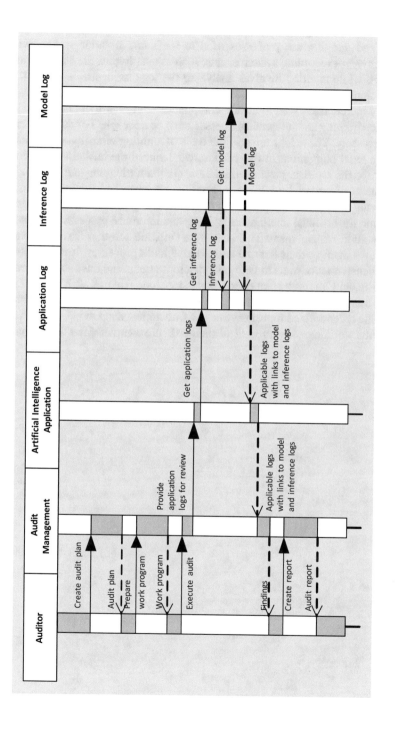

Fig. 16.4 Integration of artificial intelligence logs in auditing process

16.3   Conclusion

Logging and auditing are processes used to track and monitor system activity. Logging involves recording system events, such as user logins, file access, and system errors, while auditing involves analyzing the logs to identify security threats and suspicious activity. Logging and auditing help organizations detect and respond to security incidents, as well as ensure compliance with security policies. Artificial intelligence training and inference processes must be traceable. For this, proper logging is necessary. These logs are also the basis of auditing of artificial intelligence, which is a legal obligation. In this section, we deduced the business requirements and proposed the necessary technical implementation for logging and legal auditing in the context of artificial intelligence. For this, we identified the logging entities, the triggering actions, and the involved roles. Furthermore, we proposed integration concept into the artificial intelligence training and inference processes but also into the ERP's audit management. This shall be a software solution designed to allow organizations manage their internal and external audit processes. It should provide a comprehensive set of tools to help organizations streamline their audit processes, reduce costs, and improve compliance. It must include features such as audit planning, risk assessment, audit execution, audit reporting, and audit tracking. It should also provide a centralized repository for audit documents and evidence, as well as an integrated workflow to ensure that all audit tasks are completed in a timely manner.

Model Validation

17

In this chapter, we specify the business requirements and propose the solution concept for model validation. Statistical methods exist to validate artificial intelligence models regarding the accuracy of predictions. However, for ERP business applications, this mathematical approach alone is not enough. Additional validation from functional and business process points of view are necessary. Existing ERP techniques like A/B testing, feature toggle, business features, or switch framework must be analyzed in this context. We suggest a validation process that is appropriated for ERP software and considers the state transitions of artificial intelligence models. Finally, we propose a model validation cockpit as central environment for administration.

17.1   Problem Statement

Artificial intelligence has the ability to uncover hidden patterns and relationships by learning from the data provided by applications, rather than relying on pre-programmed rules. By incorporating artificial intelligence capabilities into ERP business processes, it becomes possible to identify overlooked opportunities, reveal concealed risks, and automate monotonous tasks or work that requires knowledge. When creating intelligent applications that are based on artificial intelligence algorithms, the artificial intelligence model usually undergoes evolution over time. After the model is trained with an initial data set, it needs to be retrained with new data that becomes available during its use. This new data reflects changes in the environment, such as deviations in customer behavior, which the artificial intelligence model captures due to its continuous retraining.

The process of retraining is one of the differences from classical systems, as we have previously discussed. It's a recurring process that leads to the creation of new versions of the artificial intelligence model. These new versions need to be validated for their predictive power and robustness before they can be put into use. However,

S. Sarferaz, *Embedding Artificial Intelligence into ERP Software*,
https://doi.org/10.1007/978-3-031-54249-7_17

in the context of ERP systems, this is a formidable task. This is because the traditional validation methods are not adequate for artificial intelligence. Typically, customers test business applications in quality systems and transport them to production systems after successful validation. Quality systems usually only contain test data, which is sufficient for testing functional correctness. But for validating artificial intelligence models, the synthetic data in quality systems is not sufficient. Therefore, training artificial intelligence models on this synthetic data would lead to inaccurate models. Hence, artificial intelligence models must always be trained in production systems where live data is available. This is the only way to ensure that the artificial intelligence algorithms learn from the correct data and identify the relevant patterns.

Live data usually cannot be copied from production to quality systems due to GDPR compliance, so developers and consultants working in the quality system would then have access to live data, which is legally prohibited. Therefore, in a quality system, only the functional correctness of artificial intelligence applications can be tested, and the quality of the artificial intelligence model cannot be validated. This validation must occur in the production system, which is a significant difference from traditional applications and brings specific requirements to the validation procedure, such as the need for new roles like the data scientist. However, testing in production ERP systems is problematic because each action impacts business processes, change documents, and audit logs. This footprint cannot be reversed due to legal compliance reasons.

Therefore, the crucial question is how to validate artificial intelligence models from a business process perspective in production ERP systems. The solution we propose is the primary focus of this chapter. Traditional validation concepts and tools are taken as granted, such as testing the functional correctness of artificial intelligence applications in quality systems or using statistical techniques to determine the quality of artificial intelligence models.

17.2   Solution Proposal

In ERP systems, there exist certain technologies that might initially seem suitable for validating a newly trained model of artificial intelligence when another model is already in use. However, upon closer examination, these technologies prove to be insufficient.

- **A/B testing**
- A/B testing is a technique used to compare two versions of an application to determine which one performs better. Essentially, it's an experiment where two or more variations of a Web page are randomly presented to users, and statistical analysis is employed to determine which version achieves better results for a specific conversion goal. In an A/B test, an application screen might be changed to create a second version of the same page. This alteration could be as minor as changing a single headline or button or as major as a complete page redesign. Half of the traffic shows the original version of the page (the control), while the

other half shows the modified version (the variation). As visitors interact with either the control or variation, their engagement is measured, collected in an analytics dashboard, and analyzed through a statistical engine. This allows for the determination of whether the changes had a positive, negative, or neutral effect on visitor behavior.

- However, A/B testing is primarily focused on validating user interfaces and therefore cannot be directly applied to artificial intelligence models. Artificial intelligence models are deeply integrated within business processes, influencing process flow and decision-making. These impacts cannot be easily reversed in ERP solutions due to legal compliance reasons. For instance, bank transfers executed by an artificial intelligence model cannot simply be erased. Thus, in our view, having two applications with the same purpose but different behaviors due to differing artificial intelligence models is not acceptable for ERP solutions. Therefore, traditional A/B testing cannot be directly applied for the validation of artificial intelligence models.
- **Feature toggle**
- Feature toggle is a method used to selectively activate or deactivate a feature. A feature refers to a business functionality at the level of a user story. Feature toggles are used to prevent the release of incomplete or substandard features to customers. These features are delivered in an inactive state, hidden from customer access by a runtime switch (feature toggle). The default status of the feature is off. In development and test systems, it can be activated per user and per client. In customer systems, the feature cannot be switched on. The feature is a temporary switch used to separate the technical upgrade of the system from the functional update. Once the feature is released, the feature toggles are removed.
- However, the focus of feature toggles is on continuous delivery, beta shipment to selected customers, and phased rollout of functionality. Therefore, from our perspective, it doesn't align with the validation of artificial intelligence models. Moreover, feature toggles are temporary. After the final release of a feature to all customers, the feature toggle is removed, and the corresponding source code is cleaned up.
- **Business feature**
- A business feature enhances an ERP core business functionality with an additional opt-in feature. When a customer selects their scope, which references one or more business features, the corresponding customizing entry is set in the central business feature customizing table. Business features are defined by the ERP vendor and are delivered to customers as table content. Having a central customizing table for all business features instead of multiple, heterogeneous implementations increases transparency into the available business features. From a development perspective, business features provide a quick and easy way to check if a customer has a certain functionality in scope. Typically, a business feature corresponds one to one to a business configuration content object, which represents the corresponding backend enablement. As with all business configuration content, the principle of incremental content

design applies, and all dependencies between business features are managed at the business configuration content level.

- However, the focus of business features is on checking whether a customer has specific customizing settings in place for the given functionality. Therefore, this ERP technology doesn't help with the validation of artificial intelligence models, as it's about proving the quality, not about checking for customizing settings.

1. **Switch framework**

A switch framework is a tool that streamlines the landscape of an ERP system by incorporating one or more industry-specific solutions into a standard system. This framework provides the ability to manage the visibility of repository objects or their components from an external source using switches. When a switch framework is utilized, all industry-specific solutions and a limited set of repository objects are delivered in a deactivated state within the system. Typically, there is no need to install an industry-specific solution, but it must be activated when necessary. The switch framework is usually incorporated into the development environment and works in close collaboration with enhancement tools. The primary objective of these enhancement tools is to offer a technology that enables the creation of enhancements without modifications and to consolidate all potential methods of modifying or enhancing repository objects. The core of the switch framework is a straightforward structure that includes an enhancement option and an implementation element that can be attached to it. The switch framework governs which enhancement implementations should be executed.

The switch framework primarily concentrates on industry verticalization and design-time artifacts. Therefore, this technology does not meet the requirements for validating models of artificial intelligence, as these models are not merely design-time entities.

Given that none of these technologies can be repurposed to verify the models of artificial intelligence from the perspective of business processes, we will move on to discuss a novel strategy. The process of validating artificial intelligence systems can be broadly divided into two categories: offline and online. The offline validation process takes place during the initial development phase, where data scientists experiment with various features, models, and hyperparameters. This involves a repetitive cycle of validating against a predetermined baseline using selected evaluation metrics. Once a model that shows satisfactory performance is developed, the next phase is to launch the model into a live environment and validate its performance using real-time data. This is known as online validation, which involves methods that are implemented post-offline validation to continuously validate and enhance the performance of models as new data comes in.

In this discussion, we will focus solely on online validation as it is the more crucial of the two. In Fig. 17.1, we depict the state transitions of artificial intelligence models, including the necessary validation steps. Let's delve into these steps:

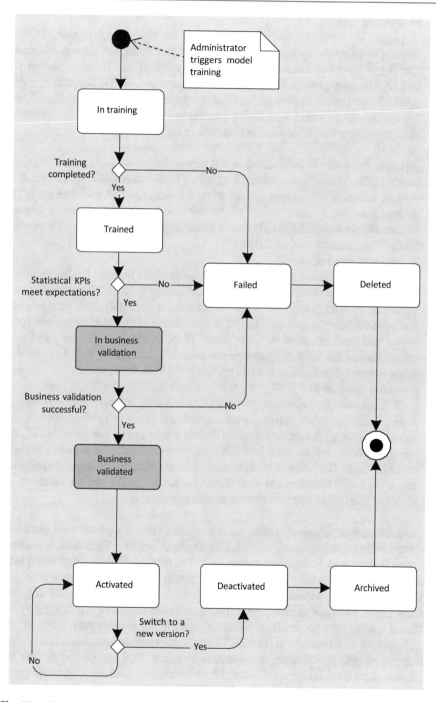

Fig. 17.1 State transition of artificial intelligence models

1. **In training**

   During the training phase, the initiation of the artificial intelligence model's training is overseen by the business administrator using the already discussed Intelligent Scenario Lifecycle Management application. The duration of the training can vary greatly, from mere minutes to several days, depending on the artificial intelligence algorithm used and the nature of the application data. There are also instances where the training process may fail, such as when a particular configuration is absent or there is insufficient training data.

2. **Trained**

   Once the model is trained, statistical key performance indicators (KPIs) are computed to determine its predictive power. The fundamental concept here is to train an artificial intelligence system using a specific dataset and then apply the derived function to data points where the target variable's value is already known. If the model's KPIs fail to meet the set expectations, the model is deemed ineffective and is labeled as failed.

3. **In business validation**

   However, KPIs only provide a static measure of the model's predictive power and are not adequate for the productive application of the artificial intelligence model. As a result, a business validation process is necessary. This process evaluates the artificial intelligence model in the context of the relevant business processes and the associated business users. If the business validation process is unsuccessful, the artificial intelligence model is labeled as failed. Typically, failed artificial intelligence models are removed from the system.

4. **Business validated**

   If the business validation process is successful, the artificial intelligence model is designated as active for productive use. From this point forward, this model handles all inference requests. Before a new model can be activated, the existing model must be deactivated, as only one model can be active in the system at a time. Deactivated models cannot be deleted due to legal compliance requirements. These models can either be stored in the online database or archived to external systems to save memory/storage space.

As previously mentioned, traditional concepts and technologies are not sufficient for the business validation of artificial intelligence models. Therefore, a specific solution is proposed, as depicted in Fig. 17.2. The fundamental idea is to run one or more validation models in the background, parallel to the productively activated artificial intelligence model. As shown in Fig. 17.2, the end user uses the artificial intelligence application to consume predictions. These requests are managed by the artificial intelligence logic class, which integrates the consumption APIs of the trained model into business processes. To run validation models concurrently with the active model, an inference dispatcher is required. This component directs the inference requests to both the validation and productively used artificial intelligence models and receives the inference responses. While the responses from the active model are provided to the artificial intelligence application, the responses from the validation models are stored locally alongside the active model's results. Therefore, for each inference call, validation data is collected, which is then made available to

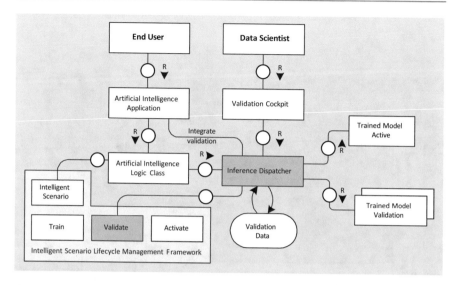

Fig. 17.2 Artificial intelligence model validation solution

the data scientist via the validation cockpit (Fig. 17.4). This allows data scientists to compare the prediction accuracy of the validation models with the productive model.

The data scientist may use additional statistical methods to determine which validation models will be put into productive use. The outcomes of these validation models could potentially be made visible to the end user through the artificial intelligence application. This would allow the end user to compare the results from the active and validation models and offer feedback. While this kind of explicit feedback is clear and understandable to the user, it could affect the user experience and present a challenge in terms of user interface design. However, it also provides valuable information for validating the artificial intelligence model. If the artificial intelligence application incorporates a mechanism for explicit feedback for model validation, then the feedback data is also stored as validation data and shown in the validation cockpit. This means that the data scientist can use the explicit feedback as a basis for making decisions. The class that contains the logic for the artificial intelligence is registered to the intelligent scenario and is therefore linked with the Intelligent Scenario Lifecycle Management framework. As already explained in previous chapters, this framework manages the life cycle of artificial intelligence applications from the perspective of the consumer. It offers the ability to check, set up, train, deploy, and monitor an artificial intelligence application. The Intelligent Scenario Lifecycle Management framework is the logical place to include the validation functionality. This implies that the validation of artificial intelligence models must be explicitly initiated by the end user of the Intelligent Scenario Lifecycle Management framework. This active decision is important because the validation process uses system resources, including storage for the validation data and CPU time for the training process. The details of the validation steps are illustrated in Fig. 17.3.

In Fig. 17.4, we propose a design for the user interface of a cockpit meant for validating artificial intelligence systems, with the aim of outlining its functional

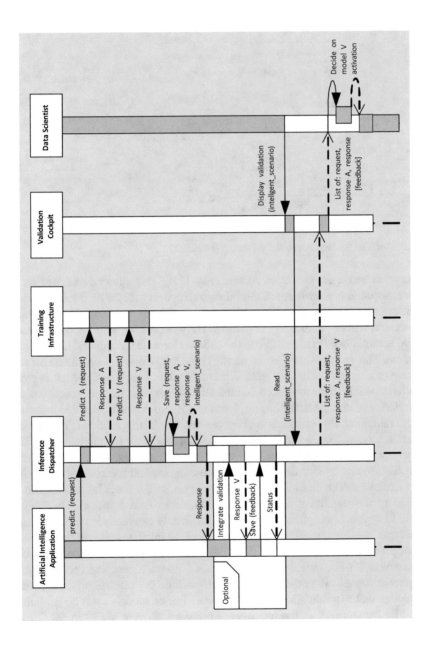

Fig. 17.3 Artificial intelligence validation process

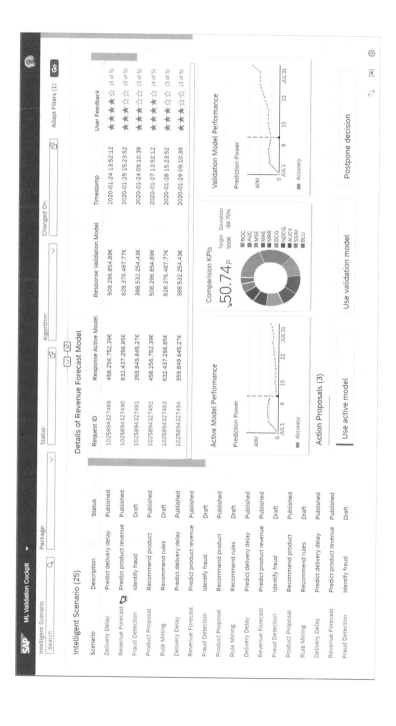

Fig. 17.4 Artificial intelligence model validation cockpit

scope. This user interface is composed of four main sections: a search area, a list page, a detailed view, and an action section. Within the search area, users have the ability to establish filter criteria to aid in the discovery of available intelligent scenarios. Examples of these search criteria could be the name of the intelligent scenario, the package it belongs to, or its current status. Intelligent scenarios that meet the established search criteria are displayed on the left-hand side of the cockpit. Users can then select the intelligent scenario that is relevant to them, and detailed information about it will be displayed on the right-hand side of the cockpit. The table in this section shows the response of the activated and validated model for each request. If available, direct feedback from the model's user can also be shown. Users have the ability to navigate to the request and compare the responses of both the activated and validated models. This comparison is facilitated by precomputed KPIs and a time-dependent display of the responses. Users also have the option to define their own KPIs or apply additional data science methods to the request and response data. Based on the analysis of this data, users can initiate various actions. These actions could include keeping the current active model, shifting to the validation model if it proves to be more accurate, or postponing the decision until more data are gathered.

17.3   Conclusion

Validation of artificial intelligence models is the process of testing the accuracy and reliability of a model's predictions. This is done by comparing the model's output with known data and making sure that the model is able to generalize well to unseen data. Validation helps to ensure that the model is not overfitting or underfitting the data and that it is able to accurately predict outcomes. Statistical methods exist to validate artificial intelligence models regarding the accuracy of predictions. However, for business applications, this mathematical approach alone is not enough. Additional validation from functional and business process points of view is necessary. Therefore, in this section, we deducted the business requirements and proposed the necessary technical solution for validation of artificial intelligence models. Validating models by providing them to specific consumer groups is not sufficient in the context of ERP as based on these, models' actions are processed, which cannot be undone due to legal compliance. To overcome this restriction, we proposed a concept making use of background inference for collecting validation data, which are analyzed with a suggested model validation cockpit.

Interface Design

18

In this chapter, we specify the business requirements and propose the solution concept for user interface design. Incorporating artificial intelligence capabilities into user interfaces needs a particular design and provisioning of new user interface technologies. Only with proper integration into the user interfaces is the instant value of artificial intelligence exploited effectively. Therefore, we propose user interface patterns like matching, recommendation, or ranking to facilitate user interface design for intelligent applications. Thus, partially completely new user interface components are necessary to serve artificial intelligence scenarios.

18.1 Problem Statement

Many individuals perceive user experience as an emotional concept rather than a logical one, which can make it challenging to justify the business benefits of investing in good user experience. However, the reality is that good user experience carries a tangible financial value, in addition to the obvious human value of enhancing people's happiness. For instance, a well-designed user experience can boost productivity, as it enables individuals to accomplish more with an ERP system. This is not only because they become more efficient but also because they become more effective, as the intelligent ERP system directs them toward the tasks that require their attention the most. Another crucial factor is the quality of data: errors in data entry can lead to significant costs later in the process. Therefore, ensuring high-quality data from the outset through a good user experience can prevent the need for later data corrections. Software that is easy to use requires minimal training, leading to substantial savings in training and subsequent support desk costs. If end users are involved in the implementation process and the user experience is tailored to meet their needs from the beginning, the number of change requests for new or different features can be reduced. Changes to a deployed user interface are more costly than changes made in advance. Additionally, the number of user errors will decrease,

S. Sarferaz, *Embedding Artificial Intelligence into ERP Software*, https://doi.org/10.1007/978-3-031-54249-7_18

reducing costs associated with poor data quality and support desk services. Beyond these measurable advantages, a high-quality user experience offers clear human value benefits. These are especially significant in the current era, where businesses compete to attract top talent who prefer to work with contemporary tools rather than outdated ones. A good user experience leads to increased user satisfaction; promotes the inclusion of all employees, including those with disabilities, by supporting accessibility; and encourages people within the company to actually use the software, instead of, for example, storing data separately on their desktops for as long as possible. If the applications are customer-facing, a good user experience can help foster and enhance customer loyalty. Lastly, from the perspective of an IT department, supplying business units with software that offers a superior user experience can strengthen the relationship with these units, as the IT department is providing software that their teams enjoy using.

An intelligently ERP system can enhance the cognitive abilities of a human user. Similar to previous generations of tools, our objective should be to equip users and enhance the results of human labor. To realize this objective, we suggest the following principles for the creation of intelligent systems:

- **Humans should be in control**
- In a corporate setting, actions initiated in an ERP system can have a concrete effect in the real world, influencing the company's objectives and earnings. Since the human user still holds the responsibility and accountability for these actions, they must always have control over the outcome.
- **Enhance human abilities**
- An intelligent system should strive to improve the skills of human experts to earn their trust and encourage successful implementation, rather than attempting to replace them. Measures such as offering improved transparency and effective tools for decision-making processes, incorporating user feedback, and presenting information in a more comprehensible manner can all enhance the individual's power and influence. On the other hand, concealing information, oversimplifying the truth, or limiting the options without adequate transparency can make the user a slave to the ERP system. The user should have the ability to comprehend and manage the intelligent system.
- **Design aligned with ethics**
- Machines perform the tasks they are programmed to do; there is no ethical judgment in an algorithm. The designers and creators of sophisticated artificial intelligence systems are involved in the ethical consequences of their use, misuse, and actions, and they have the responsibility and opportunity to influence these consequences. It is necessary to establish definite and enforceable ethical guidelines that intelligent systems must adhere to.
- **Effective automation**
- Intelligent ERP systems should minimize the effort required by a user to accomplish a task. This involves determining the appropriate level of automation for each use case. When complete automation is not possible, we should strive for increased efficiency. Intelligent systems can assist users in achieving the same outcomes with

fewer steps by integrating automation with improved use of existing information, transparency, and learning effects.

18.2 Solution Proposal

The objective of designing a user interface is to provide a consistent and high-quality user experience across all modules of an ERP system, setting the product apart from its competitors. This consistency can be achieved by creating a design system that is rooted in the company's goals and code, as well as in best practices that guarantee the quality of the development processes. These practices include conducting user research, defining personas, and adhering to guidelines. The design of the user interface aims to simplify the software, and this is achieved through five design principles:

- **Role-based:** The design or system development is tailored to specific roles within the company, such as business employees or accountants. This principle is an extension of the human-centered quality, as the design is specifically created for the workflows of a clearly defined target group, which is identified based on their role and responsibilities. Therefore, role-based design takes into account the roles that business users play, such as accounts receivables accountant or internal sales representative, and the applications are designed with these roles in mind.
- **Adaptive:** According to this principle, the ERP applications should be able to operate on various devices like notebooks, tablets, or smartphones, providing the same user experience across different scenarios and use cases. This necessitates that they are not only responsive but also allow teams to simplify the applications for mobile devices. Therefore, adaptive design means that applications can be used on different form factors such as desktop, tablet, or mobile phone. However, adaptive design goes beyond just technical responsiveness, i.e., ensuring that the same user interface will run on mobile as well as desktop, by also allowing teams to create dedicated versions of desktop apps for mobile use cases.
- **Simple:** This principle can be best understood through the 2/20/200 rule, which states that a user should be able to recognize the status (situation) within 2 seconds, identify the causes for this result in about 20 seconds, and understand the exact reasons behind this in the form of detailed information in 200 seconds. The screen should always be minimalist and organized and contain only the most important information but also serve as a quick access point for detailed information. Simplicity is easier said than done: it involves avoiding clutter on the screen, keeping only the important information in focus, and having progressive disclosure to give users access to details as they need them.
- **Coherent:** Humans tend to quickly adapt to products and behaviors. Therefore, users should always feel familiar with the system when using it. This can be achieved by avoiding repetition (consistency) and eliminating gaps or illogical jumps (coherence) during the use of different apps. Therefore, coherence means

that users of many applications feel that they all belong to the same family, i.e., they behave consistently, and they feel coherent.

- **Delightful:** The software should be enjoyable for the user to use, enabling them to build a positive emotional relationship with it. Non-functional aspects such as nice animations can contribute to this, serving as an example of pure user interface aspects that are unrelated to features and functions that support the business. Therefore, delightful means that users enjoy using the user interfaces and that they have a positive emotional connection to the software.

Depending on the use case and desired output, tasks involving artificial intelligence can be classified into several broad categories (such as classification, regression, or clustering tasks). Moreover, the specific approach for implementation can influence the user interface in a very specific way. There are two important aspects to consider when designing intelligent systems that use artificial intelligence models:

1. **Explainable Artificial Intelligence**
   The design of intelligent systems should be guided by the principle of empowering the end user. This can be accomplished by offering ample information about the underlying model and elucidating the logic behind the outcomes of an algorithm. Empowerment fosters a sense of trust between humans and machines. We delved into this topic in the chapter titled *Explanation of Results*.
2. **Feedback loop**
   Various algorithms might necessitate feedback from the end user to strengthen the underlying data model. The creation of an effective feedback loop is a complex design task that may introduce new user roles, such as data scientists, and specialized user interfaces, for instance, for the monitoring and analysis of feedback. We discussed this topic in the chapter *Model Degradation*.

As we outlined in the second part, we discovered several application patterns for artificial intelligence within the context of ERP software. In this section, we examine the general user interface design for these artificial intelligence patterns, specifically for matching, recommendation, and ranking. We concentrate on the crucial aspects to elucidate the design proposals.

18.2.1 Intelligent Matching

The process of intelligent matching uses methods derived from the field of artificial intelligence to identity items that are related and subsequently create groups of matches. This system has the capability to propose one or several matching strategies to link the items. The role of the users in this process is simply to give their approval or disapproval of these suggestions or modify them according to their specific requirements. We illustrate the varying degrees of automation involved in the matching process in Fig. 18.1.

Fig. 18.1 Matching levels

(1) **Select, validate, and rate**

This marks the initial stage of automation for an ERP system. The process of matching remains a manual task, driven by the user; however, the ERP system checks and evaluates the quality of the match when requested. Following this, the user has the option to either apply the match or make further refinements to it.

(2) **Explore and adjust**

The ERP system presents potential matches according to various methodologies. In this scenario, the users select a single method, but frequently, they are required to make adjustments.

(3) **Review and decide**

The ERP system creates the best possible matches and offers them as prioritized recommendations. The user consuming the system proposes and selects one option without needing any additional adjustment.

The process of matching involves connecting a group of items based on specific criteria, such as their similarities or the nature of their relationship. This group of items is referred to as a matching group. We've noticed some common characteristics of matching groups in the scenarios we've observed:

- **Group name**
- This is a meaningful label for the matching group. It could be, for instance, the title of the master record in a merging scenario or the name of the matching criterion.
- **Group summary**
- This is an optional explanation of what the group contains. The summary can be expressed in text form or through key/value parameters.
- **Group size**
- This refers to the total count of items within the group.
- **Quality indicator**
- This is a measure of the confidence level in a proposed match in relation to the set objective. For instance, it could be the likeness of business partner records when merging duplicates or the percentage covered when matching invoices.
- **Finalizing action**
- This is an action that can be applied to the entire group, such as approving a proposed match.

We can display the collection of matching groups to users in various formats – for instance, as a list, a grid, or even a graph. Users can then drill down into a specific group and analyze its content and match quality in detail. The way a matching group is displayed depends on the use case and can range from a simple list to a complex chart like a network graph. The level of interaction with the matched objects and groups varies depending on the matching level and the match quality. For instance, if the proposed match is not very precise, then editing the matching group becomes a crucial part of the interaction. Higher levels of automation already provide sufficiently good match proposals and only differ in strategy. Here, the following main or finalizing actions are possible:

- **Approve**
- The proposal is accepted as it is.
- **Reject**
- The proposal is either fully or partially rejected. Partial rejection involves manually editing the matching group and then accepting it. Rejection can trigger a subsequent feedback mechanism (either implicit or explicit).
- **Merge**
- This involves combining two or more groups into a superior one.
- **Split**
- This involves forming two or more groups from a single one. This can be done by selecting individual items, which are then used to form new groups.

The concept itself does not impose any restrictions on responsiveness and adaptiveness. It typically utilizes standard user interface controls and floorplans and adopts their responsiveness characteristics and guidelines.

18.2.2 Recommendations

Intelligent ERP systems can assist users by recommending suitable content or suggesting an action or input that the user might favor. In this context, we're discussing recommendation and its impact on the user interface. As previously noted, there are various types of recommendation models, such as assistance with input or suggestions for solutions. Input assistance offers recommendations for user input to fill out an entire form or just a single element of it. In both scenarios, we need to design the following micro-interactions:

- **Detect**
- From a user's perspective, we need to identify the values that the system has proposed.
- **Explain**
- From a user's perspective, we want to comprehend the reasoning behind the system's recommendation.
- **Compare**

- From a user's perspective, we need the ability to compare the existing human input against the system's recommendation.
- **Act**
- From a user's perspective, we wish to either accept or reject the system's recommendations.

The guiding principle is that human input should always win against machine input. As depicted in Figure 18.2, the ERP system can autofill blank fields with suggestions. A user's input should never be replaced by a system recommendation without the user's consent. The user's active acceptance of the ERP system's suggestion transforms it into user input. Now, let's explore the various options for input assistance:

(1) Without human input and without system recommendation
(2) With human input but without system recommendation
(3) Without human input but with system recommendation
(4) With human input and with system recommendation

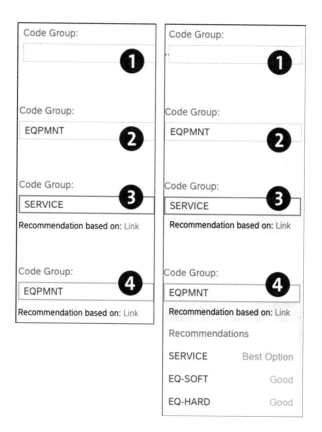

Fig. 18.2 Input assistance

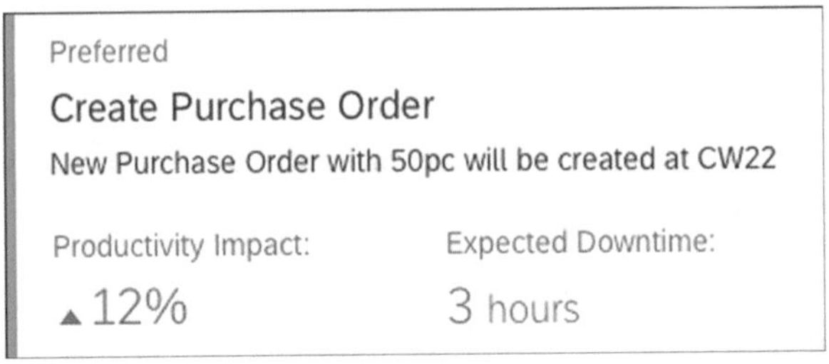

Preferred

Create Purchase Order

New Purchase Order with 50pc will be created at CW22

Productivity Impact: Expected Downtime:

▲12%   3 hours

Fig. 18.3 Recommendation item

Users have the option to either implicitly agree with the system's recommendation by submitting the entire form or they can explicitly choose an alternative if there's a disagreement. If users want to outright reject a system's recommendation, they can do so by beginning to adjust it in the input field.

In a majority of instances where solution recommendations are used, these solutions are displayed as a collection of recommended items, all of which are organized within a recommendation block. At the very least, each recommended item should possess a significant title that is associated with an action. The way these items are displayed can be further customized based on the specific use case by using a variant of the list item control. Figure 18.3 provides an example that illustrates the structure of the most complex case, complete with all optional elements:

- **Title and description**
- The recommendation should be given a concise yet meaningful title that encapsulates the recommended action. Additional details can be provided in a supplementary description. While longer texts may be cut off after the second line, it is advisable to avoid such truncation.
- **Action**
- In order to apply a recommendation, the user must perform a corresponding action. The action can be initiated by clicking on the entire list item or a specific button, depending on the design of the recommendation item.
- **Selection**
- In certain scenarios, users may need to preview the results before making a selection. In such instances, the triggers for the preview and the final action should be distinct.
- **Preferred proposal**
- Based on the specific use case, a recommendation item can be highlighted as a preferred proposal. For more information, refer to the section on ranked recommendations that follows.

A group of recommendation items constitutes a recommendation block. Figure 18.4 provides an example of the structure of a horizontal recommendation block based on a grid list:

Fig. 18.4 Recommendation block

- **Recommendation block header**
- The block toolbar contains a meaningful and short block title (1), which describes the set of proposed solutions (2). It can also offer additional functionality (3) that applies to the whole recommendation block, such as an additional explanation of the model behind the recommendations or an option to provide explicit user feedback to reinforce the underlying model.
- **Recommendation block items**
- Recommendation items (4) are the main content of the recommendation block. Depending on the use case and space constraints, they can be organized horizontally, vertically, or as a grid.
- **Ranked recommendations**
- The initial suggestion within the recommendation block can be highlighted to indicate the most favored proposition. It is advisable to underscore just a single entry, the most favored one, in the enumeration and position it at the top. If the situation demands, we can apply the use of semantic colors to enhance the emphasis.

18.2.3 Ranking

Ranking is a method that simplifies complex decision-making processes for business users by presenting the most optimal choices at the forefront. The process involves arranging items within a group based on certain criteria that align with the user's business context. These criteria could be a specific amount, the level of priority, or a particular score. When items are ranked in a table or list, the arrangement is always such that the items with the highest rank are displayed at the top. The process of ranking may involve the use of sophisticated algorithms, but this is not a necessity. Ranking can also be achieved through the application of basic rules, set thresholds, or heuristics. The concept for ranking in lists and tables consists of three fundamental elements that are grouped together in a commonly reusable component. This concept is visually represented in Fig. 18.5:

(1) **Ranking value**

The ranking is typically determined by a common value, which is usually a numerical figure that establishes the position of an object. This value could be an indirect one, such as cost or delivery duration, or it could be a score. Depending on the specific application, the score could be displayed

Fig. 18.5 Ranking
elements

as a percentage or without any measurement unit. Alternatively, a compact
visual representation like a radial microchart could be used. While it's
unusual, rankings can also be based on non-numerical values, such as the
letter-based grading systems used in academia (A+, A, A−; B+, B, B−; C+,
C, C−; D+, D, D−). Interacting with the ranking value, either by clicking or
tapping, will open a dialog box that provides detailed information about the
ranking of the item in question. If there are items in a list that, for whatever
reason, lack a ranking value, they should be placed at the end of the list. An
instance of this could be a newly added supplier that hasn't accumulated
enough data to be ranked by the system.

(2) **Ranking description**

The description associated with a ranking gives further explanation to the
ranking's value. Using words such as *best* or *alternative* can provide more precise direction without adding unnecessary complexity. It's crucial to recognize
that these ranking descriptions are greatly influenced by their context. The
choice of language and its correlation to the ranking score is determined by the
content it's associated with, the specific application, and the overall process.

(3) **Change indicator**

The modification marker simplifies the process of monitoring the ranking
value for rapidly fluctuating data sets, like live feeds used in scenarios involving
the interconnected network of physical devices, vehicles, and other items
embedded with software, sensors, and network connectivity that enables these
objects to collect and exchange data.

In order to enhance clarity and aid the user in making informed decisions, it is
advisable to furnish more detailed information about the ranking system whenever
it is feasible.

The value used for ranking is the smallest element necessary to display a ranking
for a list or table. The description of the ranking and the change indicator enhance
the fundamental value of the ranking, but they may not always be necessary. Besides
these three primary elements of the ranking component, there are two more factors
to think about:

- **Semantic colors**
- These can be used to emphasize the message of the ranking. Use semantic colors
  based on values when the aim is to highlight data points that are positive, neutral,
  or negative. Depending on the set threshold values, the color of each data point
  could be red, green, or orange.
- **Presentation variations**
- These variations allow the ranking concept to support different representations
  of the same data point. The appropriate representation depends on the role and

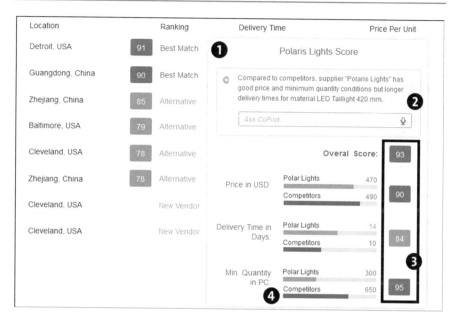

Fig. 18.6 Ranking details

use case, as well as the relative significance of ranking in the application. For instance, if the ranking is part of the dataset but isn't pertinent for the role or task, avoid using a semantic color and present the ranking like all other values in the table.

To gain additional insights into the ranking for a specific object, the user can view the ranking details as shown in Fig. 18.6. The detail dialog is triggered by clicking or tapping the RANKING indicator (1). In the ranking details, explain the position of the object in the overall ranking (2) and the individual ranking components (3). Also include a comparison (4) between the current object and the average score for all other objects. Comparing individual values with an overall score helps users assess their importance.

18.3 Conclusion

User experience has become significantly more important in recent years because companies no longer see it as a pure design function but also as an economic benefit that promises long-term competitive advantages and high employee and customer satisfaction. For this reason, the continuous development and improvement of the user experience are indispensable. Incorporating artificial intelligence capabilities into user interfaces needs a particular design and provisioning of new user interface technologies. Only with proper integration into the user interfaces is the instant value of artificial intelligence exploited effectively. In this section, we deducted the business requirements and proposed the necessary technical implementation for designing user interfaces for intelligent systems. The goal here was to optimally guide the user and focus the attention on the highest priority tasks by notifications. In addition, a wide range of other artificial intelligence design patterns facilitate the user's workflow, for example, explanations, matching, rankings, and recommendations but also predictions and forecasts.

Embedding Generative AI

19

In this chapter, we specify the business requirements and propose the solution concept for embedding Generative AI into ERP software. Generative AI has the potential to radically change the way we apply artificial intelligence in various industries and fields. By levering the strength of these sophisticated models, users without technical backgrounds can address their business challenges just by expressing them in everyday language. This creates a vast range of opportunities for both companies and individuals. In the context of ERP systems, the key questions are: What is the added value of Generative AI, what are the technical requirements, and how to embed this technology into business applications? Providing answers for those questions is the objective of this chapter.

19.1   Problem Statement

Foundation models, large language models, and generative AI are related concepts in the field of artificial intelligence, particularly in the subfield of natural language processing and machine learning. Here's a brief explanation of each term and how they depend on each other:

1. **Foundation models:** These are pre-trained machine learning models that serve as a starting point or base for more specialized models or applications. These models are usually trained on massive amounts of data and can capture general features and representations of the data. By fine-tuning these models on smaller, task-specific datasets, researchers can create models that perform well on a wide range of tasks. Examples of foundation models include OpenAI's GPT-3, BERT, and CLIP.
2. **Large language models (LLMs):** These are a type of foundation model specifically designed to handle natural language processing tasks. LLMs are trained on vast amounts of text data, enabling them to generate coherent and contextually

relevant responses, perform translation, answer questions, and more. The term large refers to the size of the model, typically measured by the number of parameters. Larger models have more capacity to learn complex patterns and representations, leading to better performance on a variety of tasks. GPT-3, with its 175 billion parameters, is an example of an LLM.

3. **Generative AI:** This term refers to the broader class of AI models that can generate new data samples based on the patterns and structures learned during training. These models can create text, images, music, or any other type of data by sampling from a learned probability distribution. LLMs are a type of generative AI, as they can generate text based on a given context or prompt.

Thus, foundation models are a general concept in machine learning, and large language models are a specific type of foundation model designed for natural language processing tasks. Both foundation models and large language models can be considered part of the broader category of generative AI, as they can generate new data samples based on learned patterns. These concepts depend on each other in the sense that large language models are a subclass of foundation models, and both of these model types can be seen as instances of generative AI. The development of more advanced foundation models and LLMs contributes to the progress in generative AI and its potential applications. As already mentioned, Generative AI refers to a type of artificial intelligence that focuses on creating new content, data, or patterns based on existing examples. These AI models are designed to generate output that resembles human-created content, such as text, images, music, or even videos. They learn from existing data and are capable of producing novel content by understanding and mimicking the underlying structure and patterns in the data. One of the most popular techniques used in generative AI is generative adversarial networks (GANs), which consist of two neural networks, a generator and a discriminator, competing against each other. The generator creates fake data, while the discriminator tries to distinguish between real and fake data. This process helps the generator improve its output, making it increasingly difficult for the discriminator to differentiate between the two. Another popular approach is variational autoencoders (VAEs), which are unsupervised learning models that learn to compress data and then reconstruct it. VAEs can generate new data by sampling from the learned compressed representation. Generative AI has numerous applications, such as creating realistic images, generating text, composing music, designing new molecules for drug discovery, and more.

Within the realm of ERP software, the primary inquiries revolve around the additional benefits brought by Generative AI, the necessary technical specifications, and the methods to incorporate this technology into business applications. Those aspects we discuss in this section. However, as the Generative AI is a brand-new research topic, those might be not final answers. Generative AI has the potential to radically change the way we apply artificial intelligence in various industries and fields. By leveraging the capabilities of these advanced models, non-technical users can now solve their business tasks simply by describing them in natural language. This opens up a wide possibility for businesses and individuals alike, empowering them to harness the capabilities of AI without requiring extensive technical expertise. Foundation models, like OpenAI's GPT series, are designed to be broadly applicable to a multitude of tasks without the need for re-training. By employing these models, businesses can optimize their processes, enhance their decision-making, and automate repetitive tasks, ultimately driving growth and innovation. The adaptability of general-purpose Generative AI models is another key advantage. These models can be fine-tuned to perform specific tasks in a relatively short amount of time, allowing organizations to quickly deploy artificial intelligence solutions tailored to their needs. To provide orientation when to apply Generative AI, we list exemplary use case patterns, which can be resolved with this technology:

1. **Content Generation:** Create articles, blog posts, social media content, mail drafts, product descriptions, or even poetry and stories based on a given theme or keywords.
2. **Question-Answering:** Build systems that answer questions based on a given context or knowledge base and extract valuable insights and information from large datasets or collections of text documents.
3. **Conversation Agents:** Develop chatbots or virtual assistants that can answer user questions, provide customer support, or engage in general conversation.
4. **Text Summarization:** Generate concise summaries of long articles, news, or research papers to help users grasp the main ideas quickly.
5. **Translation:** Translate text between different languages while maintaining the context and meaning of the original content.
6. **Sentiment Analysis:** Analyze the tone and sentiment of a piece of text, such as reviews, tweets, or comments, and classify them as positive, negative, or neutral.
7. **Text Classification:** Foundation models can be fine-tuned to categorize text into specific groups, such as spam detection, topic classification, or intent recognition.
8. **Code Generation:** Given a natural language description, generate code snippets in various programming languages or autocomplete code for developers.
9. **Data Augmentation:** Artificial intelligence models can generate new data samples for training machine learning models, improving their performance and generalization and unit tests for code evaluation.
10. **Information Extraction:** Extract structured information from unstructured text, such as names, dates, addresses, or other relevant data.
11. **Personalization:** Generate personalized content, recommendations, or experiences for users based on their preferences, interests, or past behavior.
12. **Creative Applications:** Assist with brainstorming ideas, generating names for products or companies, creating advertising slogans, writing song lyrics, generating image/video/voice.

Potential benefits of Generative AI for ERP systems are numerous and can significantly improve the user experience, streamline content creation, and enhance developer productivity. One of the key benefits is the improvement of the software and service experience for customers. By enabling interactions with the software using natural language, users can more easily navigate the system and access the functionality they need. Automation in customer support can lead to quicker resolution of issues and improved satisfaction levels. Conversational retrieval of information allows users to obtain the data they need more efficiently, making the entire user experience more enjoyable and productive. Another benefit is the assistance provided in content creation and knowledge management. Generative AI can produce or improve various types of content, such as marketing and sales copies, making it easier for businesses to communicate their value proposition to their customers. Additionally, the models can help in summarizing ERP documents and data, enabling users to quickly understand the key points and make informed decisions. Lastly, Generative AI can increase the speed and effectiveness of developers working with ERP systems. With features such as code generation from natural language and code auto-completion, developers can work more efficiently and reduce the time it takes to bring new features or improvements to market. Automated generation of documentation also ensures that developers have access to accurate and up-to-date information, further streamlining the development process. For embedding Generative AI into ERP software, the following application requirements must be considered:

1. **Vendor diversity:** It is required to be open for diverse Generative AI vendors so that ERP application development teams have the choice.
2. **Built-in Generative AI:** It is expected that the Generative AI capabilities are systematically embedded into business processes so that the features are provided to the right person, in the right place, and at the right time.
3. **Standardized implementation:** For developers, the programming model on ERP side shall be uniform, independent of the utilized Generative AI technology.
4. **Standardized operations:** For customers, the configuration and operation on ERP side shall be uniform, independent of the utilized Generative AI technology.
5. **Model adoption:** Mechanism and tooling for adopting Generative AI models are required like prompt creation, incorporating embeddings and retraining of models hosted by ERP vendor.
6. **Legal compliance:** It is demanded that the ERP application facilitating Generative AI technology is compliant to General Data Protection Regulation (GDPR), California Consumer Privacy Act (CCPA), consent management, automated decision-making, read access logging, and legal auditing.
7. **Optimized lockup:** To ensure fast lockups for Generative AI embeddings, corresponding vector search engine shall be supported.
8. **Validation:** It is required to provide validation mechanism for inputs and outputs of Generative AI, like syntax check of generated code or avoiding vulnerability injection.
9. **Life cycle customer:** Support life cycle management for customers aspects like setup of Generative AI technology, model fine-tuning, and monitoring.
10. **Life cycle provider:** Support life cycle management for provider aspects like provisioning of Generative AI models, updating models, support handling, and facilitating zero downtime.

11. **Error handling:** Mechanism and tooling for error handing and resolution, business monitoring, and provisioning of fallback models are required.
12. **Performance:** It is requested that predefined end-to-end response time for synchronous Generative AI inference calls are ensured. In the context of ERP systems, typical expectations are 150ms for instant feedback, 1000ms for simple, and 3000ms for complex interactions.
13. **Mass processing:** For mass processing, asynchronous inference calls (batch inference) must be supported, although the underlying Generative AI models typically support synchronous inferencing.
14. **Scalability:** It is required that the Generative AI technology scales with the number of calls and number of customers.
15. **Data integration:** Data extraction for Generative AI embeddings and fine-tuning shall support initial load and delta management and must be based on ERP standard technologies.
16. **Configuration:** Mechanism and tooling for configuration of Generative AI technology is required like max token, temperature, vendor, or hardware limits. Customer configurations shall not be overwritten after updates and upgrades.
17. **Extensibility:** Mechanism and tooling for extending Generative AI applications is required. Customer extensions shall not be overwritten after updates and upgrades.
18. **Localization:** It is required to implement functional localizations for Generative AI like multiple language support.
19. **Metering:** It is expected that usage metering for Generative AI consumption is supported.
20. **AI ethics:** Generative AI applications must follow the AI Ethics principles (see epilogue).

The next chapter discusses solution proposal for the above listed requirements.

19.2 Solution Proposal

This section explains how to resolve the requirements from the previous chapter. The guiding principle is to facilitate ERP application developers focusing on the business logic only while a majority of the requirements are addressed by the underlying technology and frameworks, those technology and framework-related requirements we assume as granted, e.g., performance, scalability, and optimized lookup. Conversely, in this section, we concentrate on the aspects which are specific to Generative AI and relevant for ERP application development.

Learnings from the current use cases show that Generative AI models, such as large-scale language models, are powerful tools for a wide range of applications, but they may require adaptation to perform optimally on specific tasks or domains. To achieve this, we can employ several model adoption techniques, such as:

1. **Prompt engineering:** This technique involves crafting specific tasks or questions in natural language, which can help guide the foundation model to generate more accurate and relevant responses. By carefully designing prompts, we can effectively instruct the model to focus on the desired aspects of the task, improving its overall performance.
2. **Embeddings:** Incorporating external knowledge through embeddings can significantly improve a foundation model's ability to adapt to domain-specific knowledge. Embeddings represent information in a numerical format that the model can easily process and learn from. By including domain-specific embeddings (e.g., example for good code, product documentation) or pre-trained embeddings from various sources, we can enrich the model's understanding of the domain and provide it with useful references to generate more accurate and context-aware outputs.
3. **Fine-tuning:** Another way to adapt foundation models is by fine-tuning their parameters on a small set of labeled data specific to the target task. This process involves updating the model's weights using gradient descent and backpropagation, enabling it to learn the nuances of the task and improve its performance. Fine-tuning can be particularly effective when dealing with few-shot learning scenarios, where we have limited labeled data available.

By combining these techniques, we can successfully adapt foundation models to a wide range of tasks and domains, unlocking their full potential and enhancing their performance to meet our specific needs. Those model adoption methods are a new aspect in the application development and are therefore reflected accordingly in the solution architecture depicted in Fig. 19.1. For the implementation of Generative AI applications, we could identify so far the following realization patterns:

1. **Digital assistant:** For question-answer use cases, the digital assistant solutions (chat bots) should be used. Generative AI capabilities are currently incorporated into the underlying digital assistant technologies. Applications can follow the established programming model for digital assistant and make indirectly use of Generative AI.
2. **Basic prompting:** Business applications with elementary requirements regarding prompt engineering should utilize the prompt creation capabilities of the ERP platform. Predefined prompt templates where just parameters are replaced by concrete values are an example for this category. These basic prompts are executed on Generative AI models, which are hosted externally or deployed on AI technology platform.
3. **Advanced prompting:** Business applications with sophisticated requirements concerning prompt engineering should facilitate the prompt creation capabilities of the AI technology platform. Prompts including embeddings and require therefore vector search engines are an example for this category. Prompt execution is also here based on Generative AI models, which are hosted externally or deployed on the AI technology platform.

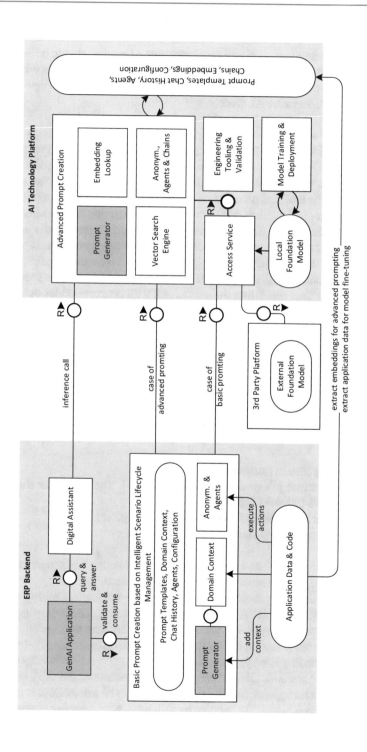

Fig. 19.1 Architecture for embedding Generative AI

4. **Model retraining:** For applications where the pretrained Generative AI models are not sufficient but fine-tuning is required, the deployment and retraining capabilities of AI technology platform for Generative AI models should be used. The idea is to train the highest layers of the underlying foundation models with application specific data. The previous three realization patterns can be then applied on these local Generative AI models.

The proposed solution architecture in Fig. 19.1 facilitates the previously explained realization patterns for embedding Generative AI into ERP. For question-answer use cases, the digital assistant technology is foreseen. Independent of the realization pattern, the Generative AI application integrates the Generative AI capability deeply into the business processes and user interfaces with consumption APIs. For harmonized implementation and operations of Generative AI, the already proposed Intelligent Scenario Lifecycle Management (ISLM) framework is used. For model adoption, the Intelligent Scenario Lifecycle Management framework shall provide basic and the AI technology platform advanced promoting capabilities.

The prompt generator utilizes the creation of prompt templates for a specific use case during design time and filling the parameters with concrete values during runtime. Let's explain this with the following example:

Prompt template for the use case Internal Job Description

- You are an assistant designed to generate appealing job descriptions for an international company named **[company_name]**.
- Users will input structured data for a job position. You should generate an html-formatted job description.
- Avoid bias based on physical appearance, ethnicity, or race. Replace inappropriate language with inclusive language or politely refuse results, if that is not possible.
- Provide the response in **[language]**.
- Generate an internal job description for **[job title]**. The candidate shall have **[Skill-01]**, **[Skill-02]** and **[Skill-03]**.
- Hiring Manager is **[manager]** and recruiter is **[recruiter]**.
- Location is **[location]** and start of work is **[start-date]**.

The above prompt template contains parameters illustrated as square brackets. During design time, such templates are defined and stored, and the corresponding Generative AI application provides the values for the parameters during runtime when the according Generative AI functionality is consumed. The prompt generator just applies text functionality and replaces the parameters with the concrete values. Storing the prompt templates on the ERP platform for basic promoting dramatically simplifies corresponding life cycle management (e.g., version dependency of templates and the ERP system). Depending on the requirements of the use case, additional context must be appended to the prompt. This can be just examples (e.g., for good job descriptions), which are handled by the component *domain context* in case of basic promoting. More complex context could be needed for advanced prompting (e.g., PDF documents containing job descriptions for different job categories), where *embedding lookup* and *vector search engine* help manage this requirement. A vector search engine is a type of search engine that uses vector representations, also known as embeddings, to search for relevant information. Unlike traditional keyword-based search engines, vector search engines use mathematical techniques to represent and process the meaning of words, phrases, sentences, or documents in a high-dimensional vector space. The key idea is that semantically similar items have similar vector representations. Vector search engines are particularly useful for information retrieval tasks, such as document retrieval, question-answer, and recommendation systems, where understanding the meaning and context of the query is essential for finding relevant results. Generated prompts can contain data privacy and protection related information (e.g., hiring manager and recruiter in the job description example above), which shall not be sent to external Generative AI models. To resolve this requirement, the effected data is anonymized before provisioned to the external Generative AI model. For this anonymization, functionality is depicted in the solution architecture, which can be implemented, for example, with the corresponding ERP database system. Further legal requirements like auditing, logging, consent management, and automated decision-making are ensured with existing and already introduced methods and tools (see chapter *Data Protection and Data Privacy*). The generated prompt is handed over to the access service as request, which then dispatches it to the external hosted or local deployed Generative AI model. The provided response is de-anonymized (anonymized parameter are replaced with original values) and sent to the Generative AI application, which validates and consumes it. Validation may be necessary, for example, to avoid security vulnerabilities like injections or just to check syntax correctness of generated coding.

For orchestrating prompts across multiple Generative AI models or to trigger actions out of Generative AI responses, corresponding chains and agents are foreseen. For extracting embeddings or application for model fine-tuning, the established data integration mechanism of ERP systems can be used (see chapter *Data Integration*). In simple scenarios, localization could be resolved within the prompt (e.g., provide the response in [language]) but may require translation infrastructure for the whole prompt too. The above-explained runtime behavior is summarized in Fig. 19.2.

The practical feasibility of the concept is illustrated in Fig. 19.3 with the above job description example, which we now explain in more detail. In the fast-paced world of recruitment, HR professionals often grapple with the challenge of creating compelling job descriptions within a limited timeframe. The quality of these descriptions significantly impacts their relevance to potential applicants, making it a crucial aspect of the recruitment process. Moreover, maintaining consistency across job descriptions is essential for effective employer branding. However, the rush to prepare for candidate interviews often leads to a compromise on the quality of job descriptions. This not only affects the caliber of applicants attracted but also hampers the overall employer branding efforts. The solution to these challenges lies in leveraging Generative AI to draft job descriptions quickly that are well-structured and reduce bias. For the implementation, job description-specific prompt template

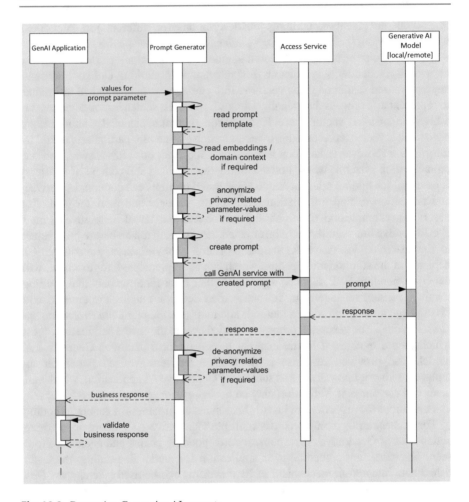

Fig. 19.2 Processing Generative AI prompts

must be defined during design time and stored in the ERP database using Intelligent Scenario Lifecycle Management. This framework also handles the connectivity the Generative AI model, which is hosted on the AI technology platform. During run-time, the HR employee specifies the concrete parameter for the prompt template. The Intelligent Scenario Lifecycle Management framework composes based on those values the prompt, sends it to the Generative AI model, and provides the result back to the application. This approach ensures that the job descriptions are not only compelling but also consistent across the board, thereby enhancing the employer's brand image. Moreover, recruiters can receive tailored interview questions based on the job description and the candidate's resume. This feature allows for a more per-sonalized and effective interview process, ensuring that the right questions are asked to assess the candidate's suitability for the role. The outcomes of this solution are manifold. Firstly, it significantly reduces the time and cost involved in creating job

Fig. 19.3 Job Description with Generative AI

descriptions. This efficiency allows HR professionals to focus on other critical aspects of the recruitment process. Secondly, it improves the quality of interviews and preparation. With tailored interview questions, recruiters can better assess a candidate's fit for the role, leading to more successful hires. Lastly, this streamlined approach to job descriptions and interview preparation increases the company's attractiveness as an employer of choice. A well-structured and unbiased job description not only attracts the right talent but also sends a positive message about the company's commitment to fairness and transparency in its recruitment process. In conclusion, the future of recruitment lies in harnessing the power of Generative AI to streamline job descriptions and interview preparation. This approach not only enhances efficiency but also improves the quality of hires, ultimately contributing to the company's success.

19.3 Conclusion

Generative AI can greatly enhance ERP systems by improving user experience, automating content creation, and boosting developer productivity. It can facilitate natural language interactions, automate customer support, assist in content creation, summarize documents, and even generate code, all of which contribute to a more efficient, enjoyable, and productive user experience and development process. Generative AI models, such as large-scale language models, have shown immense potential across various applications, but they often need customization to perform optimally in specific tasks or domains. Techniques like prompt engineering, incorporating domain-specific embeddings, and fine-tuning the model parameters on task-specific data can significantly enhance the model's performance, making these adaptation methods a crucial aspect of application development and solution architecture. The proposed solution architecture integrates Generative AI into ERP systems, using Intelligent Scenario Lifecycle Management for implementation and operations, and a prompt generator for specific use cases. It also includes data privacy measures, such as anonymization, before data is sent to external Generative AI models, and de-anonymization of responses, with validation to avoid security vulnerabilities, and uses vector search engines for advanced prompting and context understanding.

Part III

Implementation Framework and Case Studies

We deal in this part with applying the introduced concepts exemplary on SAP S/4HANA as the market leading ERP solution and illustrate how to implement intelligent business applications. Those are ERP applications with embedded artificial intelligence capabilities. We propose a framework that realizes the explained concepts and facilitates the development and operations of intelligent business applications. The concepts suggested in the previous part are built in the framework as far as possible so that developers can reuse the implementation for each artificial intelligence scenario. This increases development efficiency, reduces defect rates, harmonizes the programming model, and accelerates the introduction of new concepts. The framework abstracts from the underlying artificial intelligence technologies by providing stable APIs to the business applications. Thus, developers must not take care about the volatile artificial intelligence technologies. Uniform configuration and operations experience for artificial intelligence applications are expected. These aspects are also covered by the framework, which streamlines the entire life cycle management of artificial intelligence scenarios. Consequently, corresponding functionality is provided for the business administrator who operates the artificial intelligence applications. Having one central tool for life cycle management reduces the operations costs and simplifies the administration tasks. The mentioned framework is a patented invention of the author and is used for the implementation of all artificial intelligence scenarios in SAP S/4HANA. This fact outlines the practicability of the theoretical concepts, which were explained in the previous part. To demonstrate the workability of the concepts and framework, real-world business applications of SAP S/4HANA are depicted, which embed artificial intelligence capability. We explain scenarios in the area of finance, sourcing and procurement, sales, inventory, and supply chain as case studies. Due to time-to-mark pressure, some use cases have implemented work-arounds, which are continuously converged to the target architecture. This part is based on our investigations in Sarferaz (2021) and our patents (https://patents.justia.com/inventor/siar-sarferaz).

Implementation Framework

20

In this chapter, we propose an implementation framework that realizes the introduced concepts for embedding artificial intelligence into ERP software. The added value of the framework is to standardize the development of embedded and side-by-side artificial intelligence architecture to increase efficiency. Furthermore, the technical implementation of the previously introduced concepts is taken over by the frame-work and hidden from the developer as far as possible. Life cycle management tasks like training models, analyzing model KPIs, and deploying models are handled by the framework. Actually, the framework consists of two applications, one for imple-mentation of intelligent business applications by developers and one for operating them by administrators. The framework is used for the development of exemplary case studies of SAP's ERP solution in the next chapters and is therefore based on SAP technology. We explain the framework step by step from the developer and administrator perspective.

20.1 Approach Comparison

This chapter is dedicated to discussing the steps involved in implementing both embedded and side-by-side artificial intelligence. To begin, we will provide a brief overview of the necessary development artifacts required for each of these methods. Additionally, we will offer decision criteria for when to use which technique. The already introduced *Life Cycle Management* chapter builds the key conceptual foun-dation for the implementation of the Intelligent Scenario Lifecycle Management framework in this chapter. For the concrete realization of the framework, we utilized SAP technology. The framework covers the implementation and operations of arti-ficial intelligence applications and will be facilitated also for developing the case studies in the next chapters.

Figure 20.1 provides a visual representation of objects embedded and side-by-side artificial intelligence have in common. It also highlights the specific artifacts

© The Author(s), under exclusive license to Springer Nature
Switzerland AG 2024
S. Sarferaz, *Embedding Artificial Intelligence into ERP Software*,
https://doi.org/10.1007/978-3-031-54249-7_20

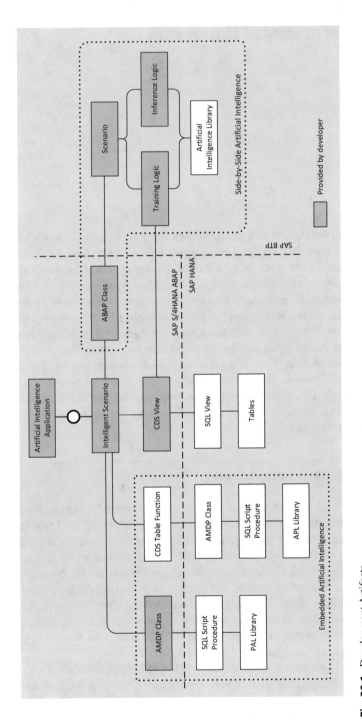

Fig. 20.1 Development Artifacts

that developers need to implement. Regardless of the type of artificial intelligence approach being used, there are certain elements – specifically, the artificial intelligence application, intelligent scenario, and CDS view (core data model view) – that are essential and are depicted in the center of Fig. 20.1. The artificial intelligence application serves as the integration point for incorporating artificial intelligence capabilities into business processes and associated user interfaces. The intelligent scenario acts as a connector for all the development components required for the artificial intelligence application and is particularly useful for managing life cycle aspects. The CDS view is designed to access application data for model training. In the case of this ABAP component, a SQL view is created on top of the application tables during the activation phase. All SQL requests are then directed from ABAP to the SQL view, ensuring maximum performance.

For use cases of embedded artificial intelligence that rely on the Automated Predictive Library (APL), there's no need for development. This is because the Intelligent Scenario Lifecycle Management framework automatically generates the necessary components. This is achievable due to the fact that the Automated Predictive Library includes the logic of artificial intelligence for both training and making predictions within its own implementation. Therefore, if the algorithms supported by the Automated Predictive Library are adequate for a particular use case, this method is the preferred choice from a development perspective, mainly because it keeps the total cost of development low.

For embedded artificial intelligence use cases that depend on the Predictive Analytics Library (PAL), a class for the ABAP Managed Database Procedure must be provided. This class includes methods for training and making predictions, which are implemented in SQLScript to include the necessary artificial intelligence logic. The Predictive Analytics Library is utilized for scenarios that require specific data validations, transformations, or feature reductions, which are not supported by Automated Predictive Library. The ABAP Managed Database Procedure (AMDP) class must implement a predefined interface and is under the control of the developer, allowing for the development of complex logic. For side-by-side artificial intelligence use cases that work alongside the SAP Business Technology Platform (SAP BTP), pipelines for training and making predictions must be provided to include the necessary artificial intelligence logic. These pipelines are either graphically modeled or coded based on operators for transformation, validation, or the inclusion of algorithms. The development object scenario serves as the connection between all development components to manage the life cycle. The training and prediction pipelines are made available by REST services to the SAP S/4HANA platform. An ABAP class is necessary to encapsulate these REST services and make them usable by ABAP methods.

Table 20.1 provides a summary of the technical capabilities of the different methods and offers criteria for deciding which approach to use. In the following section, we will explain how to implement both embedded and side-by-side artificial intelligence based on the infrastructure and programming model of SAP S/4HANA.

Table 20.1   Decision criteria for different approaches

Embedded Artificial Intelligence	Side-by-Side Artificial Intelligence
Capabilities	
• The data is stored and maintained within the SAP HANA database. • Inferences are made in real-time. • There is an extensive collection of over 100 algorithms related to artificial intelligence. • These features can be accessed through commonly used development tools. • The complexity of these functions can be concealed within views and table functions. • It is seamlessly integrated with the ABAP management and transport system. • The system comes with built-in privacy and security features. • It includes features for managing models. • The system also provides monitoring of model performance and supports automatic retraining.	• SAP Data Intelligence offers services in the cloud that allow for scalable and distributed learning and application of models. • It includes support for open-source frameworks and algorithms such as TensorFlow, Scikit-Learn, and R. • There are pre-existing models available that are designed for specific business scenarios. • Interaction with the system is facilitated through a standard REST application programming interface. • It provides algorithms and pre-trained models that can handle unstructured or fuzzy data, including images, audio, video, text, and more. • The system incorporates deep learning algorithms. • It also supports the use of Graphics Processing Units (GPUs).

(continued)

Tab. 20.1 (continued)

Decision Criteria

• The logic of business and artificial intelligence is incorporated within SAP S/4HANA platform.	• The logic of artificial intelligence is incorporated within SAP Data Intelligence, while the business logic may be grounded in SAP S/4HANA or SAP Business Technology Platform.
• Basic applications such as forecasting or identifying trends, where the algorithms don't require a lot of data, memory, or processing power.	• Intricate applications such as image recognition or natural language processing, which among other requirements, necessitate neural networks with a high demand for data, RAM, and CPU/GPU time.
• The data that is stored in SAP S/4HANA is adequate for training the model; there is no necessity for a large external data source for training purposes.	
• The necessary algorithms for artificial intelligence are supplied by SAP HANA, including Predictive Analysis Library (PAL), Automated Predictive Library (APL), and text analysis.	• A substantial amount of external data is needed for training the model, with the primary emphasis being on processing unstructured data.
	• Libraries of artificial intelligence from third-party sources are necessary.

20.2 Implementing Embedded AI Applications

As depicted earlier in Fig. 20.1, there exist two distinct types of embedded approaches to artificial intelligence, each dependent on the specific artificial intelligence library being used. The Automated Predictive Library (APL) comes with an inbuilt mechanism for executing data science procedures such as data preprocessing or transformations. This means that developers are not required to manually implement these aspects, as all the necessary artifacts are generated by the Intelligent Scenario Lifecycle Management (ISLM) framework. However, this automated process restricts the number of algorithms available in APL and their range of application. For this reason, the Predictive Analysis Library (PAL) is used for more complex scenarios where APL falls short – for instance, when the algorithms necessary for a particular use case are not supported by APL or when the predictive accuracy of the model produced is not up to par. PAL offers a wider selection of algorithms than APL and enables a more optimized implementation of an artificial intelligence use case, guided by the investigative work of data scientists. The downside, however, is that compared to APL, the development effort required is greater, as an AMDP class must be implemented.

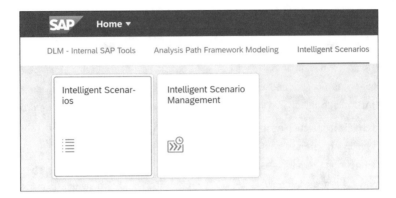

Fig. 20.2 ISLM Design-Time and Operation-Time SAP Fiori applications

In this section, we'll explain the necessary implementation steps for both flavors of embedded artificial intelligence. The implementation is based on the Intelligent Scenario Lifecycle Management framework, which consists of the two SAP Fiori applications illustrated in Fig. 20.2: the Intelligent Scenarios app and the Intelligent Scenario Management app. We can find these applications in the SAP Fiori launchpad under INTELLIGENT SCENARIOS by assigning the SAP_BR_ANALYTICS_ SPECIALIST role to the user.

The Intelligent Scenarios application is used during the design phase, allowing developers to define the intelligent scenario artifact. This artifact includes all development objects for a specific use case, regardless of whether embedded or side-by-side artificial intelligence is applied. On the other hand, the Intelligent Scenario Management application is used during operational time, enabling customers to manage the entire life cycle of their artificial intelligence models, which includes tasks such as model training and activation.

Now, let's discuss the steps involved in implementing embedded artificial intelligence based on APL.

20.2.1 Generated Approach Based on APL

Because our objective is to illustrate the technical implementation steps, we'll select a simple use case in which the tax amount will be predicted for sales orders. The implementation of all artificial intelligence use cases starts with the creation of the *intelligent scenario* design-time artifact. For this, we have to launch the Intelligent Scenarios SAP Fiori application (refer back to Fig. 20.2). In this application, the CREATE button offers the option to create an intelligent scenario for EMBEDDED artificial intelligence or SIDE-BY-SIDE artificial intelligence, as shown in Fig. 20.3.

For our use case, select the EMBEDDED option from the dropdown, and create our embedded artificial intelligence intelligent scenario with the following entries as depicted in Fig. 20.4:

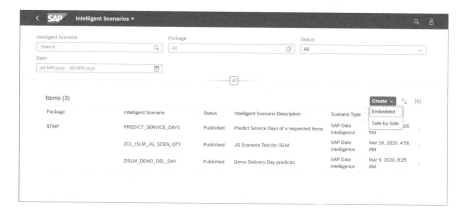

Fig. 20.3   Create Intelligent Scenarios

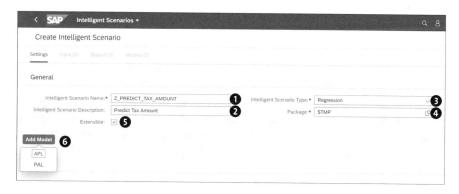

Fig. 20.4   Maintain Intelligent Scenario and Select APL Model

1. INTELLIGENT SCENARIO NAME

    Unique name of the intelligent scenario for identification.

2. INTELLIGENT SCENARIO DESCRIPTION

    Text to describe the artificial intelligence key question to be solved by the defined intelligent scenario. We've entered "Predict Tax Amount" based off of our example.

3. INTELLIGENT SCENARIO TYPE

    Type of the intelligent scenario, which represents the type of the underlying algorithms, e.g., regression or classification.

4. PACKAGE

    Package to store the development artifacts.

5. EXTENSIBLE **checkbox**

    Activation flag to allow extensibility of the intelligent scenario.

6. ADD MODEL **dropdown**

SAP HANA artificial intelligence library to be used for the intelligent scenario (APL, PAL).

Because our sample use case will be based on code generation, APL is used as the artificial intelligence library. Once APL is chosen from the ADD MODEL drop-down, the following additional information must be maintained, as shown in Fig. 20.5:

1. GENERAL

   Includes the NAME, DESCRIPTION, and PACKAGE of the intelligent scenario.

2. TRAINING DATASET

   CDS view to read and train the artificial intelligence model. Data scientists recommend which application fields are required so that the application developer can define the CDS view accordingly.

3. APPLY DATASET

   CDS view to define the consumption signature for the artificial intelligence model.

4. TARGET

   Field of the training CDS view to be predicted.

5. KEYS

   Key fields of the CDS view, which are determined automatically.

6. APPLY OUTPUT CONFIGURATION

   The checkboxes here control the prediction output fields to be generated as part of the inference API. SCORE is selected by default and represents the regression prediction. CONFIDENCE stands for the error base value on the prediction. PERCENTILE indicates the value below which a given percentage of observations in a group falls.

By completing the entry dialog in Fig. 20.5 and clicking the ADD button, the details of the intelligent scenario are displayed. In Fig. 20.6, we can see the INPUT tab with the following values:

1. INPUT

   Displays the input for the intelligent scenario, which is basically the CDS view for model training.

2. KEY **role**

   Key fields of the CDS training view are displayed.

3. INPUT **role**

   Input fields of the CDS training view with which the underlying APL algorithm is trained are displayed.

4. TARGET **role**

   The target field of the CDS training view is displayed, which will be predicted based on training using the input fields.

5. PUBLISH/SAVE DRAFT

   When we click one of these buttons, the target field of the CDS training view is displayed, which will be predicted based on training using the input fields.

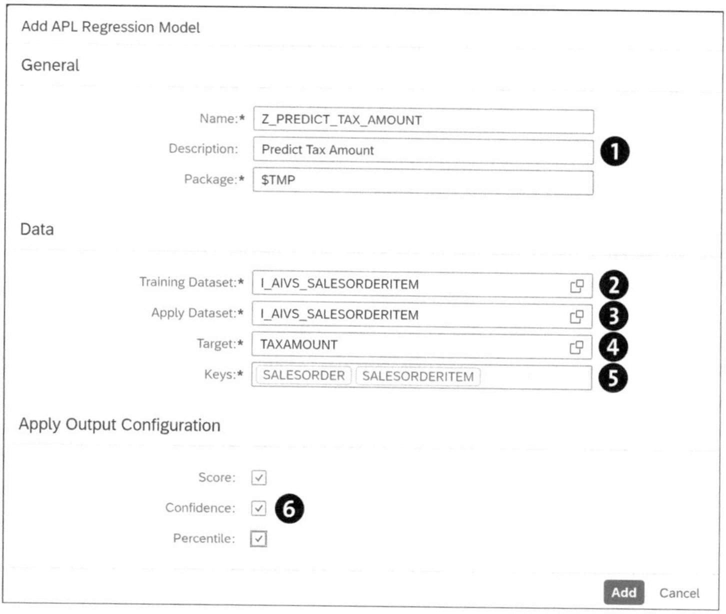

Fig. 20.5 Maintain additional information for APL-based intelligent scenario

Fig. 20.6 Display Input Section of Defined Intelligent Scenario

We can also navigate to the OUTPUT tab, as depicted in Fig. 20.7, which contains the following values:

1. OUTPUT

   Displays the output for the intelligent scenario, which is basically the consumption API of the trained model.

2. KEY **role**

Key fields of the consumption API are displayed.

3. PREDICTION **role**

Prediction fields of the consumption API with which the predicted results are exposed are displayed.

4. ABAP.APPLYCLASS

When we click the API DETAILS button, we can view the generated consumption API as an ABAP method that can be integrated into business processes and user interfaces.

5. ABAP.APPLYVIEW

When we click the API DETAILS button, we can also view the generated consumption API as a CDS table function that can be integrated into business processes and user interfaces.

As previously stated, scenarios based on APL are the most straightforward method for executing use cases implementing artificial intelligence. Therefore, once the intelligent scenario is created, the development work is essentially finished. All other required development artifacts are generated automatically. For instance, a method in ABAP and a Core Data Services (CDS) table function are created for the consumption of the trained model, as depicted in Fig. 20.7. These application programming interfaces (APIs) can be used to incorporate the outcomes of artificial intelligence into business processes and user interfaces during the design phase. The consumption APIs deliver meaningful results when the model is trained using productive data.

For this, we have to launch the Intelligent Scenario Management application (refer back to Fig. 20.2), select the defined intelligent scenario for the use case, and click the TRAIN button, as depicted in Fig. 20.8.

To reduce the volume of the training data, filter criteria can be defined in the subsequent screen, as shown in Fig. 20.9 under the TRAINING FILTERS section. In our example, the sales order number is restricted, and only the products HT-100 and

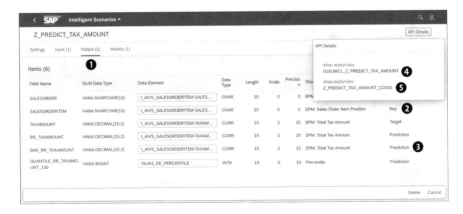

Fig. 20.7 Display output section of defined intelligent scenario

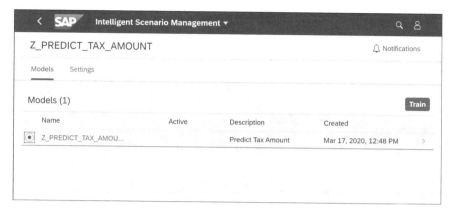

Fig. 20.8 Trigger training of defined intelligent scenario

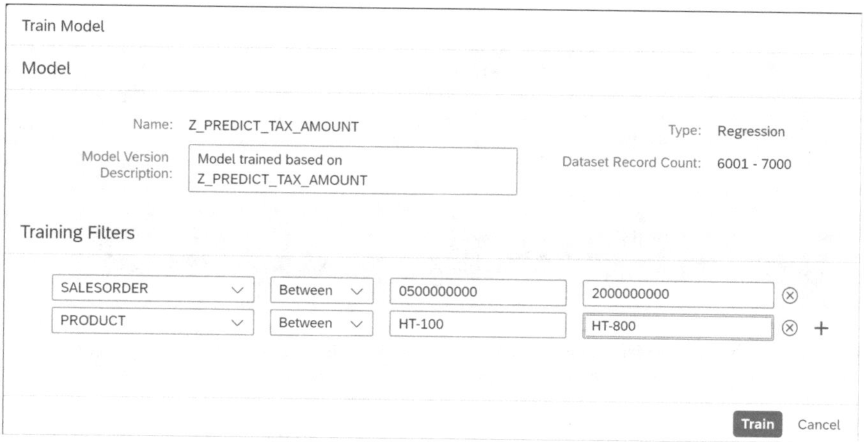

Fig. 20.9 Define filters to reduce volume of training data

HT-800 are considered. The available filter conditions are derived from the structure of the underlying CDS view for model training and vary therefore for each use case.

Once we have set our filters, click the TRAIN button. However, filtering is optional; we could also click the TRAIN button without specifying filter conditions. As illustrated in Fig. 20.10, each training run results in a new version of the model. However, only one model can be active for productive use. The following values are important:

1. MODEL VERSIONS

   Displays the different model versions that resulted from training runs.

2. ACTIVATE, DEACTIVATE, RETRAIN, and DELETE

   Models can be activated for productive usage, deactivated, retrained if the data environment changed, or deleted by clicking these buttons.

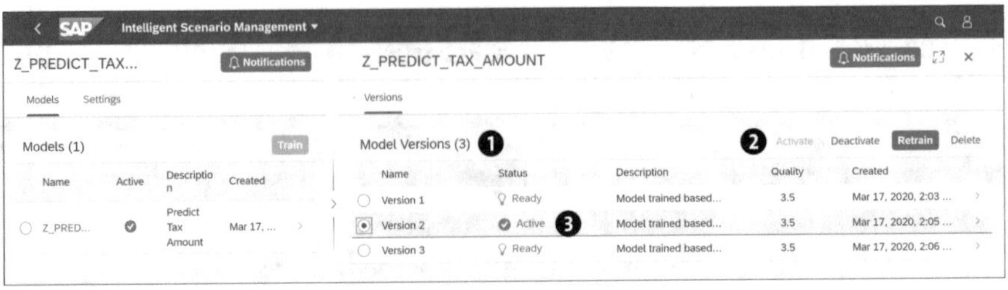

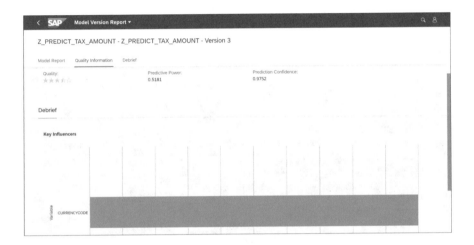

Fig. 20.10 Train multiple model versions, activate one

Fig. 20.11 Display model accuracy KPIs

3. STATUS

This attribute indicates whether the model is activated for productive usage (ACTIVE status).

To decide which model version will be activated for productive usage, we need to drill down to the model debriefing information by clicking on one of the listed model versions, thus arriving at the screen shown in Fig. 20.11. Here, the PREDICTION POWER and PREDICTION CONFIDENCE KPIs are displayed. The closer those numbers are to 1, the better the model quality is. Key influencers are also provided to show which input parameters most contributed to the trained model.

Listing 20.1 shows the generated CDS table function from Fig. 20.7, which we access via the API DETAILS button. We can use standard development tools, such as ABAP in Eclipse, to display the CDS view. With this CDS view, the trained model can be consumed and the inference results integrated into business processes or user interfaces. As already mentioned, an ABAP method for consumption is provided as well.

Listing 20.1 Generated CDS View for Model Consumption

```
@EndUserText.label: 'ISLM AutoGenerated View   Z_PREDICT_TAX_
AMOUNT_CDS01 '
@AbapCatalog.sqlViewName: 'Z_D7A03819460EAE' --ISLM Random
generated SQL name
@AbapCatalog.dataMaintenance: #DISPLAY_ONLY
@ClientHandling.type: #CLIENT_DEPENDENT
@ClientHandling.algorithm: #SESSION_VARIABLE
@VDM.private: false
@VDM.viewType: #COMPOSITE
define view Z_PREDICT_TAX_AMOUNT_CDS01
 as select from Z_PREDICT_TAX_AMOUNT_TF01
        ( p_clnt: $session.client  )
    as a
 association [1..1] to I_AIVS_SALESORDERITEM as _CKE_toBase on
 a.SalesOrder =
_CKE_toBase.SalesOrder and
a.SalesOrderItem = _CKE_toBase.SalesOrderItem
{key a.SalesOrder as SalesOrder,
key a.SalesOrderItem as SalesOrderItem,
    a.TaxAmount as TaxAmount,
    a.Rr_TaxAmount as Rr_TaxAmount,
    a.Bar_Rr_TaxAmount as Bar_Rr_TaxAmount,
    a.Quantile_Rr_TaxAmount_100 as Quantile_Rr_TaxAmount_100,
 /* Associations */
    @ObjectModel.text.element: null
    @Consumption.hidden: true
    _CKE_toBase as _CKE_toBase
}
```

The CDS view can be, for example, executed in ABAP in Eclipse. There, the DATA PREVIEW tool can be used to show the results of the CDS view, as depicted in Fig. 20.12. The RR_TAXAMOUNT column contains the predicted tax amount for dedicated sales orders.

20.2.2 Coded Approach Based on PAL

PAL offers more than 100 algorithms related to artificial intelligence and is utilized when APL falls short in addressing the needs of embedded artificial intelligence application. This might occur, for instance, when the necessary algorithm is not

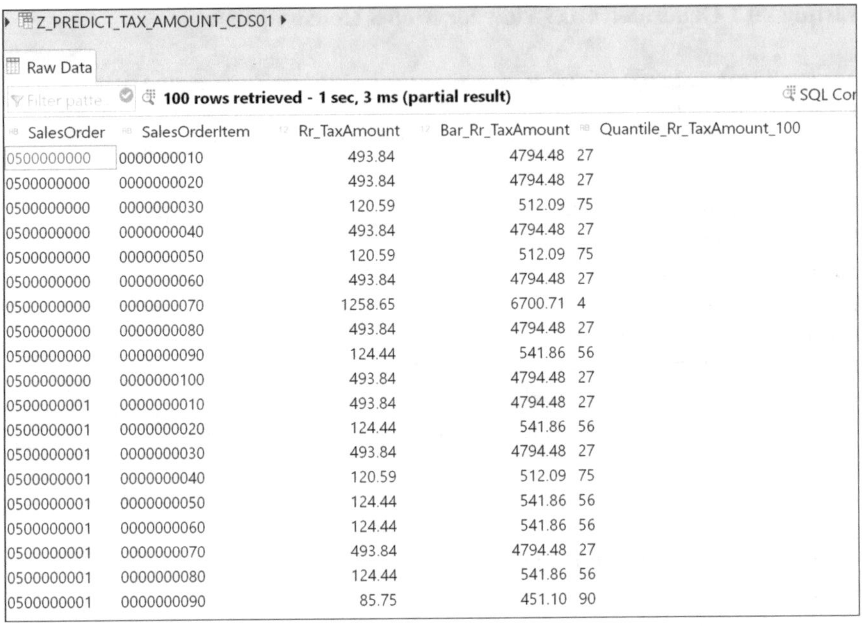

SalesOrder	SalesOrderItem	Rr_TaxAmount	Bar_Rr_TaxAmount	Quantile_Rr_TaxAmount_100
0500000000	0000000010	493.84	4794.48	27
0500000000	0000000020	493.84	4794.48	27
0500000000	0000000030	120.59	512.09	75
0500000000	0000000040	493.84	4794.48	27
0500000000	0000000050	120.59	512.09	75
0500000000	0000000060	493.84	4794.48	27
0500000000	0000000070	1258.65	6700.71	4
0500000000	0000000080	493.84	4794.48	27
0500000000	0000000090	124.44	541.86	56
0500000000	0000000100	493.84	4794.48	27
0500000001	0000000010	493.84	4794.48	27
0500000001	0000000020	124.44	541.86	56
0500000001	0000000030	493.84	4794.48	27
0500000001	0000000040	120.59	512.09	75
0500000001	0000000050	124.44	541.86	56
0500000001	0000000060	124.44	541.86	56
0500000001	0000000070	493.84	4794.48	27
0500000001	0000000080	124.44	541.86	56
0500000001	0000000090	85.75	451.10	90

Z_PREDICT_TAX_AMOUNT_CDS01
Raw Data
Filter patte   100 rows retrieved - 1 sec, 3 ms (partial result)   SQL Con

Fig. 20.12 Display inference results in ABAP in Eclipse

included in APL's offerings or when APL's automated data science processes do
not yield sufficiently accurate predictions. PAL is the go-to solution for such exceptional scenarios. In the case of PAL, the logic of artificial intelligence is crafted by
the developer, rather than being automatically generated by the framework, as is
the case with APL. This approach has the benefit of giving the developer complete
control, enabling them to fine-tune the implementation of the artificial intelligence
logic to best suit the specific use case, following the guidance of data scientists.
The developer's task is to implement an AMDP class, which adheres to predefined
interfaces and offers methods such as training and consumption. These methods
essentially embody the artificial intelligence logic and encompass aspects like preprocessing steps, data transformations, initiating the necessary PAL algorithms, and
offering an API for the consumption of the trained model. In the following section, to keep the focus on the technical implementation, we will revisit a simple
use case. Imagine being a cash specialist who classifies cash flows into various
liquidity items, such as operations and investments. By leveraging artificial intelligence, we can obtain predictive insights into liquidity items by comparing actual
and forecasted results. The actual liquidity items that are allocated can subsequently
be replaced by the predicted liquidity items suggested by the artificial intelligence
service.

The implementation of this use case is based on the PAL classification algorithm
random decision tree and starts with launching the intelligent scenarios application

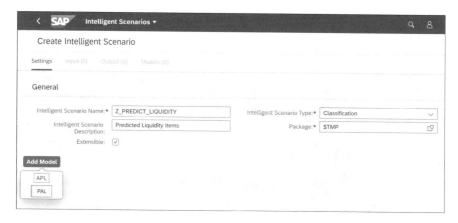

Fig. 20.13 Maintain intelligent scenario and select PAL

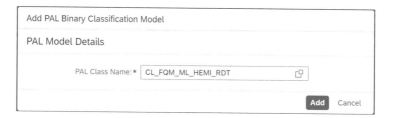

Fig. 20.14 Register AMDP class for implementing artificial intelligence logic

(refer back to Fig. 20.2). Next, we will create our intelligent scenario as depicted in Fig. 20.13. This time, we'll select CLASSIFICATION as the INTELLIGENT SCENARIO TYPE based off of our use case. Under ADD MODEL, we must select PAL.

On the next screen, we must register the CL_FQM_ML_HEMI_RDT AMDP class by entering it in the PAL CLASS NAME field, which implements the already-mentioned artificial intelligence logic (see Fig. 20.14). Click the ADD button to move forward.

The ABAP class implements methods for providing metadata like the underlying CDS view as input for training or the API signature for consuming the trained model. These kinds of metadata are processed by the ISLM framework and are also illustrated in the user interface, as shown in Fig. 20.15.

Other elements shown in Fig. 20.15, like the INPUT tab, OUTPUT tab, PUBLISH button, SAVE DRAFT button, and the semantics of the fields, remain the same as for APL in the previous section. Therefore, we can focus now on the implementation of the CL_FQM_ML_HEMI_RDT AMDP class in the ABAP Class Builder, as shown in Fig. 20.16.

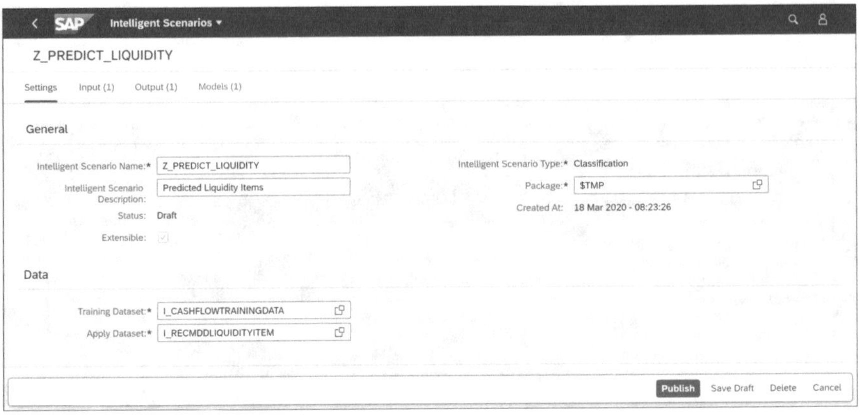

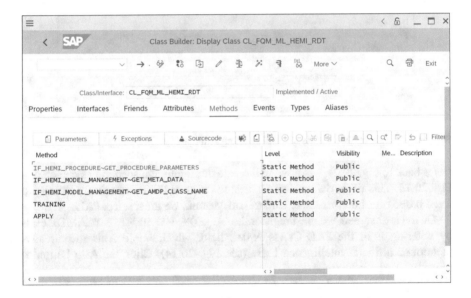

Fig. 20.15 Intelligent scenario for embedded artificial intelligence case based on PAL

Fig. 20.16 Methods of ABAP class for artificial intelligence logic

The ABAP class must implement different interfaces, so the structure and behavior of those classes are standardized, which is a prerequisite for uniform handling by the ISLM framework.

First, the method shown in Listing 20.2 provides metadata to the ISLM framework, such as the CDS view for model training or the API signature for consuming the model.

Listing 20.2 Coding for Handling ISLM Metadata

```
METHOD IF_HEMI_MODEL_MANAGEMENT~GET_META_DATA.
    DATA LR_BADI TYPE REF TO CL_FQM_ML_DETECT2_BADI.
    TRY.
      GET BADI LR_BADI.
      CATCH CX_BADI_CONTEXT_ERROR.
      CATCH CX_BADI_NOT_IMPLEMENTED.
    ENDTRY.
    CALL BADI LR_BADI->GET_META_DATA
      IMPORTING
        ES_META_DATA = ES_META_DATA.
    ES_META_DATA-TRAINING_DATA_SET = 'I_CashFlowTrainingData'.
    ES_META_DATA-APPLY_DATA_SET    = 'I_RecmddLiquidityItem'.
    ES_META_DATA-
FIELD_DESCRIPTIONS = VALUE #( ( NAME = 'LiquidityItem' ROLE =
CL_HEMI_CONSTANTS=>CS_FIELD_ROLE-TARGET )
    ( name = 'OriginSystem' role = CL_HEMI_CONSTANTS=>CS_FIELD_
ROLE-key )
    ( name = 'OriginApplication' role = CL_HEMI_CONSTANTS=>CS_
FIELD_ROLE-key )
    ( name = 'OriginDocument' role = CL_HEMI_CONSTANTS=>CS_FIELD_
ROLE-key )
    ( name = 'OriginTransaction' role = CL_HEMI_CONSTANTS=>CS_
FIELD_ROLE-key )
    ( name = 'OriginTransactionQualifier' role = CL_HEMI_
CONSTANTS=>CS_FIELD_ROLE-key )
    ( name = 'CashFlow' role = CL_HEMI_CONSTANTS=>CS_FIELD_
ROLE-key )
    ).
  ENDMETHOD.
```

Next, the method shown in Listing 20.3 is encapsulated as business add-in (BAdI) for extensibility. It implements the training logic in terms of reading the data based on the CDS view and calling the related PAL random decision tree algorithm.

Listing 20.3 Coding for Model Training

```
METHOD TRAINING
    BY DATABASE PROCEDURE FOR HDB LANGUAGE SQLSCRIPT OPTIONS
SUPPRESS SYNTAX ERRORS READ-ONLY
    USING CL_FQM_ML_DETECT_BADI=>TRAINING.
    CALL "CL_FQM_ML_DETECT_BADI=>TRAINING"(
      it_data              => :it_data,
      it_param             => :it_param,
```

```
    et_model                  => :et_model,
    et_variable_importance => :et_variable_importance,
    et_error_rate             => :et_error_rate,
    et_confusion_matrix       => :et_confusion_matrix
  );
ENDMETHOD.


METHOD IF_FQM_ML_DETECT_BADI_INTF~TRAINING
    BY DATABASE PROCEDURE FOR HDB LANGUAGE SQLSCRIPT OPTIONS
    SUPPRESS SYNTAX ERRORS.
    lt_data = select CompanyCode, CertaintyLevel, Currency,
PlanningLevel, CashPlanningGroup, GLAccount, BusinessPartner,
Customer, Supplier, PartnerCompany, CostCenter, ProfitCenter,
    Segment, BusinessArea, Material, WBSElement, PaymentMethod,
FinancialAccountType, FinancialTransactionType,
BankAccountInternalID, LiquidityItem
    from :it_data;
  /* Call PAL random decision trees algorithm */
      CALL _sys_afl.pal_random_decision_trees(:lt_data, :it_
param, :et_model, :et_variable_importance, :et_error_rate,
:et_confusion_matrix);
  ENDMETHOD.
```

Finally, the method shown in Listing 20.4 is encapsulated as a BAdI for extensibility. It implements the consumption logic in terms of applying requests to the trained model and providing inference results.

Listing 20.4 Coding for Model Inference

```
METHOD APPLY
    BY DATABASE PROCEDURE FOR HDB LANGUAGE SQLSCRIPT OPTIONS
SUPPRESS SYNTAX ERRORS READ-ONLY
    USING CL_FQM_ML_DETECT_BADI=>PREDICT_WITH_MODEL_VERSION.
  CALL "CL_FQM_ML_DETECT_BADI=>PREDICT_WITH_MODEL_VERSION"(
    it_data   => :it_data,
    it_model  => :it_model,
    it_param  => :it_param,
    et_result => :et_result
  );
  ENDMETHOD.
METHOD IF_FQM_ML_DETECT_BADI_INTF~predict_with_model_version
    BY DATABASE PROCEDURE FOR HDB LANGUAGE SQLSCRIPT OPTIONS
    READ-ONLY.
    lt_data_uuid = select to_nchar(sysuuid) as id, OriginSystem,
OriginApplication, OriginDocument, OriginTransaction,
OriginTransactionQualifier, CashFlow,CompanyCode, CertaintyLevel,
```

```
Currency, PlanningLevel, CashPlanningGroup, GLAccount,
BusinessPartner, Customer, Supplier, PartnerCompany, CostCenter,
ProfitCenter,
Segment, BusinessArea, Material, WBSElement, PaymentMethod,
FinancialAccountType, FinancialTransactionType,
BankAccountInternalID
    FROM :it_data;

lt_data_predict = select id,
CompanyCode, CertaintyLevel, Currency, PlanningLevel,
CashPlanningGroup, GLAccount, BusinessPartner, Customer,
Supplier, PartnerCompany, CostCenter, ProfitCenter,Segment,
BusinessArea, Material, WBSElement, PaymentMethod,
FinancialAccountType, FinancialTransactionType,
BankAccountInternalID
    FROM :lt_data_uuid;

    /* Execute  prediction */
    CALL _sys_afl.pal_random_decision_trees_predict(:lt_data_
predict, :it_model, :it_param, lt_result);

    /* Prediction results are mapped to the composite keys */
    et_result = select OriginSystem, OriginApplication,
OriginDocument, OriginTransaction, OriginTransactionQualifier,
CashFlow, r.score as LiquidityItem, confidence FROM :lt_data_uuid
as u INNER JOIN :lt_result as r ON u.id = r.id;
    ENDMETHOD.
```

Model training, activation, and debriefing for PAL are handled in an analogous way as for APL, as illustrated previously in Figs. 20.8, 20.10, and 20.11. Inference results are exposed by the APPLY method shown in Listing 20.4 and integrated into business processes.

20.3   Implementing Side-by-Side AI Applications

The method of using side-by-side artificial intelligence is used when the embedded artificial intelligence fails to fulfill the needs of the specific use case. This situation may arise if the suitable algorithm is not offered by SAP HANA, if external data is needed for training the model, or if the algorithm has substantial hardware demands (for instance, neural networks require a GPU and consume a significant amount of memory). For the side-by-side application of artificial intelligence, it is necessary to develop an ABAP class, CDS view, and intelligent scenario on the SAP S/4HANA ABAP platform, while the training and inference pipelines are implemented in the SAP Business Technology Platform (SAP BTP). There are several development environments available for implementing artificial intelligence on the SAP Business Technology Platform. Since the fundamental content and framework concepts are alike, we will illustrate one of them, namely, SAP Data Intelligence, as an example.

In the following section, we will use a scenario that involves predicting the delay in product delivery to demonstrate the technical implementation steps. We will first describe the required developments in SAP Data Intelligence and then proceed with the ABAP side.

20.3.1 Required Development in SAP BTP

As illustrated in Fig. 20.17, the launchpad for SAP Data Intelligence provides access to various SAP Fiori applications, of which the following three are key for artificial intelligence implementation:

1. Connection Management

    For the development of the introduced use case, Connection Management is required for setting up the connectivity to the SAP S/4HANA system in order to read the training data remotely.
2. ML Scenario Manager

    The ML Scenario Manager app is used to define all the required implementation artifacts.
3. Modeler

    The Modeler app is used to create the necessary pipelines.

We'll begin with the ML Scenario Manager application. With this app, the artificial intelligence scenario central artifact is created in SAP Data Intelligence as shown in Fig. 20.18. For this, a unique NAME must be provided (Delivery Delay Prediction in our example), and a description must be maintained in the BUSINESS QUESTION field.

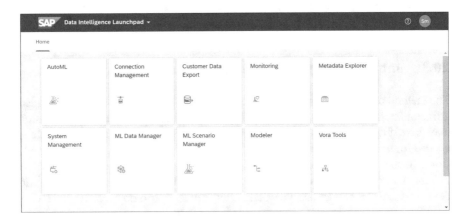

Fig. 20.17 SAP Data Intelligence launchpad

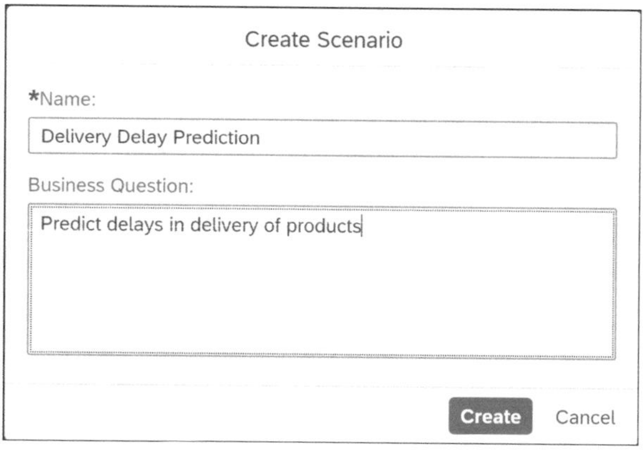

Fig. 20.18 Create artificial intelligence scenario

Fig. 20.19 Artificial intelligence scenario details

Click the CREATE button. The details of the artificial intelligence scenario are depicted in Fig. 20.19. As already mentioned, the artifact encompasses all development and operation artifacts for the use case, such as pipelines, Python coding, and deployments of the model, as follows:

1. DATASETS

   Datasets that are stored in SAP Data Intelligence and are used for the implementation of the use case, such as during data science exploration.

2. NOTEBOOKS

   SAP Data Intelligence integrates Jupyter Notebook to provide an exploration environment for data scientists. Thus, exploration and development of the use case are combined to increase efficiency.

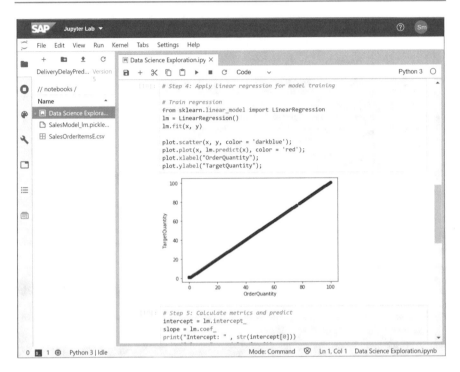

Fig. 20.20   Jupyter Notebook for data science exploration

3. PIPELINES

A pipeline is a graphical way of programming training and inference logic for a use case.

4. **URL**

Each artificial intelligence scenario has as a unique identifier, which in the current version of SAP Data Intelligence is part of the URL. We'll use this identifier later to bind the artificial intelligence scenario with the ABAP content.

The integration of Jupyter Notebook is demonstrated in Fig. 20.20 which is used by data scientists to carry out exploratory activities for a specific use case. These activities encompass data analysis, testing algorithms, and executing transformations. As illustrated in Fig. 20.20, the Scikit-Learn library, which is designed for artificial intelligence, is used to realize our artificial intelligence use case through the application of the linear regression algorithm.

By clicking the + icon in the PIPELINES section of the artificial intelligence scenario (see Fig. 20.19), new pipelines can be created as depicted in Fig. 20.21. For our use case, a training and an inference pipeline are required.

Pipelines can be created based on templates that already contain the main steps. For our use case, select PYTHON PRODUCER from the TEMPLATE dropdown for the training pipeline and the PYTHON CONSUMER template for the inference pipeline. As of the time of writing, the ISLM framework expects only one training and one inference pipeline for a side-by-side artificial intelligence use case. To identity those

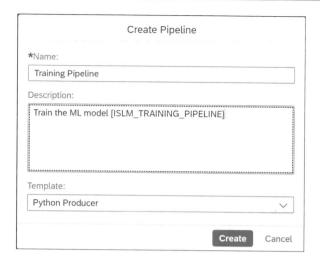

Fig. 20.21 Create training pipeline

pipelines, ISLM assumes the [ISLM_TRAINING_PIPELINE] string to be included as part of the description. This might be replaced in future versions with an explicit flag.

Figure 20.21 depicts the training pipeline modeled for our artificial intelligence use case (which we can navigate to via the previous screen, shown in Fig. 20.19). Basically, the pipeline accesses the application data online, transfers it in comma-separated value (CSV) format, trains the algorithm, stores the trained model, and computes accuracy metrics, as follows:

1. WORKFLOW TRIGGER
   The operator triggers the execution of the pipeline.
2. CLOUD DATA INTEGRATION
   The operator extracts application data from SAP S/4HANA based on the CDS extraction view for training data. The properties of this operator are detailed in Fig. 20.23.
3. FLOWAGENT CSV PROD…
   The operator transforms the application into a CSV file.
4. ALGORITHM
   The operator trains the artificial intelligence algorithm based on the application data. This operator is coded in Python.
5. ARTIFACT PRODUCER
   The operator stores the trained model.
6. SUBMIT METRICS
   The operator processes metrics for model accuracy.
7. GRAPH TERMINATOR
   The operator terminates the pipeline and releases the used system resources.

Listing 20.5 shows the coding for operator 4, ALGORITHM, shown in Fig. 20.22. The coding implemented in Jupyter Notebook (refer back to Fig. 20.20) is

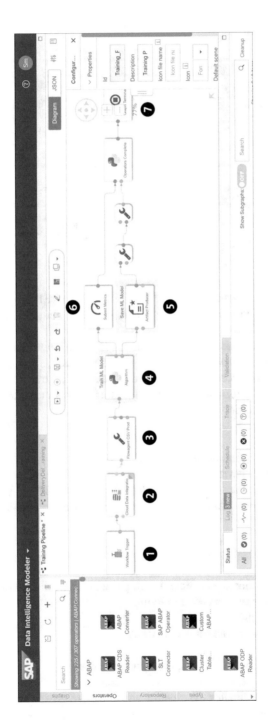

Fig. 20.22 Training pipeline

transferred to the structure, which is required by the operator. The input port of the operator receives the application data with which the Scikit-Learn linear regression algorithm is trained. Model metrics and the blob ID of the trained model are exposed by output ports of the operator.

Listing 20.5 Coding for Operator Responsible for Model Training

```python
# Python script to perform training on input data & generate
Metrics & Model Blob
def on_input(data):

# Step 1: Import libraries
import pandas as pd
import io
import numpy as np
import logging

logging.basicConfig(level=logging.DEBUG, format='%(asctime)
s - %(levelname)s - %(message)s')
api.logger.info("Your message")

# Step 2: Read data and display it
dataset = pd.read_csv(io.StringIO(data), sep=",")
x = dataset['OrderQuantity'].values.reshape(-1,1)
y = dataset['TargetQuantity'].values.reshape(-1,1)

# Step 3: Apply linear regression for model training
from sklearn.linear_model import LinearRegression
lm = LinearRegression()
lm.fit(x, y)

# Step 4: Calculate metrics and predict
intercept = lm.intercept_
slope = lm.coef_
metrics_dict = {"Intercept: " , str(intercept[0]), "Slope: ",
str(slope[0,0])}
api.send("metrics", api.Message(metrics_dict))

# Step 5: Store the model for future inference
import pickle
model_blob = pickle.dumps(lm)
api.send("modelBlob", model_blob)

api.set_port_callback("input", on_input)
```

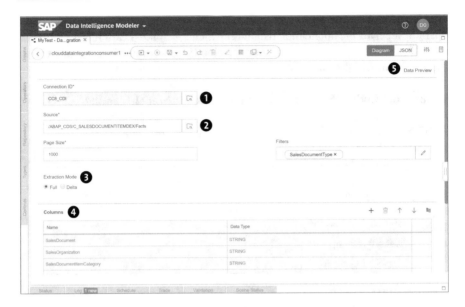

Fig. 20.23 Cloud data integration operator for reading CDS view data

By clicking on operator 2, Cloud Data Integration, in Fig. 20.22, its properties can be maintained, as shown in Fig. 20.23. According to the SAP S/4HANA artificial intelligence programming model, training data is accessed via CDS extraction views. Thus, capabilities like initial load, delta handling, and extensibility are enabled. Let's walk through the operator parameters:

1. Connection ID
   ID to connect to SAP S/4HANA system
2. Source
   CDS view to extract data for model training
3. Extraction Mode
   Extraction mode to transmit all data (Full) or only changes (Delta)
4. Columns
   Columns of the CDS view extractor that will be considered (filtering of columns)
5. Data Preview **button**
   Previews the extracted data

Next, let's review the inference pipeline for our artificial intelligence use case, which is illustrated in Fig. 20.24. In this pipeline, the trained model is loaded into RAM memory, and a listener for REST inference calls is instantiated. The details are as follows:

1. Submit Artifact Name
   This operator allows for maintaining the ID of the trained model.
2. Artifact Consumer

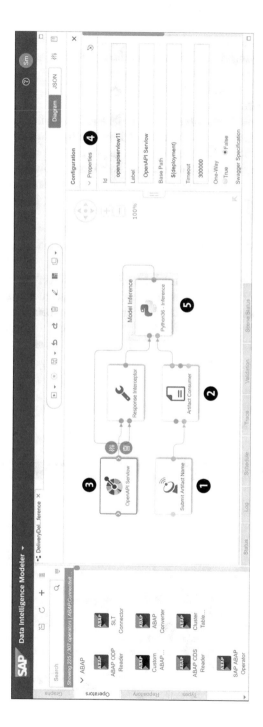

Fig. 20.24 Inference pipeline

This operator loads the trained model based on its ID.

3. OpenAPI Servlow

This operator listens for inference requests and sends inference responses back. The underlying communication protocol is REST.

4. Properties

Displays the properties of the selected operator.

5. Model Inference

This operator performs inference requests and returns the inference results.

The final step in creating content for SAP Data Intelligence involves marking the artificial intelligence scenario as released. It's important to note that only those scenarios that have been marked as released are taken into account by the ISLM framework in ABAP. To accomplish this, one needs to select the star icon on the scenario details page, as shown previously in Fig. 20.19.

20.3.2 Required Development in ABAP

The ABAP development of our artificial intelligence use case starts with the creation of the intelligent scenario. For this, the intelligent scenarios application must be launched (refer back to Fig. 20.2), and an intelligent scenario of the Side-By-Side type must be created (refer back to Fig. 20.3). Figure 20.25 shows the intelligent scenario created for our artificial intelligence use case, and the fields we must fill out are as follows:

1. Intelligent Scenario Name

Unique name of the intelligent scenario for identification.

2. Intelligent Scenario Description

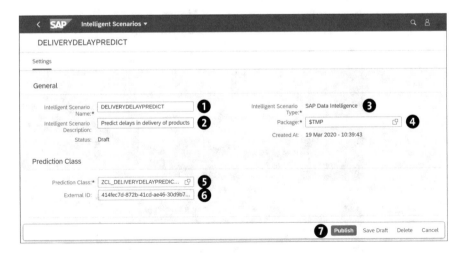

Fig. 20.25 Create intelligent scenario for side-by-side artificial intelligence

Text to describe the artificial intelligence key question to be solved by the defined intelligent scenario.

3. INTELLIGENT SCENARIO TYPE

Type of the intelligent scenario, which for our side-by-side artificial intelligence use case is SAP Data Intelligence.

4. PACKAGE

Package in which to store the development artifacts.

5. PREDICTION CLASS

The ABAP class that implements methods for metadata provisioning and inference calls. This class must be implemented specifically for the scenario using ABAP Class Builder by applying the defined interface as shown in Fig. 20.26.

6. EXTERNAL ID

ID of the corresponding artificial intelligence scenario artifact that was created for our artificial intelligence use case in SAP Data Intelligence (Refer to Fig. 20.19). Based on this ID, the ABAP content and SAP Data Intelligence content are bounded.

An intelligent scenario can be saved as draft if additional changes are expected; otherwise, it's published for use.

The prediction class of ABAP, which is registered in the intelligent scenario as depicted in Fig. 20.25, carries out the functions of metadata methods and the utilization interface of the trained model, as demonstrated in Fig. 20.26. To develop this, the ABAP Class Builder can be utilized, as shown in Fig. 20.26. To standardize the structure and behavior of the class, it must implement the IF_ISLM_INTELLIGENT_SCENARIO interface.

The process of providing metadata is carried out through methods, rather than through specific input fields in the user interface. This approach ensures the simplicity of the user interface while still allowing for the easy inclusion of

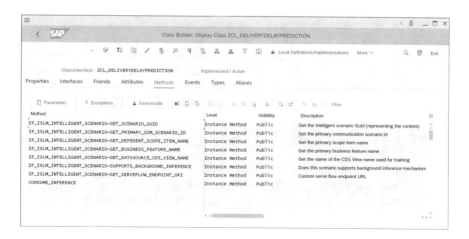

Fig. 20.26 Methods and interfaces of registered ABAP class

additional metadata. These metadata methods can take various forms, such as the name of the CDS view used for data extraction or the ID of the business feature used to activate a scope item. The ID of the scenario artifact related to artificial intelligence, which was developed in SAP Data Intelligence (as shown in Fig. 20.19), is stored as a characteristic of the class and is revealed through the method displayed in Listing 20.6.

Listing 20.6 Coding for GET_SCENARIO_GUID Method

```
METHOD IF_ISLM_INTELLIGENT_SCENARIO~GET_SCENARIO_GUID.
    "ISLM Specific: Retuen the ML scenario GUID via IF_ISLM_
INTELLIGENT_SCENARIO interface implementation
    rv_scenario_guid = me->mv_scenario_guid.
ENDMETHOD.
```

With the ID, the ABAP and SAP Data Intelligence content are correlated and processed accordingly by the ISLM framework. The method shown in Listing 20.7 implements the API for consuming the inference results using the REST protocol.

Listing 20.7 Coding for CONSUME_INFERENCE Method

```
METHOD CONSUME_INFERENCE.
DATA:
  lv_json_request_data  TYPE string,
  lr_islm_inference_provider TYPE REF TO
cl_islm_inference_provider,
  lr_islm_inference_client TYPE REF TO
cl_islm_inference_http_client.

* Initialise inference provider from ISLM
  lr_islm_inference_provider = new cl_islm_inference_
provider( me ).
  lr_islm_inference_provider->get_inference_client(
                                IMPORTING eo_http_client =
lr_islm_inference_client
                    es_bapireturn  = DATA(ls_bapiret) ).

* Check inference client is avlaible    IF lr_islm_inference_
client IS NOT INITIAL.
    lv_json_request_data ='{ "quanity":12 , "product_code":125}'.
    lr_islm_inference_client->add_request_body(
    EXPORTING  iv_header_payload = lv_json_request_data).
    lr_islm_inference_client->send_and_receive(
```

```
      IMPORTING
      ev_http_return_reason = DATA(lv_http_return_reason)
      ev_response_data      = DATA(lv_json_response_data)
      es_bapireturn         = DATA(ls_bapireturn)
      ev_http_return_code   = DATA(lv_http_return_code)
      ).


  lr_islm_inference_client->close( ).
  ENDIF.
ENDMETHOD.
```

With this, the implementation of our side-by-side artificial intelligence case is completed. The consumption API of the ABAP class provides the inference results, which can be integrated into business processes and user interfaces.

However, to provide meaningful values, first the intelligent scenario must be trained. For this, the INTELLIGENT SCENARIO MANAGEMENT application can be used (refer back to Fig. 20.2). The necessary steps are already described in the context of the embedded artificial intelligence implementation (refer back to Fig. 20.8 and Fig. 20.10). The only difference is that there are EXECUTE and DEPLOY buttons provided for side-by-side artificial intelligence. The execution step runs the training pipeline, whereas the deployment step performs the inference pipeline and provides an inference serving container.

To connect the ISLM framework to SAP Data Intelligence, the administrator must map the intelligent scenario to the HTTP destination of SAP Data Intelligence as shown in Fig. 20.27. The user interface and the menu path for accessing the transaction can vary depending on the SAP S/4HANA release, so be sure to consult the

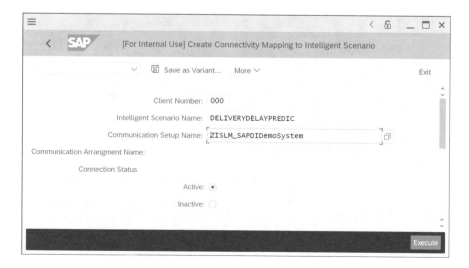

Fig. 20.27 Configure connectivity between ISLM and SAP Data Intelligence

release-specific documentation for ISLM at the SAP Help Portal (https://help.sap. com). Basically, the administrator has to access the Customizing transaction and maintain the HTTP destination for the intelligent scenario.

20.4   Conclusion

In the last chapter, we covered the technical architecture underpinning artificial intelligence in SAP S/4HANA for both embedded and side-by-side models so that in this chapter, we could dive into the technical implementation. We began with a comparison of the two models (embedded, side-by-side artificial intelligence) and then discussed how to develop and run each model. The embedded artificial intelligence is used for simple scenario with low system load The artificial intelligence libraries provided by the SAP S/4HANA platform are usually sufficient for this type of use cases. More complex scenario where neuronal networks with high hardware are demanded are implemented based on SAP Business Technology platform and referred to as side-by-side artificial intelligence. This platform supports scalable infrastructure for model training and serving, including GPU hardware. Development and operations of embedded and side-by-side artificial intelligence are based on Intelligent Scenario Lifecycle Management framework, which was explained with corresponding step-by-step guidelines. This framework standardizes the development process and harmonizes the life cycle management of the artificial intelligence applications.

Sales and Research

21

In this chapter, we explain intelligent business applications in the sales and research line of business (LoB) and how customers can benefit from this functionality. We provide a brief overview of the use case requirements, the business processes involved, and how they're addressed. The sales LoB is huge, with a lot of potential to automate and fine-tune the processes. The focus of the chapter is on conversion of sales quotations to sales orders, predicting sales forecasts, forecasting delivery delay, project cost forecasting, and digital content processing. For these use cases, the concepts and frameworks explained in this elaboration were applied, which proves the real-world feasibility of those new inventions.

21.1 Predict Conversion of Sales Quotations

In this section, our focus will be directed toward the artificial intelligence service designed to forecast the transformation of sales quotes into actual sales orders, a service that is highly beneficial for a sales manager or an internal sales representative. Figure 21.1 presents the artificial intelligence service specifically constructed for this business process, the details of which we will delve into in this section. To build the bridge to the previous chapters, we list the corresponding references points for the use case:

- AI Application Pattern: Prediction
- ERP Reference Process: Lead to Cash/Order to Fulfill
- ERP Reference Architecture: Sales/Order and Contract Management
- ERP Reference AI Technology: ERP Platform
- AI Realization Pattern: Embedded

Sales representatives have the responsibility of monitoring the conversion rate of sales quotations into actual sales orders. They must also keep an eye on open

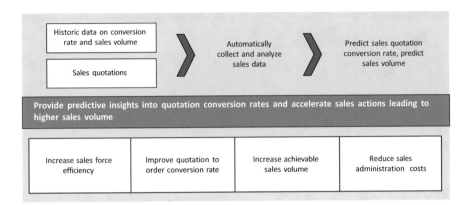

Fig. 21.1 Predict conversion of sales quotations

quotations that are available and follow up on them to boost sales volumes. One of the main challenges they face is pinpointing those quotations that aren't being transformed into sales orders as anticipated.

This process requires a significant amount of manual labor, as well as the application of their skills and expertise, and is quite time-consuming. Sales managers, on the other hand, are looking for ways to enhance the efficiency of their sales teams, improve the conversion rate from quotation to order, increase potential sales volumes, and cut down on sales administration costs, all in an effort to boost their companies' top-line growth. Artificial intelligence algorithms can be of great help in this context. They can extract information from historical system data and provide precise predictions of sales quotation conversion rates and potential overall sales volumes. This solution can handle complexity and automate the collection and analysis of sales data, eliminating the need for sales representatives to make guesswork. With this solution, sales representatives can identify which sales quotations may require additional support and action to boost sales volumes, and they can keep track of progress on an ongoing basis. The fundamental concept of the sales quotation conversion rate is to enhance overall sales volumes. The sales quotation conversion rate, also known as the sales order probability, is the likelihood that a sales quotation will be transformed into a sales order item. This probability, expressed as a percentage, along with the net value of the sales quotation, is used to calculate a total expected order value. At present, the sales order probability must be manually input either in the customer master or document category. This manually entered probability depends on manual calculations and estimates or external data that has been imported.

The feature of artificial intelligence in SAP S/4HANA that pertains to the conversion rate of quotations is a valuable service for sales managers and internal sales representatives. It provides them with predictions about achievable sales volumes and the potential conversion rates of quotations. This information is crucial in making decisions about which quotations are most likely to be transformed into sales orders, thereby boosting the current sales volume. As depicted in Fig. 21.2, the

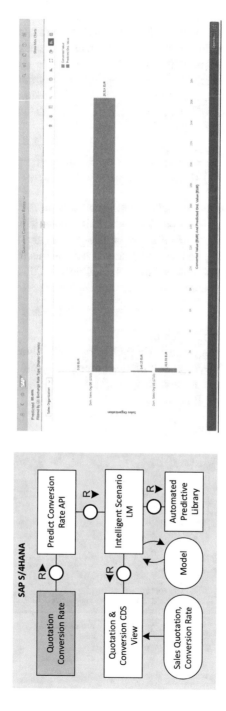

Fig. 21.2   Predict conversion of sales quotations: architecture and application

current scenario uses regression algorithms from the Automated Predictive Library. These algorithms, which are part of the Intelligent Scenario Lifecycle Management framework, are integrated into the SAP S/4HANA sales quotation business processes to enhance prediction accuracy. The business advantages of this feature are numerous. They include the ability to receive more precise sales forecasts, a reduction in manual work and analysis, and the optimization of the win/loss ratio. From the customer's perspective, the value proposition lies in gaining predictive insights into the conversion rates of quotations. This not only accelerates sales actions but also leads to an increase in sales volumes.

21.2 Predict Sales Forecasts

Next, we will focus on the artificial intelligence service that has been developed specifically for predicting sales performance. This service is particularly relevant in the context of monitoring the fulfillment of sales orders and planning sales strategies. The artificial intelligence service designed for this specific process is depicted in Fig. 21.3, which we will proceed to explain in detail in this section. To build the bridge to the previous chapters, we list the corresponding references points for the use case:

- AI Application Pattern: Prediction
- ERP Reference Process: Lead to Cash/Opportunity to Quote
- ERP Reference Architecture: Sales/Sales Force Support
- ERP Reference AI Technology: ERP Platform
- AI Realization Pattern: Embedded

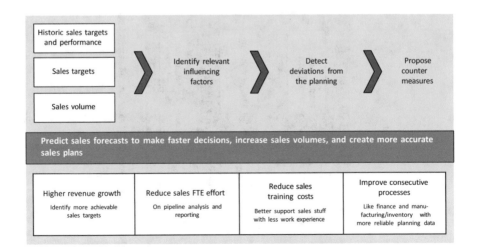

Fig. 21.3 Predict sales forecasting

Sales planning typically involves a thorough analysis that demands significant operational effort, such as gathering data from various system and external sources and formulating plans. This process also relies heavily on the expertise of a sales manager to make accurate forecasts. In order to boost sales, it's crucial for sales managers to scrutinize sales performance, assess whether sales goals are achievable or can be surpassed, and suggest appropriate subsequent steps. At present, sales forecasting is a labor-intensive process that largely depends on human expertise to establish historical data and other information sources. Sales managers are tasked with managing the operational business by comparing actual sales with planned sales, with the aim of enhancing the current sales volume. They also have the responsibility to predict the company's potential sales value, set sales goals, and devise strategies to reach these targets. Sales managers often face challenges such as the high manual effort needed to collect and analyze data from systems and external sources, repetitive and time-consuming tasks to gather information, and more. The complexity of the underlying data and uncertainty about the accuracy of the analysis and forecasting can also be daunting. There's also the constant worry of not meeting quotas, which necessitates solid knowledge and experience. Sales managers anticipate the following benefits and business value from the artificial intelligence service:

- Increased revenue growth
- Identification of more realistic sales targets
- Decreased sales full-time equivalent (FTE) effort for pipeline analysis and reporting
- More time dedicated to selling
- Lowered sales training costs
- Improved support for less experienced sales staff
- More dependable planning data to enhance subsequent processes in finance, manufacturing, and inventory

The service of artificial intelligence for predicting sales performance aids in the automatic collection and analysis of historical sales data. The system handles complexity and accuracy by identifying relevant factors that influence sales, such as customer dependencies and product categories. Sales managers can effortlessly compare the actual sales volume with the predicted and planned sales volumes by utilizing the artificial intelligence service. Predictions made through sales performance analytics expedite and simplify the process of gaining insights and taking action. Early detection of deviations from the plan allows for the planning of countermeasures, enabling informed, data-driven decisions. Furthermore, creating a decision pool for sales analysis and key performance indicators (KPIs) with an emphasis on analysis can produce tangible value for sales managers and sales staff.

The service for predicting sales performance using artificial intelligence allows us to juxtapose our actual sales volume with forecasted figures, enabling us to evaluate how well we are meeting our sales objectives. This service provides the ability to foresee the present sales performance and streamline the sales planning

Fig. 21.4 Predict sales
forecasting: architecture

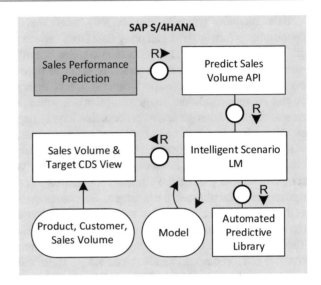

procedures. As depicted in Fig. 21.4, we are making use of time series algorithms from the Predictive Analytics Library, which are incorporated within the Intelligent Scenario Lifecycle Management framework. These are then integrated into the SAP S/4HANA business processes for predicting sales performance.

In conclusion, the depiction of sales performance predictions in Fig. 21.5 enables sales managers to accomplish several tasks:

- They can anticipate the volume of sales a business is likely to generate.
- They can juxtapose real, forecasted, and intended sales quantities across various parameters and visually represent this comparison.
- They can enhance the precision of their planning process by utilizing algorithms based on artificial intelligence. These algorithms provide predictions and suggestions, thereby minimizing the manual labor involved in sales planning and similar tasks.

The advantages to the business are manifold. They include a rise in actual sales volume due to the provision of superior insights that allow for necessary action and the offering of predictions for feasible sales volumes. There is also a general reduction in manual labor required for sales forecasting and planning. The value proposition lies in assisting sales managers with sales performance predictions. This leads to quicker decision-making, an increase in sales volumes, and the creation of more precise sales plans.

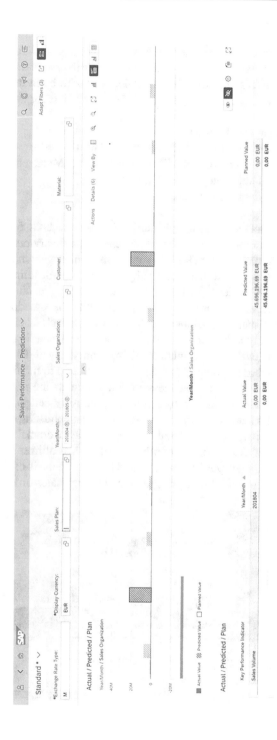

Fig. 21.5 Predict sales forecasting: application

21.3   Predict Delivery Delay

In this part of the discussion, our attention will be directed toward the service of artificial intelligence that has been designed specifically to predict the delivery dates in relation to the performance of sales order deliveries. To build the bridge to the previous chapters, we list the corresponding references points for the use case:

- AI Application Pattern: Prediction
- ERP Reference Process: Lead to Cash/Order to Fulfill
- ERP Reference Architecture: Sales/Order and Contract Management
- ERP Reference AI Technology: ERP Platform
- AI Realization Pattern: Embedded

Figure 21.6 illustrates the artificial intelligence service built for this process, which we'll unpack in this section. The effectiveness of delivery is a widely recognized key performance indicator (KPI) in supply chain management, used to gauge the success of meeting a customer's needs by the specified deadline. For those in sales roles, it's crucial to identify which sales orders are experiencing delays, determine the underlying reasons for these delays, and rectify the situation. These users often face obstacles such as postponed delivery dates, a lack of clarity regarding which orders are likely to be delayed, an insufficient understanding of the reasons behind these delays, customer complaints arising from delayed deliveries, and the additional manual labor required for recurring tasks related to monitoring delivery performance. The benefits to the business and its customers are primarily focused on enhancing customer satisfaction by minimizing delivery delays, improving the efficiency of the sales team, retaining more customers, and boosting delivery performance. The service provided by artificial intelligence plays a crucial role in overseeing the probability of a sales order item being delayed. It utilizes historical sales order data to anticipate delayed sales orders and offer an analysis of the root cause. The system presents potential delivery problems for each sales order line item for

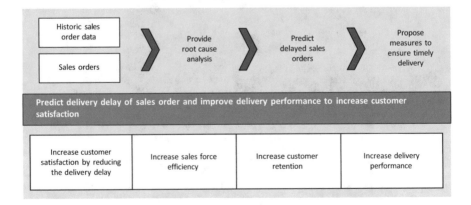

Fig. 21.6 Predict delivery delay

the sales representative's attention and suggests actions to guarantee punctual delivery.

The Predicted Delivery Delay SAP Fiori application, equipped with an artificial intelligence service, empowers a sales manager to keep an eye on the current state of delivery performance. It allows them to immediately understand the impact of the ratio of delivered items to sales orders as requested, helping to avoid significant delays in the delivery of goods. This, in turn, enhances customer satisfaction and loyalty in the long run. At present, the process of determining the expected delivery date for an item in a sales order depends on the outcome of a planning or scheduling tool, such as the available to promise (ATP) solution. However, this method does not take into account potential future deviations. The application displays the expected date of delivery creation, the requested delivery date, the predicted production and processing delays, and the overall anticipated delay in delivery for sales document items. The predicted date of delivery creation is used to concentrate on the progression of deliveries as subsequent steps to open sales orders during the training of the predicted delay of delivery creation. The expected date of delivery creation (from the confirmed schedule line of sales order items that have previously been delivered) is contrasted with the actual date of delivery creation of the relevant delivery, using historical data for this comparison. The solution compares the planned goods issue date of all deliveries for which goods issue is completed with the actual goods movement date of the subsequent deliveries to train the predicted delivery processing delay. This calculation applies to every delivery for the associated sales order item. The application then uses the maximum delivery processing delay of the aforementioned deliveries – that is, the delivery with the most significant delay – as the predicted delivery processing delay. One delivery item is considered for each of the two deliveries. The planned goods issuance date and the actual goods movement date differ for each delivery. The solution determines the predicted delivery processing delay using the longest delay. As shown in Fig. 21.7, regression algorithms from the Automated Predictive Library that use the Intelligent Scenario Lifecycle Management framework are integrated into the SAP S/4HANA sales order delivery business processes. Thus, the ability to deliver on time allows internal sales representatives to monitor the likelihood of a delay in a sales order item and take appropriate actions to prevent the delay. This increases customer satisfaction, considering the influencing criteria of the probable delay. The business benefits include reduced manual efforts to monitor and resolve issues, improved delivery performance, and hence increased customer satisfaction. The value proposition for the sales representative is to predict the delay in delivery of a sales order, improve delivery performance, and enhance customer satisfaction.

21.4   Project Cost Forecasting

Our attention will be directed toward the artificial intelligence service designed to forecast the expenses associated with enterprise projects during the planning phase of the portfolio for the forthcoming months. Figure 21.8 presents the artificial

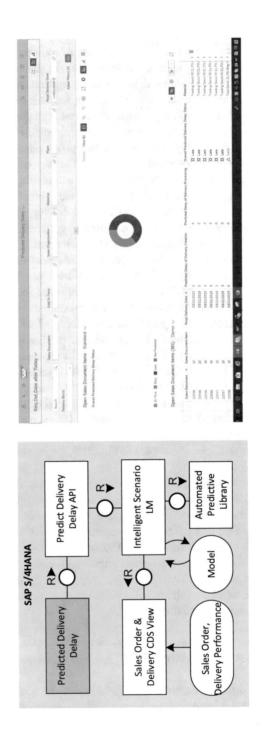

Fig. 21.7 Predict delivery delay: architecture and application

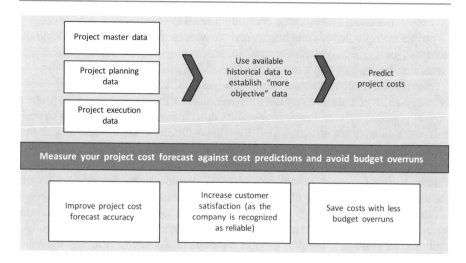

Fig. 21.8 Project cost forecasting

intelligence service specifically constructed for this process, which we will delve into with more detail in this segment. To build the bridge to the previous chapters, we list the corresponding references points for the use case:

- AI Application Pattern: Prediction
- ERP Reference Process: Idea to Market/Manage Products & Services
- ERP Reference Architecture: Research and Development/Core Portfolio and Project Management
- ERP Reference AI Technology: ERP Platform
- AI Realization Pattern: Embedded

For individuals managing projects, the primary objectives are to ensure that the projects stay within the allocated budget and prevent any budgetary excesses, provided that the given product scope, product quality, and delivery date are precisely upheld. To accomplish these goals, it's crucial to forecast as precisely as possible the expenditure of budgets and time associated with the project. Project managers often face a variety of challenges, including:

- Data that is insufficient or influenced by personal bias
- Struggles in locating the appropriate information for calculating projected costs
- Tasks that require a significant amount of time to compile all necessary information
- A high degree of manual labor and strenuous efforts required
- Factors related to politics and psychology
- Forecasting techniques that are not flawless

Project managers and financial controllers stand to gain from enhanced accuracy in project cost predictions and heightened customer satisfaction. This results in the company being perceived as dependable, cost savings due to fewer instances of exceeding the budget, and a reduction in the risk of budget overruns.

The service facilitated by artificial intelligence utilizes existing historical data to create more objective and reference data derived from the master data of the project, project planning data, and project execution data. It does this by proposing an optimal work breakdown structure (WBS). This WBS is a hierarchical model that breaks down the enterprise project into smaller, more manageable segments, represented by parts of the WBS. The solution uses reference class forecasting algorithms to learn from previous projects and provide more dependable project forecasts. By implementing the artificial intelligence service, the solution can consistently monitor and manage projects. It alerts users when there might be potential overruns, identifies available buffers, and suggests possible rescheduling and budget reallocation through a decision support mechanism. As depicted in Fig. 21.9, the scenario uses classification and k-nearest neighbors' algorithms from the Predictive Analytics Library. These algorithms are integrated into the Intelligent Scenario Lifecycle Management framework and embedded into the business processes of SAP S/4HANA Enterprise Portfolio and Project Management (EPPM). With a tight integration with business processes in Research and Development (R&D)/ Engineering and other areas like Finance or Sourcing and Procurement, the solution allows to manage enterprise projects throughout their entire life cycle. This includes project initiation, planning, execution, tracking, and closure. It can handle a variety of cross-industry projects such as investment initiatives, administrative projects, R&D projects, engineer-to-order projects, and statistical initiatives. The solution offers the following features to manage enterprise projects and their work breakdown structures:

- It allows us to manage projects within our company's organization and monitor business projects.
- It enables successful management of project progress and costs within a specified budget through project financial control.
- It enhances project efficiency and ensures the delivery of high-quality projects on time and within budget using project logistics control.

Project-based services use professional services projects to manage customer and internal projects, while Enterprise Portfolio and Project Management handles cross-industry projects with enterprise projects. There is significant potential value in using reference class forecasting to create a consistent project plan and cost structure. This allows for more accurate project cost forecasting and minimizes budget overruns.

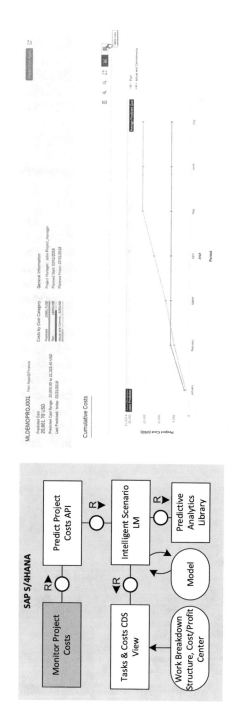

Fig. 21.9 Project cost forecasting: architecture and application

21.5   Digital Content Processing

In this section, we will focus on the service of artificial intelligence that is centered around the classification of documents and the processing of the digital content. Figure 21.10 presents the service of artificial intelligence that has been designed for this process, which we will delve into in this section. To build the bridge to the previous chapters, we list the corresponding references points for the use case:

- AI Application Pattern: Categorization
- ERP Reference Process: Idea to Market/Design to Release
- ERP Reference Architecture: Research and Development/Product Lifecycle Management
- ERP Reference AI Technology: AI Technology Platform
- AI Realization Pattern: Side-by-Side

A significant number of communications and processes that are based on paper and documents lead to a decrease in efficiency across various organizations. A large number of organizations continue to depend on these procedures; the process of digitization could significantly enhance their efficiency. In this scenario, digitization is primarily about discovering valuable data in unstructured sources such as text files and images. Customers usually need to establish various categories for classification, identify them, and sort documents based on these categories.

The challenges faced include a considerable amount of manual labor, which could be prone to errors, and a manual process of communication based on paper and documents that decreases efficiency. Clients gain from the increased business value related to cost savings and efficiency, which results in a higher rate of automation. The reduction in implementation efforts for scenarios specific to clients makes them agile and accelerates communications and procedures through digitization.

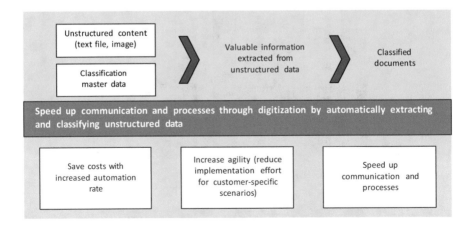

Fig. 21.10   Digital content processing

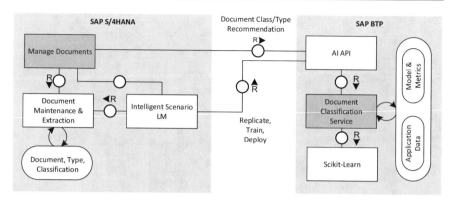

Fig. 21.11 Digital content processing: architecture

We can achieve significant savings in terms of time, money, and effort by addressing customer issues through the following strategies:

- We can rectify underperforming solutions by introducing new features, improving performance, and enhancing quality.
- We can mitigate the negative social consequences customers face and eliminate their risks by simplifying processes or removing hurdles.
- We can prevent common errors that occur during manual document handling and classification by addressing major issues, reducing concerns, and eliminating worries, thereby removing social, financial, or technical risks that could potentially cause problems.
- We can remove barriers that deter customers from adopting our solutions by introducing lower or even no initial investment costs.

As illustrated in Fig. 21.11, in this context, a few algorithms such as text analysis and classification from the Scikit-Learn library are utilized, and the service of artificial intelligence is provided on the SAP Business Technology Platform (BTP). This artificial intelligence service is consumed by the corresponding SAP S/4HANA process in a side-by-side model, delivering the necessary results.

Figure 21.12 demonstrates how the utilization of this artificial intelligence service enhances digital content processing, providing customers with several benefits:

- This service facilitates the digital transformation of business operations by extracting both structured and unstructured data from documents within the SAP Business Technology Platform, integrated with SAP S/4HANA.
- Documents are automatically categorized using the classification classes provided by SAP.
- This flexible and scalable digital content processing service allows for the easy implementation of specific use cases with minimal effort.

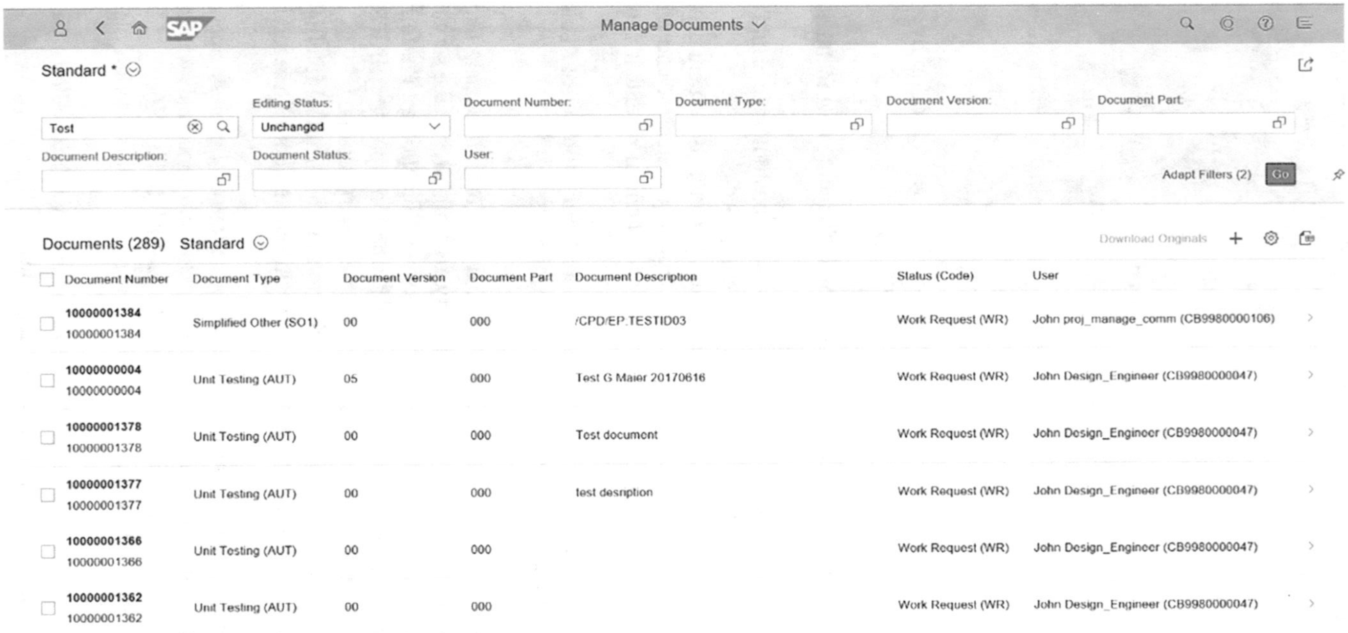

Fig. 21.12 Digital content processing: application

The application displayed in Fig. 21.12 enables the management of original software files and document information records (DIR). The master record of a document is known as the DIR. The DIR encompasses both the actual document (or the original application file) and the metadata of the document. Documents can be searched and accessed based on various filter criteria such as status, document number, document type, document version, document portion, user, and document description. Furthermore, the application supports draft compatibility, which allows users to save changes without finalizing them and continue editing at a later time. The business advantages of utilizing the digital content processing service powered by artificial intelligence include:

- Cost savings and efficiency – the service replaces manual tasks or increases automation rates by extracting structured content from unstructured content and automatically classifying documents.
- Agility – the service enables the implementation of customer-specific scenarios with minimal effort by leveraging flexible and scalable document management services such as Optical Character Recognition (OCR), rule-based content extraction, and file conversion powered by artificial intelligence.

21.6 Business Integrity Screening

Let's discuss now the artificial intelligence services that have been developed specifically for the field of governance, risk, and compliance. As organizations continue to expand and evolve due to a variety of situations and circumstances, the governance of these changes, risk management, and compliance adherence become increasingly crucial. This is where the governance, risk, and compliance solutions provided by ERP systems come into play, assisting organizations in managing their key operations and navigating potential risks. The three main areas of focus are risk analysis, regulation management, and compliance monitoring. Some of the key features of these solutions are as follows:

- Risk identification and enhancement of risk-management activities
- Efficient risk management with minimal or no complexity
- Effective prevention of fraud in business processes and improved audit management
- Enhancement of an organization's performance by safeguarding its core values

In this section, we will delve deeper into the details of how to utilize the artificial intelligence service that has been developed specifically for identifying and preventing fraud. Figure 21.13 illustrates the process involved in the artificial intelligence service designed for fraud identification and prevention in the SAP Business Integrity Screening application. We will further elaborate on this process in this section. To build the bridge to the previous chapters we list the corresponding references points for the use case:

- AI Application Pattern: Categorization and Prediction

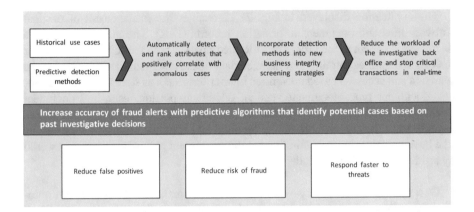

Fig. 21.13 Fraud identification and prevention

- ERP Reference Process: Idea to Market/Products and Services to Market
- ERP Reference Architecture: Research and Development/Manage Product and Services
- ERP Reference AI Technology: ERP Platform
- AI Realization Pattern: Embedded

We'll begin our discussion by examining the issues that customers encounter, their pain points and challenges, and how the SAP Business Integrity Screening application, facilitated by artificial intelligence, can provide solutions to these problems. Fraud investigators and screening experts are tasked with managing a growing number of suspicious or unusual cases that need to be evaluated and categorized on a weekly, daily, and even hourly basis. A common problem for these investigators is the time spent on cases that appear at the top of the list but end up posing little to no risk or impact to the company. Meanwhile, some high-risk cases are overlooked. These investigators would greatly benefit from focusing on fewer but more significant cases, without missing the majority of the most consequential ones. Rather than working on a random assortment of cases, predictive detection methods rank each new case based on its potential impact on the company's business. This approach not only aids companies but also makes the investigators' work more productive. Investigators who lack extensive knowledge of data science, often referred to as citizen data scientists, use the threshold parameter of predictive detection methods to manage their workload and prioritize tasks, resulting in significant improvements in efficiency and profitability. As depicted in Fig. 21.13, organizations can prevent disruptions to crucial business processes by responding more quickly to threats and establishing procedures that discourage fraud. The SAP Business Integrity Screening application aids in reducing the risk of fraud by enhancing analysis capabilities, providing greater visibility into potentially fraudulent activities, and facilitating better management decisions. This application supports fraud scenarios relevant to our organization, such as employee theft, corruption, and warranty fraud. With the backing of in-memory database technology and integration into SAP S/4HANA and other third-party sources, this application enables investigators to gather, analyze, and act on vast amounts of data in real time.

SAP Business Integrity Screening has recently introduced predictive detection techniques that employ predictive algorithms to spot potentially fraudulent activities. These techniques learn from previous investigative decisions made by SAP Business Integrity Screening. The algorithms can be frequently updated to keep up with the ever-changing strategies of fraud attacks, which can vary by the day, hour, or even minute. As depicted in Fig. 21.14, the classification and regression algorithms from the Predictive Analytics Library are used in conjunction with the Intelligent Scenario Lifecycle Management framework. These algorithms are then integrated into the SAP S/4HANA business processes. The information generated in real time is then delivered to the appropriate individuals, enabling them to make informed decisions. These decisions can lead to actions that either detect or prevent a fraud attack. Thus, SAP Business Integrity Screening empowers business analysts and investigators to perform several tasks. These include the automatic detection and ranking of attributes within classified data that have a positive correlation with anomalous cases, the integration of these attributes with existing detection methods to form new SAP Business Integrity Screening strategies, and the utilization of robust, cutting-edge algorithms related to artificial intelligence. In essence, this solution provides several benefits. It can detect new suspicious patterns, reduce the number of false positives, and seamlessly integrate artificial intelligence algorithms into the established SAP Business Integrity Screening framework.

21.7 Conclusion

In this section, we focused on the artificial intelligence services and embedded use cases built for the sales and research line of business (LoB). Figure 21.15 gives an overview of the order-to-cash process.

The process shown in Fig. 21.15 outlines the many steps involved, which include everything from handling quotations to creating sales orders, executing these orders, delivering products, managing returns, and providing invoices. The sales manager and the in-house sales team have specific requirements that can be met by harnessing the power of artificial intelligence. In this conversation, our main focus is on the completion and management of sales orders. Here are some examples of applications that we considered in this chapter, using artificial intelligence algorithms based on the Intelligent Scenario Lifecycle Management framework:

- Sales Quotation predicts conversion of sales quotations to sales orders
- Sales Performance predicts sales forecasts
- Delivery Performance predicts delivery delays

Furthermore, we considered the artificial intelligence services and embedded use cases built for the research and development (R&D)/engineering line of business

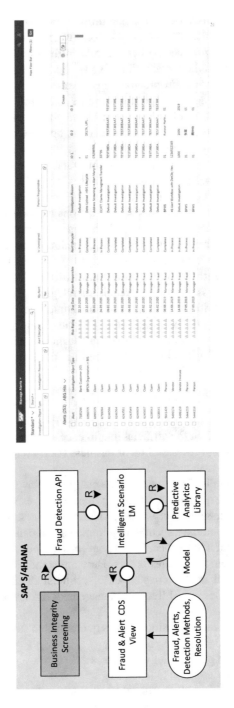

Fig. 21.14 Fraud identification and prevention: architecture and application

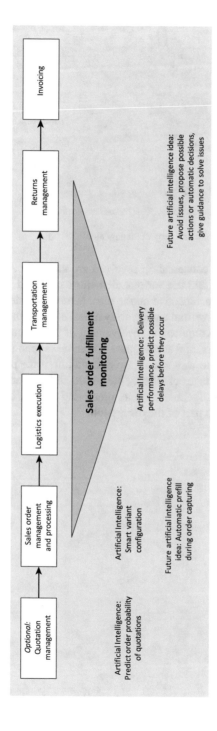

Fig. 21.15 Order-to-cash process with artificial intelligence

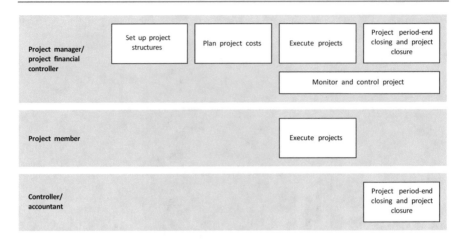

Fig. 21.16 Enterprise portfolio and project management

(LoB). Particularly, our conversation revolved around the management of project and portfolio life cycles and the various elements associated with it. Figure 21.16 offers an encompassing perspective on the management of enterprise portfolios and projects. This clearly shows that a wide array of tasks within the enterprise portfolio management procedures require the involvement of project managers, team members, financial supervisors, and accountants. These tasks span from the early phases of project planning all the way to the implementation of the project and even continue to the concluding stages of closing the period and further. The potential applications of artificial intelligence, such as predicting project costs and processing digital content, were also part of the discussion.

Sourcing and Procurement

22

In this chapter, we explain intelligent business applications in the sourcing and procurement line of business (LoB) and how customers can benefit from this functionality. We provide a brief overview of the use case requirements, the business processes involved, and how they're addressed. The sourcing and procurement LoB is huge, with a lot of potential to automate and fine-tune the processes. The focus of the chapter is on contract consumption, resolution for invoice payment block, supplier deliver prediction, new catalog items, image-based busing, and intelligent approval workflow. For these use cases, the concepts and frameworks explained in this elaboration were applied, which proves the real-world feasibility of those new inventions.

22.1 Contract Consumption

Our attention will now shift to the service based on artificial intelligence that is designed around the functionality of quantity contract consumption in SAP S/4HANA. This service is capable of forecasting contract consumption and expiration in advance, thereby enabling buyers to renegotiate contracts. The artificial intelligence service designed for this specific process is depicted in Fig. 22.1, which we will delve into in this section. To build the bridge to the previous chapters, we list the corresponding references points for the use case:

- AI Application Pattern: Prediction
- ERP Reference Process: Source to Pay/Source to Contract
- ERP Reference Architecture: Procurement/Sourcing and Contract Management
- ERP Reference AI Technology: ERP Platform
- AI Realization Pattern: Embedded

© The Author(s), under exclusive license to Springer Nature
Switzerland AG 2024
S. Sarferaz, *Embedding Artificial Intelligence into ERP Software*,
https://doi.org/10.1007/978-3-031-54249-7_22

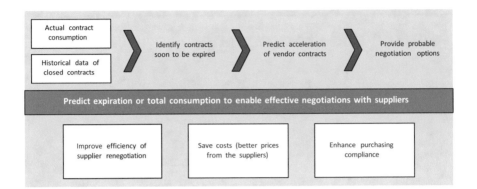

Fig. 22.1 Predict contract expiration and consumption

Leaders in procurement need to revisit and revise contracts that are nearing their end, with the aim of securing more favorable terms. Keeping an eye on when contracts are due to expire can be a complex task, as they often run out earlier than anticipated. The advantages for customers include the ability to negotiate with suppliers earlier and, more effectively, securing better prices for products, forecasting contract end dates in advance, and improving adherence to purchasing rules.

Algorithms based on artificial intelligence can pinpoint contracts that are nearing their end and estimate the likelihood of a contract running out earlier than predicted. A predefined set of key performance indicators enables in-depth analysis of data from the SAP S/4HANA, improving business usability by offering visual predictions and suggesting potential negotiation strategies. Essentially, the sourcing and procurement features of SAP S/4HANA allow businesses to control spending across all major categories, decrease direct costs and administrative workload, and reduce the overall time taken to complete a cycle. When combined with predictive services from the SAP Business Technology Platform, the sourcing and procurement process is further improved, offering new insights into when contracts are likely to be consumed.

The system uses historical data from completed contracts to forecast when vendor contracts will be fully utilized. This allows the purchaser to strategically plan for contract renegotiations with suppliers in a timely manner. SAP S/4HANA is already equipped to analyze contract consumption for both quantity and value contracts, providing a monthly breakdown of contract usage. With the introduction of a service that uses artificial intelligence to predict contract consumption, businesses can further refine their contract negotiation strategies, decrease overall expenses, and improve their management of vendors. As shown in Fig. 22.2, regression algorithm from the Automated Predictive Library is used within the Intelligent Scenario Lifecycle Management framework. These are integrated into the SAP S/4HANA procurement business processes, enabling the system to provide advance predictions for when contracts will expire.

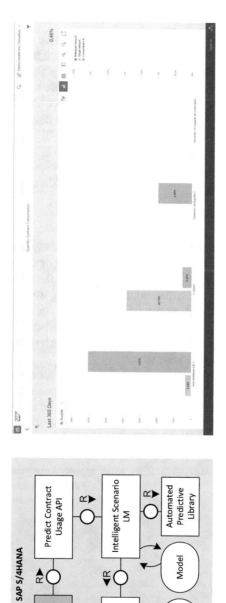

Fig. 22.2   Contract consumption: architecture and application

22.2   Resolution for Invoice Payment Block

Our focus will now be on the artificial intelligence service that has been developed to center around the payment blocks for invoices, which could potentially jeopardize the cash discounts available to the buyer. The diagram labeled as Fig. 22.3 illustrates the artificial intelligence service that has been designed specifically for this procedure, a topic we will delve into in this section. To build the bridge to the previous chapters, we list the corresponding references points for the use case:

- AI Application Pattern: Recommendation
- ERP Reference Process: Source to Pay/Supplier Invoice Management
- ERP Reference Architecture: Procurement/Invoice Management
- ERP Reference AI Technology: ERP Platform
- AI Realization Pattern: Embedded

The process of invoicing has already been significantly transformed by digital technology and automation. The only time a purchaser or accountant needs to step in is when an invoice payment is halted. The onus is on the purchaser to address the root cause of the issue to lift the payment block. During this process, the purchaser may face several hurdles, such as resolving the reason for a payment block, which is often a lengthy and costly process. Often, a manual process is initiated whenever there's an anomaly in a payment, leading to missed cash discounts for buyers and lost business opportunities for suppliers.

Incorporating an embedded service facilitated by artificial intelligence, algorithms are used to cross-verify invoices with existing purchase orders and procurement regulations. Despite the high level of automation in matching invoices, there are always exceptions that necessitate manual intervention from purchasers or accounts payable specialists. These exceptions could be unexpected additional costs in the invoice or discrepancies in quantity or price. Such exceptions are not only time-consuming but also expensive. If a reason for blocking arises, supplier invoices

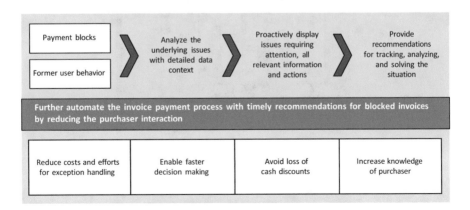

Fig. 22.3 Resolve invoice payment block

are automatically halted, and the accountable purchaser must address the underlying issues. The process can be made even more efficient by using recommendations to monitor, analyze, and resolve the situation. Quicker processing times can also assist buyers in not missing out on cash discounts for early or prompt payments.

The process illustrated in Fig. 22.4 takes advantage of regression algorithms from the Automated Predictive Library, making use of the Intelligent Scenario Lifecycle Management framework, and is integrated into the SAP S/4HANA business procedures. Businesses typically seek advantages such as cost reduction and minimized effort, expedited decision-making, prevention of cash discount losses, and the ability for employees to concentrate on more critical tasks rather than maintaining these manual tasks. Suppliers also stand to gain from quicker invoice payments, cash discounts, and cost savings. The unique selling point is the automation of the invoice payment process with timely suggestions for blocked invoices, thereby reducing the time a purchaser spends on manually removing payment blocks. In summary, the payment block cash discount at risk provides accountants and purchasers the ability to:

- Actively show issues that need attention, consolidating all relevant information and actions in one location
- Examine the root causes with a detailed data context
- Get suggestions based on previous user behavior
- Prevent a loss of cash discounts

Some of the business advantages include mitigating the impact of exception handling and repetitive tasks, process automation for quicker decision-making, prevention of cash discount losses, and allowing employees to concentrate on significant tasks.

22.3   Supplier Delivery Prediction

We will now concentrate on the artificial intelligence service that has been developed specifically for managing purchase order processing, with the aim of forecasting the delivery dates for items in a purchase order. The diagram labeled as Fig. 22.5 illustrates the structure of this artificial intelligence service designed for this particular task, which we will delve into and explain in detail in this section. To build the bridge to the previous chapters, we list the corresponding references points for the use case:

- AI Application Pattern: Prediction
- ERP Reference Process: Source to Pay/Procure to Receipt
- ERP Reference Architecture: Procurement/Operational Procurement
- ERP Reference AI Technology: ERP Platform
- AI Realization Pattern: Embedded

Fig. 22.4 Resolution for invoice payment block: architecture and application

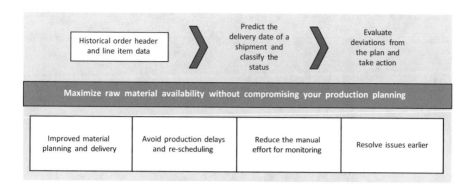

Fig. 22.5 Predict delivery date for purchase order items

During the procurement process, it's common for the necessary production materials to come from a variety of suppliers. When there's a delay in delivery, it can disrupt the timely production at factories, necessitating the costly rescheduling of assembly lines. Delays in the delivery of indirect materials can also significantly postpone the provision of necessary products or services to employees. Algorithms based on artificial intelligence can identify these supplier delivery delays under various circumstances and forecast the likelihood of future delays. As shown in Fig. 22.6, these regression and classification algorithms use the Automated Predictive Library and take advantage of the Intelligent Scenario Lifecycle Management framework to incorporate artificial intelligence into the SAP S/4HANA business processes.

The artificial intelligence algorithm that predicts supplier delivery enables buyers to forecast when a shipment will arrive and categorize its status. This empowers the buyer to relay this information to the product lifecycle management (PLM) department and ultimately keep up with the material requirements planning (MRP) and security optimization service (SoS) manually. Future releases with enhanced artificial intelligence capabilities could further streamline this process, eliminating the need for the MRP engineer and the design engineer to manually update any records in the system. Some of the business advantages of this approach include:

- Enhanced reliability in planning and delivering materials
- Prevention of production delays and rescheduling
- Reduced manual efforts to monitor and address issues more quickly and proactively
- Current lead time information for goods and services at the master level for both direct and indirect procurement

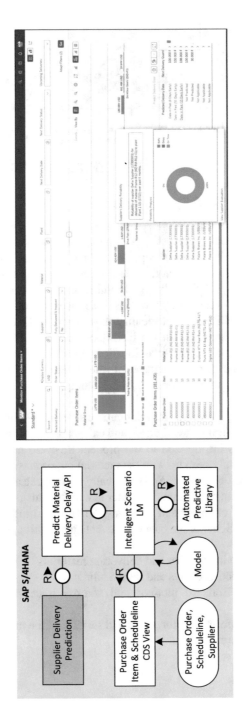

Fig. 22.6 Supplier delivery prediction: architecture and application

22.4   Proposal of New Catalog Item

Let's focus now on the service of artificial intelligence that has been designed around the processing of purchase orders and the suggestions offered in the catalog items. The artificial intelligence service designed for this procedure is depicted in Fig. 22.7, which we will delve into in this section. To build the bridge to the previous chapters, we list the corresponding references points for the use case:

- AI Application Pattern: Recommendation
- ERP Reference Process: Source to Pay/Source to Contract
- ERP Reference Architecture: Procurement/Operational Procurement
- ERP Reference AI Technology: AI Technology Platform
- AI Realization Pattern: Side-by-Side

A purchasing manager is responsible for the internal procurement of goods and items, as well as maintaining the internal catalog current. The purchasing manager faces a number of challenges. Users generate vast quantities of free-text items, and examining and analyzing these free-text items always requires a significant amount of effort. Furthermore, free-text items result in purchases that are prone to errors, and it's difficult to consistently keep the internal catalog updated. The purchasing department would greatly benefit from enhancing the optimization of catalog coverage and minimizing the purchases prone to errors, ultimately reducing the overall time spent on processing purchase orders.

The proposed establishment of a service for artificial intelligence in the catalog item is set to allow the algorithm to assume control of the investigative tasks and resources that are in high demand by users. This would enable these items to be automatically included in the catalog. The process of creating purchase orders would be automated, thereby guaranteeing automated suggestions for items that should be incorporated into the catalog. Ultimately, this would assist the purchasing

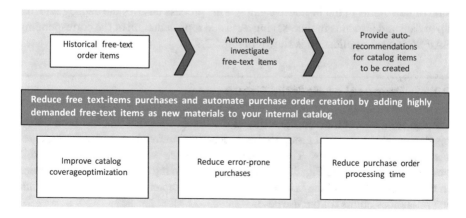

Fig. 22.7 Convert free-text order items to catalog items

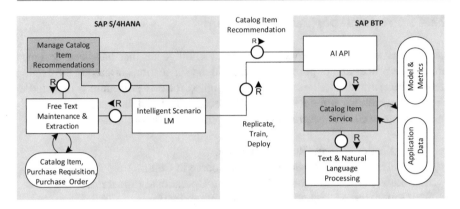

Fig. 22.8 Proposal of new catalog items: architecture

manager in achieving their objective of minimizing the number of free-text items to the greatest extent possible. When users generate a large number of free-text items, computational methods can assist in determining the appropriate time to introduce a new item into the catalog. If there is a significant demand from users, existing materials are automatically incorporated into the catalog. As previously mentioned, through the use of capabilities inherent in artificial intelligence and statistical models, the service dedicated to artificial intelligence offers automated suggestions for the creation of new catalog items. These suggestions are further enhanced with insights collected by the algorithm used in the artificial intelligence service. As shown in Fig. 22.8, the algorithms from the TensorFlow library are employed, and the service for artificial intelligence is constructed using the SAP Business Technology Platform (SAP BTP). The corresponding SAP S/4HANA process utilizes this artificial intelligence service in a side-by-side model and delivers the necessary results.

The value proposition of this artificial intelligence-based service emphasizes the importance of utilizing past experiences to suggest or execute the automated inclusion of new items in the in-house catalog. This process ensures the catalog remains up to date and also aids in time-saving. A visual representation of the corresponding SAP S/4HANA application is shown in Fig. 22.9.

22.5   Proposal of Material Group

We will now concentrate on the artificial intelligence service that has been developed to suggest a material group for items described in free text during the procurement requisition process. The artificial intelligence service designed for this procedure is depicted in Fig. 22.10, and we will delve into the details of this service in this section. To build the bridge to the previous chapters, we list the corresponding references points for the use case:

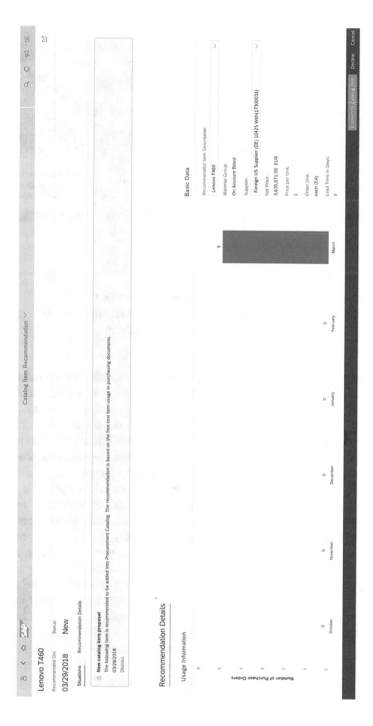

Fig. 22.9 Proposal of new catalog items: application

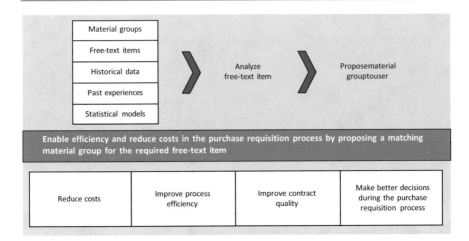

Fig. 22.10 Propose material group for free-text items

- AI Application Pattern: Recommendation
- ERP Reference Process: Source to Pay/Source to Contract
- ERP Reference Architecture: Procurement/Operational Procurement
- ERP Reference AI Technology: AI Technology Platform
- AI Realization Pattern: Side-by-Side

Operational buyers are tasked with identifying and correcting misallocated material groups, which helps minimize inadvertent purchases in incorrect categories. The procurement department often faces issues with employees unintentionally making purchases under the wrong categories. When employees create free-text items, they frequently assign a material group that doesn't match the item in question. This necessitates a labor-intensive and resource-heavy manual process to assign the correct material group to the free-text item. Buyers must manually adjust the material group, allowing the appropriate team member to take over. This manual process is costly in terms of both resources and processes. Automating this process can offer customers several benefits, including cost reduction through automatic material group assignment, improved process efficiency, decreased risk of error-prone purchases, and enhanced decision-making in the purchase requisition process. The suggested material group for free-text items service, facilitated by artificial intelligence, aids in decreasing the instances of incorrectly assigned material groups. This artificial intelligence service recommends a suitable material group for the required free-text item to the requester during the purchase requisition creation. This recommendation is based on the capabilities of artificial intelligence and statistical models. The service uses algorithms from the TensorFlow library and is constructed with the SAP Business Technology Platform (SAP BTP), as depicted in Fig. 22.11. The corresponding SAP S/4HANA process uses this artificial intelligence service in a side-by-side model and, as shown in Fig. 22.12, delivers the necessary results.

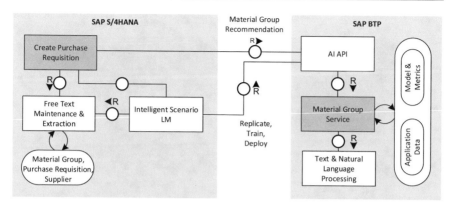

Fig. 22.11 Propose material group: architecture

The advantages that businesses can gain from utilizing services powered by artificial intelligence are numerous and include the following:

- There's a significant reduction in the need for manual tasks.
- There's an enhancement in process efficiency, which in turn leads to a decrease in expenses.
- There's a lower likelihood of making purchases that are prone to errors.

A more accurate categorization of free-text items into material groups can help in managing purchases that are susceptible to mistakes. The recommendation for a suitable material group is derived from historical experiences and data. These models, powered by artificial intelligence, learn and offer suggestions based on past data. They utilize predictive algorithms to automatically suggest materials and categories for the free-text items, thereby improving the user experience for the purchasers. The main benefit offered is the ability to increase efficiency and lower expenses in the process of purchase requisition.

22.6   Materials Without Purchase Contract

Let's focus now on the artificial intelligence service that has been developed with the aim of minimizing expenditure that is not contractually covered. This is achieved by giving priority to materials that lack purchase contracts and offering alternatives. Figure 22.13 illustrates the artificial intelligence service designed for this procedure, the details of which we will delve into in this section. To build the bridge to the previous chapters, we list the corresponding references points for the use case:

- AI Application Pattern: Ranking
- ERP Reference Process: Source to Pay/Source to Contract
- ERP Reference Architecture: Procurement/Operational Procurement

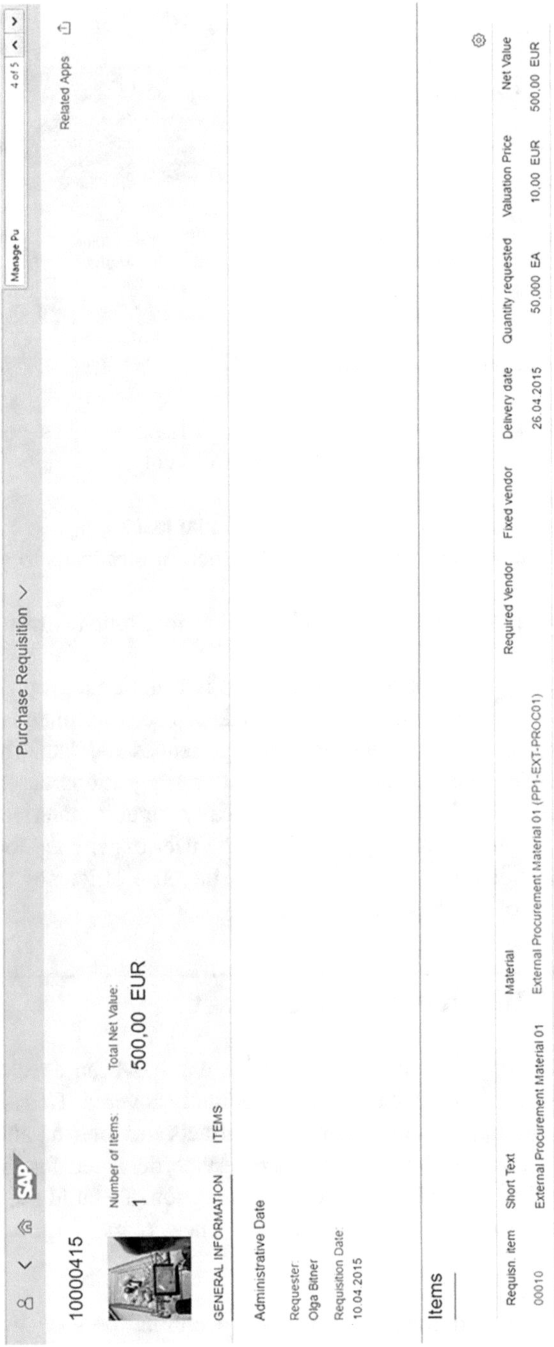

Fig. 22.12 Propose material group: application

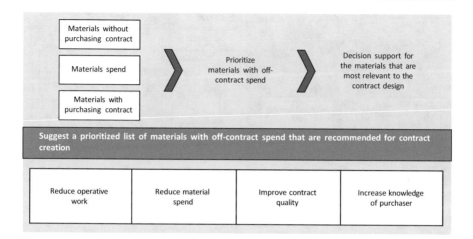

Fig. 22.13 Materials without purchase contract

- ERP Reference AI Technology: AI Technology Platform
- AI Realization Pattern: Side-by-Side

Buyers are required to pinpoint items that lack associated contracts and generate quotation requests based on comparable items that do have existing contracts. It's crucial for buyers to rank items according to factors such as quantity and worth when forming a quotation request and, subsequently, a contract for those items. The execution of corporate procurement tasks presents a multitude of challenges for buyers. The absence of a purchase contract for specific items leads to an increase in overall expenditure due to frequent off-contract ordering. The process of formulating a quotation request from the ground up is often more laborious than creating one based on a similar item. The task of ranking a list of off-contract items can also be time-consuming. The procurement department stands to gain significantly if this off-contract expenditure can be managed in an intuitive manner. This approach could lead to cost reductions, as quotation requests for items that are frequently ordered off-contract are generated using a ranked list of items. This would allow buyers to be prepared well in advance for early and effective negotiations with suppliers, resulting in more favorable purchase prices for items. Consequently, the process of creating quotation requests becomes more efficient. The illustration in Fig. 22.14 demonstrates that the implementation of artificial intelligence is grounded on the SAP Business Technology Platform (SAP BTP). The service for proposing contracts uses historical data for the purpose of training. In this context, historical purchase orders, contracts, and material expenditures are taken into consideration. Proposals that are rejected by the purchasing staff are factored into the operations of the artificial intelligence service.

The artificial intelligence service identifies materials that are most deserving of being included in a contract. The TensorFlow library's algorithms are utilized for

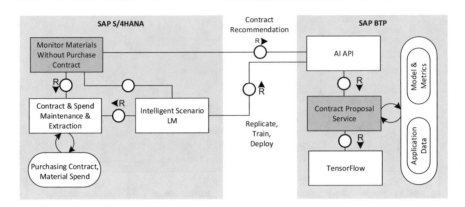

Fig. 22.14 Materials without purchase contract: architecture

the artificial intelligence. The corresponding SAP S/4HANA process uses this artificial intelligence service in a side-by-side model and delivers the necessary outcomes by offering suggestions for creating a Request for Quotation (RFQ). To economize, purchasers must refrain from ordering off-contract. In this regard, the artificial intelligence algorithm assists the buyer in identifying materials that lack a contract and associating them with similar ones that have contracts based on certain factors. It then suggests these materials for an RFQ as depicted in Fig. 22.15. The solution enables procurement leaders to perform the following actions:

- Foresee contract negotiations in line with the company's guidelines and practices
- Initiate and conduct efficient negotiations with suppliers regarding frequently ordered materials
- Establish predictive models and execute the scenarios
- Utilize a pre-established set of key performance indicators (KPIs) that facilitate the creation of robust analytics on SAP S/4HANA

Some of the business advantages for the customers encompass the following:

- Improved usability for businesses to visualize the options for recommendations with predictions
- Opportunities for purchasers to initiate and conduct efficient negotiations with suppliers
- Achieving more favorable purchasing prices for materials from the suppliers
- Obtaining improved purchasing compliance.

The advantages offered to both purchasers and buyers include minimizing purchases that are not part of a contract and simplifying the process of contract negotiations, all in line with the company's established practices. The service based on artificial intelligence provides an advantage to purchasers and buyers by facilitating early and effective negotiations with suppliers, leading to significant cost savings.

Fig. 22.15 Materials without purchase contract: application

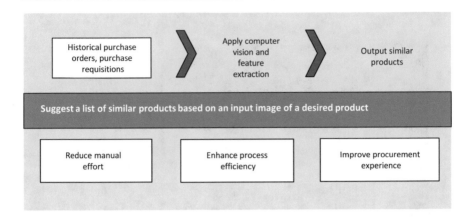

Fig. 22.16 Image-based buying

22.7   Image-Based Buying

We will now delve into the specifics of the application and the operations related to image-based procurement in the purchasing requisition procedure. Figure 22.16 displays the service designed using artificial intelligence for this process, the details of which we will explore in this segment. To build the bridge to the previous chapters, we list the corresponding references points for the use case:

- AI Application Pattern: Recommendation
- ERP Reference Process: Source to Pay/Procure to Receipt
- ERP Reference Architecture: Procurement/Operational Procurement
- ERP Reference AI Technology: AI Technology Platform
- AI Realization Pattern: Side-by-Side

We are already witnessing a variety of interactions between humans and systems in the current technological landscape, and this trend is only expected to grow as technology continues to evolve. Systems involved in procurement, which must handle images and complex algorithms, need to be trained to identify the most suitable internal material or catalog item that corresponds to a given image. This allows a user to simply snap a photo using their mobile device, triggering a cross-content search that automatically generates the corresponding purchase request. This significantly improves the procurement process for buyers and can result in substantial cost reductions. Often, there are discrepancies between the item descriptions provided by the user and the buyer, leading to delays in the procurement process due to incorrect material procurement or unnecessary additional costs incurred from procuring undesired material items. By addressing this problem, user efficiency can be dramatically improved while also ensuring that generated purchase requests are pre-validated. The functionality of artificial intelligence significantly aids workers when they are conducting a cross-catalog search to order items. The algorithms that are used come from the TensorFlow library, and the artificial intelligence service is

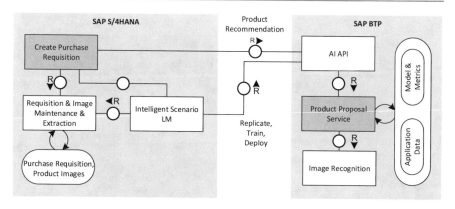

Fig. 22.17 Image-based buying: architecture

constructed using the SAP Business Technology Platform (SAP BTP), as shown in Fig. 22.17.

The product proposal service uses historical data for training, which may include historical catalog data in CSV format. The service takes an image of a product provided by the end user as input to locate this item and other similar items in the catalog. The recommendation includes the product identification numbers from the customer catalogs that the artificial intelligence service identifies as relevant, based on the product image uploaded by the end user. As shown in Fig. 22.18, the corresponding SAP S/4HANA process uses this artificial intelligence service and provides the necessary results. The process is expedited by uploading an image and conducting a cross-catalog search, which automatically generates a purchase requisition. Some of the main features include:

- Comparing images taken with catalog item images in the cross-catalog search index to identify matching patterns in the pictures.
- Detecting similar images by initially normalizing the images – for instance, flipping, rotating, or adjusting brightness and colors – to enhance the probability of finding similarities.
- The cross-catalog search results display the best matching items based on their similarity scoring (items are identified by internal catalog IDs).

Images can be added to the shopping cart either from a local laptop or from a specialized image-based buying app that could prepare a draft shopping cart. The utilization of this artificial intelligence service brings numerous significant advantages. These include the simplicity it offers to the user and the ability to bypass costly exception handling. The service also guarantees that the products ordered adhere to compliance standards, and it prevents purchases outside of the catalog. This leads to substantial financial savings, a factor that is highly valued in procurement departments.

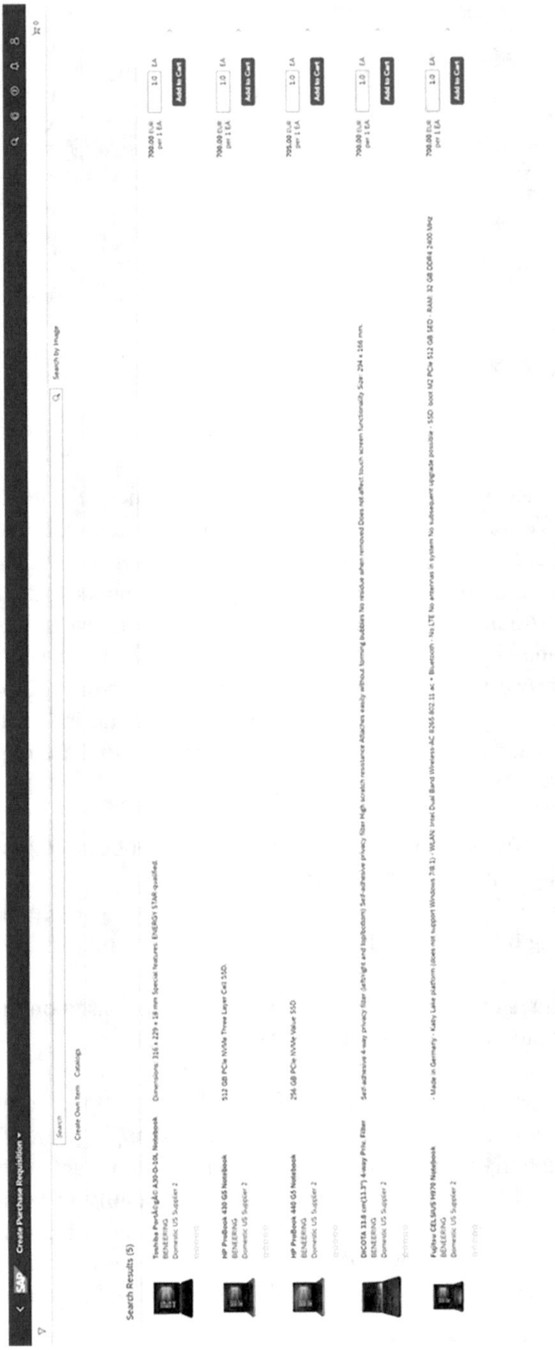

Fig. 22.18 Image-based buying: application

22.8   Intelligent Approval Workflow

The process of acquiring goods or services is systematic and adheres to certain standards. We will delve into the specifics of how to semi-automate this process and make it smarter by incorporating lessons from past experiences and integrating artificial intelligence. Figure 22.19 illustrates the artificial intelligence system designed for this procedure, which we will dissect and explain in this part of the discussion. To build the bridge to the previous chapters, we list the corresponding references points for the use case:

- AI Application Pattern: Recommendation
- ERP Reference Process: Source to Pay/Procure to Receipt
- ERP Reference Architecture: Procurement/Operational Procurement
- ERP Reference AI Technology: AI Technology Platform
- AI Realization Pattern: Side-by-Side

The service facilitated by artificial intelligence scrutinizes the procedures involved in approving purchases and autonomously gives the green light to requests that typically aren't turned down – specifically, those with a historical approval rate of over 90%.

The algorithms of artificial intelligence are capable of discerning the patterns for automatic approval, patterns that might be challenging for buyers to detect on their own. This significantly enhances the productivity of the purchasing department and leads to cost savings. The algorithms used are sourced from the TensorFlow library, and the service of artificial intelligence is constructed using the SAP Business Technology Platform (SAP BTP) as illustrated in Fig. 22.20.

The service, known as the work item approval proposal service, uses historical data for its training process. This data could include historical approval data for purchase requisitions in CSV format. The data related to purchase requisitions carry information about a particular purchase requisition, enabling the service to ascertain

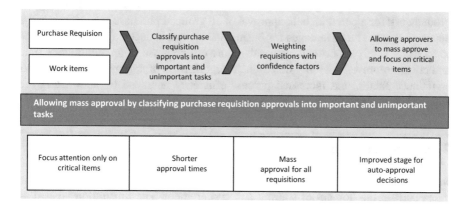

Fig. 22.19 Intelligent approval workflow

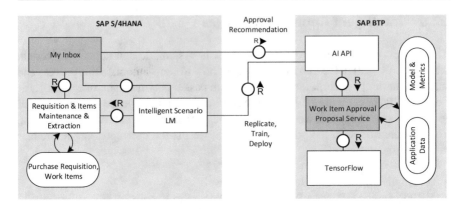

Fig. 22.20 Intelligent approval workflow: architecture

the confidence level for approving a purchase requisition. The confidence level provided is a percentage, calculated based on the history of approved or rejected items from past purchase requisitions. As shown in Fig. 22.21, the established level of certainty is displayed to the approver within the My Inbox application, accompanied by the approval percentage that is associated with the contributing influential factors for clarification. The corresponding SAP S/4HANA process utilizes this artificial intelligence service in a side-by-side model, providing the necessary outcomes. In essence, those who approve based on function or finance in the procurement sector are typically overwhelmed with a multitude of approval tasks daily. The goal of the intelligent approval workflow is to classify purchase requisition approvals into significant and insignificant tasks by assigning them a confidence factor, thereby enabling them to focus on the crucial items. This not only saves time and reduces costs but also allows them to devote more attention to their strategic work. Several key elements are considered when assigning a confidence factor to the purchase requisition approvals. These include the ability to easily differentiate between critical and less critical approvals, directing the authorizer's focus solely toward critical tasks, categorizing all tasks based on their confidence factor, and setting the groundwork for a potential bulk approval of all grouped purchase requisitions at the approval stage. The advantages for businesses include reduced approval times due to focusing solely on critical approvals, more efficient use of an authorizer's time and effort, improved usability due to the categorization of approvals based on their confidence factor, and increased process efficiency achieved by automating the approval decisions.

22.9 Conclusion

In this section, we focused on the artificial intelligence services and embedded use cases built in the domain of souring and procurement. The illustration labeled as Fig. 22.22 provides a comprehensive look at the detailed steps involved in the

Fig. 22.21 Intelligent approval workflow: application

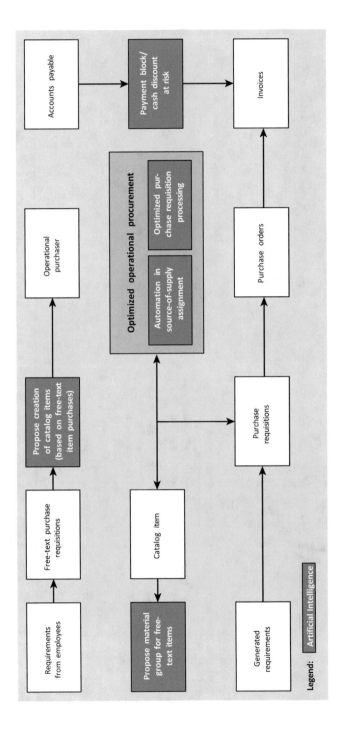

Fig. 22.22   Source to pay process with artificial intelligence

procure-to-pay process. We will now take a moment to examine the *source to pay* business process and understand how the capabilities of artificial intelligence are integrated within this process. Every business entity, as part of its operations, needs to acquire various materials, which could include raw materials and services. These materials can be obtained through the company's own production methods or through the process of external procurement.

At a high level, the procure-to-pay process consists of the following processes:

• Material requirements planning	• Goods receipt
• Supplier selection	• Goods receipt invoice
• Request for quotation	• Invoice verification
• Purchase requisition	• Payment to suppliers
• Purchase order	

In the subsequent sections, we looked into some of these processes and how artificial intelligence services are embedded or consumed with SAP S/4HANA. All the use cases were implemented based on the concepts and frameworks proposed in this elaboration. This is a proof of the real-world applicability of the underlying inventions.

Inventory and Supply Chain

23

In this chapter, we explain intelligent business applications in the inventory and supply chain line of business (LoB) and how customers can benefit from this functionality. We provide a brief overview of the use case requirements, the business processes involved, and how they're addressed. The inventory and supply chain LoB is huge, with a lot of potential to automate and fine-tune the processes. The focus of the chapter is on stock in transit, demand-driven replenishment, defect code proposal, early detection of slow, and nonmoving stock. For these use cases, the concepts and frameworks explained in this elaboration were applied, which proves the real-world feasibility of those new inventions.

23.1   Stock in Transit

In this section, we will concentrate on the artificial intelligence system that has been developed to revolve around the functionality of stock in transit. This system is designed to forecast any delays in the movement of stock between various plants or storage locations. The artificial intelligence service designed for this specific process is depicted in Fig. 23.1. We will delve into the details of this service in the following section. To build the bridge to the previous chapters, we list the corresponding references points for the use case:

- AI Application Pattern: Prediction
- ERP Reference Process: Plan to Fulfill/Make to Inspect
- ERP Reference Architecture: Supply Chain/Inventory
- ERP Reference AI Technology: ERP Platform
- AI Realization Pattern: Embedded

The majority of customers require the movement of inventory between different storage sites or factories, making it essential to establish stock transport orders. The

© The Author(s), under exclusive license to Springer Nature
Switzerland AG 2024
S. Sarferaz, *Embedding Artificial Intelligence into ERP Software*,
https://doi.org/10.1007/978-3-031-54249-7_23

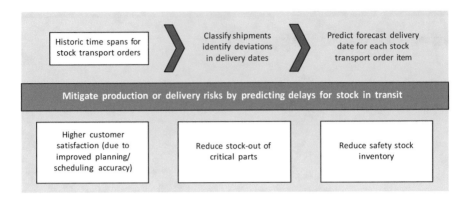

Fig. 23.1 Stock in transit

SAP S/4HANA Overdue Materials-Stock in Transit SAP Fiori application allows clients to monitor materials that are in the process of being transported or open stock transport orders that have not yet been acknowledged by the receiving factory. This is particularly useful when these materials have, for instance, surpassed the anticipated transit time. Typically, customers have a predetermined timeline for the duration it should take to transfer materials between two factories.

The responsibility of ensuring that the materials reach the production plant on time falls on the inventory manager. This involves overseeing the movement of materials across various storage locations or plants. Stock transport orders are established to facilitate the transfer of stocks and to keep track of materials in transit, ensuring they are delivered on time. Inventory managers often face challenges such as a lack of transparency into delayed deliveries between storage sites or difficulty in estimating the duration of stock transfers, among others. These challenges can have a negative impact on the time and cost associated with the downstream delivery of finished goods, raw materials, or work in progress (WIP). This could potentially affect the quality of the finished products, especially if the goods are perishable or time-dependent. Customers stand to benefit significantly from enhanced planning and scheduling accuracy, which can help mitigate scenarios of critical stock shortages and improve turnover. This would ultimately lead to a reduction in the amount of safety stock inventory. The prediction of the arrival date, or the forecast delivery date, is accessible during the creation of the stock transport order, due to the integrated predictive modeling built into the functionality. The ability to predict the forecast delivery date of a shipment yields substantial benefits. The value proposition of this solution is its ability to reduce production or delivery risks by predicting delays for stock in transit. Businesses that send and receive goods from their plants need to monitor the status of materials in transit. When delays, shortages, or other issues occur, the company must be able to react and take appropriate action promptly.

The Materials Overdue-Stock in Transit application in SAP S/4HANA provides a summary of the open shipments, enabling the business user to take action. The application, with its integrated predictive modeling, can forecast shipment dates for each goods movement. This insight allows users to manage delivery delays, production scheduling, and other downstream activities. The accuracy of the results improves as users retrain the model with the most recent behaviors and data stored in ERP. As demonstrated in Fig. 23.2 in the current scenario, regression algorithms from the Automated Predictive Library that use the Intelligent Scenario Lifecycle Management framework are integrated into the corresponding SAP S/4HANA business processes to predict the arrival of stock in transit between locations. Thus, the artificial intelligence service designed to predict the arrival of stock in transit enables warehouse and inventory managers to do the following:

- Forecast the arrival date of a shipment and categorize its status
- Establish predictive models and train and execute the scenarios
- Utilize a prebuilt set of KPIs for robust analytics on ERP data with drilldown functionality
- Obtain early and effective visibility into stock transport orders
- Utilize new integration capabilities with ERP to gain real-time insights into the production line of business scenarios with predictive analytics

Some of the business advantages include reducing stock shortages and excesses, which ultimately leads to better inventory cost management; optimizing and automating the business process of tracking stock in transit, which helps achieve more reliable planning and scheduling of goods in transit processes; and improving usability for the business by visualizing data with predictions. With this new artificial intelligence functionality, warehouse managers and inventory managers can reduce cost outages and stock overages, manage inventory costs more effectively, and predict the shipment duration in days.

23.2   Demand-Driven Replenishment

In this section, our attention will be directed toward the artificial intelligence service that has been designed to cater to the needs of demand-driven replenishment. This service is specifically aimed at managing the dynamic adjustment of buffer levels for materials being transferred in stock. The artificial intelligence service that has been developed for this particular process is depicted in Fig. 23.3. We will delve into the details of this service in the current section. To build the bridge to the previous chapters, we list the corresponding references points for the use case:

- AI Application Pattern: Prediction
- ERP Reference Process: Plan to Fulfill/Plan to Optimize Fulfillment
- ERP Reference Architecture: Supply Chain/Inventory
- ERP Reference AI Technology: ERP Platform
- AI Realization Pattern: Embedded

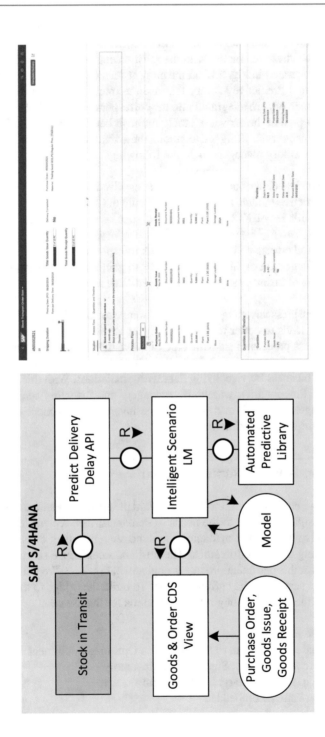

Fig. 23.2 Stock in transit: architecture and application

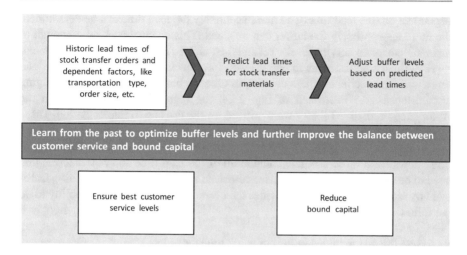

Fig. 23.3 Demand-driven replenishment

The role of an inventory manager is crucial in ensuring that production facilities or customers receive necessary materials on time. They are also responsible for overseeing the planning and execution of replenishment, as well as maintaining appropriate buffer levels. However, due to inadequate supply chain analytics and fluctuating demand signals, the task of planning, tracking, and managing buffer levels can be both costly and time-consuming for inventory managers. The potential benefits for businesses and their customers from effective inventory management are significant. These include a decrease in safety stock inventory, a reduction in the costs associated with carrying inventory, fewer days of inventory, and a decrease in obsolete inventory.

The solution is designed to analyze and categorize products that require adjustments to their buffer levels. It then selects those products that are relevant for demand-driven replenishment. By managing buffer levels for products transferred from stock based on predicted lead times, the system can generate optimal replenishment orders and buffer-level proposals. The value proposition of this service is its ability to use data to optimize buffer levels. This balance between customer service levels and capital investment is crucial. Predicting the individual lead times for stock transport orders is key for inventory and warehouse managers to effectively manage their stock at their facilities or storage locations. Lead time refers to the delay between the start and completion of a process. For instance, the lead time for the delivery of a new car from the manufacturer, following an order, could range from 2 weeks to 6 months. These lead times are predicted, and tasks are then set in motion to maintain the inventory buffer values. These new values can be incorporated into the application to manage buffer levels with decoupled lead times. In the planning approach of demand-driven replenishment, a critical component is the dynamic adjustment of buffer levels. One essential input for recalculating buffer levels is the lead time for buffer replenishment. Buffer levels are proportionally dependent on this lead time. The more accurately the lead time can be determined, the more appropriately the buffer can be sized. This ensures it is large enough to maintain customer service levels, yet small enough to minimize capital investment.

Historically, adjustments to buffer levels have been suggested based on the lead times and the specific business context, in order to best adapt to the ever-changing circumstances. As illustrated in Fig. 23.4, the regression algorithms from the Automated Predictive Library were utilized for the use case implementation. These algorithms use the Intelligent Scenario Lifecycle Management framework and are integrated into the corresponding SAP S/4HANA business processes. This integration allows for a more accurate calculation of the lead time and buffer levels that need to be maintained. Thus, the demand-driven replenishment functionality, facilitated by artificial intelligence, provides the inventory manager with the ability to do the following:

- Assess the historical lead times of stock transfer orders
- Take into account the contextual information of orders to identify patterns and dependencies

The advantage of using this artificial intelligence service in business is that it guarantees the highest possible customer service levels at the lowest possible cost, specifically, the capital tied up in buffered stock.

23.3   Defect Code Proposal with Text Recognition

Before we delve into the specifics of the proposed scenario for handling defective code, it's important to first understand the general process of defect management and how quality management processes these defects. Figure 23.5 illustrates the service designed using artificial intelligence to facilitate this process, which we will examine in detail in this part of the discussion. To build the bridge to the previous chapters, we list the corresponding references points for the use case:

- AI Application Pattern: Recommendation
- ERP Reference Process: Plan to Fulfill/Make to Inspect
- ERP Reference Architecture: Manufacturing/Quality Management
- ERP Reference AI Technology: ERP Platform
- AI Realization Pattern: Embedded

The process of handling defects can be divided into several categories:

1. Suggesting a defect code accompanied by a textual and visual explanation
2. Warning about similar defects
3. Suggesting the underlying cause of defects
4. Suggesting tasks related to defects
5. Grouping similar defects together

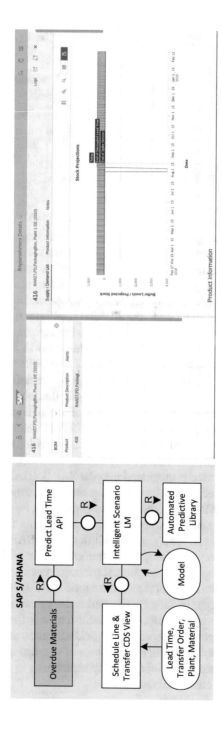

Fig. 23.4 Demand-driven replenishment: architecture and application

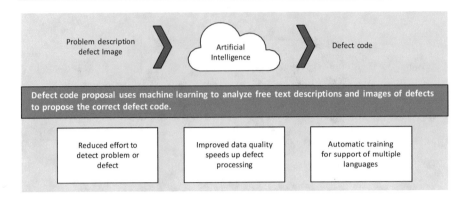

Fig. 23.5 Defect code proposal

These defects are managed and dealt with at different stages by the quality technician and the quality engineer. It's important to note the roles of the quality technician and the quality engineer in reporting and analyzing defects, respectively, and how these roles contribute to the overall context of defect processing. The various steps involved in reporting and analyzing defects are outlined and numbered accordingly. Now, let's shift our attention to the artificial intelligence service that revolves around suggesting defect codes with textual and visual explanations in the field of quality management. Let's examine the steps illustrated in Fig. 23.5. Suppose a quality technician wishes to receive suggestions for a specific defect code group and code based on a textual explanation and an image of the defect during the defect recording process, with the aim of finding the code that best matches the defect. Drawing from existing defects with textual explanations and images that correspond to a matching defect code group and code, the artificial intelligence algorithm suggests a defect code group and code for a new defect, provided a textual explanation and an image are available, while the quality technician is recording the defect. This artificial intelligence service is integrated into the SAP S/4HANA business process and assists the quality technician by providing recommendations and suggestions while working in the SAP Fiori launchpad. As depicted in Fig. 23.6, in the current scenario, classification and k-nearest neighbors algorithms from the Automated Predictive Library and text analysis capabilities from SAP HANA, using the Intelligent Scenario Lifecycle Management framework, are utilized and integrated into the SAP S/4HANA quality management business processes.

The construction of the artificial intelligence model takes into account a range of elements, including the type of defect, a detailed and brief explanation of the defect, and an image or picture of the defect. This information is then used to suggest a defect group and corresponding code, utilizing classification algorithms. The model's value lies in its ability to simplify the process of suggesting defect codes based on historical patterns, thereby allowing quality technicians to devote more of their time to the discovery of additional defects.

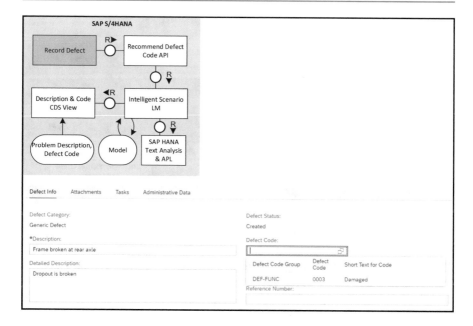

Fig. 23.6 Defect code proposal: architecture and application

23.4   Early Detection of Slow and Non-moving Stocks

In this part, we are going to concentrate on the service of artificial intelligence that is designed to identify slow-moving and stagnant stock in inventory management at an early stage. Figure 23.7 presents the specific artificial intelligence service created for this procedure, the details of which we will delve into within this section. To build the bridge to the previous chapters, we list the corresponding references points for the use case:

- AI Application Pattern: Prediction
- ERP Reference Process: Plan to Fulfill/Deliver Product to Fulfill
- ERP Reference Architecture: Supply Chain/Inventory
- ERP Reference AI Technology: ERP Platform
- AI Realization Pattern: Embedded

The role of a production and inventory planner involves strategizing the transfer of inventory among various locations. This could mean relocating stock to a nearby warehouse or dealer location where inventory turnover is high. The planner's responsibility is to ensure that each location maintains an optimal stock quantity to facilitate efficient inventory movement. Artificial intelligence services can be instrumental in this process, as they can identify slow-moving and stagnant stock ahead

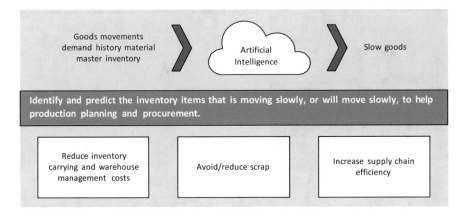

Fig. 23.7 Early detection of slow and non-moving stock

of time. This allows for the categorization of products into different groups based on historical data and information. Artificial intelligence algorithms are capable of scanning for slow-moving and non-moving stock across a range of locations, including plants, warehouses, and dealers. These algorithms can forecast potential slow-moving and non-moving materials in advance, thanks to their predictive capabilities. This artificial intelligence service also monitors for new demands or requirements, which could come in the form of purchase requisitions, sales orders, or demands for spare parts. It can even anticipate expected orders and recommend material movements to prevent stock from becoming slow-moving or non-moving. The effectiveness of these artificial intelligence algorithm can be greatly enhanced by historical sales, procurement, and manufacturing data. A substantial amount of data on past inventory movements can be particularly useful in refining the algorithm. As illustrated in Fig. 23.8, the approach involves the use of regression and time series algorithms from the Automated Predictive Library. These are integrated into the Intelligent Scenario Lifecycle Management framework and embedded into the corresponding SAP S/4HANA business processes. This integration allows for improved prediction of slow-moving and non-moving stock.

The software helps to monitor items that are not selling quickly, which the inventory employees are responsible for. By selecting the preferred display currency, the user can assess the amount of money tied up in these slow-selling products. Furthermore, the clerk can consume the slow-moving indicator to keep tabs on items with low usage, based on the ratio of usage to stock. The slow-moving indicator enables to compare different items based on their rate of consumption. Consequently, the user can identify and compare key items using our own set of criteria. Items should be monitored that have not been used within a specific period based on an analysis. The solution then provides a list of unused items that meet the filtering criteria. The common business advantages for clients include the following:

• Decrease in the costs of holding inventory

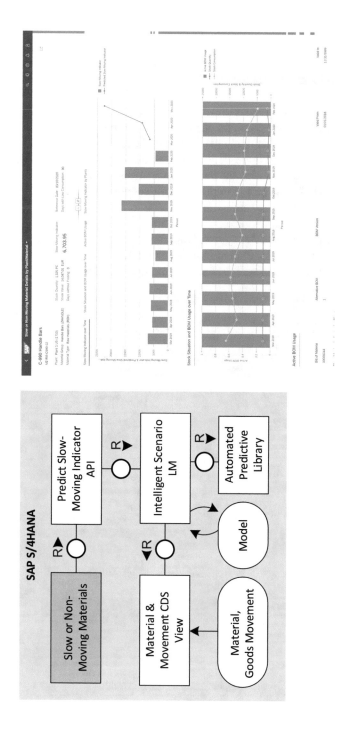

Fig. 23.8 Early detection of slow and non-moving stock: architecture and application

- Improved planning of production, procurement, and associated costs
- Enhanced efficiency of the supply chain

23.5   Automate Root Cause Analysis

Our focus will be now directed toward the prerequisites for mechanizing the functionality of root cause analysis for firms involved in component production. This enables them to more effectively oversee the schedules of their quality engineers and production experts. Figure 23.9 illustrates the way in which artificial intelligence can enhance and mechanize root cause analysis, a topic we will delve into in this section. To build the bridge to the previous chapters, we list the corresponding references points for the use case:

- AI Application Pattern: Recommendation
- ERP Reference Process: Plan to Fulfill/Make to Inspect
- ERP Reference Architecture: Manufacturing/Quality Management

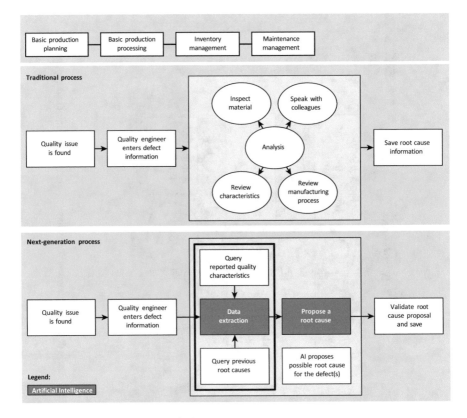

Fig. 23.9 Automate root cause analysis

- ERP Reference AI Technology: ERP Platform
- AI Realization Pattern: Embedded

In conventional procedures, the quality engineer identifies issues through a comprehensive process that involves examining the materials, engaging in discussions with a range of colleagues and individuals, scrutinizing the distinct traits of the problems discovered in the manufacturing process, and recording these findings. Subsequently, an in-depth analysis of the root cause is carried out, drawing upon these diverse pieces of information and insights.

The suggested approach utilizes a service based on artificial intelligence that suggests potential root causes for various defects, drawing from historical data on root causes and different quality characteristics. The algorithms of this artificial intelligence service sift through the provided data and identify a range of possible root causes. This can assist the quality engineer in devising a solution, thereby minimizing the downtime of equipment and assets. The Predictive Analytics Library of SAP HANA is used for the algorithmic aspect, while Intelligent Scenario Lifecycle Management is used for implementation and operation. The application, as depicted in Fig. 23.10, concisely presents the most important facts and responsibilities related to inspection management that are relevant to us currently. Information is displayed on cards, allowing us to quickly view, filter, and react to information while focusing on the most important tasks. The most important information is displayed on the cards, ordered by relevance. For example, the Inspection Lots Without Usage Decision card shows the percentage distribution of inspection lots based on their results recording status, followed by a donut chart that shows the number of inspection lots without usage decision in the header.

The user can then decide whether to make usage decisions for inspection lots with different result recording statuses or for inspection lots without a usage decision at all. The application provides value by offering the following cards:

- Inspection Lots Without Inspection Plan: This page, sorted by creation date, shows open inspection lots that do not have an inspection plan.
- Inspection Lots Without Usage Decision: This shows the total number of inspection lots without a recommended use.
- Inspection Lots Ready for Usage Decision: This shows the percentage of inspection lots that are ready for usage decision out of all inspection lots, i.e., inspection lots with results recording status finished and those without deviations.
- Inspection Lots with Defects: This shows the number of defects produced for inspection lots, based on the lot origin. By default, the number of defects produced on the current day is shown.
- Top Defective Materials: This shows the total number of defects produced by the worst materials. By default, the number of defects produced on the current day is shown.
- Top Defects: This shows the number of defects produced by the defect code and defect code group. By default, the number of defects produced on the current day is shown.

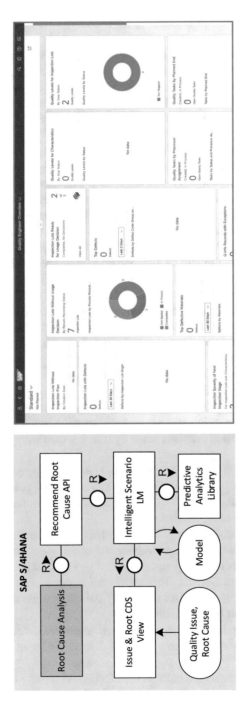

Fig. 23.10 Automate root cause analysis: architecture and application

- Inspection Severity of Next Inspection Stage: This shows how many quality levels were developed for inspection lots and attributes.
- Quality Level for Inspection Lots: This shows the number of inspection lot quality levels that have been established.
- Quality Level for Characteristics: This shows the number of qualities that have been developed for a characteristic.
- Action Limit Violations: This shows the number of times action limits have been exceeded in the past six days and today.
- Q-Info Records with Exceptions: This shows the number of quality information records with exceptions, either by block level or release date.
- Quality Tasks by Planned End: This shows the number of open quality tasks with projected completion dates for the last 30 days and the upcoming 30 days.
- Quality Tasks by Processor Assignment: This shows the number of active, high-quality tasks by processor assignment.

23.6 Optimize Inspection Plans

Next, our focus will be directed toward the requirements for enhancing inspection strategies with the aim of enabling production operators and quality inspectors to reduce expenses. To build the bridge to the previous chapters, we list the corresponding references points for the use case:

- AI Application Pattern: Recommendation
- ERP Reference Process: Plan to Fulfill/Make to Inspect
- ERP Reference Architecture: Manufacturing/Quality Management
- ERP Reference AI Technology: AI Technology Platform
- AI Realization Pattern: Side-by-Side

As depicted in Fig. 23.11, artificial intelligence has the potential to offer recommendations and augment the inspection strategies, a concept we will delve into in this section. In a conventional method, those involved in production and quality inspection are required to examine the quality features and the outcomes of the inspection. Subsequently, they verify the diverse quality demands of the customers, leading to the quality engineer making modifications to the detailed inspection plans. The suggested solution takes advantage of algorithms based on artificial intelligence and the past traits of the inspection plans and their outcomes and then offers suggestions on how the inspection plans could be modified. This has the potential to significantly lessen the manual work that quality engineers need to put into reviewing all the inspection plans.

The diagram depicted in Fig. 23.12 demonstrates the utilization of the side-by-side method, where application data is replicated to the SAP Business Technology Platform (SAP BTP) for the purpose of training models. The suggested inspection schemes are incorporated into the SAP S/4HANA business procedures via the use of REST API. The management of the models is overseen by Intelligent Scenario

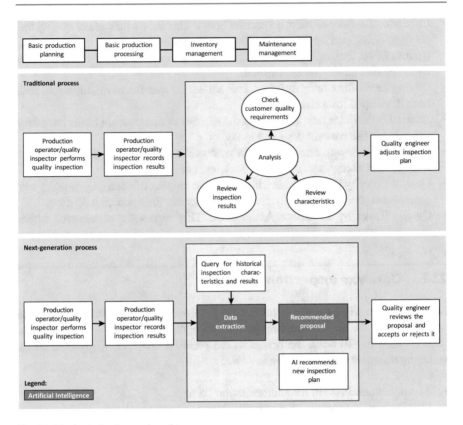

Fig. 23.11 Optimize inspection plans

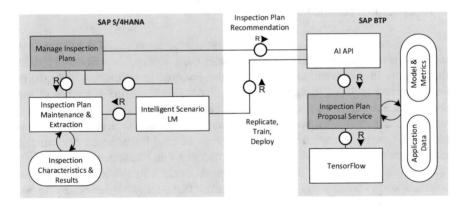

Fig. 23.12 Optimize inspection plans: architecture

Lifecycle Management. Inspection plans can be devised for a multitude of objectives, such as inspecting models, conducting audits, preliminary series inspections, inspections upon receipt or issue of goods, inspections during stock transfers, and inspections in the context of repetitive manufacturing. The inspection plan is associated with rate routing and the master recipe. However, the functions of inspection planning in these task list types only slightly differ.

There is no need for further preparation of inspection plans for inspections related to production. Inspection features are established by routings (inspections during production), rate routings, master recipes (inspections during production in the process industry), or maintenance job lists (calibration inspection). The structure of the inspection plan is similar to that of the route plan. The inspection plan header is assigned one or more operations, which are then linked to the inspection characteristics and testing tools (production resources/tools). Inspection specifications from a lower level may supersede those at the inspection plan level (inspection plan header, operation, and inspection characteristic). The structure of the inspection plan header is similar to that of the routing. The details outlined in the plan heading provide the framework for the entire document. The plan header specifies the following details: Plan data, information about dynamic modification and inspection points, information about external numbering in results recording, and information about engineering change management. One or more inspection activities are assigned to the inspection plan heading. The organizational structure of the inspection operations is similar to that of a routing operation. Each inspection operation can be assigned a variety of inspection characteristics.

The standards for assessing the quality of materials can be established using the solution depicted in Fig. 23.13, which is designed to create and oversee inspection plans. This application allows to incorporate tasks and features into the inspection plans, as well as pinpoint the elements that require scrutiny.

The software features a worklist page where inspection plans can be sifted through using a variety of filters. Common components of inspection plans include:

- The inspection plan's header, which provides an overview of the entire plan
- The inspection procedure, which outlines the sequence in which the inspection should be carried out
- The inspection characteristic, which selects the particular aspect of the items that needs to be inspected

23.7   Defect Recording

In Sect. 23.3, we considered the processing and recording of defects, particularly in relation to the inventory and supply chain sectors. Certain aspects of these functionalities can also be applied to the industry of component manufacturing. The solution created for this context is depicted in Fig. 23.14, which will be the focus of our discussion in this section. To build the bridge to the previous chapters, we list the corresponding references points for the use case:

- AI Application Pattern: Recommendation
- ERP Reference Process: Plan to Fulfill/Make to Inspect

Fig. 23.13 Optimize inspection plans: application

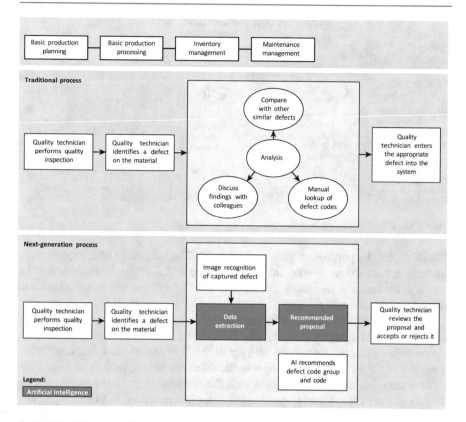

Fig. 23.14 Defect recording

- ERP Reference Architecture: Manufacturing/Quality Management
- ERP Reference AI Technology: AI Technology Platform
- AI Realization Pattern: Side-by-Side

The service of artificial intelligence is integrated into the SAP S/4HANA business process, offering a more efficient way to suggest defect codes based on historical patterns. This allows quality technicians to dedicate more of their time to discovering a wider range of defects. In Sect. 23.3, we explored a similar application in the inventory and supply chain sectors, but our focus was on text recognition in the context of suggesting defect codes.

In the component manufacturing sector, there are certainly some areas of overlap, but the intention here is to concentrate on the aspect of image recognition and the algorithms of artificial intelligence that suggest defect codes and groups of defect codes based on similarities with other defects. As demonstrated in Fig. 23.15, a side-by-side method is applied using the generic image recognition capability of the SAP Business Technology Platform (SAP BTP), which is tailored for this specific use case. Information about defects, including images, is pulled from SAP

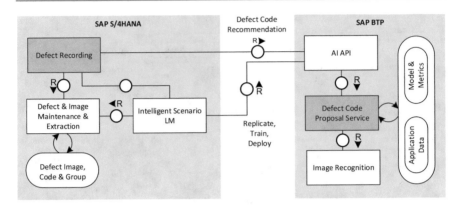

Fig. 23.15 Defect recording: architecture

S/4HANA for the purpose of training the model. The operations of life cycle management are overseen by the Intelligent Scenario Lifecycle Management. The results of the inference are made available as a REST API and are incorporated into the underlying business process.

Defects of multiple kinds can be generated. Depending on the category, the user has the ability to input a variety of data for a defect. On the SAP Fiori launchpad, it's possible to display the unique tiles for each of the numerous defect categories. General flaws are separate from any specific reference object, such as an inspection lot or a material, and can be logged with the application depicted in Fig. 23.16. Defects that are categorized as production flaws incorporate data from the production order that is relevant to the manufacturing process. Information such as the material, unit of measurement, and work center are derived from the manufacturing order if we provide one. Issues that are classified under the category of warehouse-specific information are encompassed in warehouse defects. This information pertains to details about the plant, storage location, or the area supplying production. In order to record imperfections, the users have the ability to establish own distinct categories of defects. Furthermore, they have the capability to define information that is specific to a certain context, which can be maintained and updated, for instance, while documenting errors.

23.8   Conclusion

In this section, we focused on the artificial intelligence services and embedded use cases built for the inventory and supply chain management area of business. We also briefly touched on the scenarios for warehouse management; most of that functionality is linked to inventory management in the context of manufacturing. Inventory management deals with the process of tracking the value and quantities of all the goods our company has in stock, whereas warehousing is the act of storing goods that will be sold or distributed later. Typically, inventory management manages the

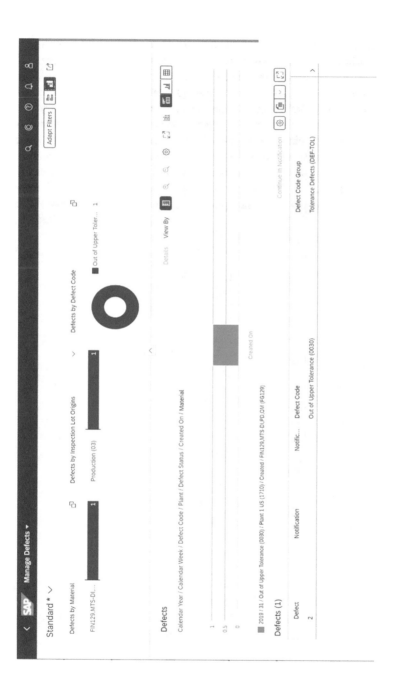

Fig. 23.16 Defect recording: application

products or materials a company sells to its customers in order to make profit. As part of the supply chain, inventory management includes several different aspects, such as controlling and overseeing purchases from suppliers and customers, maintaining the storage of stock, controlling the amount of product for sale, and order fulfillment. There are three core steps: Purchasing inventory, storing inventory, and profiting from inventory. In general, inventory types can be grouped into four classes: raw material, work in process, finished goods, and maintenance, repair, and operating supplies (MRO) goods. In the component manufacturing industry, we have a lot of requirements for streamlined procure-to-pay, idea-to-design, accelerated plan-to-product, optimized order-to-cash, HR, project services, and core finance to help address and solve a few challenges. We looked into various scenarios to understand how artificial intelligence can improve and enhance the processes for better business outcomes. The use cases were founded on the concepts and frameworks proposed in this elaboration, which proves the real-world applicability of the inventions.

Finance

24

In this chapter, we explain intelligent business applications in the finance line of business (LoB) and how customers can benefit from this functionality. We provide a brief overview of the use case requirements, the business processes involved, and how they're addressed. The finance LoB is huge, with a lot of potential to automate and fine-tune the processes. The focus of the chapter is on accounts receivable, accounts payable, accounting, and financial period-end close. For these use cases, the concepts and frameworks explained in this elaboration were which proves the real-world feasibility of those new inventions.

24.1 Cash Application

The SAP Cash Application enhances the cash application process by automating the laborious task of reconciling incoming bank payments with the respective receivable invoices. To build the bridge to the previous chapters, we list the corresponding references points for the use case:

- AI Application Pattern: Matching
- ERP Reference Process: Finance/Invoice to Cash
- ERP Reference Architecture: Finance/Financial Operations
- ERP Reference AI Technology: AI Technology Platform
- AI Realization Pattern: Side-by-Side

This is a solution based in the cloud that leverages artificial intelligence to offer predictions for matching, using historical data as its basis. Consequently, as depicted in Fig. 24.1, the side-by-side artificial intelligence is used with the SAP Business Technology Platform (SAP BTP) to develop the services and ultimately the artificial intelligence application of SAP S/4HANA that are discussed in this chapter. In the SAP S/4HANA system, there is a feature that allows for scheduling the underlying

© The Author(s), under exclusive license to Springer Nature
Switzerland AG 2024
S. Sarferaz, *Embedding Artificial Intelligence into ERP Software*,
https://doi.org/10.1007/978-3-031-54249-7_24

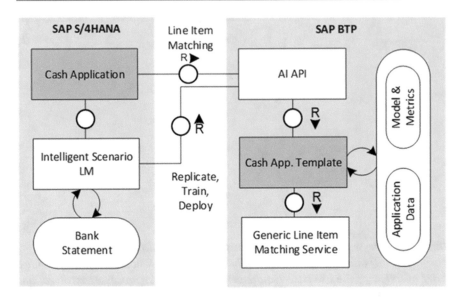

Fig. 24.1   AI architecture of SAP cash application

integration process. This process is designed to extract historical data and then replicate it to the SAP Business Technology Platform. This replication process is used for both training and inference purposes. Once this process is complete, a different program can be selected for additional processing.

For instance, the system can be set up to extract data related to open receivable items. This data is then replicated to the SAP Business Technology Platform where it is scored. When the customer decides to reprocess their bank statement items, the system proposes prediction results. The integration and operation that involves artificial intelligence between SAP S/4HANA and the SAP Business Technology Platform is managed by the Intelligent Scenario Lifecycle Management (ISLM) framework. The ISLM framework is responsible for replicating application data, executing training jobs, and deploying models for inference. On the SAP Business Technology Platform, the integration with SAP S/4HANA is standardized using an Artificial Intelligence Application Programming Interface (AI API). This interface is essentially a collection of APIs that are used for model management. These APIs can be utilized for tasks such as triggering training jobs or providing model metrics. As a result, the integration contract between SAP S/4HANA and the SAP Business Technology Platform can be abstracted from the underlying artificial intelligence technology. This ensures that the contract remains stable. There is also a generic line item matching (GLIM) service that can be used to implement any line item matching use cases. This artificial intelligence service is specialized for the SAP Cash Application. This allows it to serve the specific line item matching requirements for this use case. The process of clearing line items in the SAP Cash Application is illustrated with a representative system screenshot, as shown in Fig. 24.2.

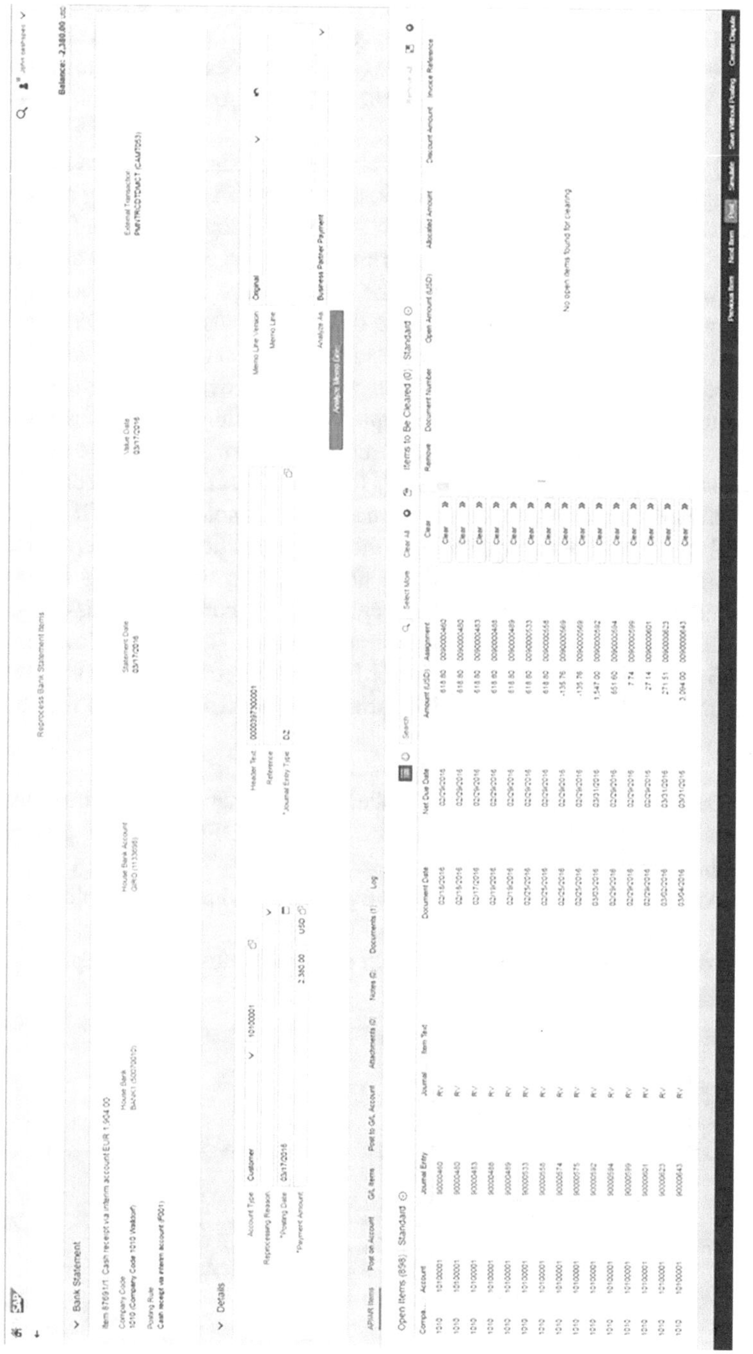

Fig. 24.2 Reprocess bank statement items

The depicted functionality of artificial intelligence is utilized to enhance the efficiency of the clearing process. Now, let's delve into the various features that are included in the SAP Cash Application. Figure 24.3 provides a detailed explanation of the process flow in context of the *finance* business process for an account receivable clerk. We will clarify how and where the SAP Cash Application can be beneficial in streamlining the process.

In many businesses, the accounts receivable team or shared services team must put in a significant amount of manual work, from the point of receiving an order to the point where the payment is processed. As these businesses expand their customer base, the accounts receivable department must be capable of handling the increased volume of payments without the need to hire additional accountants. Simultaneously, they must ensure that the days sales outstanding (DSO) is kept under control by making sure that cash does not remain in customers' accounts for an extended period. Current custom rules can provide a degree of automation, but they are often difficult and expensive to implement, and they may not cover all scenarios as many payments lack complete remittance information. A large number of payments still require manual processing, for instance, if the payment does not include complete invoice references, if the master data is not current, or if customers pay several invoices at once. Applications that utilize artificial intelligence and are smoothly integrated into existing business processes can be extremely beneficial. They can relieve the accounts receivable teams from the burdensome task of reconciliation, allowing them to focus on more strategic tasks. The process flow depicted in Fig. 24.3 illustrates the comprehensive order-to-cash process, which is enhanced with artificial intelligence services. This process is broken down into the following steps:

1. The Remittance Advice Extractor application automatically extracts payment information from unstructured documents, such as PDFs, emails, or papers, for use in the payment clearing process.
2. The accounts receivable team verifies the proposal and proceeds to the payment clearing phase.
3. Standard clearing rules are used to match open receivables with the payments.

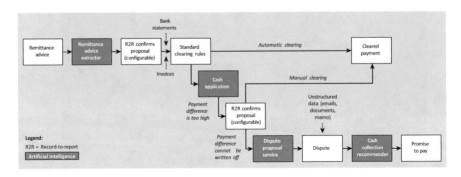

Fig. 24.3 Accounts receivable end-to-end process

4. Payments that cannot be processed using the standard rules are sent to the SAP Cash Application, which generates matching proposals based on artificial intelligence models that use historical financial clearing information.
5. If the payment difference is too large, the accounts receivable team either manually clears the payment or rejects it. This triggers additional process steps that are supported by other artificial intelligence SAP Fiori apps, such as the Dispute Proposal Service and Cash Collection Recommender.

The artificial intelligence services incorporated into the SAP Cash Application are further broken down into several topics due to the numerous updates that have been made to assist accounts receivable (AR) and accounts payable (AP) staff. The next section will first discuss receivables line item matching.

24.1.1 Receivables Line Item Matching

The SAP Cash Application is designed to automatically pair incoming payments with outstanding receivables. This significantly enhances the efficiency of the traditionally laborious clearing process, making it possible to carry out with minimal user intervention. The application leverages artificial intelligence to facilitate a seamless setup and to boost the rate of automatic matches. The artificial intelligence service integrated into the SAP Cash Application for the purpose of matching line items in receivables is illustrated in Fig. 24.4. We will delve into the details of this feature in the following section.

It's important to note that the role of an accounts receivable clerk involves aligning incoming bank payments with customer invoices, ensuring that payments are correctly recorded against the receivables. There are several challenges that these clerks face in their routine tasks:

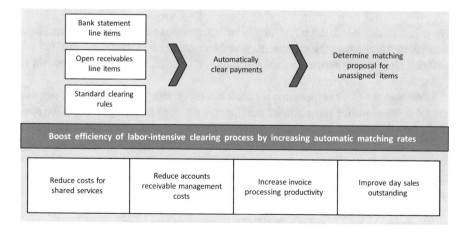

Fig. 24.4   Receivables line item matching

- They often encounter payment information that is either incomplete, such as missing an invoice reference, or incorrect.
- They have to manually process mismatched payments, a task that is not only labor-intensive but also prone to errors.
- Their work is time-sensitive.

Customers, on the other hand, are looking for certain improvements and benefits that would enhance the value of the business:

- They want to see an improvement in Days Sales Outstanding (DSO).
- They are looking for a reduction in the costs of managing accounts receivable.
- They want to increase the productivity of invoice processing.
- They are seeking to reduce the costs associated with shared services.

The artificial intelligence service assists the accounts receivable clerk by automatically aligning the payments with open receivables, eliminating the need for manual data matching. In this context, algorithms such as random forest and XGBoost from the Scikit-Learn library are utilized. We won't discuss the technical mechanism of these algorithms, focusing instead on their business application. These algorithms learn the matching criteria from the historical actions of accountants, with the models running overnight to provide the necessary results. This can facilitate early identification of payment issues from customers who consistently send payments with incorrect invoice numbers. If the system is customized, it can clear the payments accordingly. The primary value proposition of this artificial intelligence service is to enhance the efficiency of labor-intensive clearing processes by increasing the rates of automatic matching.

24.1.2 Receivables Line Item Matching with Payment Advice Information Extraction

We will now delve into the payment advice information extraction feature and how it caters to the needs of the customers. The functionality and the added value of the artificial intelligence service is depicted in Fig. 24.5, which we will elaborate on in this section.

How does the clerk responsible for accounts receivable and the team in charge of shared services utilize this artificial intelligence service? Before going into the specifics, let's first understand the prerequisites. The clerk handling accounts receivable has the task of documenting the payment advice notes that are received in a non-digital format from clients. These payment advice notes contain the necessary information for clearing customer accounts for invoice payments. The clerk encounters several challenges in this process:

- The payment advice notes might be ambiguous or incorrect.
- Manually extracting information from payment advice notes is not only time-consuming but also prone to errors.

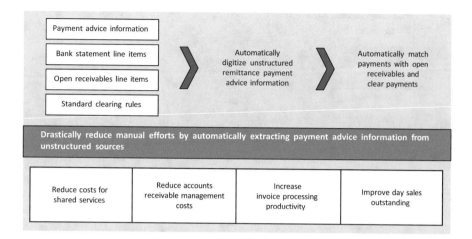

Fig. 24.5 Payment advice information extraction

- Manually matching payment advice notes with customer invoices can be a complex task. Often, due to technical hurdles, payment advices are not entered into the system, and the effort can only be used for manual clearing of payments.

There are several potential outcomes and benefits that the clerk handling accounts receivable and the shared services team can achieve to enhance the overall business value of their company:

- Enhancement in the efficiency of full-time equivalent (FTE) invoice processing
- Improvement in the productivity of FTE invoice receipt and processing
- Decrease in payment processing and supplier inquiries along with associated personnel costs
- Reduction in invoice errors made by external workforce

In this context, algorithms from the TensorFlow library are used. The artificial intelligence service automatically digitizes unstructured remittance advices or payment advices and extracts additional payment information from unstructured advices (such as email, PDF, paper). This extracted information is then used to automate the clearing process via the SAP Cash Application. The matching process is carried out automatically and, on a large scale, manages a wide range of customer communication preferences. The primary value proposition of the artificial intelligence service is to minimize manual effort by automatically extracting payment advice information from unstructured sources and using it to automate the clearing process. The service was implemented as depicted in Fig. 24.1.

24.1.3 Receivables Line Item Matching with Lockbox Information

Let's delve into the construction of the lockbox information functionality and how it caters to the requirements of customers. An illustration of the service powered by

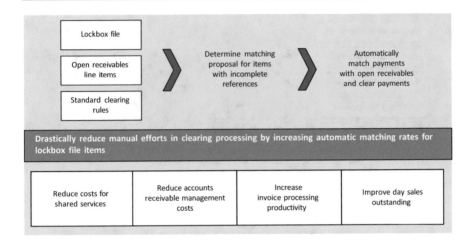

Fig. 24.6 Receivables line item matching with lockbox information

artificial intelligence is provided in Fig. 24.6, which we will dissect in this segment. With the growing prevalence of digital transactions, the information about remittances has become separated from the payments themselves. This separation poses a challenge in promptly identifying the payer or the receivable. The quality and details of remittance information provided with checks can vary, leading to similar quality issues in lockbox entries. These issues can be compounded by any errors made during manual data entry at the bank. The conventional lockbox program offers basic automation, which relies on perfect matching of reference numbers. However, this might necessitate additional manual work or further investment in automation.

Entries in the lockbox can be forwarded to SAP Cash Application for enhancement via a program based on artificial intelligence. This process utilizes the algorithms found in the TensorFlow library. The artificial intelligence model is designed to recognize accounts and receivables by analyzing the given data and historical trends. For instance, the artificial intelligence models are capable of learning the connections between the accounts and magnetic ink character recognition (MICR) or locating receivables using incomplete reference numbers. The enhanced payment advice proposals are then sent back to SAP S/4HANA, where they are verified by an accountant and cleared using the lockbox feature available in SAP S/4HANA. There is also an option for automatic clearing. The enhanced fields include alternative customer, alternative company code, invoice number, and alternative account type.

The lockbox feature offers several business advantages such as:

- Boosting efficiency and minimizing errors in the finance department
- Allowing the finance team to concentrate on strategic tasks and grow with the business
- Accelerating the processing of incoming payments to decrease DSO

- Seamlessly integrating with SAP S/4HANA Cloud and SAP S/4HANA on-premise to extract value from historical data and maintain the current processing workflow
- Learning from accountant behavior and starting to work for us immediately
- Constantly adapting and not requiring ongoing maintenance

The account receivable clerk is responsible for documenting the advice notices received in non-electronic form from customers. The payment advice note provides the necessary information for clearing the customer accounts for invoice payments. The account receivable clerk often faces challenges such as:

- Payment advice notes may be unclear and/or incorrect.
- Manual extraction from payment advice notes is labor-intensive and prone to errors.
- Manual reconciliation (matching) of payment advice notes and customer invoices is complex. Often payment advices are not entered into the system due to technical barriers, and effort can be used only for a manual clearing of payments.

By utilizing the lockbox feature and the artificial intelligence service, several benefits can be achieved:

- Enhanced invoice processing FTE efficiency.
- Increased invoice receipt and processing FTE productivity.
- Decreased payment processing and supplier inquiries headcount costs.
- Reduced external workforce invoice errors.

The lockbox feature allows us to automatically digitize unstructured remittance advices/payments advice and extract any additional payment information from unstructured advices. This additional information can be used to prepare the automated clearing process via SAP Cash Application. The account receivable clerk would greatly benefit from using this lockbox app because it automates and scales the matching process. It also allows for managing a wide range of customer communication preferences. The value proposition is to significantly reduce manual efforts by automatically extracting payment advice information from unstructured sources such as emails, PDFs, and paper and use it to automate the clearing process. The service was implemented as depicted in Fig. 24.1.

24.1.4 Payables Line Item Matching

We will now consider the payables line item functionality and how it caters to the requirements of customers. The artificial intelligence service is outlined in Fig. 24.7, which we will delve into and clarify in this part of the discussion.

Payments that customers send to their suppliers are considered outgoing payments, and they appear as debit items on a bank statement. When a supplier initiates

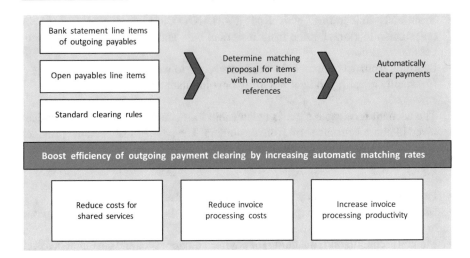

Fig. 24.7 Payables line item matching

a payment to settle an invoice, the amount is directly deducted from the customer's bank account. However, these payments are often not automatically cleared by the system due to the limited information provided on the bank statement. An artificial intelligence service can identify and suggest corresponding payables and then automatically clear them. This service offers several benefits:

- It learns from the behavior of the account and begins to function immediately.
- It continuously adapts and does not require constant maintenance.

In this context, the random forest and XGBoost algorithms from the Scikit-Learn library are utilized. The basic data needed for this process includes outgoing invoices, vendor payments, and bank statement items for outgoing payments. The accountant's role is to ensure that the received payment is applied to the relevant payable item. They must match the incoming payments initiated by the supplier with the correct payable item. This task is labor-intensive and requires investigative work to match a payment amount using the minimal information available on the bank statement. However, the use of artificial intelligence can lessen the labor needed to match payments with payables and allow for a concentrated effort on more complex issues. This process also leads to:

- Improved productivity among staff
- Decreased manual errors
- Quicker month-end close due to automated clearing

Customers can anticipate a quicker clearing process that combines standard rules with clearing generated by artificial intelligence. Manual effort is only needed for cases that the model has not yet managed. Clearing enabled by artificial intelligence, as opposed to manual clearing, allows for scalability and accuracy, and it utilizes the customer's expertise contained in the system data. The main benefit is to enhance the efficiency of outgoing payment clearing by increasing the rate of automatic matching. The service was implemented as depicted in Fig. 24.1.

24.2 Accounting and Financial Close

In this part, we will delve into a few of the services that have been developed for accounting and financial period-end close, utilizing the capabilities of artificial intelligence. These services are particularly focused on revenue accounting and reporting, which are essential for handling the process of recognizing revenue and accounting for it in compliance with legal requirements. These requirements are often dictated by international regulations such as the International Financial Reporting Standards, as well as the Accounting Standards Codification.

Inventory accounting is a method used to assess and keep track of the physical inventory and work-in-progress stock, in compliance with legal regulations and the needs of management accounting. Every movement of goods is evaluated in the material ledger which enables simultaneous, real-time assessment of stock in various currencies. A key aspect is its ability to handle large amounts of logistics data efficiently. The valuation of the physical inventory can be done either at a standard cost or a moving average, which is calculated automatically. Furthermore, it is possible to manually adjust the costs of materials and the value of the inventory. There is also the option to periodically value the material inventory in accordance with legal requirements (like lowest value, Last In First Out, or First In First Out) or product cost management needs (like actual costing or standard costing). We have the capability to execute a local close for one or multiple companies within our corporate group on a monthly, quarterly, or yearly basis or at any other intervals, with a customizable range of closing operations. Local accounting standards and/or the standards used by the group can be considered. A consolidation foundation can be utilized to generate and oversee the financial data compilation for corporate close, either for legal reasons or for consolidated management reporting purposes. This procedure provides a high level of flexibility in the data collection process, as well as the ability to configure different accounting principles. The accounting solution to automate the process of collecting consolidation data can be seamlessly integrated with it.

As illustrated in Fig. 24.8, the side-by-side artificial intelligence is applied. This involves the replication of historical data related to goods receipt/invoice receipt (GR/IR) postings, purchase orders, accruals, and sales orders to the SAP Business Technology Platform (SAP BTP) for the purpose of training models and conducting batch inference. For each of the use cases outlined, a specific artificial intelligence service is offered and made accessible as REST endpoints for seamless integration into business processes and user interfaces. The artificial intelligence capabilities are typically presented in a process-oriented language and visual format, enabling business users to utilize them without the need for extensive data science

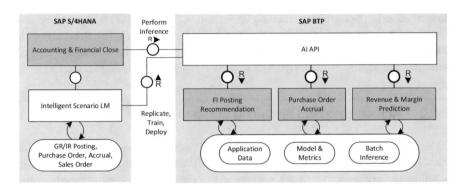

Fig. 24.8 AI architecture of accounting and financial close

knowledge. Life cycle management operations are bundled with artificial intelligence learning APIs (AI APIs) and coordinated by the Intelligent Scenario Lifecycle Management (ISLM) framework. An example system screenshot of the goods and receipts accounting reconciliation solution is shown in Fig. 24.9. Next, we will briefly explore the process and how artificial intelligence services can enhance it, starting with the financial account reconciliation with goods receipt/invoice receipt (GR/IR).

24.2.1 Clear Goods Receipts and Invoice Accounts

The illustration in Fig. 24.10 explains how the service based on artificial intelligence enhances the procedure of reconciling goods receipt and invoice accounts within the framework of financial account reconciliation. In this section, we will delve into the specifics of this process. To build the bridge to the previous chapters, we list the corresponding references points for the use case:

- AI Application Pattern: Recommendation
- ERP Reference Process: Finance/Record to Report
- ERP Reference Architecture: Finance/Accounting and Financial Close
- ERP Reference AI Technology: AI Technology Platform
- AI Realization Pattern: Side-by-Side

The reconciliation of Goods Receipt/Invoice Receipt (GR/IR) accounts is a process designed to handle exceptions for all purchase order items where discrepancies exist between the receipt of goods and the receipt of invoices. These discrepancies can either be written off or the underlying cause can be traced through various domains such as accounting, purchasing, logistics, and supplier interactions.

This process is often fraught with challenges due to the significant manual labor involved in generating reports, collecting all pertinent information, investigating the root cause, and resolving the issue through communication with different

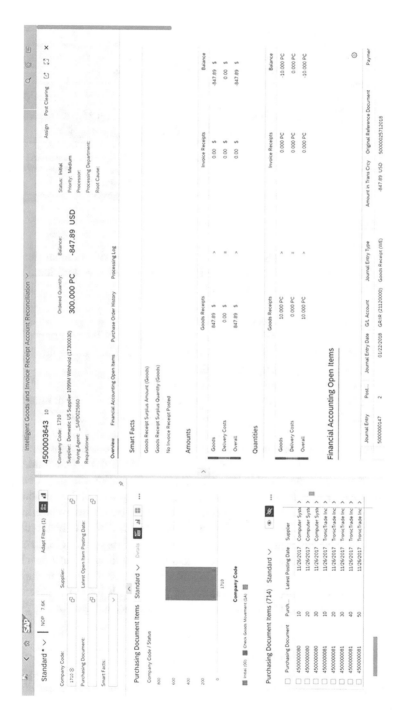

Fig. 24.9 Intelligent goods and invoice account reconciliation

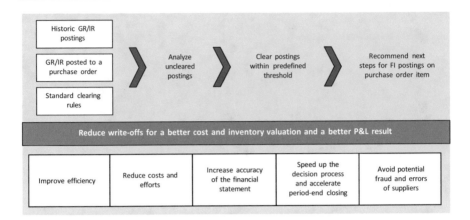

Fig. 24.10 Clear goods receipts and invoice accounts

departments. These efforts can cause delays in the closing of financial periods. However, if this process could be automated, customers could reap additional business benefits. Some of these benefits include:

- Enhancing the precision of financial statements
- Decreasing the number of write-offs, which in turn increases the accuracy of cost and inventory assessments, as well as improves profit and loss outcomes
- Improving the accuracy of supplier liabilities
- Preventing potential fraud and errors from suppliers
- Ensuring compliance with corporate rules, which necessitates the maintenance of GR/IR accounts in accordance with the Sarbanes-Oxley Act (SOX)

The challenges in this area can be addressed through the robust reporting capabilities of embedded predictive analytics algorithms in SAP S/4HANA Cloud. SAP S/4HANA offers real-time insights into all relevant information through a simple and flexible SAP Fiori user interface, which includes integrated collaboration features. Moreover, the ability to monitor process information facilitates process analysis and optimization. Ultimately, efficiency is enhanced through intelligent suggestions provided by the artificial intelligence service. This service aids in accelerating the closing of financial periods by reducing manual labor and providing real-time data analysis. The value proposition here is the potential for companies to achieve better profit and loss outcomes; reducing write-offs leads to improved cost and inventory assessments. The service was implemented as depicted in Fig. 24.8.

24.2.2 Accruals Management

Figure 24.11 presents an artificial intelligence service designed to aid in comprehending the workings of accrual management and the process of predicting

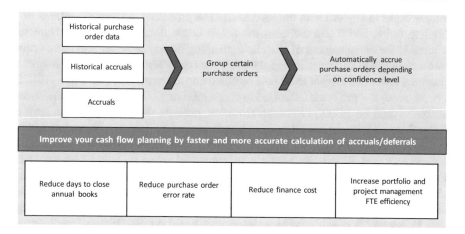

Fig. 24.11 Accruals prediction

accruals. We will delve deeper into this topic in the following section. To build the bridge to the previous chapters, we list the corresponding references points for the use case:

- AI Application Pattern: Prediction
- ERP Reference Process: Finance/Record to Report
- ERP Reference Architecture: Finance/Accounting and Financial Close
- ERP Reference AI Technology: AI Technology Platform
- AI Realization Pattern: Side-by-Side

The functionality of predicting accruals provides estimates and forecasts of accruals, which are crucial for planning cash flow. The system's proposed linear value can be modified based on the understanding of the purchase order, the business owner's feedback, and the values reported so far. Some of the challenges faced include the difficulty in estimating accruals as projects seldom operate in sync, the system suggesting linear values, adjustments consistently relying on accountants' understanding of the purchase order, reported values being outdated, and the necessity of the business owners' feedback. To mitigate these problems, we can utilize existing data to categorize certain purchase orders and use historical data from previous purchase orders to suggest how the accruals for these orders should be handled. This information is used for developing the artificial intelligence service that addresses these issues.

The use of artificial intelligence services can lead to significant improvements in various areas. These include shortening the time it takes to finalize the annual accounts, reducing the error rate in purchase orders, enhancing the efficiency of portfolio and project management resources, and cutting down on financial costs. Customers stand to gain from the automatic accumulation of purchase orders and the precise calculation of the total accruals. This artificial intelligence service, which works in tandem with the SAP S/4HANA processes, utilizes algorithms like random forest and XGBoost from the Scikit-Learn library. The main advantage offered is the enhancement of cash flow planning through quicker and more accurate computation of accruals and deferrals. Accruals are projected amounts on a purchase order that are yet to be paid or billed due to the current status of a project. For instance, if a project is estimated to cost a total of 12,000 over a year, the linear accrual would be 1,000 per month. However, projects seldom progress in such a linear fashion; it might be that nothing is paid in the first 3 months instead of 3,000, but by the eighth month, the project is 80% complete, so 9,600 should be paid instead of 8,000. At present, accruals are estimated by an accountant who adjusts the linear value suggested by the system based on their understanding of the purchase order, the feedback of the business owner, and reported values to date. The use of artificial intelligence services can address this issue by essentially using existing data to categorize certain purchase orders and, based on their history, predict how they should accrue. Each purchase order that is accrued automatically reduces manual work. An accurate total accrual value helps prevent incorrect cash flow planning and unnecessary capital costs. The typical end-of-period closing activity also includes any accruals that need to be posted when liabilities arise for a third party with associated costs. The SAP S/4HANA accrual engine provides flexible configuration options to manage these types of accrual costs. The monthly accrual amounts can optionally be reviewed, and accruals can be approved. The service was implemented as depicted in Fig. 24.8.

24.2.3 Predictive Accounting

Figure 24.12 provides a detailed explanation of the artificial intelligence service that was developed to assist in comprehending the workings of the predictive accounting procedure. This service is designed to predict future income, expenses, and cash flow. In this section, we will delve deeper into the specifics of this service. To build

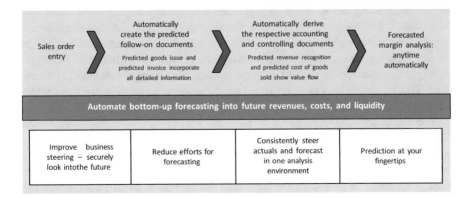

Fig. 24.12 Predictive accounting

the bridge to the previous chapters, we list the corresponding references points for the use case:

- AI Application Pattern: Prediction
- ERP Reference Process: Finance/Record to Report
- ERP Reference Architecture: Finance/Accounting and Financial Close
- ERP Reference AI Technology: AI Technology Platform
- AI Realization Pattern: Side-by-Side

In the conventional method of accounting, the accounting team is required to complete a range of closing tasks before stakeholders could assess the company's performance. This approach doesn't allow for immediate access to data for on-the-spot business decision-making. This leads to several improvements and modifications in the ERP system to expedite the closing process and decrease the number of closing tasks, thereby shortening the overall closing cycle. This approach is often referred to as continuous accounting because it allows for real-time data access without having to wait for the completion of the closing cycle. With the rapid evolution of business and industry processes, there was a need for predictive accounting data for future periods, as well as a single source of truth table, like the Universal Journal, prompting the transition from continuous to predictive accounting. The predictive accounting service in SAP S/4HANA, facilitated by artificial intelligence, allows to broaden the scope of accounting. This is the next evolution of continuous accounting, aiding organizations in future business operations planning and strategy development. This feature focuses on the revenue generated by organizations based on incoming sales order data, even in the absence of a goods receipt or invoice booking. Essentially, predictive accounting extends the primary reporting with forward-looking data. SAP offers SAP Fiori apps as a standard feature to visualize the impact of predictive accounting on gross margin and similar metrics. The process involves two steps:

1. Incoming sales orders are converted into predicted revenue
   This provides a comprehensive summary of all sales orders and their values for a specific time period, irrespective of the billing status. Predicted goods issued and billing documents are recorded in the prediction ledger.
2. Commitments are converted into anticipated expenditures
   This includes cost allocations to a work breakdown structure (WBS), order, cost center, and supplier. Commitments for derived characteristics such as profit center, segment, and functional area can be also viewed.
   The advantages of predictive accounting are numerous:

- It allows for accurate forecasting of future revenue based on predicted receivables and profit margins from sales orders.
- It provides report availability for future working capital based on predicted revenue and anticipated expenditures.
- It helps identify exceptions and opportunities.

- It provides an overview of future cash flow and other similar reports based on predictive data for future periods.

The service was implemented as depicted in Fig. 24.8.

24.3 Conclusion

In this section, we focused on use cases in the finance line of business (LoB) and how customers could benefit from this functionality. We gave a brief overview of the use case requirements, the business processes involved, and how they were addressed. As we can imagine, the finance LoB is huge, with a lot of potential to automate and fine-tune the processes. This can help the account receivable (AR)/ accounts payable (AP) clerks, the accountants, and finance controllers. We discussed the topics centering on AR/AP and accounting and financial period-end close. These scenarios were implemented by applying the side-by-side artificial intelligence approach. Thus, application data needed to be replicated, individual artificial intelligence services were provided serving the use cases, and life cycle management was handled with Intelligent Scenario Lifecycle Management (ISLM). The successful application of the proposed concepts and frameworks on the finance scenarios validated the practicability of the inventions explained in this elaboration.

Epilogue: Ethical Considerations

25

We conclude the elaboration with ethical considerations of artificial intelligence in context of business applications. Although artificial intelligence positively impacts the economy and our society, at the same time, it raises public concerns, such as negative effects on jobs or loss of human control in automated decision-making. Thus, the success of artificial intelligence depends on its broad social acceptance. Therefore, in this final epilogue, we briefly discuss ethical guiding principles to steer the development and deployment of artificial intelligence software.

25.1 Guiding Principle

Artificial intelligence helps in economy and society challenges but raises also concerns, e.g., elimination of jobs or loss of human control. In practice, however, most of those concerns is more fiction than facts. Artificial intelligence evolves evolutionary rather than revolutionary, giving us time to prepare for the changes and challenges ahead. Nevertheless, those concerns must be taken seriously. Certainly, artificial intelligence impacts the labor market as additional tasks are automated. Employees are liberated from routine and repetitive activities, allowing them to shift to higher-value tasks that depend on capabilities unique to human beings, e.g., creativity or emotionality. Thus, existing jobs are transformed through artificial intelligence, and new jobs are created for designing, operating, and using intelligent systems. Conversely, the future of work will be marked by human-machine collaboration. Automated decision-making based on artificial intelligence entails consumer protection issues in terms of neutrality and objectiveness of algorithms. Good software design can mitigate this. The design of intelligent systems shall have human in control as guiding principle. In a business environment, actions triggered in a system have a tangible outcome in the real world that impacts the goals and profits of the company. As the responsibility and accountability for these actions still lie with the human user, humans must always remain in control of the outcome. Intelligent systems shall augment human capabilities so that users can better understand and control the software. Providing sufficient information about the underlying artificial intelligence model and explaining the reasoning behind the results of algorithms should be essential part of designing intelligent applications in order to build trust between human and machine. Furthermore, artificial intelligence development must respect ethical values and legal standards. The success of artificial intelligence depends on its broad social acceptance. SAP defined the following guiding principles to steer the development and deployment of artificial intelligence business application (SAP AI Guiding Principles, 2021):

- Driven by values: We acknowledge that there is potential for AI to be used in ways that are inconsistent with these guiding principles and the operational standards we are building, just like there is with any technology. We shall uphold the United Nation Guiding Principles on Business and Human Rights (United Nation Human Rights, 2011), legal requirements, and generally acknowledged international standards as we create artificial intelligence software. Where appropriate, AI Ethics Steering Committee shall assist in advising teams on how these guiding principles apply to particular use cases. We shall make an effort to stop the improper usage of our technology where it conflicts with our values.
- Design for people: We work hard to develop inclusive artificial intelligence software solutions that aim to empower and enhance the skills of our diverse userbase. We employ artificial intelligence to help people reach their full potential by delivering human-centered user experiences using intuitive and augmentative technology. To do this, we closely collaborate with users as we create our solutions in a multidisciplinary, demographically varied context.
- Enable business beyond bias: Bias has a bad effect on everyone, including our consumers and artificial intelligence software. This is especially true when there is a chance that discrimination or unfair effects on underrepresented groups would result. As a result, we insist that our technical teams fully comprehend the business issues they are attempting to resolve as well as the level of data quality required. Our teams should be more diverse and multidisciplinary, and we are looking into new technology ways to reduce bias. We are also steadfastly committed to assisting our clients in establishing even more varied firms by utilizing artificial intelligence to create cutting-edge items.
- Strive for transparency and integrity: Depending on their level of technical sophistication and intended use, our systems are subject to strict criteria. Our clients will be made aware of their input, capabilities, intended use, and limitations, and we will give them the tools to monitor and regulate it. They are in charge of the distribution of our items and always will be. In order to increase system openness, we will conduct research and aggressively support industry collaboration.
- Uphold quality and safety standards: Quality assurance procedures, which we continuously update as necessary, is applied to our AI software just like it is to any other product we produce. Our artificial intelligence software goes through extensive testing in real-world situations to firmly establish their suitability for

use and that the product requirements are met. To maintain and further enhance the quality, safety, reliability, and security of our systems, we collaborate closely with our clients and users.

- Place data protection and privacy at the core: Every product and service must include data protection and privacy as a basic component. We are transparent about the how, why, where, and when our artificial intelligence software uses customer and anonymized user data. This dedication to data security and privacy is shown in our compliance with all relevant legal standards as well as in the research we carry out in collaboration with top academic institutions to create the newest approaches and tools for strengthening privacy.

- Engage with the wider societal challenges of artificial intelligence: The afore-mentioned areas are mostly under our control, but there are a number of new concerns that call for a much wider conversation that cuts across fields, countries, and cultural, philosophical, and religious traditions. These include, but are not restricted to, inquiries about:
  - Impact on the economy, including how business and society should work together to prepare students and workers for an AI economy and how society may need to change how it distributes wealth, ensures social safety, and develops its economy.
  - Impact on society, including the worth and significance of labor for individuals and the potential for AI programs to serve as social companions and caregivers.
  - Normative issues include how artificial intelligence should handle moral conundrums and what uses of artificial intelligence, particularly in terms of security and safety, should be regarded acceptable.

In addition, there are further challenges that require a much broader discourse across industries, disciplines, borders, and cultural, philosophical, and religious traditions.

25.2 Ethics Policy

In this section, the guiding principles for artificial intelligence are explained in further detail in the ethics policy (SAP AI Ethics Policy, 2022). Particularly, the AI ethics policy clarifies how the guiding principles are related to artificial intelligence use cases. It outlines the objectives, requirements, and responsibilities for staff members involved in the creation, use, and sale of artificial intelligence business applications.

25.2.1 Human Agency and Oversight

Teams should take into account the following when developing artificial intelligence business applications as they relate to Human Agency and Oversight:

- A human's rights and freedoms should always outweigh those of an artificial intelligence business application, with the exception of situations when it is expressly permitted by local laws that are in force.
- When applicable local law is silent, human oversight must be accomplished by means of an effective governance system. This will be determined on a case-by-case basis and may include, but not be limited to, human-in-the-loop, human-on-the-loop, or human-in-command.
- In accordance with the data privacy and protection policy of an enterprise, human oversight must be implemented in cases where humans may be directly impacted by a decision made by artificial intelligence business applications to ensure that it does not compromise human autonomy or have unexpected effects.
- As much as is practicable, an explanation of how decisions were made by an artificial intelligence business application utilized in automated decision processes must be given.
- To ensure the artificial intelligence business application behaves as intended by the developers and does not have any unintended behavior, outputs, or usage, appropriate extensive testing and governance shall be conducted during development and deployment where the visibility of human oversight of the artificial intelligence system may be limited or unknown after deployment.

25.2.2 Addressing Bias and Discrimination

Artificial intelligence systems learn from the behaviors and existing social structures of the cultures they study. Therefore, data-driven technologies have the potential to replicate, reinforce, and magnify societal patterns of marginalization, inequality, and prejudice that may be embedded in data sources utilized to develop artificial intelligence. In addition, artificial intelligence business applications may be able to reproduce the prejudices and preconceptions of its developers as many of the characteristics, metrics, and analytical frameworks of the models that enable data mining are chosen by their creators. Finally, data samples utilized to develop algorithmic systems' training and testing processes may not be properly representative of the populations or historical contexts from which they are inferring conclusions. This may apply in situations when the initial datasets were collected from businesses, industries, or other organizations that are inappropriate for the artificial intelligence business application being created and implemented. These biases may have a negative effect on the creation and results of artificial intelligence business applications, which may therefore have an adverse effect on users or clients. When there is a chance of fostering discrimination or unfairly affecting underrepresented groups, extra caution must be exercised. As it relates to resolving bias and discrimination in artificial intelligence systems, teams need to take the following into account:

- In addition to the restrictions outlined by the data privacy and protection policy of enterprises, artificial intelligence systems must not be created or used to de-anonymize data that has previously been anonymized in a way that could lead to the identification of certain people or groups.

- Artificial intelligence business applications must not purposefully produce unfairly skewed results.
- The data used to train artificial intelligence systems must, where applicable, be as inclusive as possible, represent a diverse cross-section of the population or historical events, and be as free as possible from any historical or socially constructed biases, inaccuracies, errors, and mistakes (or account for and mitigate them).
- In order to minimize direct or indirect prejudice, discrimination, or marginalization of groups or individuals, teams must make an effort to identify unfairly biased outputs and take technological or organizational remedies, such as minimizing bias in training data.
- Developers must make every effort to include impacted/affected users when evaluating and verifying that outputs are inclusive and devoid of discrimination.
- Processes must be in place to test and monitor for potential biases during the development, implementation, and use phase of artificial intelligence business applications.
  - It must be trained and evaluated using datasets that are as large, representative, accurate, and generalizable as is practical.
  - Target variables, characteristics, procedures, or analytic structures that are irrational, unethical, or impossible to validate in accordance with the guiding principles shall not be included in the model architectures.
  - It must be created and implemented without having any unintentionally negative effects on system users or any direct or indirect beneficiaries.
  - A fairness function should be used to assess artificial intelligence systems for impartial results where it is practical to do so.
- Regardless of the users' age, gender, abilities, or traits, artificial intelligence business applications must be user-centric, addressing the broadest variety of relevant end users and adhering to pertinent accessibility requirements.

25.2.3 Transparency and Explainability

In accordance with their level of technical expertise and intended use, artificial intelligence business applications are subject to strict requirements. Along with the technical resources required for training and prediction, we must effectively express to clients their input, capabilities, intended use, and restrictions. Since artificial intelligence agents lack moral accountability, it is impossible to hold them responsible for their deeds. By prioritizing both the transparency of the process by which the artificial intelligence business application is built and the transparency and interpretability of its decisions and behaviors, procedures must be put in place to ensure that developed artificial intelligence systems are objective and viable as planned. As it relates to the transparency and explainability of artificial intelligence business applications, teams should take the following into account:

- To enable transparency and traceability, the data sets and procedures utilized to generate an artificial intelligence system's judgment, including those for data collection and data labeling as well as the algorithms employed by the created artificial intelligence business applications, must be recorded.
- As part of the development process, the capabilities and constraints must be described in a way that is acceptable for the current use case. This must provide details on the artificial intelligence system's accuracy level (performance metric), as well as its capabilities and restrictions.
- If the data subject requests it, products that use artificial intelligence business applications in the processing of personal data shall, in accordance with data privacy and protection policy, offer as much transparency as possible regarding how the artificial intelligence was used in plain and straightforward language.
- In accordance and compliance with data privacy and protection policy, artificial intelligence software that use automated decision-making or profiling must be able to, upon request from the data subject, provide explanations that, to the extent possible, explain the data segment the subject was placed into and the reasons they were placed there. In addition, if the data subject asks for them, the decision's justifications must be disclosed. The justification must give the data subject justification for contesting the judgment.
- The methodologies used for creating, analyzing, and validating the artificial intelligence business applications, as well as the results or decisions it makes, must all be completely documented as part of the development process.
- Where appropriate, when communicating directly with people (including through "Chatbots" or Conversational AI):
  - Artificial intelligence business applications must be identified to the proper end users as such.
  - Where applicable and practical, a choice must be given to allow a user to choose human interaction over engaging with an artificial intelligence system.
  - Artificial intelligence systems must be created in a way that discourages people from feeling empathy or attachment for the artificial intelligence software.
  - Users of artificial intelligence systems must be clearly informed that social interaction is simulated.
- Based on the use case, artificial intelligence system developers shall make every effort to ensure that the decisions, recommendations, and outputs of the artificial intelligence system are as visible as feasible. The user interface (UI) or application logs can be used for this to enable the best understanding and traceability of these.
- The user must be informed that confidence levels are commonly used by artificial intelligence systems, and if necessary, the user must be provided with the actual confidence level of a given output.
- The goal, limitations, requirements, and judgments of the artificial intelligence system must be specified and documented in a way that is transparent to the non-technical general reader or user.

- Software/conditions involving black boxes and/or deep neural networks:
  - Where developers has created so-called black box algorithms, further explicability measures must be offered. Traceability, auditability, and open documentation and disclosure of the software's capabilities should be among them.
  - An explanation of the output must be made available wherever possible; if this is not practicable, users must be informed that the output might not be completely comprehensible.
  - The need for this information will depend on the circumstances and the gravity of the repercussions.
- The context and setting in which an artificial intelligence system will work must be considered during development so that, despite the best of intentions, humans are not likely to suffer harm as a result of the deployment of artificial intelligence systems.
- This policy shall apply to the complete software solution to the degree that a third-party artificial intelligence system (e.g., TensorFlow) is embedded in the solutions.

25.2.4 Civic Society

Artificial intelligence business applications must be designed to enhance, complement, and empower human cognitive, social, and cultural abilities rather than to prevent or limit behaviors appropriate for a free society. As it relates to civic society, teams should take the following into account when designing or implementing artificial intelligence systems:

- Artificial intelligence systems cannot be created or implemented for human surveillance that uses biometrics, facial recognition, or other distinguishing characteristics to target specific people or groups with the intention of violating their human rights.
- Artificial intelligence systems must not be created or used for activities that discriminate against or exclude certain individuals or groups from opportunities and advantages that artificial intelligence may bring to the general public.
- Artificial intelligence systems may not be created or used to unfairly manipulate people or groups in public spaces or the media or for other similar purposes.
- Artificial intelligence systems must not be created or used to subvert democratic elections or public discourse.
- Development and deployment of artificial intelligence systems must adhere to the guiding principles, which aims to lessen the environmental impact of business operations.

25.3 Use Case Assessment Process

As stated in SAP AI Ethics Policy (2022), professionals shall handle ethical problems and trade-offs connected to the usage of artificial intelligence systems through reasoned, context-relevant, and evidence-based decision making rather than through

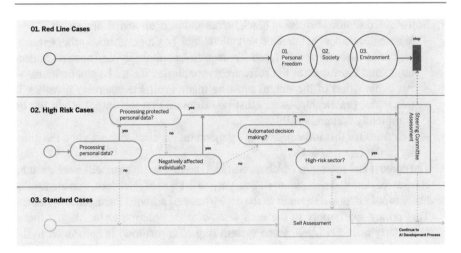

Fig. 25.1 Use case assessment process

intuition or random discretion. Teams should first submit the problem for consideration by their unit in cases where a use case presented for an artificial intelligence business application may violate the defined policy at any point in the lifetime or to decide whether or not to pursue the application of a given use case. This holds true even if the teams just have reservations or worries.

Figure 25.1 illustrates the assessment process for artificial intelligence use cases by differentiating the use cases in the categories red line, high risk, and standard cases (SAP AI Ethics, 2022).

The so-called red lines outlined in the ethics policy should not apply to any artificial intelligence use cases. Under the objectives of artificial intelligence, they are classified as being seriously immoral. We must immediately stop creating, deploying, and selling our use case if it was designed with these goals in mind. Let's recap the red lines:

- Personal freedom – human surveillance that uses biometrics, facial recognition, or other distinguishing characteristics to target specific people or groups with the intention of violating or abusing those people's rights. Discrimination that prevents certain people or groups from having equal access to the advantages and opportunities that AI offers to the general community. Data that has already been anonymized is de-anonymized, which could lead to the identification of specific people or groups.
- Society – manipulation of people or groups through public forums, the media, or control of other similar purposes with the intention of misleading or unfairly manipulating them. Undercutting democratic electoral systems or discussion methods that undermine human dialogue. Intentional negative effects on system users and/or those who are both directly and indirectly affected by it.
- Environment – development and deployment of artificial intelligence systems must be done with little to no overt environmental damage.

We categorize certain artificial intelligence application cases as high-risk scenarios. We base these standards on the types of artificial intelligence that have historically resulted in unfavorable outcomes for particular people or entire communities (see, for instance, Amazon's case of a discriminatory AI recruiting tool). High-risk use cases are allowed, but before they can be further developed, used, or sold, they must first be evaluated according the process depicted in Fig. 25.1:

- Processing personal data: If not for anonymized data and the process of anonymization, does the use case handle any data belonging to a named or identifiable natural person for instructional reasons or during productive usage?
- Processing protected personal data: Does the use case involve processing particular categories of personal data, such as information on a person's sexual orientation, religion, or biometrics (including face imaging)?
- Negatively affected individuals: Could the use case interfere with or restrict a person's fundamental rights or freedom? Could it harm people's well-being (health and safety)?
- Automated decision-making: Does the use case demonstrate totally or partially automated decision-making (covering situations in which there is no human intervention and in which there is human supervision but recommender systems are excluded)?
- High-risk sector: Do any of the following sectors (employment/human resources, healthcare, law enforcement) apply to the use case?

If the answer is Yes to question 1 and at least one of the questions 2–5, the artificial intelligence steering committee approval is necessary. All other scenarios fall in the category standard case and can be developed after a brief self-assessment.

25.4 Conclusion

Artificial intelligence holds the promise of opening up a wealth of options for organizations, governments, and society as a whole. Artificial intelligence could, however, potentially lead to social, political, and economic upheavals. Additionally, the pace at which the technology entered widespread use surpassed the governmental policymakers' ability to provide the essential direction for the technology to evolve into a sustainable and secure development for artificial intelligence utilization. Due to these factors, we must establish explicit ethical guidelines that have to be followed in the development, implementation, usage, and sale of artificial intelligence technologies. The commitment of the business to preserve and support the Universal Declaration of Human Rights is the cornerstone of artificial intelligence ethics. The prohibition of discrimination and harassment of people based on personal characteristics, such as culture, race, ethnicity, religion, age, gender, sexual orientation, gender identity, and physical or mental handicap, among others, is a crucial component of this commitment. In addition, the objective for artificial intelligence business applications includes safeguarding people from harm, treating everyone equally and justly, guaranteeing that everyone has the right to the same freedom and dignity under the law, and defending civil, political, and social rights. The artificial intelligence ethics policy aims to make sure that artificial intelligence solutions are created, implemented, used, and sold in accordance with the enterprise's fundamental organizational values and the defined guiding principles for artificial intelligence. By matching policy requirements to the appropriate stages of development process, this chapter offered teams involved in the creation of artificial intelligence as a roadmap for how to execute the artificial intelligence ethics policy throughout all phases of the artificial intelligence life cycle.

Bibliography

Aberdeen Group. (2006, November). *Best practices in extending ERP*. Research brief.

Aberdeen Group. (2007). *The total cost of ERP ownership*. Research brief.

Aberdeen Group. (2008). *The ERP in manufacturing benchmark report*.

Aberdeen Group. (2009). *The ERP in action: Epicor*.

Adam, F., & O'Doherty, P. (2000). Lessons from enterprise resource planning implementation in Ireland - Towards smaller and shorter ERP projects. *Journal of Information Technology, 15*(4), 305–316.

Akerkar, R. (2019). *Artificial intelligence for business*. Springer.

Akkermans, H. A., & Helden, K. V. (2002). (2002). Vicious and virtuous cycles in ERP implementation: A case study of interrelations between critical success factors. *European Journal of Information Systems, 11*, 35–46.

Akkermans, H. A., Bogerd, P., & Yucesan, E. (2003). The impact of ERP on supply chain management: Exploratory findings from a European Delphi study. *European Journal of Operational Research, 146*(2003), 284–301.

Aktürk, C. (2021). Artificial intelligence in enterprise resource planning systems. A bibliometric study. *Journal of International Logistics and Trade., 19*(2), 69.

Aladwani, A. M. (2001). Change management strategies for successful ERP implementation. *Business Process Management Journal, 7*(3), 266–275.

Alaskari, O., Pinedo-Cuenca, R., & Ahmad, M. M. (2019). Framework for selection of ERP system: Case study. *Procedia Manufacturing, 38*, 69–75.

Al-Ghourabi, A. (2023). *Artificial intelligence in business and technology*. Kindle.

Al-Mashari, M. (2000). Enterprise-wide information systems: The case of SAP R/3 application. In *Proceedings of the 2nd International Conference on Enterprise information systems*, pp. 3–8.

Al-Mashari, M., & Zairi, M. (2000). Revisiting BPR: A holistic review of practice and development. *Business Process Management Journal, 6*(1), 10–42.

Al-Mashari, M., Al-Mudimigh, A., & Zairi, M. (2003). Enterprise resource planning: A taxonomy of critical factors. *European Journal of Operational Research, 146*(2), 352–364.

Al-Mashari, M., Ghani, S. K., & Al-Rashid, W. (2006). A study of the critical success factors of ERP implementation in developing countries. *International Journal of Internet and Enterprise Management, 4*(1), 68–95.

Al-Mudimigh, A., Zairi, M., & Al-Mashari, M. (2001). ERP software implementation: An integrative framework. *European Journal of Information Systems, 10*(4), 216–226.

Aloini, D., Dulmin, R., & Mininno, V. (2007). Risk management in ERP project introduction: Review of the literature. *Information & Management, 44*(6), 547–567. https://doi.org/10.1016/j.im.2007.05.004

Al-Okaily, A., Al-Okaily, M., & Teoh, A. P. (2021). Evaluating ERP systems success: Evidence from Jordanian firms in the age of the digital business. *VINE Journal of Information and Knowledge Management Systems*. ISSN: 2059-5891.

S. Sarferaz, *Embedding Artificial Intelligence into ERP Software*, https://doi.org/10.1007/978-3-031-54249-7

Alpaydin, E. (2014). *Introduction to machine learning*. MIT Press.

Alsharari, N. M., Al-Shboul, M., & Alteneiji, S. (2020). Implementation of cloud ERP in the SME: Evidence from UAE. *Journal of Small Business and Enterprise Development*. ISSN 1462-6004.

Alvarez, R. (2000). *Examining an ERP implementation through myths: A case study of a large public organization* (pp. 1655–1661). Proceedings of the Americas Conference of Information Systems.

AMR Research. (1997). *Enterprise resource planning software report, 1997–2002*. AMR Research.

Anderson, E. E., & Chen, Y.-M. (1997). Microcomputer software evaluation: An econometric model. *Decision Support Systems, 19*(2), 75–92.

Anderson, J., & Narasimhan, R. (1997). Assessing implementation risk: A technological approach. *Management Science, 25*, 512–521.

Anexinet, R.B. (2006). *Top 10 ERP implementation pitfalls*. Retrieved from http://www.anexinet.com/pdfs/ERP_top10pitfalls3-2006.pdf

Anguelov, K. (2021). Applications of artificial intelligence for optimization of business processes in the Enterprise resource planning systems. In *12th National conference with international participation*.

Avital, M., & Vandenbosch, B. (1999). SAP implementation at metallica: An organizational drama. In *International conference on information systems ICIS*.

Ayağ, Z., & Ozdemir, R. G. (2007). An intelligent approach to ERP software selection through fuzzy ANP. *International Journal of Production Research, 45*(10), 2169–2194.

Aydogmus, H. Y., Kamber, E., & Kahraman, C. (2021). ERP selection using picture fuzzy CODAS methods. *Journal of Intelligent & Fuzzy Systems, 40*(6).

Bacharach, S. B., Bamberger, P., & Sonnenstuhl, W. J. (1996). The organizational transformation process: The micro politics of dissonance reduction and the alignment of logics of action. *Administrative Science Quarterly, 41*, 477–506.

Bancroft, N., Seip, H., & Sprengel, A. (1998). *Implementing SAP R/3: How to introduce a large system into a large organization* (2nd ed.). Manning Publications.

Barki, H., & Pinsonneault, A. (2002). Explaining ERP implementation effort and benefits with organizational integration. *Cahier du Gresi, 20*(1), 54.

Barth, C., & Koch, S. (2019). Critical success factors in ERP upgrade projects. *Industrial Management & Data Systems., 119*(3), 656.

Becerra-Fernandez, I., Murphy, K., & Simon, S. (2000). Integrating ERP in the business school curriculum. *Communications of the ACM, 43*(4), 39–41.

Berchet, C., & Habchi, G. (2005). The implementation and deployment of an ERP system: An industrial case study. *Computers in Industry, 56*(6), 588–605.

Berett, S. (2002). Unleashing the integration potential of ERP systems: The role of process-based performance measurement systems. *Business Process Management Journal, 8*(3), 254–277.

Bernroider, E., & Koch, S. (2001). ERP selection process in midsize and large organizations. *Business Process Management Journal, 7*(3), 251–257.

Beskese, A., Corum, A., & Anolay, M. (2019). A model proposal for ERP system selection in automotive industry. *International Journal of Industrial Engineering, 26*(3).

Bhatt, N., Guru, S., Thanki, S., & Sood, G. (2021). Analysing the factors affecting the selection of ERP package: A fuzzy AHP approach. *Information Systems and e-Business Management, 19*, 641–682.

Bingi, P., Sharma, M. K., & Godla, J. K. (1999). Critical issues affecting an ERP implementation. *Information Systems Management, 16*(3), 7–14.

Biolcheva, P., & Molhova, M. (2022). Integration of AI supported risk management in ERP implementation. *Computer and Information Science, 15*(3), 37.

Bishop, C. M. (2006). *Pattern recognition and machine learning. Information science and statistics*. Springer.

Boddington, P. (2023). *AI ethics*. Springer.

Boersma, K., & Kingma, S. (2005). Developing a cultural perspective on ERP. *Business Process Management Journal, 11*(2), 123–136.

Bonner, M. (2000). Roadmap to ERP success. *Control Magazine, 26*(08), 14.

Bourrasset, C., Boillod-Cerneux, F., & Sauge, L. (2018). Requirements for an enterprise AI benchmark. In *Technology conference on performance evaluation and benchmarking*.

Bowersox, D. J., Closs, D. J., & Hall, C. T. (1998). Beyond ERP—The storm before the calm. *Supply Chain Management Review, 1*(4), 28–37.

Bradford, M., & Florin, J. (2003). Examining the role of innovation diffusion factors on the implementation success of enterprise resource planning systems. *International Journal of Accounting Information Systems, 4*, 205–225.

Bradley, J. (2008). Management based critical success factors in the implementation of enterprise resource planning systems. *International Journal of Accounting Information Systems, 9*(3), 175–200.

Brown, R. M., & Stephenson, K. (1981). The evaluation of purchased computer software. *Mid-South Business Journal, 7*, 8–11.

Brown, C., & Vessey, I. (1999). ERP implementation approaches: Toward a contingency framework. In *International conference on information systems ICIS*.

Bruce, P., & Bruce, A. (2020). *Practical statistics for data scientist*. O'Reilly.

Bueno, S., & Salmeron, J. L. (2008). Fuzzy modeling enterprise resource planning tool selection. *Computer Standards and Interfaces, 30*(3), 137–147.

Bzdok, D., Altman, N., & Krzywinski, M. (2018). Statistics versus machine learning. *Nature Methods, 15*, 233.

Caldwell, B., & Stein, T. (1998). Beyond ERP—New IT agenda—A second wave of ERP activity promises to increase efficiency and transform ways of doing business. *Information Week, 711*, 34–35.

California Consumer Privacy Act (CCPA). (2023). *State of California Department of Justice*. Retrieved from https://oag.ca.gov/privacy/ccpa

Canhoto, A., & Clear, F. (2020). Artificial intelligence and machine learning as business tools: A framework for diagnosing value destruction potential. *Business Horizons, 63*(2), 183.

Cantu, R. (1999). *A framework for implementing enterprise resource planning systems in small manufacturing companies, Master's thesis*. St. Mary's University.

Carmona, D. (2019). *The AI organization*. O'Reilly.

Casati, F., Govindarajan, K., & Jayaraman, B. (2019). Operating enterprise AI as a service. In *International Conference on Service-Oriented Computing*.

Chang, Y. (2020). What drives organizations to switch to cloud ERP systems? The impacts of enablers and inhibitors. *Journal of Enterprise Information Management., 33*(3), 600.

Chang, W., Schmelzer, M., Kopp, F., Hsu, C., Su, J., Chen, L., & Chen, M. (2019). A deep learning facial expression recognition based scoring system for restaurants. In *International Conference on Artificial Intelligence in Information and Communication (ICAIIC)*, pp. 251–254.

Charlier, R., & Kloppenburg, S. (2017). *Artificial Intelligence is not the future, it is already happening and widely*. Retrieved from https://www.pwc.nl/nl/assets/documents/artificialintelligence-in-hr-a-no-brainer.pdf

Chau, P. Y. K. (1995). Factors used in the selection of packaged software in small businesses: Views of owners and managers. *Information and Management, 29*(2), 71–78.

Chaubard, F. (2023). *AI for retail: A practical guide to modernize your retail business with AI and automation*. Wiley.

Chen, I. J. (2001). Planning for ERP systems: Analysis and future trend. *Business Process Management Journal, 7*(5), 374–386.

Chen, S., & Wang, J. (2019). Cloud-based ERP system selection based on extended probabilistic linguistic MULTIMOORA method and Choquet integral operator. *Computational and Applied Mathematics, 38*.

Chen, A. N., Goes, P. B., Gupta, A., & Marsden, J. R. (2006). Heuristics for selection robust database structures with dynamic query patterns. *European Journal of Operational Research, 168*, 200–220.

Chen, D., Doumeingts, G., & Vernadat, F. (2008). Architectures for enterprise integration and interoperability: Past, present and future. *Computers in Industry, 59*, 647–659.

Chen, H.-H., Chen, C.-S., & Tsai, L. H. (2009). A study of successful ERP—From the organization fit perspective. *Journal of Systemics, Cybernetics and Informatics, 7*(4), 8–16.

Chen, L., Jiang, M., Jia, F., & Liu, G. (2021). Artificial intelligence adoption in business-to-business marketing: Toward a conceptual framework. *Journal of Business & Industrial Marketing, 37*(5).

Chugh, R., Sharma, S. C., & Cabrera, A. (2017). Lessons Learned from enterprise resource planning (ERP) implementations in an Australian Company. *International Journal of Enterprise Information Systems, 13*(3), 23–35.

Chung, S. H., Tang, H.-L., & Ahmad, I. (2011). Modularity, integration and IT personnel skills factors in linking ERP to SCM systems. *Journal of Technology Management & Innovation, 6*, 1–3.

Ciborra, C., Braa, K., Cordella, A., et al. (2000). *From control to drift—The dynamics of corporate information infrastructures*. Oxford University Press.

Cohen, M. (2022). *Practical linear algebra for data science*. O'Reilly.

Colmenares, L. E. (2004). Critical success factors of enterprise resource planning systems implementation in Venezuela. In *Americas Conference on Information Systems (AMCIS) Proceedings paper 21*, pp. 134–139.

Cotteleer, M. J., & Bendoly, E. (2006). Order Lead-time improvement following enterprise information technology implementation: An empirical study. *MIS Quarterly, 30*(3), 643–660.

Cubric, M. (2020). Drivers, barriers and social considerations for AI adoption in business and management: A tertiary study. *Technology in Society, 62*, 101257.

Czekster, R. M., Webber, T., Jandrey, A. H., & Macron, C. A. M. (2019). Selection of enterprise resource planning software using analytic hierarchy process. *Enterprise Information Systems, 13*(6), 895.

D'Ascoli, S. (2022). *Artificial intelligence and deep learning with python*. Independently published.

Davenport, T. H. (1998). Putting the enterprise into the enterprise system. *Harvard Business Review, 76*(4), 121–131.

Davenport, T. H. (2000). *Mission critical: Realizing the promise of enterprise systems*. Harvard Business School Press.

Davenport, T. H., & Ronanki, R. (2018). Artificial intelligence for the real world. *Harvard Business Review*.

Davenport, T. H., Harris, J. G., & Cantrell, S. (2004). Enterprise systems and ongoing process change. *Business Process Management Journal, 10*(1), 16–26.

Davidson, R. (2020). *Top ERP software vendors in 2020 company comparison list*. Retrieved from https://softwareconnect.com/erp/top-vendors/

Deutsch, C. (1998). Software that can make a grown company cry. *The New York Times, 148*(51), 1–13.

Dixit, A. K., & Prakash, O. (2011). Study of issues affecting ERP implementation in SMEs. *International Refereed Research Journal, 2*(2), 77–85. Retrieved from www.researchersworlld.com

Domingos, P. (2015). *The master algorithm: How the quest for the ultimate learning machine will remake our world*. Basic Books.

Dong, L. (2000). A model for enterprise systems implementation: Top management influences on implementation effectiveness. In *Americas conference on information systems AMCIS, USA*.

Duda, R. O., Hart, P. E., & Stork, D. G. (2000). *Pattern classification* (2nd ed.). Wiley-Interscience.

Earley, S. (2020). *The AI-powered enterprise*. LifeTree.

Edwards, L., & Veale, M. (2017). *Slave to the algorithm? Why a 'right to an explanation' Is probably not the remedy you are looking for*. Social Science Research Network.

El Sawah, S., El Fattah, A. A., Tharwat, A., et al. (2008). A quantitative model to predict the Egyptian ERP implementation success index. *Business Process Management Journal, 14*(3), 288–306.

Escalle, C. X., Cotteleer, M. J., & Austin, R. D. (1999). *Enterprise resource planning (ERP): Technology note*. Harvard Business School Publishing.

Essex, D., Diann, D., & O'Donnell, J. (2020). *Enterprise resource planning*. Retrieved from https://searcherp.techtarget.com/definition/ERP-enterprise-resource-planning

Esteves, J., & Pastor, J. A. (2001). *Analysis of critical success factors relevance along SAP implementation phases.* In *Seventh Americas Conference on Information Systems*, pp. 1019–1025.

European Commission. (2018). *Guidelines on automated individual decision-making and profiling for the purposes of regulation 2016/679 (Wp251rev.01).*

European Commission. (2019a). EU high-level expert group on artificial intelligence. In *Ethics guidelines for trustworthy AI.* European Commission.

European Commission. (2019b). *Policy and investment recommendations for trustworthy artificial intelligence.*

Everdingen, Y., Hillergersberg, J., & Waarts, E. (2000). ERP adoption by European midsize companies. *Communications of the ACM, 43*(4), 27–31.

Ewusi-Mensah, K. (1997). Critical issues in abandoned information systems development projects. *Communications of the Association for Computing Machinery (ACM), 40*(9), 74–80.

Federici, T. (2009). Factors influencing ERP outcomes in SMEs: A post-introduction assessment. *Journal of Enterprise Information Management, 22*(1–2), 81–98.

Finney, S., & Corbett, M. (2007). ERP implementation: A compilation and analysis of critical success factors. *Business Process Management Journal, 13*(3), 329–347.

Fisher, D. M., Fisher, S. A., Kiang, M. Y., et al. (2004). Evaluating mid-level ERP software. *Journal of Computer Information Systems, 45*(1).

Foster, D. (2023). *Generative deep learning.* O'Reilly.

Gantz, J., & Reinsel, D. (2012). *The digital universe in 2020: Big data, bigger digital shadows and biggest growth in the far east.*

Gargeya, V. B., & Brady, C. (2005). Success and failure factor of adopting SAP in ERP system implementation. *Business Process Management Journal, 11*(5), 501–516.

Gartner, I. (2019). *Gartner says 5.8 billion enterprise and automotive IoT endpoints will be in use in 2020.* Retrieved from https://www.gartner.com/en/newsroom/press-releases/2019-08-29-gartner-says-5-8-billion-enterprise-and-automotive-io

Gattiker T., Goodhue D.L. (2000). Understanding the plant level costs and benefits of ERP: Will the ugly duckling always turn into a swan? In *33rd Hawaii International Conference on Science Systems HICSS, Maui, Hawaii.*

Gattiker, T., & Goodhue, D. L. (2005). What happens after ERP implementation: Understanding the impact of interdependence and differentiation on plant-level outcomes? *MIS Quarterly, 29*(3), 559–585.

Gaughan, D., Natis, Y., Alvarez, G., & O'Neill, M. (2020). *Future of applications: Delivering the composable enterprise.* Gartner. Retrieved from https://www.gartner.com/en/doc/465932-future-of-applications-delivering-the-composable-enterprise

Gavali, A., & Halder, S. (2019). Identifying critical success factors of ERP in the construction industry. Asian. *Journal of Civil Engineering, 21.*

General Data Protection Regulation (GDPR). 2023. *Council of the European Union.* Retrieved from https://www.consilium.europa.eu/en/policies/data-protection/data-protection-regulation

George Saadé, R., Nijher, H., & Chandra Sharma, M. (2017). Why ERP implementations fail—A grounded research study. In *Proceedings of the 2017 SITE conference* (pp. 191–200). Informing Science Institute.

Geron, A. (2019). *Hands-on machine learning with Scikit-learn, Keras & TensorFlow.* O'Reilly.

Gianclaudio, M., & Comandé, G. (2017). Why a right to legibility of automated decision-making exists in the general data protection regulation. *International Data Privacy Law, 7*(4).

Gibson, N., Holland, C., & Light, B. (1999a). A case study of a fast track SAP R/3 implementation at Guilbert. *Electronic Markets, 9*(3), 190–193.

Gibson, N., Holland, C., & Light B. (1999b). Enterprise resource planning: A business approach to systems development. In *32nd Hawaii international conference on science systems HICSS, Maui, Hawaii.*

Glass, R. L. (1998). Enterprise resource planning: Break through and/or term problem? *Data Base, 29*(2), 14–15.

Gobeli, D. H., Koeing, H. F., & Mirsha, C. S. (2002). Strategic value creation. In P. Phan (Ed.), *Technological entrepreneurship* (pp. 3–16). McGraw Hill.

Goldenberg, B. (1991). Analyze key factors when choosing software. *Marketing News, 25*, 23.

Goldkuhl, G. (2002). Anchoring scientific abstractions ontological and linguistic determination following socio-instrumental pragmatism. In *European conference on research methods in business and management* (pp. 29–30).

Goodfellow, I., Bengio, Y., & Courville, A. (2016). *Deep learning* (Adaptive computation and machine learning series). MIT Press.

Gordon, C., & Upadhyay, M. A. (2021). *The AI dilemma*. BPB Publications.

Goundar, S., Nayyar, A., Maharaj, M., Ratnam, K., & Prasad, S. (2021). *How artificial intelligence is transforming the ERP systems. Enterprise systems and technological convergence.* Information Age Publishing.

Grabski, S. V., Leech, S. A., & Lu, B. (2003). Enterprise systems implementation risks and controls. In G. Shanks, P. B. Seddon, & L. P. Willcocks (Eds.), *Second-wave enterprise resource planning systems: Implementing for effectiveness.* Cambridge University Press.

Gregor, S., & Hevner, A. R. (2013). Positioning and presenting design science research for maximum impact. *MIS Quarterly, 37*(2), 337–355.

Growth Business. (2017). *The rise of the AI recruiter: Is HR tech the next to challenge human intuition?* Retrieved from https://www.growthbusiness.co.uk/rise-ai-recruiter-hr-technext-challenge-human-intuition-2550350/

Grus, J. (2019). *Data science from scratch*. O'Reilly.

Guenole, N., & Feinzig, S. (2018). *The business case for AI in HR*. Retrieved from https://forms.workday.com/content/dam/web/en-us/documents/case-studies/ibm-business-case-ai-in-hr.pdf

Gunasekaran, A., Ngai, E. W. T., & McGaughey, R. E. (2006). Information technology and systems justification: A review for research and applications. *European Journal of Operational Research, 173*, 957–983.

Hadidi, M., Al-Rashdan, M., Hadidi, S., & Soubhi, Y. (2020). Comparison between cloud ERP and traditional ERP. *Journal of Critical Reviews, 7*(3).

Han, S. W. (2004). ERP-enterprise resource planning: A cost-based business case and implementation assessment. *Human Factors and Ergonomics in Manufacturing, 14*(3), 239–256.

Hanseth, O., Ciborra, C. U., & Braa, K. (2001). The control devolution: ERP and the side effects of globalization. *The Data Base for Advances in Information Systems, 32*(4), 34–46.

Haq, R. (2020). *Enterprise Artificial Intelligence transformation*. Wiley.

Hastie, T., Tibshirani, R., & Friedman, J. (2009). *The elements of statistical learning: Data mining, inference, and prediction* (Springer series in statistics). Springer.

Hechler, E., & Oberhofer, M. (2020). *Deploying AI in the enterprise*. Apress.

Hecht, B. (1997). Choose the right ERP software. *Datamation, 43*(3), 56–58.

Hevner, A., & Chatterjee, S. (2010). *Design research in information systems*. Springer.

Hilpisch, Y. (2020). *Artificial intelligence in finance*. O'Reilly.

Hitt, L. M., Wu, D. J., & Zhou, X. (2002). Investment in enterprise resource planning: Business impact and productivity measures. *Journal of Management Information Systems, 19*(1), 71–98.

Holland, C., & Light, B. (1999). A critical success factors model for ERP implementation. *IEEE Software, 16*(3), 30–36.

Hong, K. K., & Kim, Y.-G. (2002). The critical success factors for ERP implementation: An organizational fit perspective. *Information and Management, 40*(1), 25–40.

Hoofnagle, C. J., Sloot, B., & Zuiderveen, B. F. (2019). The European Union general data protection regulation: What it is and what it means. *Information & Communications Technology Law, 28*(1), 65.

Hsiuju, R. Y., & Chwen, S. (2008). Aligning ERP implementation with competitive priorities of manufacturing firms: An exploratory study. *International Journal of Production Economics, 92*, 207–220.

Hurwitz, J., & Kirsch, D. (2018). *Machine learning for dummies*. Wiley.

Huyen, C. (2022). *Designing machine learning systems*. O'Reilly.

Hyvonen, T. (2003). Management accounting and information systems—ERP vs BoB. *European Accounting Review, 12*(1), 155–173. Retrieved from http://ssrn.com/abstract=369323

Iakimets, A. (2020). *What are packaged business capabilities?* Elastic Path Software Retrieved from https://www.elasticpath.com/blog/what-are-packaged-business-capablities

Ibrahim, A. M. S., Sharp, J. M., & Syntetos, A. A. (2008). A framework for the implementation of ERP to improve business performance: A case study. In Z. Irani, S. Sahraoui, A. Ghoneim, et al. (Eds.), *Proceedings of the European and Mediterranean conference on information systems (EMCIS).*

IDC. (2020). *Worldwide enterprise resource planning software market shares, 2020: The advance of modular and intelligent ERP systems.*

IDC. (2021). *IDC FutureScape: Worldwide enterprise resource management software market shares, 2021: Digital-first world propelling the market.*

IDC. (2022a). *IDC FutureScape: Worldwide artificial intelligence and automation 2023 predictions.*

IDC. (2022b). *IDC FutureScape: Worldwide Intelligent ERP 2023 predictions.*

IDC. (2022c). *IDC market forecast: Worldwide Artificial Intelligence Software Forecast, 2022–2026.*

Insights, F. (2018). *How AI builds a better manufacturing process.*

Jacobs, F. R., & Bendoly, E. (2003). Enterprise resource planning: Developments and directions for operations management research. *European Journal of Operational Research, 146*, 233–240.

Jalan, S. (2020). *Applications of data science in ERP.* Retrieved from https://medium.com/swlh/applications-of-data-science-in-erp-5e98347d4d07

James, G., Witten, D., Hastie, T., & Tibshirani, R. (2013). *An introduction to statistical learning: With applications in R* (Springer texts in statistics). Springer.

Jamison, T. A., Layman, P. A., Niska, B. T., et al. (2005). *Evaluation of enterprise architecture interoperability.* Air Force Institute of Technology.

Janich, P. (1997). *Kleine Philosophie der Naturwissenschaften.* BeckscheReihe 1203.

Janich, P. (2005). *Was ist Wahrheit? Eine philosophische Einführung.* C.H. Beck.

Janich, P. (2006). *Was ist information? Kritik einer Legende.* Suhrkamp.

Jarrar, Y. F., Al-Mudimigh, A., & Zairi, M. (2000). ERP implementation critical success factors-the role and impact of business process management. In *International Conference on Management of Innovation and Technology* (Vol. 1, pp. 122–127).

Jarvinen, Z. (2020). *Enterprise AI for dummies.* For Dummies.

Johansson, B. (2007). *Why focus on roles when developing future ERP systems.* Retrieved from www.3gerp.org

Juma, M., & Shaalan, K. (2020). Cyberphysical systems in the smart city: Challenges and future trends for strategic research. In *Swarm intelligence for resource management in internet of things* (pp. 65–85). Elsevier.

Kaddoumi, T., & Tambo, T. (2022). Democratizing Enterprise AI success factors and challenges. In *European Mediterranean and Middle Eastern Conference on Information Systems.*

Kalling, T. (2003). *ERP systems and the strategic management processes that lead to competitive advantage* (Vol. 16, p. 46). Information Resources.

Kamhawi, E. M. (2008). Enterprise resource-planning systems adoption in Bahrain: Motives, benefits, and barriers. *Journal of Enterprise Information Management, 21*(3), 310–334.

Kanaracus, C. (2011, August 11). *Epicor sued over alleged ERP project failure, computer world.* Retrieved from http://www.computerworld.com

Katsov, I. (2022). *The theory and practice of Enterprise AI.* Grid Dynamics.

Ke, W., & Wei, K. K. (2008). Organizational culture and leadership in ERP implementation. *Decision Support Systems Journal, 45*(2), 208–218.

Kearns, M., & Roth, A. (2019). *The ethical algorithm: The science of socially aware algorithm design.* Oxford University Press.

Keil, M., & Tiwana, A. (2006). Relative importance of evaluation criteria for enterprise systems: A conjoint study. *Information Systems Journal, 16*(3), 237–262.

Kelleher, J. D., & Tierney, B. (2018). *Data Science.* The MIT Press Essential Knowledge series.

Kerzel, U. (2020). Enterprise AI canvas integrating artificial intelligence into business. *Applied Artificial Intelligence, 35.*

Kholeif, A. O., Abdel-Kader, M., & Sherer, M. (2007). ERP customization failure: Institutionalized accounting practices, power relations and market forces. *Journal of Accounting and Organizational Change, 3*, 250–269.

Kimberling, E. (2006). *7 critical success factors to make your ERP or IT project successful.* Retrieved from http://it.toolbox.com/blogs/erp-roi/7-criticalsuccess-factors-to-make-your-erp-or-it-project-successful-12058

Kimberling, E. (2011). *Back to school: When will ERP software customers learn to avoid failure?* Retrieved from http://panorama-consulting.com/back-to-school-when-will-erp-software-customers-learn-to-avoid-failure/

Kiran, T. S., & Reddy, A. V. (2019). Critical success factors of ERP implementation in SMEs. *Journal of Project Management, 4*(4).

Kleppmann, M. (2017). *Designing data-intensive applications.* O'Reilly.

Konstantas, D., Bourrières, J. P., Léonard, M., et al. (2005). Interoperability of enterprise software and applications. In *Proceedings of the first conference on interoperability of enterprise software and applications, INTEROP-ESA'05* (pp. 409–420). Springer.

Krishnan, N. (2020). *Enterprise Artificial Intelligence and machine learning for Managers: A practical guide to AI and ML for business and government.* C3.ai.

Krumbholz, M., Galliers, J., Coulianos, N., & Maiden, N. A. M. (2000). Implementing enterprise resource planning packages in different corporate and national cultures. *Journal of Information Technology, 15*(4), 267–280.

Kumar, V. (2010). Application of analytical hierarchy process to prioritize the factors affecting ERP implementation. *International Journal of Computer Applications, 2*(2), 0975–8887.

Kumar, K., & Hillegersberg, J. V. (2000). ERP experiences and evolution. *Communications of the ACM, 43*(4), 22–26.

Kumar, V., Maheshwari, B., & Kumar, U. (2002). Enterprise resource planning systems adoption process: A survey of Canadian organizations. *International Journal of Production Research, 40*(3), 509–523.

Kumar, V., Maheshwari, B., & Kumar, U. (2003). An investigation of critical management issues in ERP implementation: Empirical evidence from Canadian organizations. *Technovation, 23*(10), 793–807.

Laboni, B., Avijit, D., & Ranajay, M. (2021). *Machine learning with SAP.* SAP Press.

Lakshmanan, V. (2020). *Machine learning design patterns.* O'Reilly.

Lall, V., & Teyarachakul, S. (2006). Enterprise resource planning (ERP) system selection: A data envelopment analysis (DEA) approach. *Journal of Computer Information Systems, 47*(1), 123–127.

Langenwalter, G. (2000). *Enterprise resources planning and beyond: Integrating your entire organization.* St. Lucie Press.

Laughlin, S. (1999). An ERP game plan. *Journal of Business Strategy, 20*(1), 32–37.

Leon, A. (2007). *ERP demystified.* McGraw-Hill Education (India).

Liao, X. W., Li, Y., & Lu, B. (2007). A model for selecting an ERP system based on linguistic information processing. *Information Systems, 32*(7), 1005–1017.

Light, B., Holland, C. P., & Wills, K. (2001). ERP and best of breed: A comparative analysis. *Business Process Management Journal, 7*(3), 216–224.

Li-Ling, H., & Minder, C. (2004). Impacts of ERP systems on the integrated-interaction performance of manufacturing and marketing. *Industrial Management & Data Systems, 104*(1), 42–55.

Lindley, J. T., Topping, S., & Lindley, L. (2008). The hidden financial costs of ERP software. *Managerial Finance, 34*(2), 78–90.

Mabert, V. A., Soni, A., & Venkataramanan, M. A. (2000). Enterprise resource planning survey of us manufacturing firms. *Production and Inventory Management Journal, 41*, 52–58.

Mabert, V. A., Soni, A., & Venkataramanan, M. A. (2003). Enterprise resource planning: Managing the implementation process. *European Journal of Operational Research, 146*(2), 302–314.

Mackinnon, W., Grant, G., & Cray, D. (2008). Enterprise information systems and strategic flexibility. In *Proceedings of the 41st Hawaii international conference on system sciences* (p. 402).

Mahraz, M., Benabbou, L., & Berrado, A. (2020). A compilation and analysis of critical success factors for the ERP implementation. *International Journal of Enterprise Information Systems., 16*(2), 107.

Maione, G. (2021). *Artificial intelligence and the public sector: The case of accounting* (Artificial intelligence and its contexts). Springer.

Manoilov, I. T. (2023). *ERP systems and AI* (Vol. 1). Electronic Journal Economics and Computer Science.

McKinney, W. (2022). *Python for data analysis*. O'Reilly.

McKinsey & Company. (2019). *Industry 4.0: Capturing value at scale in discrete manufacturing*. Retrieved from https://www.mckinsey.com/~/media/McKinsey/Industries/Advanced%20 Electronics/Our%20Insights/Capturing%20value%20at%20scale%20in%20discrete%20 manufacturing%20with%20Industry%204%200/Industry-4-0-Capturing-value-at-scale-in-discrete-manufacturing-vF.ashx

Menon, S. A., Muchnick, M., Butler, C., & Pizur, T. (2019). Critical challenges in Enterprise resource planning (ERP) implementation. *International Journal of Business and Management, 14*(7), 54.

Momoh, A., Roy, R., & Shehab, E. (2010). Challenges in enterprise resource planning implementation: State-of-the-art. *Business Process Management Journal, 16*(4), 537–564.

Moon, Y. B., & Phatak, D. (2005). Enhancing ERP system's functionality with discrete event simulation. *Industrial Management & Data Systems, 105*(9), 1206–1224.

Moon, Y. B., & Young, B. (2007). Enterprise resource planning (ERP): A review of the literature. *International Journal of Management and Enterprise Development, 4*(3), 235–264.

Moore, G. E. (1965). Cramming more components onto integrated circuits. *Electronics, 38*(8), 114–117.

Motwani, J., Mirchandani, D., Madan, M., et al. (2002). Successful implementation of ERP projects: Evidence from two case studies. *International Journal of Production Economics, 75*(1), 83–96.

Mueller, J. P., & Massaron, L. (2021). *Artificial intelligence for dummies*. For Dummies.

Murphy, K. P. (2012). *Machine learning: A probabilistic perspective* (Adaptive computation and machine learning series). MIT Press.

Muscatello, J. R., & Parente, D. H. (2006). Enterprise resource planning(ERP): A post implementation cross-cross analysis. *Information Resource Management Journal, 3*, 61–81.

Nagai, E. W. T., Law, C. C. H., & Wat, F. K. T. (2008). Examining the critical success factors in the adoption of enterprise resource planning. *Computers in Industry, 59*(6), 548–564.

Nah, F., Faja, S., & Cata, T. (2001). Characteristics of ERP software maintenance: A multiple case study. *Journal of Software Maintenance, 13*(6), 1–16.

Nah, F. F.-H., Zuckweiler, K. M., & Lau, J. L.-S. (2003). ERP implementation: Chief information officers' perceptions of critical success factors. *International Journal of Human-Computer Interaction, 16*(1), 5–22.

Natarajan, P., & Rogers, B. (2021). *Demystifying AI for the enterprise*. Productivity Press.

Nazemi, E., Tarokh, M. J., & Djavanshir, R. R. (2012). ERP: A literature survey. *International Journal of Advanced Manufacturing Technology, 61*, 999–1018.

Nelson, B. (2020). *AI concepts for business applications*. Business Expert Press.

Nelson, H. (2023). *Essential Math for AI*. O'Reilly.

Nield, T. (2022). *Essential math for data science*. O'Reilly.

Nohria, N., William, J., & Roberson, B. (2003). What really works. *Harvard Business Review, 81*(7), 42–52.

Olhager, J., & Selldin, E. (2003). Enterprise resource planning survey of Swedish manufacturing firms. *European Journal of Operational Research, 146*(2), 365–373.

Parasuraman, R., Thomas B., & Sheridan, A. (2000). Model for types and levels of human interaction with automation. *IEEE Transactions on Systems, Man, and Cybernetics—Part A: Systems and Humans, 30*(3).

Parijat, U., & Dan, P. K. (2009). ERP in Indian SME's: A post implementation study of the underlying critical success factors. *International Journal Of Management Innovation System, 1*(2), 1–10.

Parikh, T. (2018). The ERP of the future: Blockchain of things. *International Journal of Scientific Research in Science, Engineering and Technology, 4*(1), 1341–1348.

Park, K., & Kusiak, K. (2005). Enterprise resource planning (ERP) operations support systems for maintaining process integration. *International Journal of Production Research, 43*(19), 3959–3982.

Parr, A., & Shanks, G. (2000). A model of ERP project implementation. *Journal of Information Technology, 15*(4), 289–304.

Parthasarathy, S., & Padmapriya, S. T. (2023). Understanding algorithm bias in artificial intelligence-enabled ERP software customization. *Journal of Ethics in Entrepreneurship and Technology., 3*, 79.

Pawlowski, S., Boudreau, M., & Baskerville, R. (1999). Constraints and flexibility in enterprise systems: A dialectic of system and job. In *Americas conference on information systems*. AMCIS.

Pierson, L. (2021). *Data science for dummies*. For Dummies.

Polivka, M., & Dvorakova, L. (2021). Selection of the ERP system with regard to the global 4th industrial revolution. In *The 20th international scientific conference globalization and its socio-economic consequences* (Vol. 92).

Prahalad, C. K., & Krishnan, M. S. (2008). *The new age of innovation: Driving co-creating value through global networks*. McGraw Hill.

Provost, F., & Fawcett, T. (2021). *Data science for business*. Upfront Books.

Ptak, C., & Schragenheim, E. (2000). *ERP: Tools, techniques, and applications for integrating the supply chain*. St. Lucie Press.

Purnendu, M., & Gunasekaran, A. (2003). Issues in implementing ERP: A case study. *European Journal of Operational Research, 146*, 274–283.

Raja, P., Sheridan, T. B., & Christopher, W. (2000). A model for types and levels of human interaction with automation. *IEEE Transactions on Systems, Man, and Cybernetics*.

Ranganathan, C., & Brown, C. V. (2006). ERP investments and the market value of firms: Toward an understanding of influential ERP project variables. *Information Systems Research, 17*(2), 145–161.

Rao, S. S. (2000). Enterprise resource planning: Business needs and technologies. *Industrial Management and Data Systems, 100*(1–2), 81–88.

Rasmy, M. H., Tharwat, A., & Ashraf, S. (2005). *Enterprise resource planning (ERP) implementation in the Egyptian organizational context* (pp. 1–13). European Mediterranean Conference on Information Systems.

Ratkevičius, D., Ratkevičius, Č., & Skyrius, R. (2012). ERP selection criteria: Theoretical and practical views. *Ekonomika, 91*(2), 97–116.

Rebstock, M., & Selig, J. (2000). Development and implementation strategies for international ERP software projects. In *8th European conference on information systems ECIS*, Vol. 2, pp. 932–936.

Reid, A. (2023). *The AI renaissance*. Kindle.

Reis, J., & Housley, M. (2022). *Fundamentals of data engineering*. O'Reilly.

Richter, M., & Flückiger, M. D. (2013). *Usability Engineering kompakt. Benutzbare Produkte gezielt entwickeln* (3rd ed.). Springer (IT kompakt). Retrieved from http://site.ebrary.com/lib/alltitles/docDetail.action?docID=10691416

Robb, D. (2011, January). *Enterprise ERP buyer's guide: SAP, Oracle and Microsoft*. Retrieved from www.enterpriseappstoday.com

Robinson, A., & Dilts, D. (1999). OR & ERP: A match for the new millenium? *OR/MS Today, 1999*, 30–35.

Rogerson, S., & Fidler, C. (1994). Strategic information systems planning: Its adoption and use. *Information Management & Computer Security Journal, 12*(3), 12–17.

Rohit, K., & Zafar, K. (2021). A research study on the ERP system implementation and current trends in ERP. *Shanlax International Journal of Management, 8*(2).

Rosario, J. G. (2000). On the leading edge: Critical success factors in ERP implementation projects. *Business World (Philippines), 27*, 27.

Rosemann, M., Scott, J., & Watson, E. (2000). Collaborative ERP education: Experiences from a first pilot. In *Proceedings of the Americas conference on information systems AMCIS*.

Ross, J. W., & Weill, P. (2002). Six decisions your IT people shouldn't make. *Harvard Business Review, 80*(11), 84–92.

Rowe, F., Elamrani, R., Bidan, M., et al. (2005). Does ERP provide a cross-functional view of the firm? Challenging conventional wisdom for SMEs and large French firms. In *26th international conference on information systems*, Los Vegas, pp. 11–24.

Ruivo, P., Johannson, B., Sarker, S., & Oliveira, T. (2020). The relationship between ERP capabilities, use, and value. *Computers in Industry, 117*, 1–15.

Russell, S., & Norvig, P. (2020). *Artificial intelligence: A modern approach*. Pearson.

Sadagopan, S. (1999). *The world of ERP: A managerial perspective* (pp. 1–16). Tata McGraw-Hill Publishing Company.

Samara, T. (2015). *ERP and information systems: Integration or disintegration*. Wiley.

SAP AI Ethics. (2022). *Building trustworthy & ethical AI systems*. Retrieved from https://www.sap.com/products/artificial-intelligence/ai-ethics.html

SAP AI Ethics Policy. (2022). *SAP global artificial intelligence ethics policy*. Retrieved from https://sap.sharepoint.com/teams/SAPOneAssets/Library/company_policies_and_guidelines/Global_AI_Ethics_Policy_1.0_English.pdf

SAP AI Guiding Principles. (2021). *SAP's guiding principles for artificial intelligence*. Retrieved from https://www.sap.com/products/artificial-intelligence/ai-ethics.html?pdf-asset=940c6047-1c7d-0010-87a3-c30de2ffd8ff&page=1

SAP Human Rights Commitment. (2022). *SAP global human rights commitment statement*. Retrieved from https://www.sap.com/documents/2016/01/a8c6d366-577c-0010-82c7-eda71af511fa.html

Sarferaz, S. (2022). *Compendium on Enterprise resource planning*. Springer.

Sarferaz, S. (2023). *ERP-Software: Funktionalität und Konzepte*. Springer.

Sarferaz, S., & Banda, R. (2021). *Implementing machine learning with SAP S/4HANA*. Rheinwerk Verlag.

Saueressig, T., Gilg, J., Betz, O., & Homann, M. (2021a). *SAP S/4HANA cloud - An introduction*. SAP Press.

Saueressig, T., Stein, T., Boeder, J., & Kleis, W. (2021b). *SAP S/4HANA architecture*. SAP Press.

Schonefeld, M., & Vering, O. (2000). Enhancing ERP-efficiency through workflow-services. In *Proceedings of 2000 Americas Conference on Information Systems* (pp. 640–645). AMCIS.

Schuler, K., & Schlegel, D. (2021). A framework for corporate artificial intelligence strategy. In *International conference on digital economy*.

Scott, E. J. (1999, May 13) The FoxMeyer drugs' bankruptcy: Was it a failure of ERP? In *Proceedings of the 5th Americas Conference on Information System*, pp. 223–225.

Shah, I. (2019). *Intro to data science: A step-by-step guide to learn data science*. Retrieved from https://towardsdatascience.com/intro-to-data-science-531079c38b22

Shahin, D., & Sulaiman, A. (2009). Successful enterprise resource planning implementation: Taxonomy of critical factors. *Industrial Management and Data Systems, 109*(8), 1037–1052.

Shalev-Shwartz, S., & Ben-David, S. (2014). *Understanding machine learning: From theory to algorithms*. Cambridge University Press.

Sharif, A. M., Irani, Z., & Love, P. E. D. (2005). Integrating ERP using EAI: A model for post-hoc evaluation. *European Journal of Information Systems, 14*(3), 162–174.

Shehab, E., Sharp, M., Supramaniam, L., et al. (2004). Enterprise resource planning: An integrative review. *Business Process Management Journal, 10*(4), 359–386.

Siriginidi, S. R. (2000a). Enterprise resource planning: Business needs and technologies. *Industrial Management & Data Systems, 100*, 81.

Siriginidi, S. R. (2000b). Enterprise resource planning in reengineering business. *Business Process Management Journal, 6*, 376.

Soh, C., Kien, S. S., & Tay-Yap, J. (1999). Enterprise resource planning: Cultural fits and misfits: Is ERP a universal solution? *Communications of the Association for Computing Machinery (ACM), 43*(4), 47–51.

Soh, C., Kien, S., & Tay-Yap, J. (2000). Cultural fits and misfits: Is ERP a universal solution? *Communications of the ACM, 43*(4), 47–51.

Somers, T., Nelson, K., & Ragowsky, A. (2000). Enterprise resource planning ERP for the next millennium: Development of an integrative framework and implications for research. In *Americas conference on information systems AMCIS.*

Soni, N., Sharma, E., Singh, N., & Kapoor, A. (2020). Artificial intelligence in business: From research and innovation to market deployment. *Procedia Computer Science, 167*, 2200.

Spathis, C., & Constantinides, S. (2003). The usefulness of ERP systems for effective management. *Industrial Management and Data Systems, 103*(9), 677–685.

Spathis, C., & Constantinides, S. (2004). Enterprise resource planning systems' impact on accounting processes. *Business Process Management Journal, 10*(2), 234–247.

Sprott, D. (2000). Componentizing the enterprise application packages. *Communication of the ACM, 43*(2), 63–69.

Sridharan, V., & LaForge, R. L. (2000). Resource planning: MRP TO MRPII AND ERP. In P. M. Swamidass (Ed.), *Encyclopedia of production and manufacturing management.* Springer. https://doi.org/10.1007/1-4020-0612-8_818

Stapleton, G., & Rezak, C. J. (2004). Change management underpins a successful ERP implementation at Marathon Oil. *Journal of Organization Excellence, 23*(4), 15–21.

Stensrud, E. (2001). Alternative approaches to effort prediction of ERP projects. *Information & Software Technology, 43*(7), 413–423.

Stewart, G. (2000). Collaborative ERP curriculum developing using industry process models. In *Americas conference on information systems AMCIS.*

Straub, D. (2009). Editor's comments: Why top journals accept your paper. *Management Information Systems Quarterly, 33*, 3.

Sumner, M. (2000). Risk factors in enterprise-wide/ERP projects. *Journal of Information Technology, 15*(4), 317–327.

Swan, J., Newell, S., & Robertson, M. (1999). The illusion of 'best practice' in information systems for operations management. *European Journal of Information Systems, 8*(8), 284–293.

Swanton, B. (2004, September 21). Build ERP upgrade costs into the business change program – Not the IT budget. *Computer Weekly, 2004*, 28–28.

Tarantilis, C. D., Kiranoudis, C. T., & Theodorakopoulos, N. D. (2008). A web-based ERP system for business services and supply chain management: Application to real-world process scheduling. *European Journal of Operational Research, 187*, 1310–1326.

Thanh, N. (2022). Designing a MCDM model for selection of an optimal ERP software in organization. *Systems, 10*(4).

Themistocleous, M., Irani, Z., & O'Keefe, R. M. (2001). ERP and application integration, exploratory survey. *Business Process Management Journal, 7*(3), 195–204.

Tiwana, A., & Keil, M. (2006). Functionality risk in information systems development: An empirical investigation. *IEEE Transactions on Engineering Management, 53*(3), 412–425.

Tongsuksai, S., Mathrani, S., & Taski, N. (2019). Cloud enterprise resource planning implementation: A systematic literature review of critical success factors. In *IEEE Asia-Pacific Conference on Computer Science and Data Engineering.*

Tsai, W. H., Chien, S. W., Hsu, P. Y., et al. (2005). Identification of critical failure factors in the implementation of enterprise resource planning (ERP) system in Taiwan's industries. *International Journal of Management and Enterprise Development, 2*(2), 219–239.

Tsai, W. H., Lee, P. L., Shen, Y. S., et al. (2009). The relationship between ERP software selection criterion and ERP success. In *Proceedings of international conference on industrial engineering and engineering management* (pp. 2222–2226). IEEE.

Umble, E., & Umble, M. (2002). Avoiding ERP implementation failure. *Industrial Management, 44*(1), 25–33.

Umble, E. J., Haft, R. R., & Umble, M. M. (2003). Enterprise resource planning: Implementation procedures and critical success factors. *European Journal of Operational Research, 146*(2), 241–257.

United Nation Human Rights. (2011). *Guiding principles on business and human rights.* Retrieved from https://www.ohchr.org/Documents/Publications/GuidingPrinciplesBusinessHR_EN.pdf

Vahrenkamp, R. (2021). *Enterprise resource planning system.* Retrieved from https://wirtschafts-lexikon.gabler.de/definition/enterprise-resource-planning-system-51587/version-274748

Van der Aalst, W. (2014). Data scientist: The engineer of the future. In *Proceedings of the I-ESA conference* (Vol. 7). Springer.

Van der Aalst, W. (2016). Data science in action. In *Process mining: Data science in action* (pp. 3–23). Berlin, Heidelberg, Springer.

Vander, P. J. (2017). *Python data science handbook.* O'Reilly.

Varga, E. (2019). Introduction to data science. In *Practical data science with python 3: Synthesizing actionable insights from data* (pp. 1–27). Apress.

Vasiliev, Y. (2022). *Python for data science.* No Starch Press.

Venable, J., Pries-Heje, J., & Baskerville, R. (2016). FEDS: A framework for evaluation in design science research. *European Journal of Information Systems, 25*, 77–89.

Verville, J., & Halingten, A. (2002). An investigation of the decision process for selecting an ERP software: The case of ESC. *Management Decision, 40*(3), 206–216.

Verville, J., & Halingten, A. (2003). A six-stage model of the buying process for ERP software. *Industrial Marketing Management, 32*(7), 585–594.

Wailgum, T. (2009). *10 famous ERP disasters, dustups and disappointments, CIO.* Retrieved from http://www.cio.com

Wei, C. C., & Wang, M. J. J. (2004). A comprehensive framework for selecting an ERP system. *International Journal of Project Management, 22*, 161–169.

Wei, C. C., Chien, C. F., & Wang, M. J. J. (2005). An AHP-based approach to ERP system selection. *International Journal of Production Economics, 96*(1), 47–62.

Weiss, T. R., & Songini, M. L. (2002). Hershey upgrades R/3 ERP system without hitches. *Computerworld, 36*(37), 25.

Wier, B., Hunton, J., & Hassabelnaby, H. R. (2007). Enterprise resource planning systems and non-financial performance incentives: The joint impact on corporate performance. *International Journal of Accounting Information Systems, 8*(3), 165–190.

Wight, O. W. (1984). *Manufacturing resource planning: MRP II – Unlocking America's productivity potential* (pp. 53–54). Wiley. ISBN: 0-471-13274-8.

Willis, T. H., & Willis-Brown, A. H. (2002). Extending the value of ERP. *Industrial Management & Data System, 102*(1), 35–38.

Wilson, J. (2002). Responsible authorship and peer review. *Science and Engineering Ethics, 8*(2), 155–174.

Winter, R. (2008). Design science research in Europe. *European Journal of Information Systems, 17*, 470–475.

Witten, I. H., Frank, E., Hall, M. A., & Pal, C. J. (2016). *Data mining: Practical machine learning tools and techniques* (4th ed.). Morgan Kaufmann.

Wong, B., & Tein, D. (2003). Critical success factors for ERP projects. In *Proceedings of the National Conference of the Australian Institute of Project Management*, pp. 1–8. Retrieved from http://cms.3rdgen.info/3rdgen_sites/107/resource/orwongandtein.pdf

Woo, H. (2007). Critical success factors for implementing ERP: The case of a Chinese electronics' manufacturer. *Journal of Manufacturing Technology Management, 18*(4), 431–442.

Woollacott, E. (2019). *Intelligent ERP: The foundation of digital transformation.*

Yajiong, X., Huigang, L., William, R., et al. (2005). ERP implementation failures in China: Case studies with implications for ERP vendors. *International Journal of Production Economics, 97*(3), 279–295.

Yang, J. B., Wu, C. T., & Tsai, C. H. (2007). Selection of an ERP system for a construction firm in Taiwan: A case study. *Automation in Construction, 16*(6), 787–796.

Yathiraju, N. (2022). Investigating the use of an artificial intelligence model in an ERP cloud-based system. *International Journal of Electrical, Electronics and Computers., 7*(2), 1–26.

Yurtyapan, M. S., & Aydemir, E. (2021). ERP software selection using intuitionistic fuzzy and interval grey number-based MACBETH method. *Grey Systems: Theory and Application, 12*(1).

Zadeh, A. H., Sengupta, A., & Schultz, T. (2020). Enhancing ERP learning outcomes through Microsoft dynamics. *Journal of Information Systems Education, 31*(2), 83–95.

Zdravkovic, M., Panetto, H., & Weichhard, G. (2021). AI-enabled enterprise information systems for manufacturing. *Enterprise Information Systems, 16*(4).

Zhang, L., Lee, K. O., & Banerjee, P. (2002). Critical success factors of enterprise resource planning systems implementation success in China. In *Proceedings of the 36th Hawaii International Conference on System Sciences*, pp. 1–10.

Ziaee, M., Fathian, M., & Sadjadi, S. J. (2006). A modular approach to ERP system selection: A case study. *Information Management & Computer Security, 14*(5), 485–495.

Printed in the United States
by Baker & Taylor Publisher Services